Scientifica
Kids in Lab Coats

For Key Stage 3 Science

Peter Ellis • Phil Godding • Derek McMonagle
Louise Petheram • Lawrie Ryan
David Sang • Jane Taylor

7

Published in 2004 by:
Nelson Thornes Ltd
Delta Place
27 Bath Road
CHELTENHAM
GL53 7TH
United Kingdom

06 07 / 10 9 8 7 6 5 4 3 2

A catalogue record for this book is available from the British Library

ISBN 0 7487 7980 9

Illustrations by Mark Draisey, Ian West, Bede Illustration
Page make-up by Wearset Ltd

Printed and bound in China by Midas Printing International Ltd

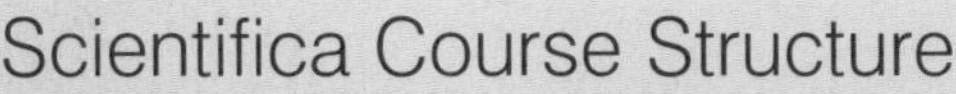

0 7487 7980 9
Levels 4–7
Student Book

0 7487 7984 1
Complete teacher guidance for Levels 4–7

0 7487 8010 6
Teacher Resource Pack for total learning support and extension

0 7487 8017 3
ICT Power Pack for Supercharged lessons!

0 7487 7981 7
Levels 3–6
Student Book

0 7487 7987 6
Complete teacher guidance for Levels 3–6

0 7487 8011 4
Formative and summative progression tracking

0 7487 8013 0
CD-ROM and Online Test and Assessment

0 7487 9199 X
Ultimate SEN support

0 7487 9013 6
Fantastic science reading

0 7487 9184 1
Low cost.
take-home
personalise

CONTENTS

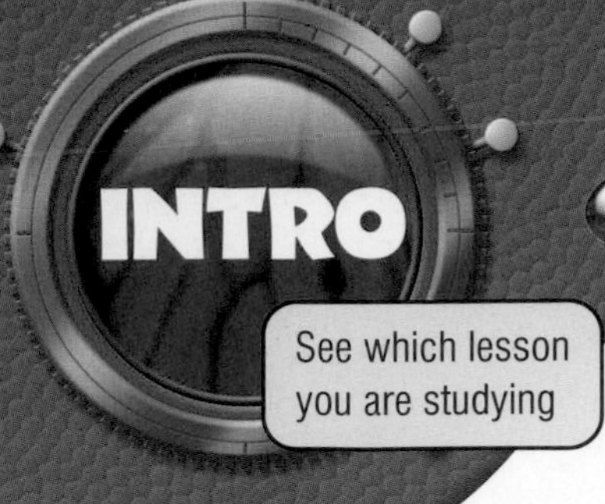

SCIENTIFICA

See which lesson you are studying

This shows what you should hope to learn in this lesson. If you don't understand these things at the end, read through the pages again, and don't be afraid to ask teacher!

LEARN ABOUT
How Scientifica works

You can use the things you learn in Science in other subjects too. These panels will help you watch out for things that will help you in other lessons like Maths, Geography and Citizenship. Sometimes they will contain handy hints about other sections of the book.

CHALLENGE

It's really important to develop good computer skills at school. These ICT Challenges will provide lots of interesting activities that help you practice.

Welcome to Scientifica

Why should Science textbooks be boring? We think Science is amazing, and that's why we've packed this book full of great ideas. You'll find tons of amazing facts, gruesome details, clever activities and funny cartoons. There's lots of brilliant Science too!

Here are some of the main features in Scientifica. There are lots more to discover if you look…

Get stuck in

Whenever you see a blue-coloured panel, it means it's time to start doing some science activities. This blue panel provides a set of simple instructions you can follow. Your teacher may also have a sheet to help you and for you to write on.

Meet the Scientifica crew!

Throughout the book you may see lots of questions, with four possible answers. Only one is correct. The answers **are in different colours**. If the teacher gives the class coloured cards to vote with, it will be easy to show your vote.

Q1 Did you really understand what you just read?

Q2 Are you sure?

Q3 Won't these questions help you check?

SUMMARY QUESTIONS

At the end of each lesson, there is a set of questions to see if you understood everything.

★ See those stars at the beginning of each question?

They tell you whether a question is supposed to be Easy (★), Medium (★★) or Hard (★★★).

Freaky insects, expanding bridges, boiling hot super stars... These are the most fantastic facts you can find!

Find out how scientists worked out what we know so far. Don't worry! There's plenty for the scientists of the future to find out.

Gruesome science

Lethal clouds of poison gas, dead human skin cells, killer electric eels... Sometimes Science can be just plain nasty! Why not learn about that too?

UNIT REVIEW

There are loads of homework questions at the end of each Unit. There are lots of different types too. If you complete all the SAT-style questions, the teacher may be able to tell you what Level you are working at. Do your best to improve as you go along!

DANGER! AVOID THESE COMMON ERRORS

'Er, the Sun goes out like a light-bulb at night, right?' People make mistakes about science all the time. Before you leave the topic, this will help you make sure you're not one of them!

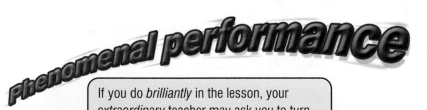

Phenomenal performance

If you do *brilliantly* in the lesson, your *extraordinary* teacher may ask you to turn towards the back of this *fantastic* book. There are lots of *super* activities for you to try in the *Phenomenal Performance* section.

Key words

amazing
brilliant
phenomenal

Keywords are a handy way of remembering a topic. Some might be scrambled up though!

We think you'll enjoy Scientifica, and hopefully Science too. Best of luck with your studies!

The (other) Scientifica crew – *Lawrie, David and Jane*

7A Cells

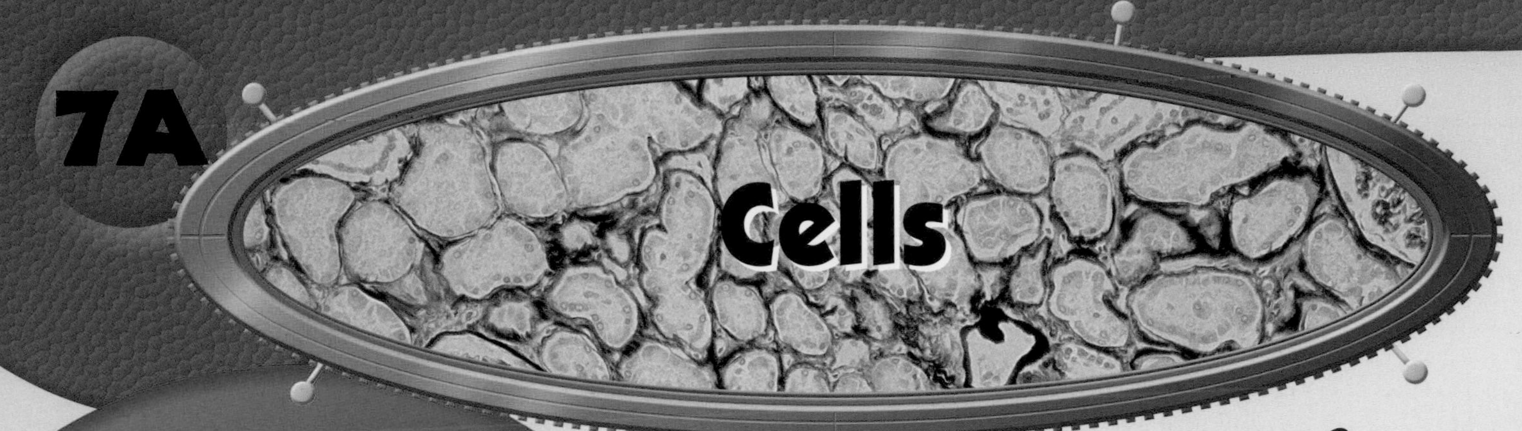

COMING SOON

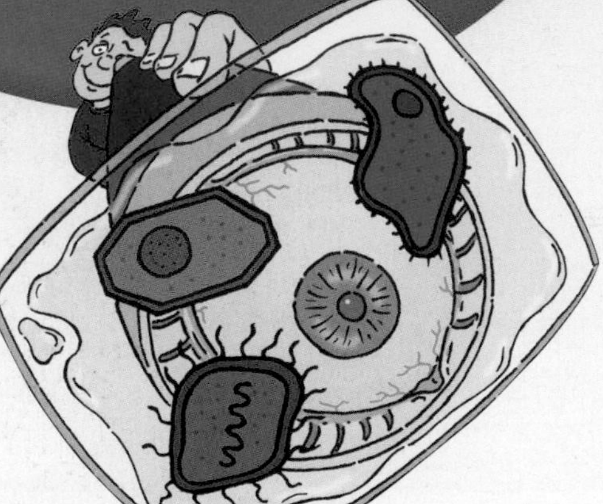

What's it all about?

All living things are made of **cells**. You can't see them without help, because they are much too small. If you could magnify a drop of red-looking blood you would see that it is really a clear yellow liquid packed with millions of tiny red objects. These are **red blood cells**; they carry oxygen round the body. There are many other types of cell in animals and plants.

Some very small living things, such as bacteria and baker's yeast, have only one cell. In this unit, you will look at many different sorts of cell and how they are arranged. You will find out how you can observe things too small to be seen with your eyes.

What do you remember?

You already know about:

- the life processes in living things.
- the parts of a plant and its flower.
- the function of the heart, skeleton and muscles.

1 List the life processes, here is the first letter of each to start you off:
M... R... S... G... R... E... N...

2 Which organ does which job?
heart **root** **lungs** **leaf**
1 obtains water from the ground
2 pumps blood
3 makes food using light
4 obtains oxygen from the air

3 Look at the picture. It is something familiar magnified using a microscope. Can you identify it?

What is this?

Ideas about cells

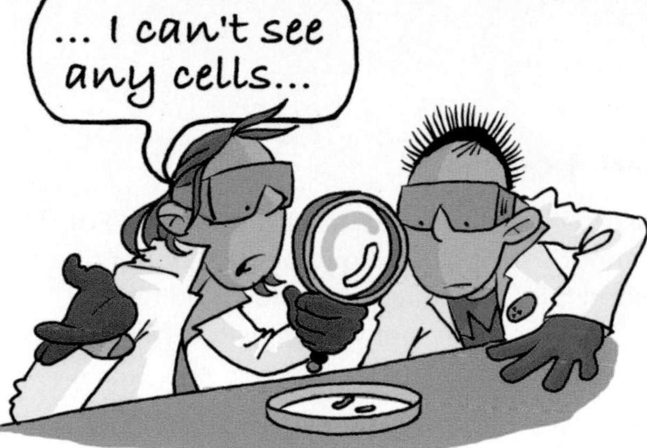

QUESTIONS

The students at Scientifica are about to find out about cells.

a) Why can't Molly or Mike see any cells?

b) Is Reese correct – is the liver an organ? List three organs in the human body and give their jobs.

c) Molly is worried that her cells are dying. Can you explain where new cells come from?

Looking at microscopes

LEARN ABOUT
- how to focus a microscope
- observing cells with a microscope

Too small to see

Even if you look closely, it is hard to see what skin is made of. This is because our eyes cannot see anything smaller than about one tenth of a millimetre. Red blood cells are only seven thousandths of a millimetre across so we have to magnify them with a **microscope** to see them.

A microscope uses two lenses to magnify the view of a small sample of material, called a **specimen**.

The view that you see – the image – is **magnified** as it passes through the first lens. It is magnified again as it passes through the second lens.

ICT CHALLENGE

Use a flex-cam to help you explain the features of a specimen on a slide to the rest of your group.

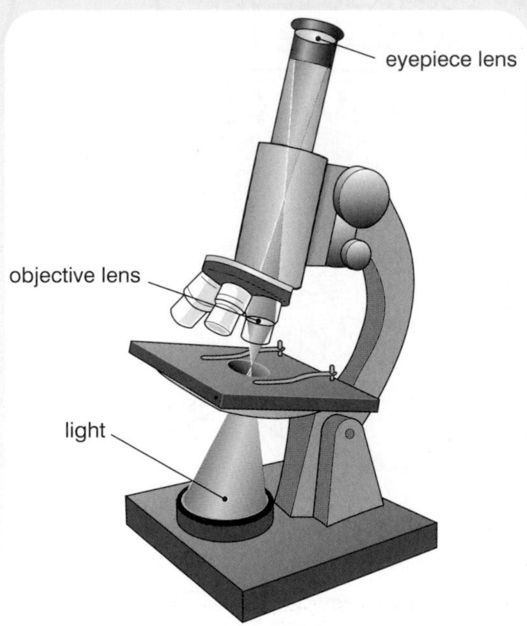

The parts of a microscope

LINK UP TO PHYSICS

Lenses change the direction of the rays of light.

Calculating magnification

When the lens near the specimen, called the objective lens, magnifies four times (×4) and the lens nearest the eye magnifies ten times (×10), the specimen is magnified forty times ($4 \times 10 = 40$) larger than real life.

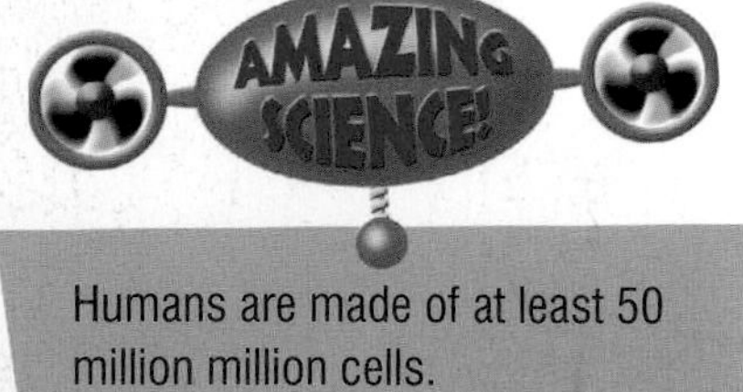

Humans are made of at least 50 million million cells.

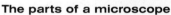

Q1 Imagine you are looking at a specimen using a ×10 objective lens and a ×10 eyepiece lens. By how much is the image magnified?

Seeing cells

The specimen is cut into very thin slices called **sections**. These are thin enough for light to pass through. One section is put on a microscope **slide** with a drop of water. It is then covered with a **cover slip**.

The circular area that you can see when you look down the microscope is the field of view.

The picture shows a section of plant stem stained and viewed through a microscope. We can see that it is made up of many small, rounded, shapes packed together. These are the cells.

How many different kinds of cell can you see in this picture?

When the cells are cut across to make a section they appear rectangular or roughly circular.

Cells are almost transparent. Scientists have developed **stains**, which dye particular parts of the cell. These make the structures clearer to see.

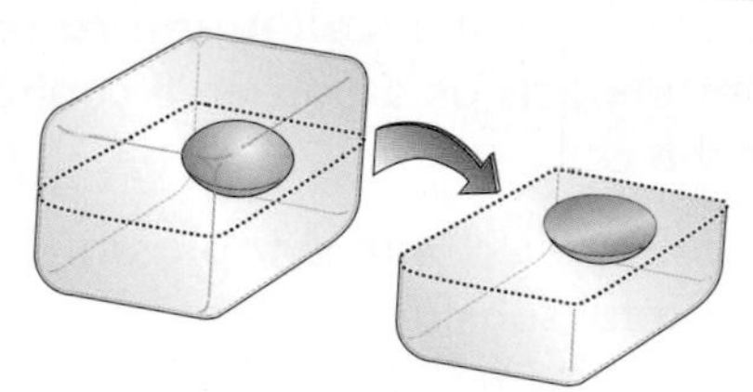

A cell that is shaped like a cube looks like a square when you see it in a section

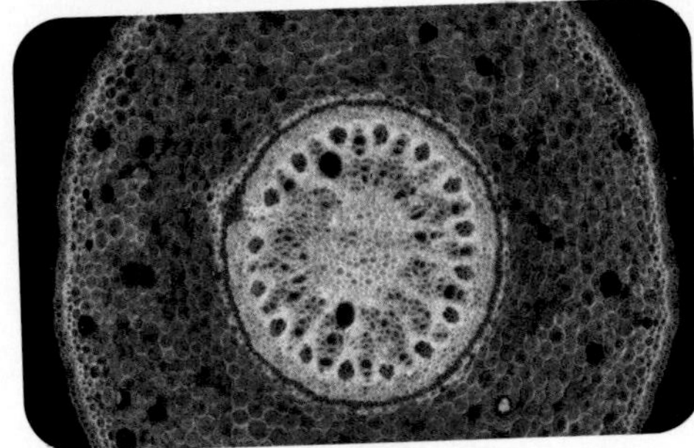

This section of plant stem has been stained and magnified

Using a microscope

- Set up your microscope and practise focusing so that you can see a specimen on a slide clearly.
- Look at a clear plastic ruler under the microscope using ×40 magnification. Can you see the millimetre markers? How far is it from one side of the field of view to the other?
- Use your microscope to look at prepared sections of plants and animals. Choose one of the slides that interests you and find out about the features you can see.

SUMMARY QUESTIONS

1 ☆ Explain what each of the following is:
a) a slide **b)** a cover slip **c)** a section **d)** a stain

2 ☆☆ Make a flow chart of the actions you would take to look at a prepared slide with a microscope.

Key words

cover slip
magnification
microscope
section
slide
specimen
stain

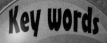

Plant and animal cells

Learn about
- cell structure
- the differences between animal and plant cells

Cells

All living things are made of **cells**. These are the smallest building blocks of animals and plants.

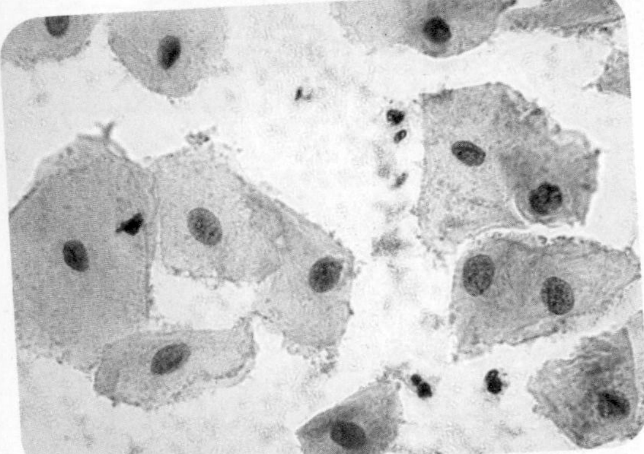

These cells come from the inside of someone's cheek. They have been stained to show the nucleus more clearly.

What's in a cell?

Animal and plant cells have a similar structure, but plant cells have some extra features.

Every cell has a thin **cell membrane** surrounding it. The cell membrane acts as a barrier. It controls what substances can enter or leave the cell.

Every cell is filled with **cytoplasm**. Cytoplasm is a watery gel with many useful substances dissolved in it. There are very small structures in the cytoplasm but they are too small to see with a laboratory microscope.

Every cell has a **nucleus** somewhere in the cytoplasm. The nucleus directs the cell's activity. It is sometimes described as the 'control centre'. It controls which activities happen, when, and for how long. The nucleus has a set of instructions, called **genes** that enable it to do these activities.

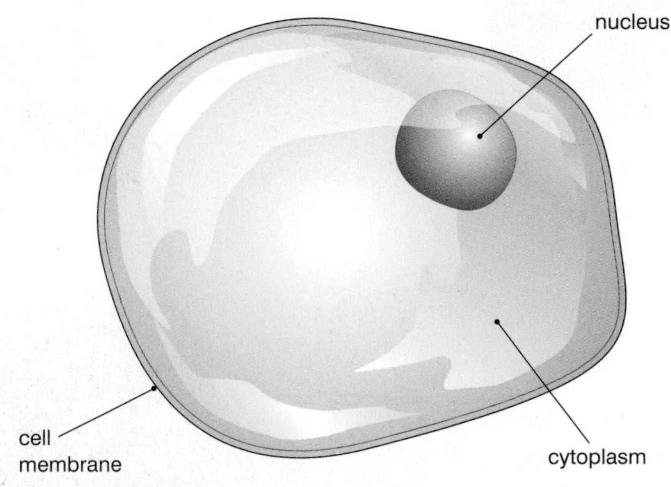

Animal cell

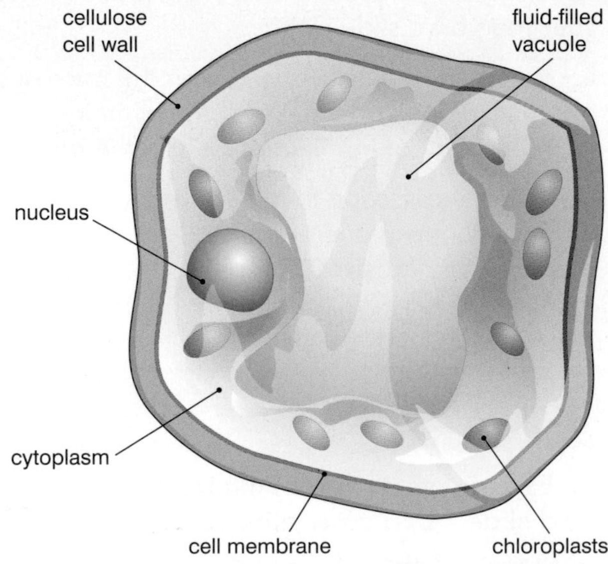

Plant cell

Plant cells

Cells in plants also have:

- A **cell wall**, which is a layer outside the cell membrane. The cell wall is made of a tough substance called cellulose. It is strong and keeps the cell's shape.
- Green **chloroplasts** in the cytoplasm. These give plants their green colour. Chloroplasts use light energy to make sugars. The sugars are an energy source for the cell. Plant roots and other underground parts are usually white because they do not have chloroplasts.
- A large bubble of fluid called a **vacuole** inside the cell. The fluid is a solution of useful materials, such as sugars and minerals. The vacuole swells when a plant has plenty of water, pushing out the cell wall. This helps to keep a plant upright and hold its leaves out firmly. If a plant is short of water, we can see its leaves become floppy and wilt.

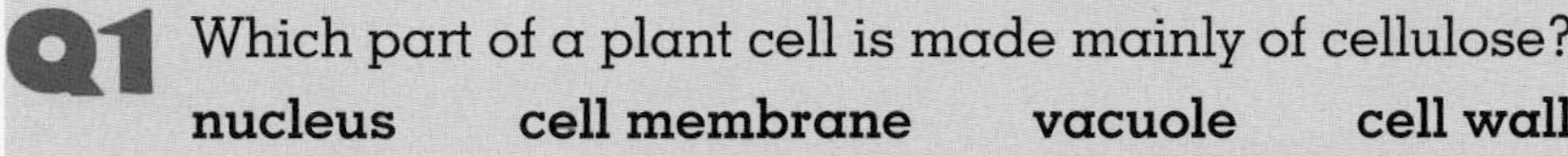

Q1 Which part of a plant cell is made mainly of cellulose?

nucleus **cell membrane** **vacuole** **cell wall**

a) Pondweed cells are packed with green chloroplasts.
b) The cell walls around onion cells act as a support. The cells are not all the same shape.

Viewing plant and animal cells

- Prepare a section of the skin you find between the layers in an onion. Use a microscope to identify the cell wall and cytoplasm.
  a) Make a careful drawing of a few cells. Label the cell wall and nucleus. Try to estimate how long a cell is along its longest edge.
- Use a microscope to look at a leaf from pondweed (*Elodea*). Draw a few cells; label the cell wall and chloroplasts.
  b) Can you think of a reason why pondweed leaf cells have chloroplasts but onion epidermis does not?
- A haemocytometer is a special slide used to count cells such as red blood cells. Look at a drop of yeast suspension in a haemocytometer using a digital camera and TV. Each of the squares you can see bounded by a single line has sides of 0.02 mm.
  c) Estimate how many yeast cells could fit along one side of one square.

SUMMARY QUESTIONS

1 ☆ Look at the diagram.
a) Identify A, B, C and D.
b) Which of these is made mainly of water?
c) Which makes a plant cell appear green?

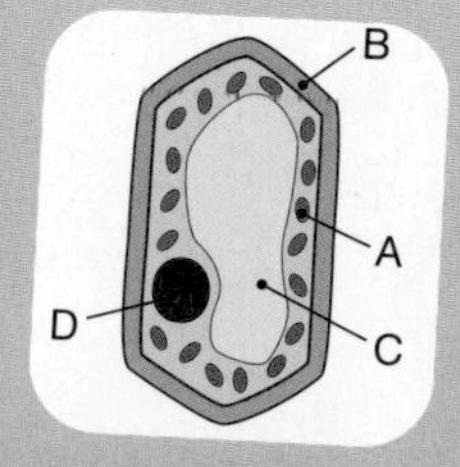

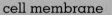

2 ☆☆ Using the headings 'Animal and plant cells' and 'Only in plant cells' sort the following into two groups:

nucleus cell wall chloroplast cytoplasm vacuole cell membrane

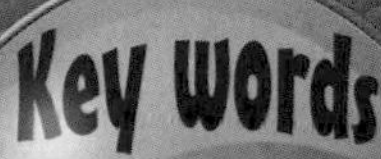

cell
cell membrane
cell wall
chloroplast
cytoplasm
gene
nucleus
vacuole

Different cells

LEARN ABOUT
- how cells are adapted for different functions
- how cells are organised into tissues

Specialised cells

Animal and plant cells may share features, such as a cell membrane, but they are not all alike. The body uses different kinds of cell to do different jobs, just as we use a car to go shopping but a lorry to do deliveries.

The cells in different parts of the body are made for different functions. There are cells in the eye specialised for detecting light. Cells in the stomach make digestive juices. Cells in the blood carry oxygen.

Specialised cells have features, or **adaptations**, that make them efficient at their job. Cells with the same function in different places have the same specialisations.

There are cells in the lungs that absorb oxygen from the air. They are similar to cells in a fish's gill that absorb oxygen from the water. Both are large and flat, and very thin. These features make absorbing as efficient as possible.

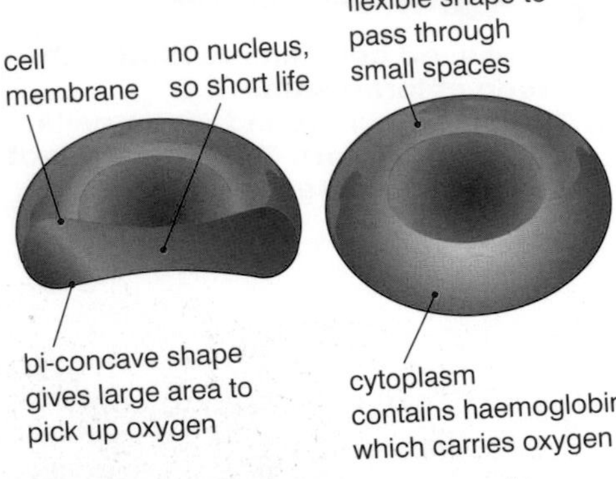

Red blood cells carry oxygen to every part of the body. They have to be able to pass through tiny blood vessels and take in or release large amounts of oxygen quickly.

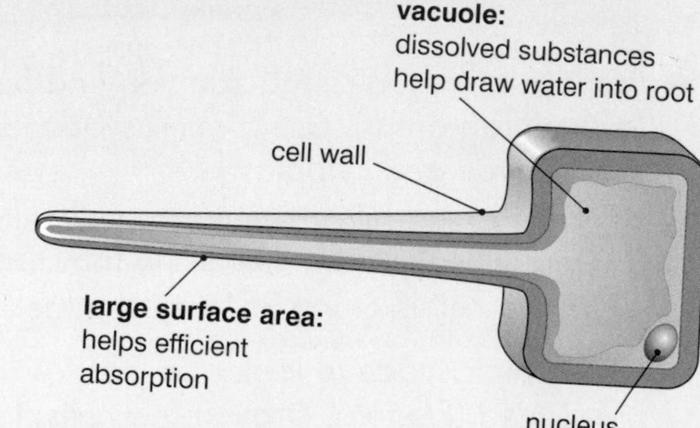

Root hair cells absorb water and minerals from the soil

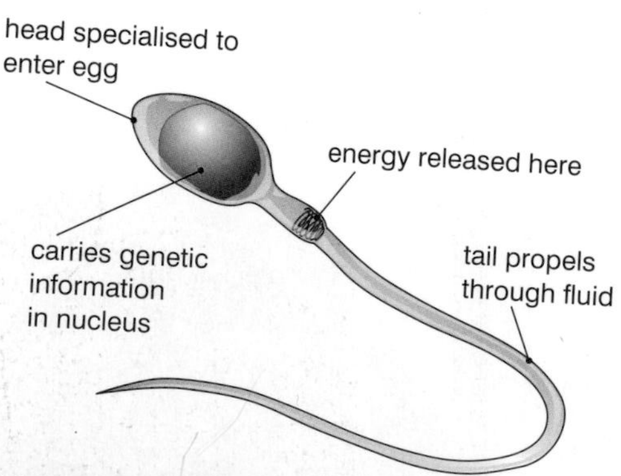

A sperm cell delivers a nucleus, containing genes, to an egg. It can travel speedily for a long distance for its size, and penetrate an egg cell to deliver the information.

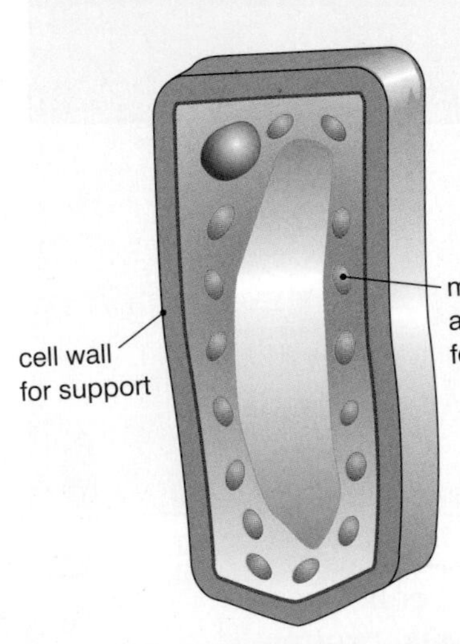

Palisade cells make sugars for the plant. The long thin shape packed with chloroplasts traps as much light as possible.

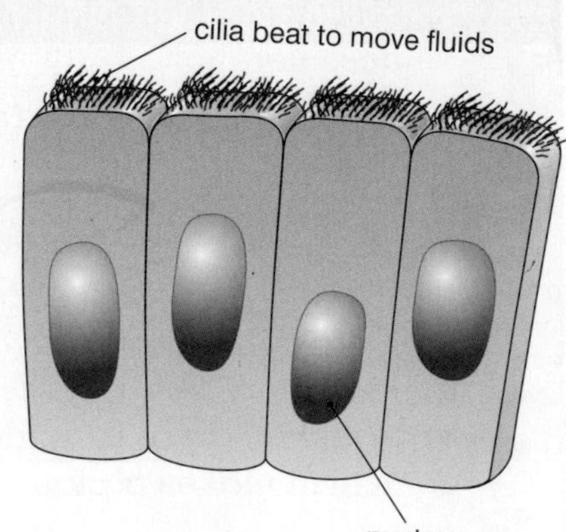

Epithelium cells, like these, line tubes in the body. They move substances along these tubes. The hair-like cilia beat to create a current in the fluid in the tubes.

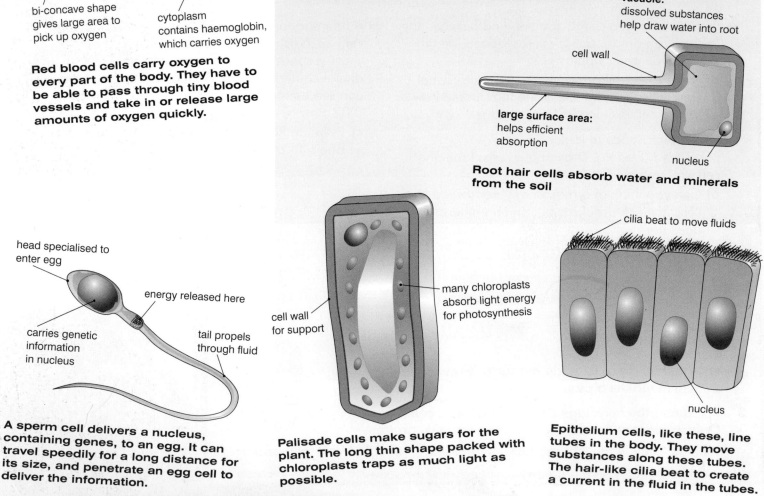

Viewing cell adaptations

- Potato plants make starch and store it in the potato. Prepare a microscope slide with a very thin section of potato and two drops of iodine stain. Iodine makes starch grains turn blue.
- Use a microscope to find starch grains.
  a) Are all the grains the same?
  b) How many are there in a cell?
  c) Draw two or three cells with starch grains.
  d) What do you think the potato uses starch for?
- Cut a very thin section of lemon rind and look at it with a microscope. Try to locate the oil pockets where the lemon stores the oils that give it its smell.
- Use a flex-cam or digital microscope to show one of your slides while you talk to other groups about what you have observed.

Gruesome science

The main ingredient of the dust in your house is skin cells that have fallen off you and your pets.

Using science

People have a blood transfusion when they have lost a lot of blood. Often this is because of a severe injury, but it could be after giving birth, or during an operation, or if they have a blood disorder.

People can be given whole blood, but some patients may need just the red cells or just plasma (the liquid part). Blood that is separated into cells and plasma can be kept longer. A fit adult blood donor makes up the 475 cm^3 donated in a few weeks without any ill effects.

SUMMARY QUESTIONS

1 ☆ Match the cell to the funtion:
a) photosynthesis **b)** moving mucus along the windpipe **c)** absorbing
Choose from: red blood cell root hair cell palisade cell sperm cell epithelium with cilia

2 ☆☆ Look at the cells in the picture.
List the features that you can see in a cell.
Are they plant or animal cells?
Which feature was the most important in making your decision?

3 ☆☆☆ Using recycled or scrap materials and craft materials, make a model of one of the cells you have learnt about.

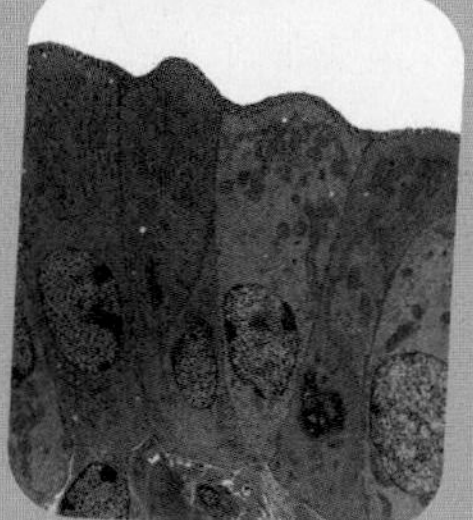

Are these plant or an animal cells?

Key words

adaptations
epithelium cell
palisade cell
red blood cell
root hair cell
specialised
sperm cell

LEARN ABOUT

- tissues
- how tissues are grouped to make organs
- locating your major organs

Working together

The different parts of a human body do not work on their own. Each part of the body relies on activities done by other parts. For example, when you run around playing football or netball your leg muscles need oxygen. They rely on the lungs to absorb oxygen and blood to carry it from the lungs to the muscles.

Tissues and organs

A **tissue** is a group of similar cells that carry out a specialised activity. A layer of specialised cells makes the tissue that lines the nose and windpipe. Its job is to protect the lungs from dust and microbes. A different layer of specialised cells in the lungs absorbs oxygen from the air.

Organs carry out the major life functions such as breathing, feeding and reproduction. Organs such as the lungs, liver or the eye contain many different types of tissue. Each does its own specialised part of the function.

Q1 List as many organs as you can think of that are involved in feeding and digestion.

Q2 All the life functions need a network of organs working together. How do organs work together to supply a leg muscle, for example?

Your skin is your largest organ – it's as big as a duvet cover.

Finding out about organs

- Make a map of the human organs involved in the following processes: breathing, circulation, digestion, detecting changes in the environment, and reproduction.
- Find out about organ transplants. Why can't you have organs from *any* donor? Some people think that doctors should automatically be able to use organs or transplants, unless some one has 'opted-out' by specifically saying that they don't want their organs used. What do you think?

Systems

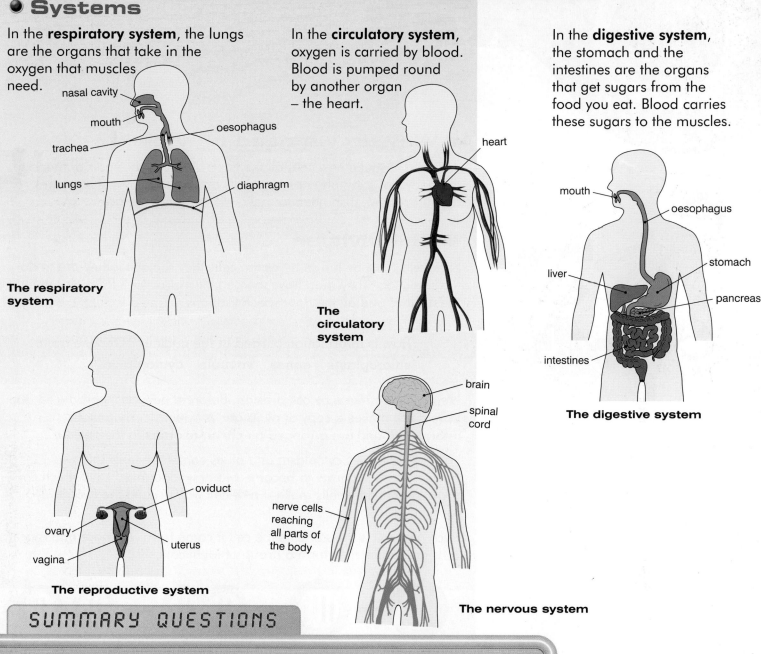

In the **respiratory system**, the lungs are the organs that take in the oxygen that muscles need.

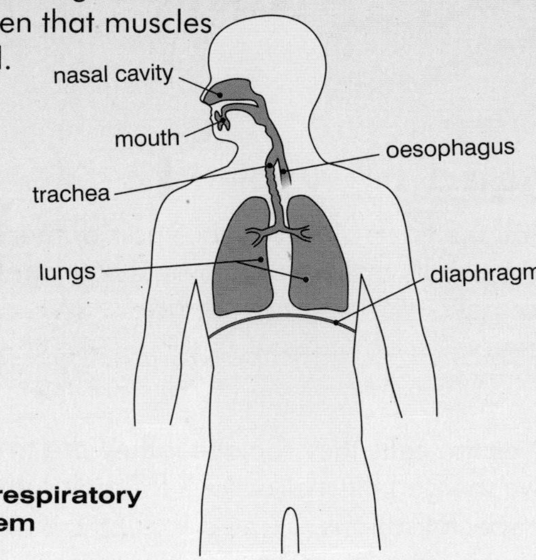

The respiratory system

In the **circulatory system**, oxygen is carried by blood. Blood is pumped round by another organ – the heart.

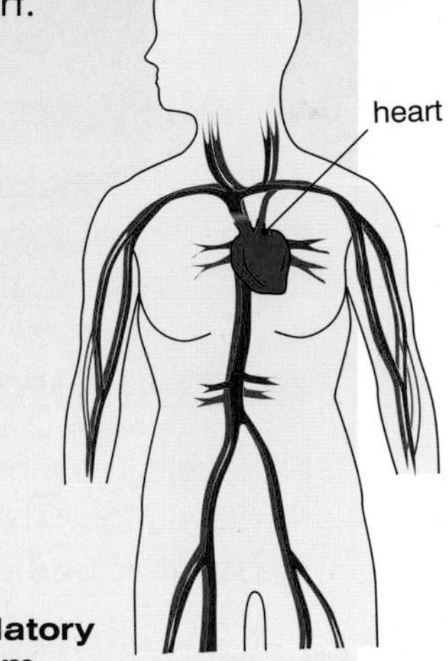

The circulatory system

In the **digestive system**, the stomach and the intestines are the organs that get sugars from the food you eat. Blood carries these sugars to the muscles.

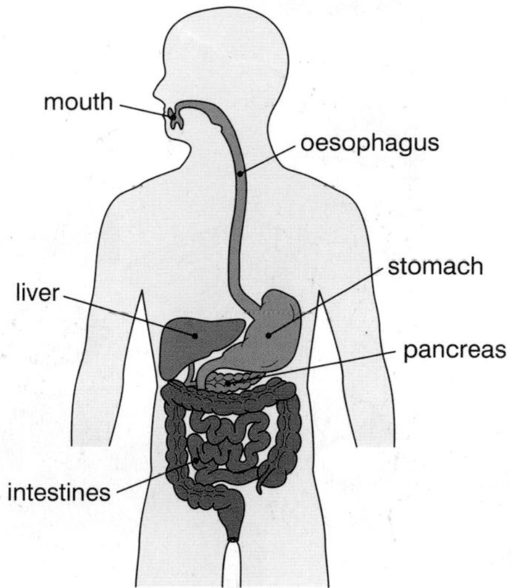

The digestive system

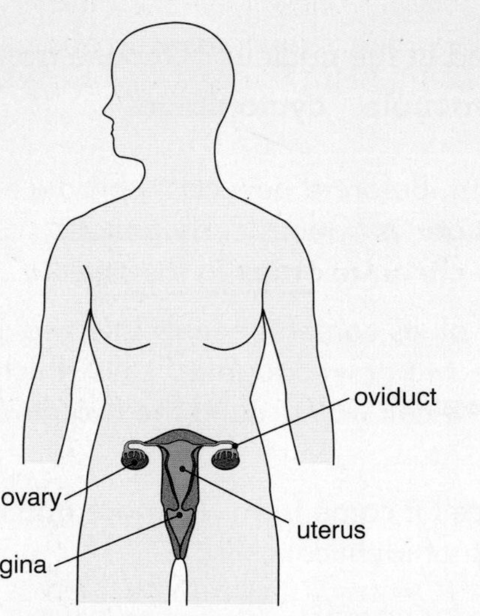

The reproductive system

brain

spinal cord

nerve cells reaching all parts of the body

The nervous system

SUMMARY QUESTIONS

1 ☆ Read 'working together' again. Identify one organ mentioned in the paragraph.

2 ☆ The diagram shows some of the organs in a human body.

Identify each organ and explain what it does.

3 ☆☆☆ Look back over the first section of this unit (pp.4–9). Make a mind map around the theme of 'cells'. Use colours to help build the map.

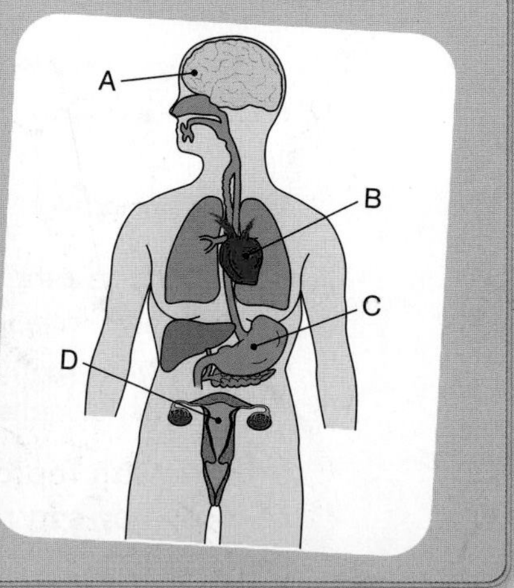

Key words

circulatory
digestive
nervous
organ
reproductive
respiratory
system
tissue

7A5 Making more cells

Learn about

- how cells make more cells

Why do we need new cells?

We need to make new cells all the time. We have to repair damage to the body. For example, new skin cells are needed to heal scratches and grazes. We also need to make more cells as we grow.

Cell division

New cells must be the same as the cells they replace if they are to do the same job. They must have the genetic instructions for their job in the nucleus and all the right specialisations.

Q1 How is information carried in the nucleus? Choose from:
chloroplasts genes vacuole cyctoplasm

New cells are made by cell division. Before a new cell is produced, the parent cell makes a copy of all its genes. Genes carry genetic information and are arranged on **chromosomes** in the nucleus.

The cell divides its cytoplasm and all its contents evenly into two halves. These separate to become two new 'daughter' cells which can grow larger. Plant cells make a new cell wall around the two newly forming cells.

Each new cell is the same as the cell it came from. As more and more cells are made, they form a group of identical cells.

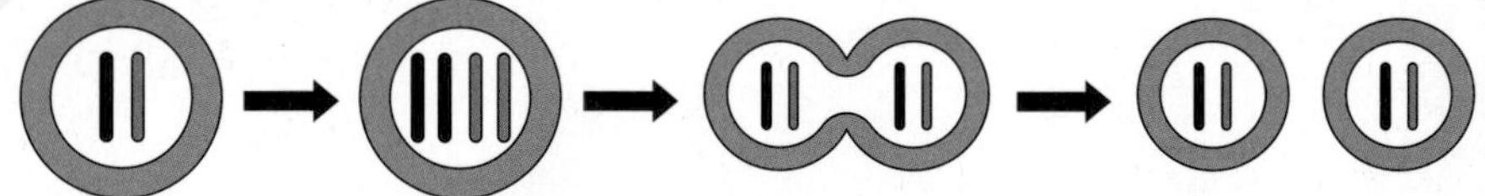

the cell is ready to divide | each chromosome makes an identical copy of itself | the cell starts to divide into two | two new daughter cells, each identical to the cell they came from

How cells divide

Binary fission and clones

Bacteria and other creatures such as the protozoans, found in ponds and damp places, have only *one* cell. They reproduce by the same process of copying their genes and sharing the cell contents between two daughter cells. This is **binary fission**.

Bacteria can reproduce very quickly. In a warm moist place with plenty of food they can reproduce as often as every 20 minutes. This sort of reproduction is called **asexual reproduction**. It does not need two individuals contributing to the offspring.

You have to make about 25 million new red blood cells every day to replace the ones that die.

Q2 You have a dish with all the things bacteria need to grow well. If you start at 9 a.m. with one bacterium that can divide every 20 minutes, estimate how many will you have by 3.30 p.m. Choose from:

500 5000 50 000 550 000

A cluster of cells that have identical genes is described as a **clone** of cells. As bacteria reproduce by binary fission they will make a clone of identical bacteria.

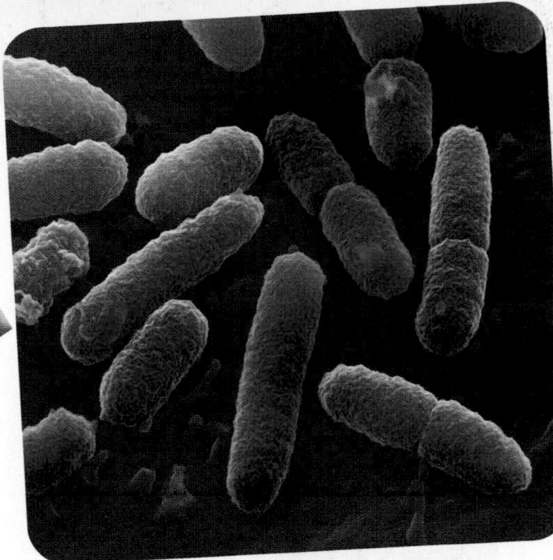

E.coli bacteria can divide every 9 minutes. You can see the 'waist' where the two new cells are separating.

Fruit clones

Strawberry plants naturally make clones of themselves. They grow stems, called runners, along the surface of the soil. About 30 cm away from the parent plant, cells in the shoot tip divide and develop into a cluster of roots. Then some new leaves grow, forming a new plant.

The new plant is identical to its parent, because it is made from its parent's cells and carries the same genes.

The strawberries on the new plants will be every bit as tasty as their parent's fruit!

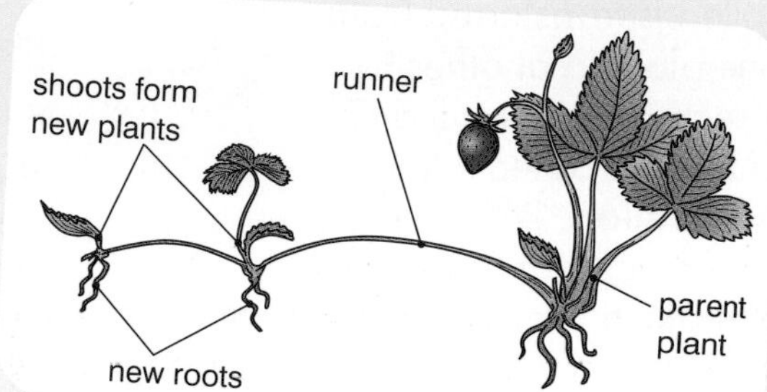

Making more strawberry plants

Making clones

- Your class has decided to grow some strawberry plants to raise money at the school's Spring Fair. There is a suitable parent plant in the Biology lab. Write a plan for your class project to produce at least 20 plants for the fair.

SUMMARY QUESTIONS

1. ☆ What is: **a)** cell division? **b)** binary fission?
2. ☆☆ Genes are important in controlling the flavour of a strawberry. Explain why the strawberries on the new plants will taste the same as those on the parent plant.
3. ☆☆☆ Can you think why producing new plants on runners is a good thing for strawberry plants?

Key words

asexual reproduction
binary fission
cell division
chromosome
clone

Pollen and ovules

LEARN ABOUT

- how pollen and ovules are specialised for their function

Pollen catches in the bee's hair and is carried to other flowers

Flowers

Flowers are reproductive organs. They have stamens that make **pollen**, and ovaries with **ovules**. Pollen and ovules contain specialised cells that will eventually produce a new plant.

Pollen is transferred from one plant to another by insects or by the wind. This process is called **pollination**. Pollination is the first step of the process of making seeds.

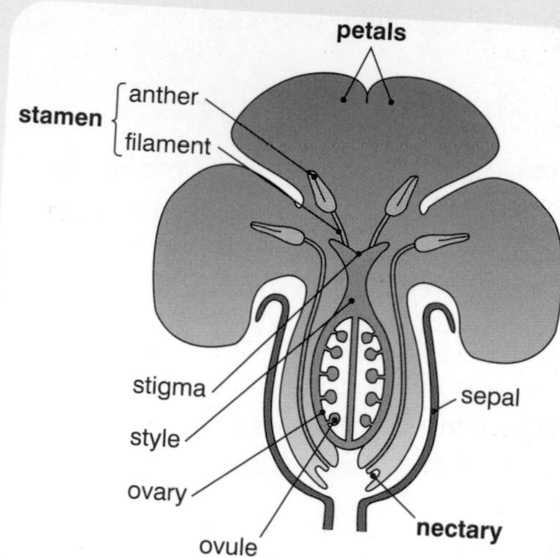

Flower structure

Pollen

A pollen grain has a hard protective coat round the outside that stops it drying out.

Pollen grains are adapted for their function. Some are very light with a surface that helps them to float in air. Others have projections that attach to the hairs of insects. A group of cells inside the grain are specialised to deliver a nucleus, containing genes, to an ovule.

Q1 Are the pollen grains in the picture below adapted for transfer by insects or birds?

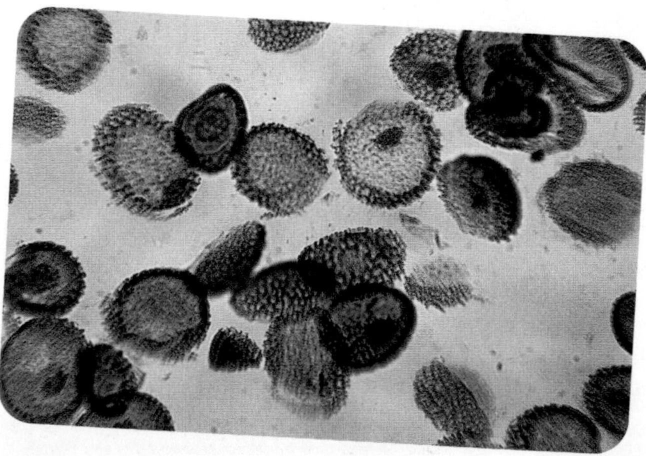

Pollen

Ovules

Some of the cells inside the ovule store nutrients for the seed when it starts to grow. Other cells provide an egg nucleus that is needed to make the new plant.

Fertilisation

A sticky sugary solution on the top of the stigma traps incoming pollen. This solution stimulates the pollen grain to grow a long tube. The pollen tube pushes down between the cells to the ovary.

When it has reached the ovule, the pollen tube releases a nucleus. It combines with the egg nucleus in the ovule. This is **fertilisation**. The nucleus gives genes to the fertilised ovule, which can now develop into a seed.

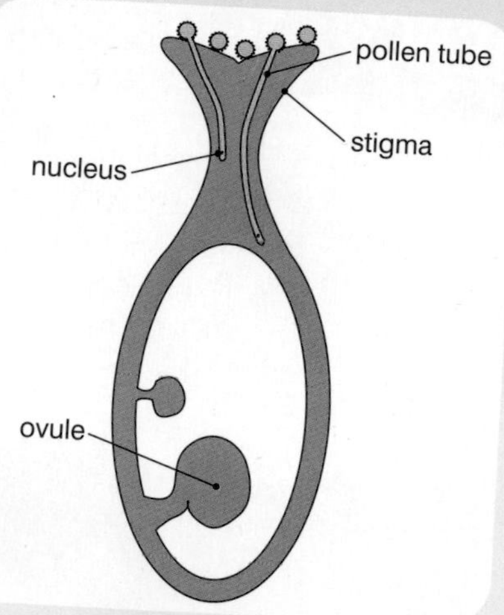

Fertilisation

The developing seed grows a tough outer coat and builds up a store of nutrients. The nutrients supply the young seedling until it can make food for itself.

When seeds germinate, the cells of the young plant divide rapidly. These new cells quickly organise themselves into a shoot, roots and eventually leaves.

ICT CHALLENGE

Search on the Internet for images of pollen grains; compare the shapes of those dispersed by wind with those dispersed by an insect.

Viewing pollen

- Look at pollen grains with a flex-cam or a microscope – can you see any features that would adapt it to be carried by the wind or an insect?
- Grow pollen grains in a sugary solution similar to that on a stigma. Use a microscope to compare how two different sorts of pollen grow.
  a) Look at the flower your pollen came from. Roughly how far would the pollen tube have to grow to reach the ovule from the stigma?

SUMMARY QUESTIONS

1 ☆ Explain the difference between pollination and fertilisation.

2 ☆☆ Using your previous knowledge, and what you have learned from this unit, make a flow chart of how plants reproduce.

Key words

fertilisation
ovules
pollen
pollination

7A
Read all about it!
IDEAS AND EVIDENCE

Antony van Leeuwenhoek (1632–1723)

Antony van Leeuwenhoek, born in Holland in 1632, was an early microscopist. He knew about the microscope used by Robert Hooke to observe animal and plant materials. Hooke's microscope could magnify objects to about 20 or 30 times natural size. Hooke gave us the word 'cell'.

Leeuwenhoek took this newly invented technology, developed it and used it to discover new things. He knew how to make and use lenses and also that he needed good lighting to see clearly. His skills enabled him to build microscopes that magnified over 200 times, with much clearer and brighter images. Some of his 500 simple microscopes still survive.

As Leeuwenhoek had not studied science at University, he did not have pre-existing ideas about how a scientist should work. He worked in a different way to others and developed new techniques to find out about living things. Some of these are part of the scientific method we use today. He was willing to alter his ideas when his observations did not fit with what he had expected.

Leeuwenhoek followed his interest in the natural world to discover bacteria, single-celled pond creatures, sperm cells and red blood cells. He wrote careful descriptions of his observations and used an illustrator to prepare the drawings. These are so good that anyone today could recognise his specimens. Leeuwenhoek regularly sent his findings to the Royal Society in London. The Royal Society published his work, making microscopic life available to other scientists.

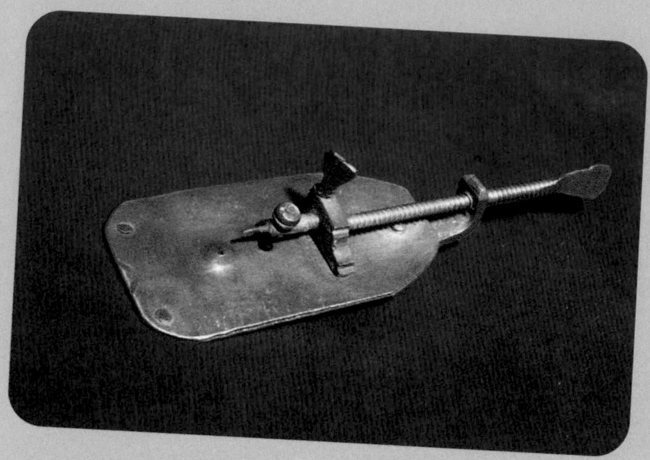

A letter, dated December 25, 1702, gives descriptions of many single-celled pond creatures including ***Vorticella***:

'In structure these little animals were fashioned like a bell, and at the round opening they made such a stir, that the particles in the water thereabout were set in motion thereby. And though I must have seen quite 20 of these little animals on their long tails alongside one another very gently moving, with outstretched bodies and straightened-out tails; yet in an instant, as it were, they pulled their bodies and their tails together, and no sooner had they contracted their bodies and tails, than they began to stick their tails out again very leisurely, and stayed thus some time continuing their gentle motion: which sight I found mightily diverting.'

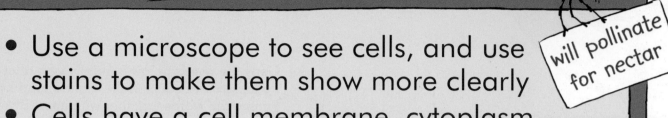

will pollinate for nectar

- Use a microscope to see cells, and use stains to make them show more clearly
- Cells have a cell membrane, cytoplasm and a nucleus
- Plant cells also have cell walls, chloroplasts and a large vacuole
- Plant and animal cells are made by cell division
- Bacteria reproduce by binary fission

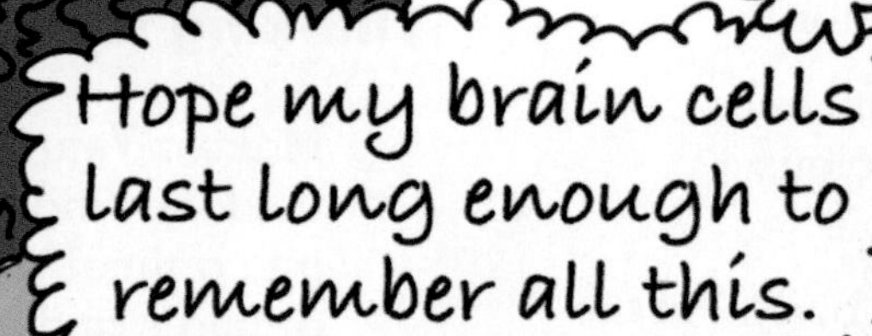

Hope my brain cells last long enough to remember all this.

In mathematics *multiplying* and *dividing* are different, almost the opposite of each other. But when we talk about making more cells, or bacteria, they mean the same thing! When cells reproduce we use *dividing,* as they appear to split into two. Yet they are *multiplying* at the same time, because there are more cells at the end of the process.

Spelling: *cells* are what living things are made of, but we *sell* cars.

Key words

cells
cell division
divide
observations

UNIT REVIEW

REVIEW QUESTIONS

1 Copy and complete, using the words below.
The **field of view** is the area that you can see when looking down a . . . . The lenses enlarge the image. To see cells, a . . ., which is a thin slice of material, is cut and placed on a glass slide. It is covered with a . . . . The . . . is calculated by multiplying the magnifying power of the eyepiece lens by the magnifying power of the objective lens. Inside a cell you will be able to see the . . ., a rounded structure that controls the cell's activity. It is surrounded by . . . . Plant cells have a more regular structure because they have a . . . . A tissue is a group of specialised . . . that carry out a particular job. New cells are made by . . .: the process a cell undergoes when it divides to make two new cells.

cover slip cells cytoplasm microscope nucleus magnification cell wall cell division section

2 Draw two different types of plant cell. On each diagram label the nucleus, cytoplasm, cell wall and vacuole.

3 Copy the outline of the human body. Put the letter of each organ in the correct place on the outline. At the side of the outline write what each organ does.

A heart
B lungs
C brain
D liver
E kidney
F uterus (womb)

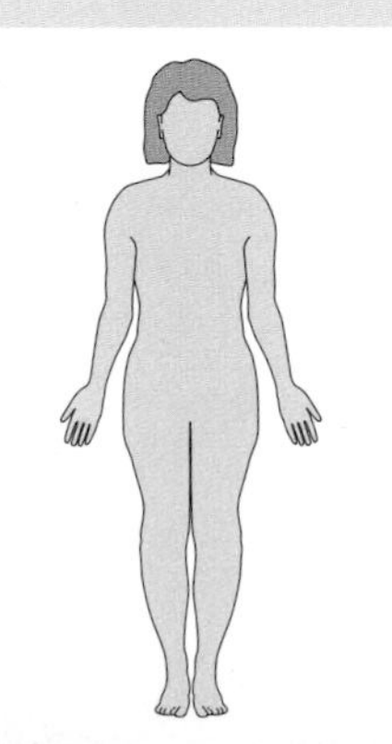

4 Copy the words below carefully with a lot of space around each. Make a mind map by joining the words together with lines. By each line, write a word or short phrase that explains the link between the two. One part has been done for you as an example.

cells binary fission cell division cell membrane cell wall chloroplast cover slip cytoplasm microscope nucleus ovule palisade cell red blood cell section specimen sperm stain slide specialised cells vacuole

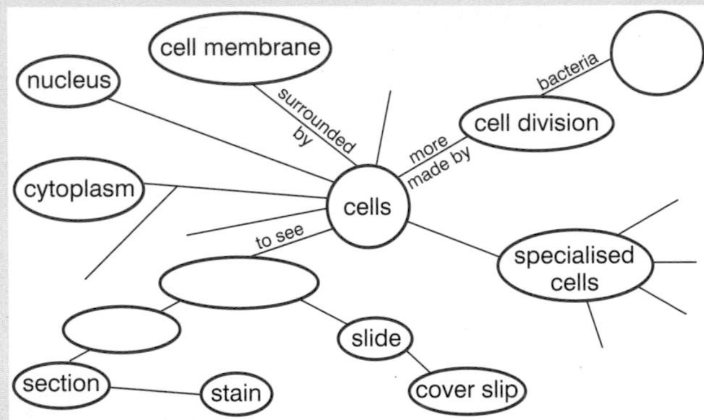

Thinking skills

5 Make a Venn diagram, like the one below, of the following words and phrases. Group them into animal only (A), plant only (P), and animals and plants (A&P).

cell membrane cell wall chloroplast cytoplasm nucleus ovule palisade cell red blood cell sperm vacuole pollen root hair cell tissue organ egg

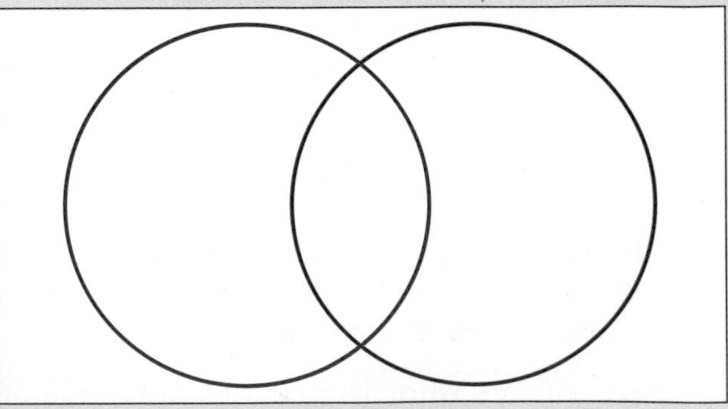

Ways with words

6 Physicists, chemists and biologists use the word 'nucleus' in different ways. Write a sentence using 'nucleus' as a biologist studying cells would use it.

SAT-STYLE QUESTIONS

1 The diagram shows a cell from a leaf.

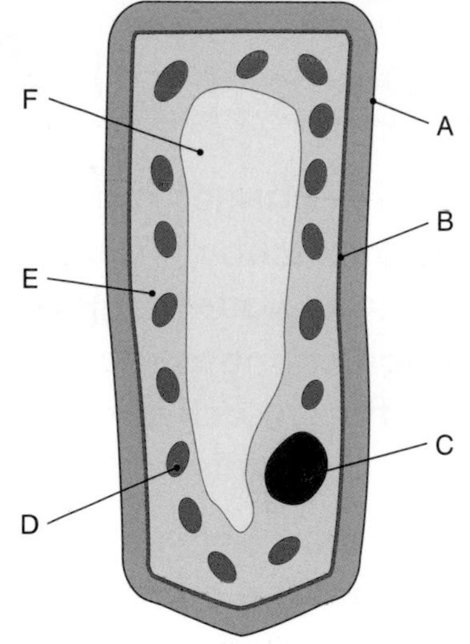

a Match the parts of the cell with a letter on the diagram.

cell wall cytoplasm nucleus vacuole chloroplast (5)

b Which parts are also found in animal cells? (2)

2 The diagram shows a cell from the lining of the windpipe.

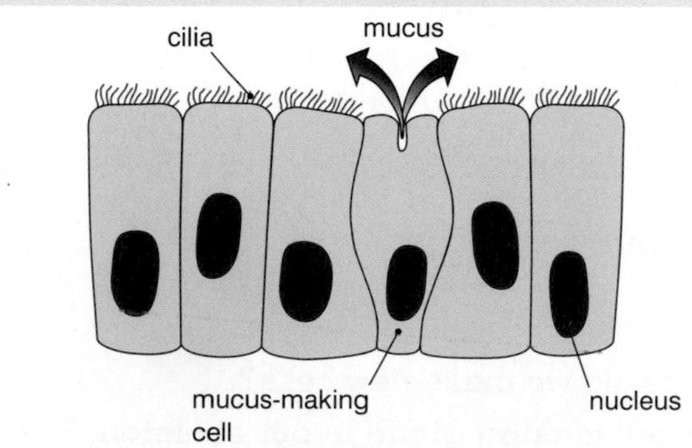

a What is the function of the nucleus in this cell? (1)

b Give one way in which the cell is adapted for its function of keeping the lungs free of dust and bacteria. (1)

c What word describes a group of similar cells that work together? (1)

3 Josh and Arun had been researching bees for a project. Bees see blue, violet and ultra-violet light best. They wondered if bees collecting nectar and pollen were more likely to visit flowers with these colours. They made model flowers out of filter paper, coloured with food dye, and dropped sugar solution on the centre. They made some blue and some pink flowers. They used a security marker pen that shines under UV light to mark dots on some of the pink and blue flowers.

Arun and Josh placed the model flowers near a flowerbed in the school grounds. They recorded the number of bees visiting the flowers. Arun predicted that bees would visit blue flowers more frequently than pink.

Flower colour	Number of visits by bees
blue	6
blue with UV spots	8
pink	4
pink with UV spots	7

a Why did they put sugar on the flowers? (1)

b Josh and Arun wanted to make this a 'fair test'. What factors do they need to think about to make it a fair test? (2)

c Does the data support Arun's prediction? (1)

d Is there another explanation for these results? (1)

e Does the data support the statement that bees can detect UV reflections from flowers? (1)

Key words

Unscramble these:

reclean emblem

toy clamps

specci moor

nice mens

suites

7B Reproduction

Coming soon

What's it all about?

Your life changes many times. You are born, you go to school. You leave school, move house, get your first job . . . Your body passes through changes too. Each new stage of life has different activities, different ways of doing things, and different worries.

Somewhere between the age of 10 and 14 you begin the changes of **adolescence**. Your body grows and your emotions change. Your mind matures and learns to cope with different ideas. Life is confusing sometimes. The changes take several years.

By the end of this unit you will know a bit more about how your body develops during adolescence.

What do you remember?

You already know about:

- human and animal life cycles.
- how plants reproduce.
- cells.

1 Sort these stages into the correct order:

teenager baby pensioner
parent child adult

2 How do we make new cells?

a cell making gland in our skeleton
from eggs
by existing cells dividing
they sprout under your skin

3 Working in small groups, take turns describing the life cycle of a pet to the rest of your group.

Ideas about growing up

I prefer tankinis, they cover you up more.

A week? But I heard that periods only last for a day!

embarrassing innit?

My sister's having a baby.

My big sister and my mum are always arguing over every little thing.

I'm not even allowed a kitten – it's less bother than babies.

QUESTIONS

The Scientifica kids are about to find out more about adolescence. What can you tell them?

a) How does your body change as you pass from child to adult?

b) How do your emotions change?

c) Was Mike right? Do periods last for one day?

d) What does a baby need to grow healthily?

Growing up

LEARN ABOUT
- the changes in puberty
- how the changes are controlled
- human growth

Changes

Since Year 5, you have learned more about the world, you have developed your social skills and you have become more independent. But have you ever wondered if your trousers had shrunk? Well guess what, your legs are growing more than the rest of you.

These differences accompany a growth spurt that begins around the time that most pupils change from primary to secondary school.

Growing

You can see how children grow in the graph. Boys and girls grow in the same way until around 12 years old. After that they differ, because boys become taller and heavier than girls.

Puberty starts sometime between about 10 and 14 and lasts for two or three years. In this time your skeleton and muscles enlarge so that you become taller and wider. Your reproductive organs complete their growth and take on their adult tasks.

Your physical growth and body changes are one part of adolescence. Your mind and emotions change too.

Changing

Some of the changes in puberty are very obvious. Boys and girls grow more fine hair all over the body and coarser hair in their armpits and groin. They begin to smell more strongly, because glands in their skin become active.

Q1 What can you do to stay 'fresh as a daisy'?

Girls develop breasts and wide hips, but boys develop broad shoulders. Boys grow hair on their faces, and their larynx grows larger – leading to a deeper voice. A boy's penis and testicles grow and start to produce sperm. Girls begin to have their periods.

Q2 Look at the growth curve (left).
Choose two ages when girls have a growth spurt.
Choose one age when girls and boys grow at the same rate.
How much taller do boys grow compared to girls?

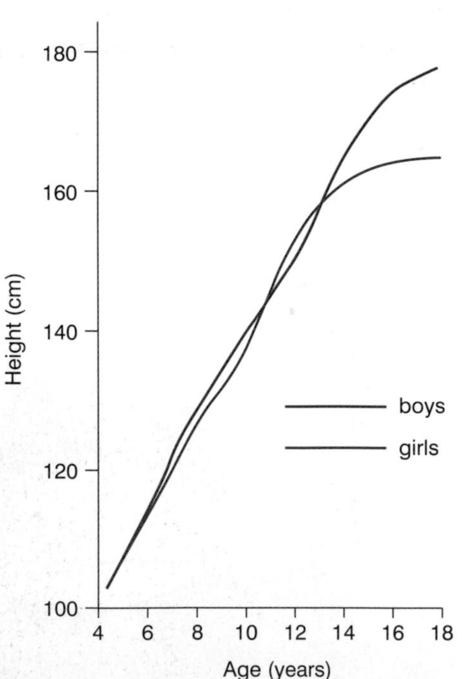

Typical growth curves for boys and girls

Carrying out surveys

- How have you grown since the start of Year 6? Make a list of your changes. Think about shoe size, clothes size, height and weight. What other changes can you think of?
- Carry out a height survey of your class. Choose two other features to measure. Think about how to measure every one in the same way, so that a fair comparison can be made.
  a) How are you going to set out your data?
  b) What would be the best way to present your findings?
  Repeat this at the end of the year. Compare the data.

What causes the changes?

The physical changes are the result of **hormone** action. Hormones are chemicals made by specialised glands and circulated by your blood. They affect many parts of the body.

A hormone is released by a part of the brain called the **pituitary gland**. It makes the reproductive organs mature. The reproductive organs make other hormones that cause the changes that you can see.

These hormones also affect your interests, moods and emotions. The changes continue until your late teens. You become more aware of the opposite sex and more concerned about your appearance. You are expected to behave like an adult, not a child.

You may feel that everyone else is coping better. Problems with spots, stray hairs, smells, sprouting breasts or cracking voices make things worse. Fortunately most young people get through the changes without too much turmoil. They emerge as self-confident, mature individuals.

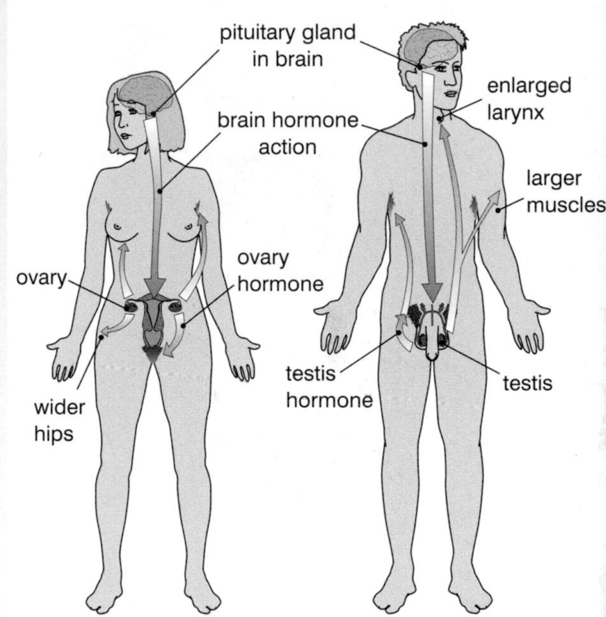

The female sex organs **The male sex organs**

SUMMARY QUESTIONS

1 ☆ Make three lists headed 'Boys', 'Girls' and 'Both sexes'.
List each change under the appropriate heading.
sex organs get bigger hair grows on face and chest
breasts get larger hair grows in armpits and between legs
ovaries start to make hormones voice gets deeper periods start

2 ☆ What controls puberty?

3 ☆☆ Molly Kewell had a chart on her wall and her height was marked on it every three months. Use the data below to construct a growth chart for Molly. Is her growth pattern normal?

Age	3½	5	6	6½	7	7½	8	8½	9	10	10½	11	11½	12	13	14
Height (cm)	91	101	107	110	112	115	118	120	123	128	131	134	137	142	149	153

Key words
adolescence
hormones
pituitary gland
puberty
sex organs

About girls and boys

LEARN ABOUT
- the reproductive organs
- sperm and eggs
- fertilisation

New individuals

Two special cells are needed to make a new life. They are a **sperm** cell made by the father and an **egg** cell made by the mother. An egg cell is also called an ovum. Neither can develop into a human baby by itself, because each has only half the genes needed to make a whole individual.

Q1 Where in the cell are genes found?

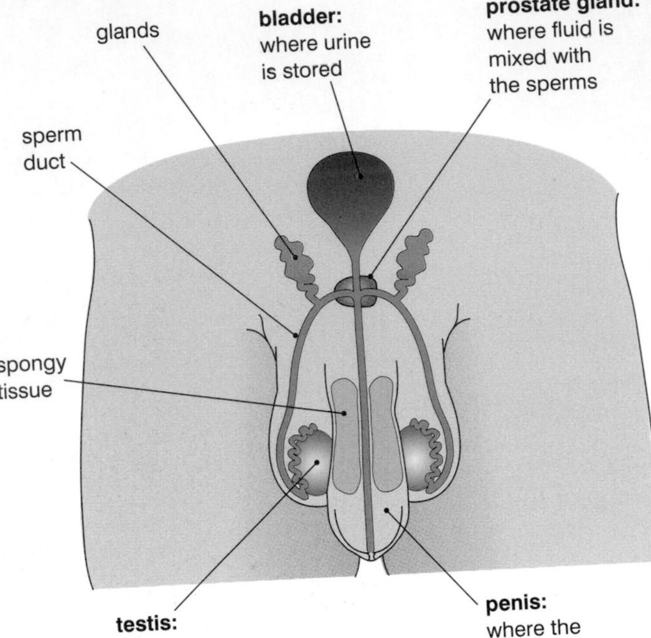

The male reproductive system

Testes and sperm

Men make sperm cells in two **testes**. These are inside the scrotum, near the penis. Testes start to make sperm during puberty and they carry on for life. The testes also make the hormone **testosterone** that makes boys develop bigger muscles, a deeper voice and more body hair.

Sperm are very small cells with little cytoplasm. They are specialised for taking genes in the nucleus to an egg.

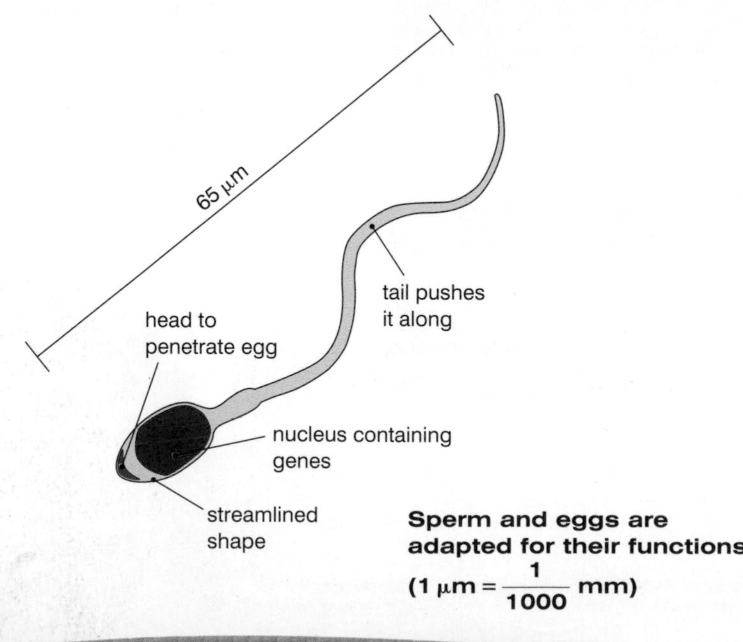

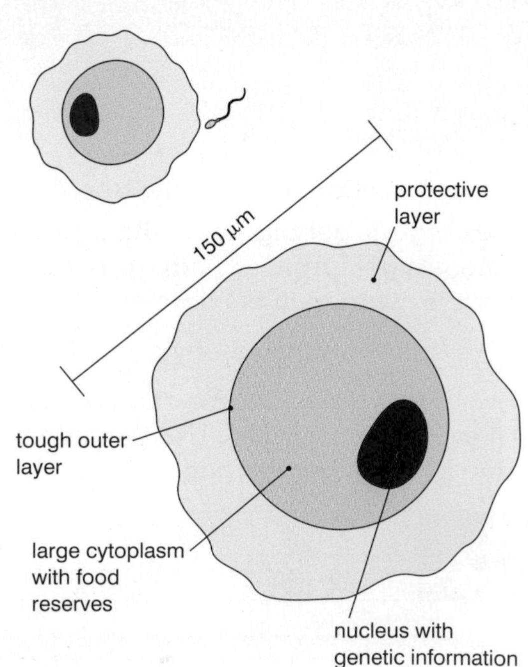

Sperm and eggs are adapted for their functions

$(1\ \mu m = \frac{1}{1000}\ mm)$

Ovaries and eggs

Egg cells are also adapted for their job. They are much larger than sperm and carry some food materials for a few days after they are released.

Eggs are made by two **ovaries**. Each month one ovary releases an egg. The egg passes through the **oviduct** towards the uterus. The ovaries produce hormones that affect the uterus and the rest of the body. One of these hormones is responsible for a woman's softer skin, her breast growth and broader hips.

The female reproductive system

oviduct: where one egg passes to the uterus each month

uterus: where a fertilised egg grows into a baby

ovary: where eggs develop

sperm swim up towards the oviduct where they could meet an ovum. They die after a few days

cervix

bladder: where urine is stored

sperm swim to the uterus from the vagina

vagina: where the baby comes out

Fertilisation

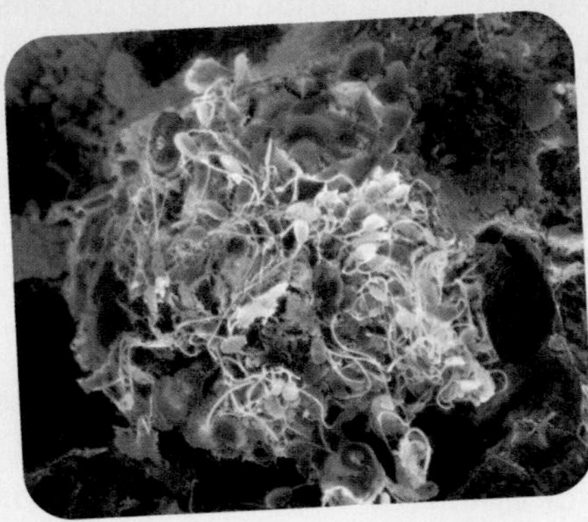

The penis is usually soft, but during sexual intercourse it becomes swollen, firmer, and erect. When it is erect, it can be inserted into the vagina. Sperm pass from the testes along the sperm duct to the penis.

A fluid is mixed with the sperm that helps to keep the sperm alive as they make the long journey to an egg. Sperm are released into the vagina by ejaculation.

Sperm swim through the cervix into the uterus. From there they swim into the oviduct to meet the egg. Many sperm die on the way, but there are so many in each ejaculate that there are plenty left to reach the egg.

Hundreds of sperm cluster round the egg but only one succeeds in pushing into the membrane around the egg cell. The sperm nucleus passes into the egg, while the rest of the sperm cell remains outside. This is **fertilisation**.

The fertilised egg cell now has the genes it inherited from the mother combined with the genes from the father.

The tube in the oviduct is the same width as a human hair.

Drawing paths

- Label the reproductive organs on a suitable diagram. Write the function of each organ by its label.
- On the female diagram, use blue arrows to show the path the egg takes before it is fertilised. Use red arrows to show the path taken by sperm. Mark the place where fertilisation takes place with an X.

SUMMARY QUESTIONS

1 ☆ Explain how sperm and eggs are adapted for their function.

2 ☆☆ Some people find it hard to conceive a baby because of problems with their reproductive organs. Men may make too few sperm and women may have their oviducts blocked, or make too little pituitary hormone. Explain why these make it hard to conceive a baby.

Key words

egg
fertilisation
ovary
oviduct
sperm
testis (plural testes)
testosterone

LEARN ABOUT

- how eggs are produced

What is a period?

A girl's periods are the outward sign of a regular cycle of activity in the ovaries and uterus that produces an egg. It is called the menstrual cycle.

All of the thousands of eggs in a woman's ovaries were already there when she was born.

The first half of the cycle

The ovary contains thousands of undeveloped eggs. At the start of each cycle, a **hormone** from the brain activates one egg. The egg develops in a small pocket of cells. At the same time, the ovary releases a hormone that prepares the uterus to receive a fertilised egg.

The **uterus** is made of muscle with a lining. It can grow larger to accommodate a developing baby. In the first half of each cycle its lining grows.

Ovulation

When the egg is ready it is released from the ovary. This is **ovulation**. The egg enters the oviduct and is swept down the tube. The egg lives for about 12–24 hours after it has been released, unless it is fertilised.

Sex and relationships are tricky areas for teenagers.

Q1 The cells lining the oviduct have hair-like **cilia**. How can these help the egg travel down the tube? Is it:

They push it down using the cilia

They make a current in the fluid in the tube that carries the egg

Once the egg has been released, the ovary makes another hormone that thickens the uterus lining and also stops any more eggs maturing.

If the egg is fertilised by a sperm in the oviduct, it will start to develop as it travels. When it reaches the uterus, a fertilised egg attaches, or **implants**, in a crevice in the lining.

If there is no fertilised egg, the uterus lining breaks up and is lost through the vagina. This is having a period, or **menstruation**. By this time, a new egg starts growing so menstruation also marks the first day of the next cycle.

Q2 Some women have difficulty having children because they do not develop and release eggs from their ovaries. How could doctors use knowledge of the menstrual cycle to help these women?

Ovulation to menstruation takes about 14 days, but the first half of the cycle varies slightly from person to person. On average, the whole cycle takes about 28 days. The hormone changes towards the end of the cycle can make girls and women feel irritable and uncomfortable.

Though every one needs a healthy diet, girls who have begun their periods should eat plenty of foods containing iron. Girls need iron to replace the red blood cells they have lost in their period.

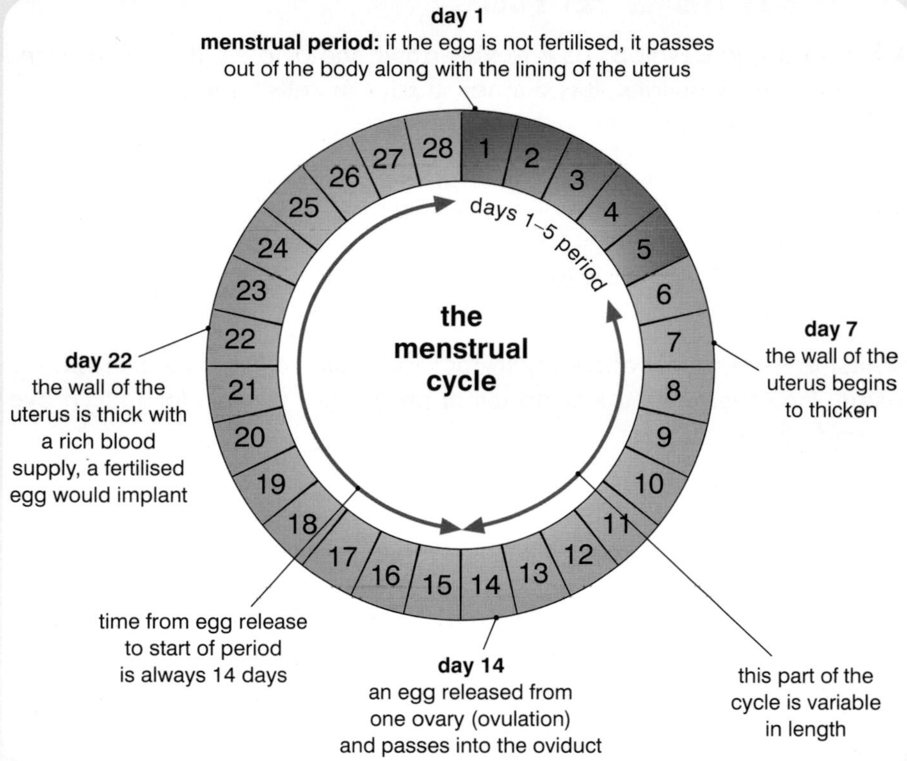
day 1
menstrual period: if the egg is not fertilised, it passes out of the body along with the lining of the uterus
days 1–5 period
the menstrual cycle
day 7
the wall of the uterus begins to thicken
day 22
the wall of the uterus is thick with a rich blood supply, a fertilised egg would implant
time from egg release to start of period is always 14 days
day 14
an egg released from one ovary (ovulation) and passes into the oviduct
this part of the cycle is variable in length

Monthly cycles

Look at the calendar information below. It shows some of the dates in Mrs Stevenson's menstrual cycle.

- If her cycles are regular, when will she expect her next period to start?
- Sperm can live for up to 3 days after release. On which days could she conceive a baby, if there were sperm in her oviducts?
- She is going on holiday on 4 August for two weeks. Will she need to be prepared for having a period while she is away?

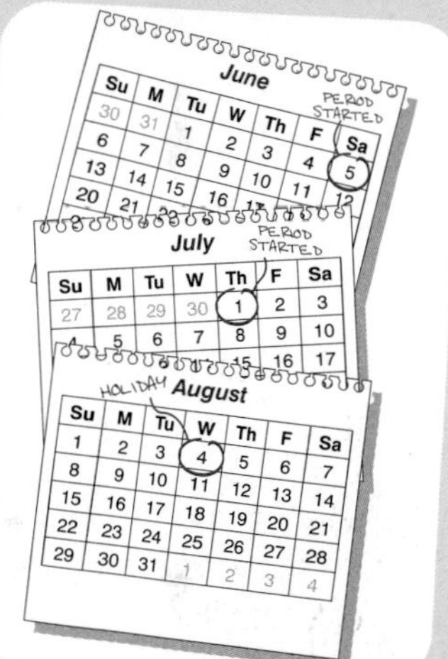
June
PERIOD STARTED
July
PERIOD STARTED
HOLIDAY
August

SUMMARY QUESTIONS

1 ☆ What is the difference between menstruation and ovulation?

2 ☆☆ Use the information you have read to suggest how a woman might realise that she is pregnant.

3 ☆☆☆ Why do girls need more iron in their diets than boys?

Look at the table of nutrients in foods. Choose two foods that would be good for a girl having heavy periods.

Food	Composition per 100 g	
	protein (g)	iron (mg)
chocolate	8.4	1.6
cheese	26.0	0.4
baked beans	5.1	1.4
rice	6.5	0.5
spinach	2.7	3.0
beef	30.9	3.0

Key words

hormone
implants
menstrual cycle
menstruation
ovulation
uterus

Pregnancy

LEARN ABOUT
- how a foetus develops in the uterus
- what the placenta does

What is a foetus?

A fertilised egg develops as it travels down the oviduct. It starts as one cell, but quickly divides. It is a small cluster of cells by the time it arrives at the uterus.

The ball of cells implants in the lining of the uterus. It grows into a **foetus**. The foetus is not referred to as a baby until it is born. A membrane bag, called the **amnion,** grows round the foetus. The amnion is filled with **amniotic fluid** that supports and cushions the growing foetus.

At first there is plenty of room, so that the foetus can move around inside. However, by the last stages of pregnancy it is too large to move around so much.

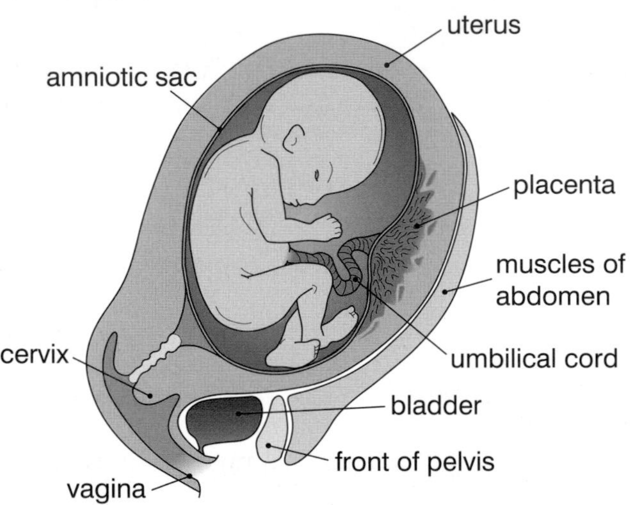

The time taken for a foetus to grow from fertilisation to birth is the **gestation period**. Human babies take about 38 to 40 weeks to develop enough to be born.

The foetus grows quickly and needs oxygen, water and food materials. The **placenta** supplies these to the foetus. The mother's blood flows through her side of the placenta, bringing useful materials.

Blood from the foetus passes through the **umbilical cord** to the placenta. Wastes then pass by **diffusion** into the mother's blood. The foetus' blood, carrying useful substances, returns to its own blood system.

The Asian elephant is the mammal with the longest gestation period, averaging 650 days.

Q1 Which of the mother's organs have supplied the food materials and oxygen needed by the foetus?

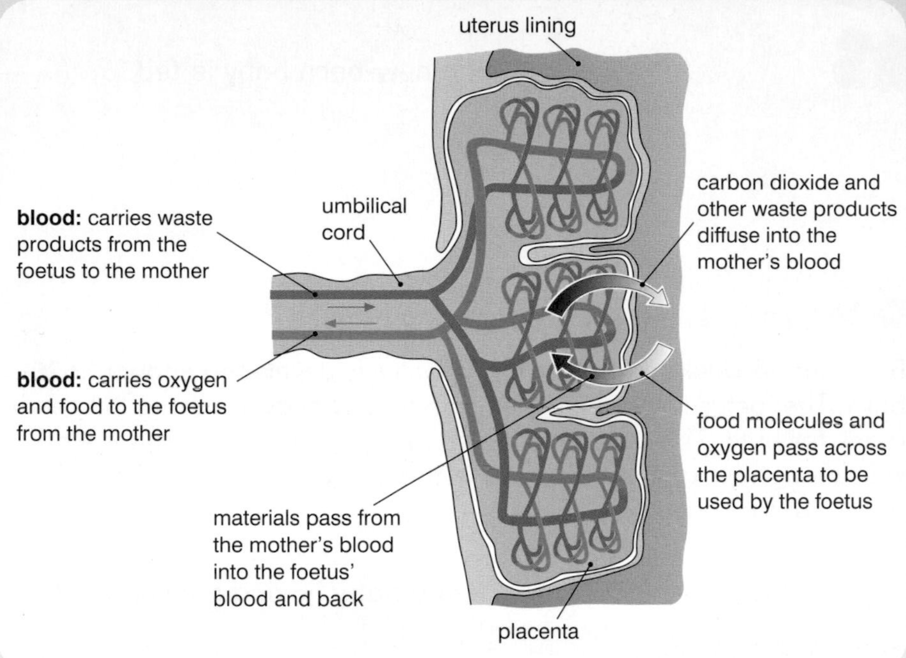

The placenta

Bless you!

The foetus is protected from infections while it is developing inside its mother's body. Her blood carries antibodies that protect the baby from most infectious microbes.

Many harmful substances in the mother's blood cannot pass through the barrier of the placenta, which keeps the baby safe.

Unfortunately, alcohol and chemicals in cigarette smoke can pass through and damage the developing foetus.

Very rarely, two eggs are started in the ovaries at the same time. If they are fertilised by two sperm, two babies begin to develop as **non-identical twins**.

Occasionally, the ball of cells implanted in the uterus lining becomes separated into two clusters of cells. Both groups grow separately into babies. They are **identical twins,** because they have the same genetic information in their cells. They have all their inherited features in common.

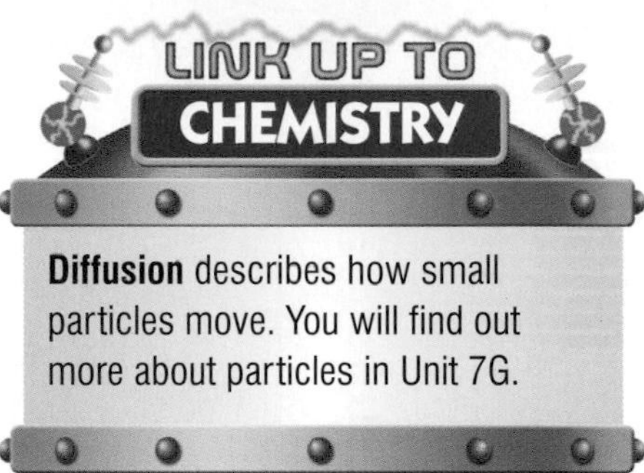

LINK UP TO
CHEMISTRY
Diffusion describes how small particles move. You will find out more about particles in Unit 7G.

Making a model

- Make a model of a developing foetus in the uterus using household materials.

SUMMARY QUESTIONS

1 ☆ Describe how identical and non-identical twins come about.

2 ☆☆ How do genes pass from mother to foetus?

3 ☆☆ Describe how the placenta supplies and protects the foetus.

Key words

amnion
amniotic fluid
diffuse
foetus
gestation period
placenta
umbilical cord
blood: carries oxygen and food to the foetus from the mother

7B5 The first few months

Learn about
- birth
- how a new-born baby is fed

What happens at birth?

By about 38 weeks of pregnancy, a foetus is developed enough to be born. The foetus turns in the uterus so that its head is next to the cervix ready for birth. The lungs, the liver and other important organs work well enough for a baby to survive in the outside world. It will also have a layer of fat under the skin.

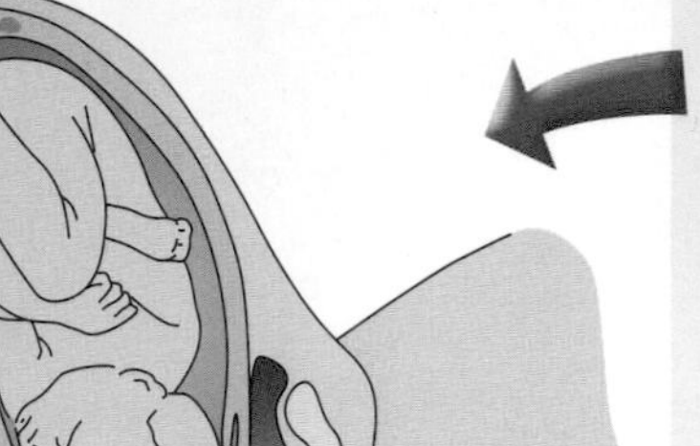

A baby being born

Q1 What are the advantages of a baby having a layer of fat?

The uterus is held closed by a ring of muscle, the cervix. During birth the cervix muscles relax (**dilate**) to allow the baby to pass through into the vagina. The baby is pushed out by very powerful contractions of the uterus.

Once the baby has been delivered, the umbilical cord is cut. The placenta is also pushed out after the baby.

Baby care

The new-born baby needs milk to provide **nutrients**. Milk is made by **mammary glands** in its mother's breasts.

Human milk has exactly the right balance of nutrients for the baby. The baby's digestive system will not be ready for other foods for several months. It also carries **antibodies** that protect the baby from infectious microbes.

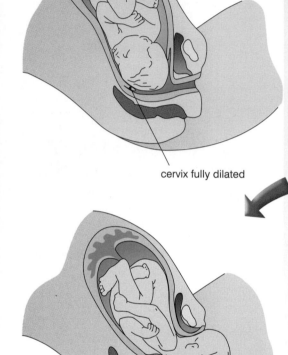

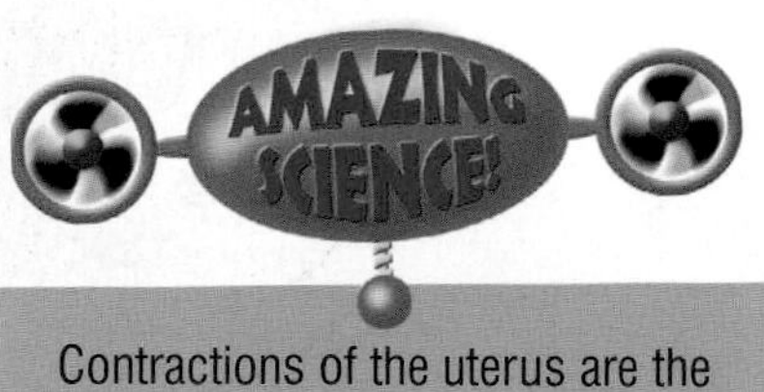

Contractions of the uterus are the most powerful muscle action humans can do.

Breast is best

- There is a lot of interest in differences between babies that have been breast-fed and those that have been bottle fed with formula milk. Doctors and other health professionals say that 'breast is best'. Find out why breast-feeding is better for a baby.

Development

New babies can locate their food source, turning their heads when their cheeks are touched. Within weeks, they can recognise their main carer. They will interact with the people around them – crying, babbling, reaching and smiling.

Babies grow rapidly in the first few months, learning to control their limbs. At the same time, their sociability and thinking skills develop. Babies enjoy being with people, being shown books and toys, and seeing the world.

Here you will look at parenting skills and family life.

Special-care babies

Premature babies are born weeks before their due time. They need special care to survive, because many of their important organs have not developed enough. These babies have a very thin skin and no body fat so they cannot keep warm. They are nursed in incubators, in warm air.

Their lungs are stiff, and so they cannot breathe well, and the digestive system cannot cope well with formula milk. Occasionally they are fed with nutrient solution that passes through a tube into the blood in the umbilical cord.

The babies are given light therapy, or a blood transfusion, to help with problems caused by an underdeveloped liver. Sometimes a baby needs help with breathing to obtain enough oxygen from the air. The incubator is monitored and computer-controlled to keep conditions as steady as in the uterus.

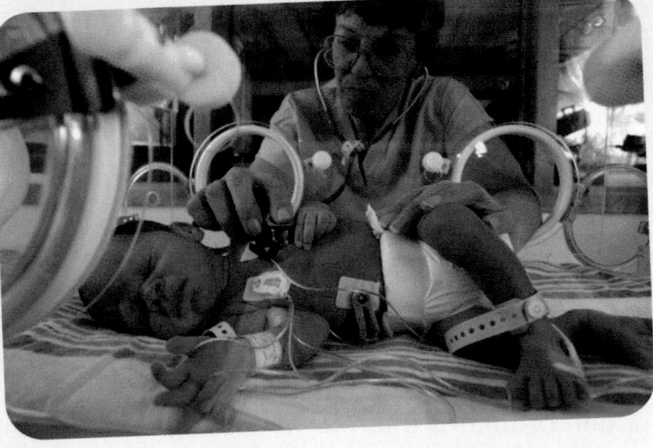

The air in the incubator is kept at body temperature and has a higher oxygen concentration than normal air

SUMMARY QUESTIONS

1 ☆ How do new-born babies obtain the nourishment they need?

2 ☆ Give one advantage of breast-feeding.

3 ☆☆☆ Some people think that a child's ability to do well in primary school is linked with the amount of interesting and new experiences they had in the first six months of life. What sort of activities, toys and experiences do you think a young baby would enjoy? Re-read the paragraph above on development for some clues.

Key words

antibodies
dilate
mammary glands
nutrients

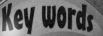

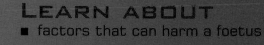

LEARN ABOUT

- factors that can harm a foetus

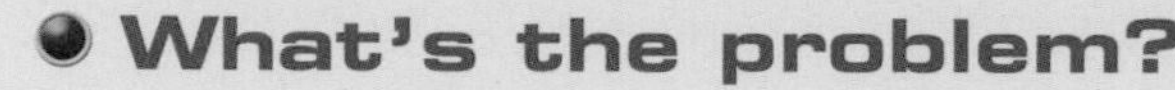

What's the problem?

The foetus is very easily harmed during the first few weeks of development. At this time the mother may not even realise she is pregnant!

Vitamins

A woman is encouraged to have a good diet *before* conceiving a baby as well as during the pregnancy. That way she has good stores of important nutrients. If she does not have enough vitamins the baby may suffer.

Microbes

The placenta usually stops microbes passing to the foetus. Unfortunately the **rubella virus**, also called German measles, can pass through. The virus grows in the foetus' developing nervous system and heart, and damages them. There is less chance of a pregnant woman catching rubella if everyone is vaccinated against it.

Pregnant women should also avoid foods made with unpasteurised milk or raw egg. They may contain *Listeria* bacteria that can cause a miscarriage.

Smoking

Cigarette smoke contains poisonous chemicals, including carbon monoxide and nicotine. **Smoking** reduces the amount of oxygen the blood can supply to the foetus. Its growth slows down (see Table 1).

Babies that weigh less than 2.5 kg ($5\frac{1}{2}$ lb) at birth often have serious health problems after birth. They are more likely to die and have a bigger risk of long-term disability.

Smoking is also linked with premature birth. Women who smoke are more likely to have complications in pregnancy and there is a greater risk of the baby dying. Some of the effects on the baby's development seem to last through to the child's school years.

Learn about the dangers of smoking and drinking.

Table 1 Effects of smoking on birth weight. Reduction in weight (g) compared to babies born to non-smoking mothers (various research studies)

Country studied	Brazil	USA	Norway	Japan
Reduction weight for smokers' babies (g)	−142	−189	−182	−96

Alcohol and drugs

Doctors take special care when prescribing medicines for pregnant women because the drug may harm the developing baby. Too much **alcohol** in wine and spirits can affect the foetus. Other sorts of drug can also pass through the placenta and may harm the baby.

Drinking more than four alcoholic drinks a week can affect the foetus

Designing posters

- Design a poster to persuade pregnant women to give up smoking or reduce the amount of alcohol they drink during pregnancy.
- Look up the vitamin and mineral content of foods. Make a list of attractive foods or dishes that a pregnant woman could add to her diet to maintain her iron and vitamin levels.

SUMMARY QUESTIONS

1 Everyone is offered the MMR vaccine that protects against measles, mumps and rubella. Some people think that it is more important that girls are vaccinated. Why do you think this is?

2 Table 1 (on the previous page) and Table 2 (below) show data about the birth weight of babies and the amount their mothers smoked. The data is collected from several research studies in different countries. Look at the data.

a) Is the effect of smoking the same in every country?
b) If you were collecting data on smoking and birth weight, what other factors would you consider to be affecting the baby's birth weight?
c) Is there a safe amount to smoke?
d) Does having a father who smokes affect the baby?
e) Why doesn't this data prove that smoking damages babies?

Table 2 Smoking and birth weight (The reduction in weight is the average figure for smokers' babies when compared to babies of non-smoking mothers.)

Country	Balkans	USA	Czech	Canada	UK	Norway	Japan
No. of cigarettes per day	1–9	15–19	15–19	20–24	25+	smoking father/ non-smoking mother	smoking father/ non-smoking mother
Reduction in weight (g)	−89	−288	−245	−207	−289	−88	−11

alcohol
rubella
smoking
virus

7B7 Growth and reproduction

LEARN ABOUT
- reproduction in other animals

Do all animals reproduce in the same way?

Some animals produce thousands of young, but just a few reach maturity. Others produce few young, but care for them so that they are likely to reach maturity. Each pattern has its own advantages and disadvantages.

Mammals

Most mammals **reproduce** in the same way as humans. They keep eggs inside their body, and fertilise them there. This is **internal fertilisation**. There is a very good chance that sperm will fertilise an egg when they are both inside the female's body.

Mammals also develop their young inside their body. This gives the young a good start, because they have a constant supply of **nutrients**. They are also kept warm, cushioned and protected from predators and other dangers.

Parental care after birth also protects them from dangers, so they have a good chance of surviving to independence.

Q1 Look at the photo; how can you tell the pig is a mammal?

Pigs are good mothers and protect their young from dangers

Find data on the amount of care given by an animal to its offspring, and the number of offspring it has. Is there a relationship between the two?

Fish

Fish have a different pattern of reproduction. When the adults mate, they release eggs and sperm into the water together. The sperm swim to the eggs to fertilise them. This is **external fertilisation**.

The embryos are usually left to develop by themselves. Many of the young die or are eaten by predators. Only a few of the thousands of eggs released by a female each year become adult fish. Many aquatic animals use this pattern.

Stickleback male builds a nest

Other animals

Birds and reptiles have internal fertilisation, but the young develop in eggs outside the body. The parents usually care for the eggs and may care for the young. Within just a few weeks after the eggs were laid, the young are living independently.

Investigating reproduction

- Working in groups, choose three very different animals to investigate: such as a trout, a crocodile and a robin; or a locust, a starfish and a mouse. Find out about how they reproduce and make a presentation comparing their patterns of reproduction.
- Find out how a developing bird or reptile meets its needs inside an egg.

Crocodiles are very good mothers who carry their young down to the water in their mouths after hatching.

Insects

Insects have a hard outside skeleton that stops them from getting larger all the time. Instead, they pass through growth stages after hatching from the eggs.

The young, called larvae or nymphs, lack many adult features. At the end of each growth stage the hard skeleton splits and the young insect climbs out. It has a new, soft skeleton and some new features.

It expands itself as much as it can until the new skeleton has hardened. This leaves it 'room to grow' inside the new skeleton. Once it is mature, it does not grow anymore.

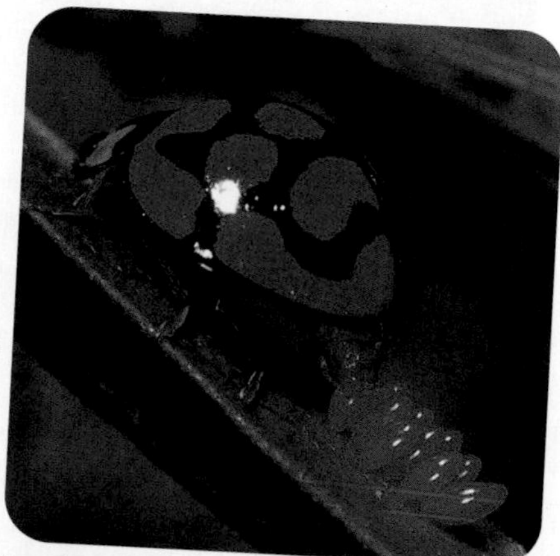

Ladybirds lay their eggs on plants with plenty of aphids for their young to eat

SUMMARY QUESTIONS

1 ☆ Give one advantage of internal fertilisation and one of internal development.

2 ☆☆ Draw two overlapping circles to make a Venn diagram. Label them 'Lays eggs' and 'Internal fertilisation'.

Put the following animals in the diagram.

chicken salmon cobra leopard spider ladybird robin deer goldfish cat human turtle crocodile

Key words

external fertilisation
internal fertilisation
nutrients
reproduction

Infertility and IVF

Lots of would-be parents cannot have children. Often this is due to a problem in the complex reproductive system. A blocked tube, not enough sperm produced to survive, or hormone levels too low to trigger egg maturation are some of the commoner problems.

Scientists have developed techniques to assist families to have children.

In **IVF** (in-vitro fertilisation) hormones are used to ensure that a woman releases eggs. The eggs are caught as they leave the ovary. The eggs are mixed with sperm in a glass dish so they can be fertilised. Healthy fertilised eggs that have begun to develop are returned to the body. Eggs, fertilised eggs and sperm can be 'banked' by freezing them. The parents can then use them later.

The first human baby conceived outside the body – Louise Joy Brown – was born on 25 July 1978. Louise was born in Oldham County Hospital, Oldham, Lancashire, UK.

Spots

Almost everyone between the ages of 12 and 17 gets spots. They happen when the openings of hair follicles in the skin become plugged. Oil from glands in the skin and dead skin cells mix together and plug the follicle. **Acne** is a condition where people have a large number of large spots. It is often linked to the hormone changes of puberty. It affects people whose skin glands make a large amount of oil. Having large pores, or large glands, stress, certain medications, and using particular cosmetics can also cause acne. Though there is no cure for acne, it is controllable with treatments. The most important thing is to wash your face *gently* and rinse thoroughly with clear water. This helps to remove oil, bacteria and dead skin cells on your skin. Hard scrubbing, harsh soaps and very hot water can make things worse.

You do not have to avoid chocolate, soft drinks and nuts because they do not have a major effect on acne. However, a balanced diet with plenty of water is best for all aspects of your health.

IDEAS AND EVIDENCE

It has been hard to prove that cigarette smoke or a shortage of vitamins harm babies. Research starts when children are being born with a particular health problem that cannot easily be explained. Researchers collect data about affected babies and their families. They look for **links** and **correlation** in the data.

Spina bifida, for example, is more common in babies born at certain times of the year. The researchers develop several **ideas** that can explain the facts. One possibility is that there are fewer fresh vegetables available at certain times of the year. Another is that it is colder at certain times of the year and babies do not get as much fresh air and sunshine. Both of these could be the cause, or linked to the cause, of spina bifida.

These ideas have to be tested as much as possible and more detailed data collected. The data is analysed very carefully to try to eliminate other factors that could be contributing to the problem.

However researchers often cannot carry out an experiment to test the ideas because of ethical problems. An experiment might involve giving a vitamin found in fresh vegetables to one group of mothers, while preventing the mothers in another group from having any. If the second group had more babies with spina bifida that would support the idea that lack of the vitamin is the cause. But, in doing the experiment researchers would have harmed babies in the second group who might have been healthy on the mother's usual diet. This would be **unethical**.

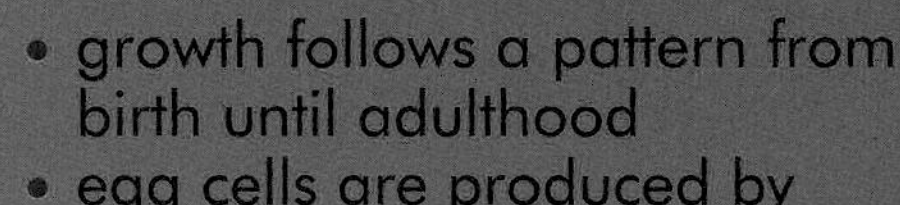

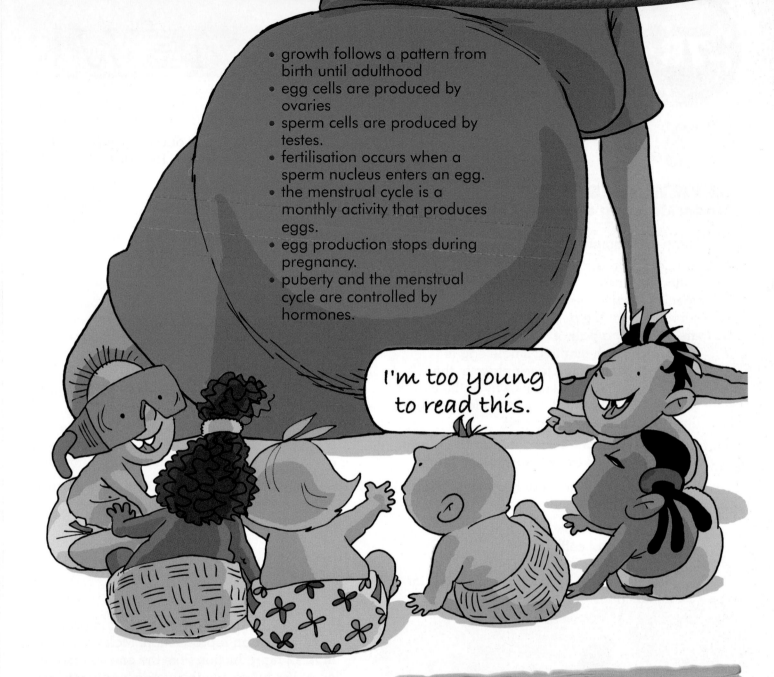

- growth follows a pattern from birth until adulthood
- egg cells are produced by ovaries
- sperm cells are produced by testes.
- fertilisation occurs when a sperm nucleus enters an egg.
- the menstrual cycle is a monthly activity that produces eggs.
- egg production stops during pregnancy.
- puberty and the menstrual cycle are controlled by hormones.

I'm too young to read this.

Word Game

Link the letters together with a word, the first has been done for you:

```
u n b o l t
t         e
e         s
r         t
u         e
s         s
```

DANGER! AVOID THESE COMMON ERRORS

Sperm are *cells* that can move independently. Eggs are also *cells*. Testes and ovaries are *organs* that produce these special cells.

Key words

acne
correlation
ethical
infertility
in-vitro fertilisation

UNIT REVIEW

REVIEW QUESTIONS

Understanding and applying concepts

1 Copy and complete, using the words below.

Animals reproduce using special sex cells called . . . and . . . . These cells are produced in special organs. The male . . . are found in the scrotum, near the penis. The female sex cells are made by a pair of . . . located in the abdomen. Each month a single egg is released. Fertilisation takes place in the . . . . The fertilised egg makes its way to the uterus where it . . . in the wall. If it is not fertilised, the lining of the . . . is discharged.

testes oviduct eggs implants uterus ovaries sperm

2 Describe the changes that boys and girls go through at puberty.

3 Look at the cell below.

- a What type of cell is this?
- b What is its function?
- c Give two ways in which it is adapted for its function.

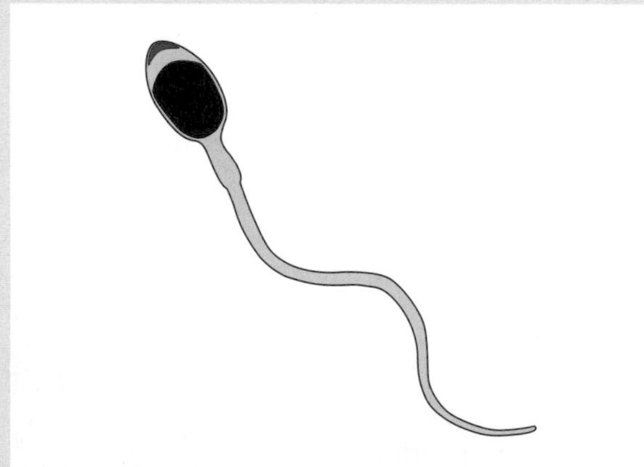

4 Describe how a foetus obtains oxygen and nutrients from its mother. How does it get rid of carbon dioxide?

5 Fish and frogs use external fertilisation, but reptiles and birds use internal fertilisation. Explain the difference between internal and external fertilisation. Give one advantage and one disadvantage of each method.

Thinking skills

6 Work in pairs to decide which is the odd one out in each group. Write down your reason for your decision.

a	testes	ovary	sperm
b	infant	teenager	growth
c	menstruation	uterus	ovulation
d	uterus	amniotic sac	placenta
e	mammary gland	moustache	hormone

7 Bob and Alice have decided it is time to start a family. Alice has a regular menstrual cycle of 28 days. She started her last period on 6 October – on what days in October is she most likely to conceive?

Ways with words

8 All the words below are important in your study of human reproduction. Make a 'concept map' of reproduction (like the one you made on p. 18), by joining the words together with lines. By each line, write a word or short phrase that explains the link between the two.

**baby egg
fertilisation foetus
hormone mammary glands
menstruation ovary
ovulation placenta
sperm testes
uterus umbilical cord**

SAT-STYLE QUESTIONS

1 This diagram shows part of the female reproductive system:

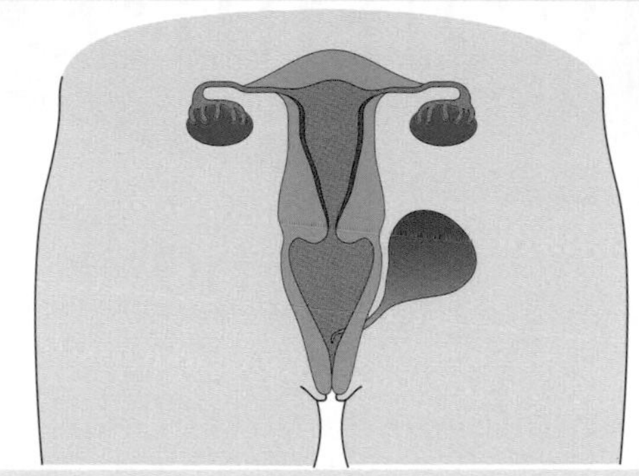

a Where does fertilisation take place? (1)
b Where are the sperm deposited? (1)
c Where is the ovum released? (1)
d Where does the fertilised egg implant? (1)
e What happens at fertilisation? (1)

2 Look at the diagram of a developing foetus:

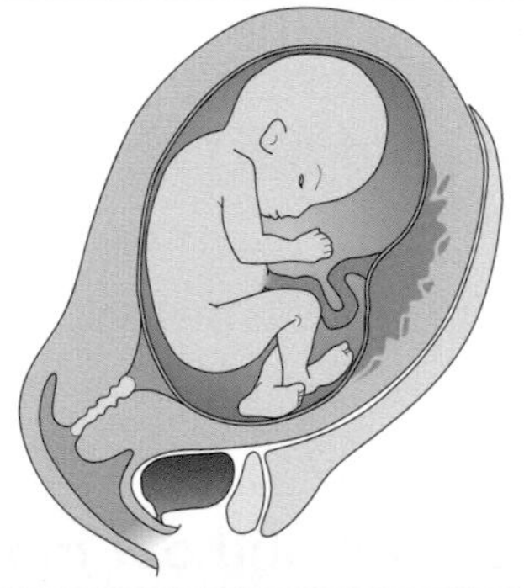

a What links the foetus to the placenta? (1)
b How does the foetus get the food and oxygen that it needs? (2)
c How is the baby pushed out during birth? (2)
d Describe how a baby obtains its food after it is born. (1)

3 Lizzie kept pet rats. She bought two young female rats when they were six weeks old. She measured Millie and Coco from nose to tail tip every Sunday.

Week	Millie's length (cm)	Coco's length (cm)
1	24.0	22.5
2	25.5	24.0
3	27.5	25.5
4	29.0	26.5
5	—	—
6	32.5	29.5
7	34.5	31.0
8	36.0	32.0

a Which rat was the longest? (1)
b Which rat grew most quickly in the first four weeks? (1)
c Use the information in the table to plot a graph.
- Put the number of weeks on the horizontal axis – this is the **independent variable.**
- Put the length of rat on the vertical axis – this is the **dependent variable.**
- Label each axis and write the units on each.

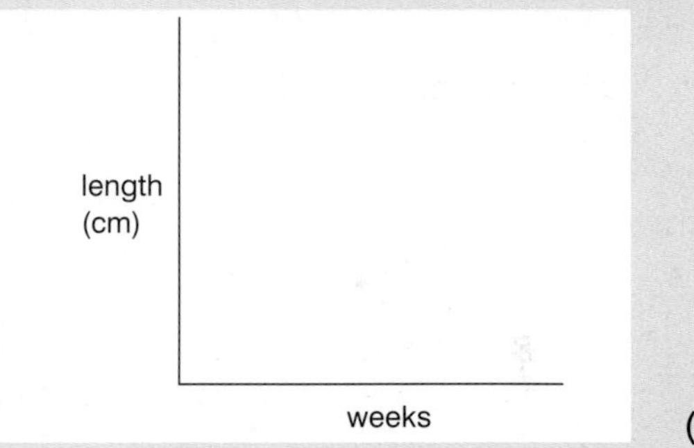

(5)

d Lizzie had to spend one weekend with her Grandma and she could not measure her rats.
Use your graph to predict the length of each rat in Week 5. (1)
e How old were the rats in Week 6? (1)
f Give one reason why Lizzie's measurements might not be accurate. (1)

Key words

Unscramble these:
stoufe
cantaple
minicoat lidfu
stumer nation
pry tube

7C

Environment and feeding relationships

COMING SOON

What's it all about?

What's your favourite food? Chips? Chocolate? Feeding is one of the features of life. The food we eat gives us energy. All animals and plants need energy. Plants use light energy to make their food. Animals eat plants or other animals for energy.

Food made by plants provides energy for herbivores. In turn, these animals are food for predators. Plants, animals that feed upon them and the predators link together in food chains.

Animals and plants also need water and shelter. They must be able to cope with the climate too.

In this unit you will find out more about the features that help animals and plants survive. You will also explore how animals and plants depend on each other.

What do you remember?

You already know that:

- different animals and plants live in different environments.
- animals and plants depend on each other to live.
- some animals feed on other animals.
- some animals feed on plants.

1 Arrange these following animals and plants into a food chain.

bird **lettuce** **slug** **cat**

2 Match the organism to its habitat

desert	common frog
freshwater	shark
woodland	camel
sea	polar bear
arctic	squirrel

3 Name a

carnivore **herbivore** **predator** **prey**

Who's eating whom?

SHE SWALLOWED THE CAT TO EAT THE BIRD,
SHE SWALLOWED THE BIRD TO EAT THE SPIDER,
SHE SWALLOWED THE SPIDER TO EAT THE
I DON'T KNOW WHY SHE SWALLOWED

I told you it looked hungry

It was this big, but it was too slippery to lift out of the water.

If we stay out of the Sun, we can try to find our way home at night.

QUESTIONS

a) What do you know about the feeding pattern in the song?

b) Can you explain why predators need sharp teeth and claws?

c) Can you tell the fishermen why fish have smooth, slippery scales?

d) How does being underground help desert animals survive?

Environmental influences

LEARN ABOUT
- different environments
- how organisms are adapted to their environment

What's the problem?

Polar bears have thick fur to reduce heat loss in the cold Arctic **environment**. Low temperature is a physical factor in the environment.

Animals and plants are **adapted** to cope with the problems caused by physical factors in their environment.

You can see the main physical factors in the table.

The chief factors affecting animals and plants
how hot or how cold it is during the year
how much the temperature changes each day
how much water there is in the soil for plants
how much drinking water there is
when, and how much, it rains or floods
how much oxygen there is in the surroundings
how much light there is
what's in the soil

Life in water

Animals and plants living in water do not need such strong skeletons as on land because water supports some of their mass. **Streamlining** helps animals to pass through water because it reduces resistance and friction.

Q1 The barracuda's fins help it control movement in three directions – what do you think they are?

This predatory barracuda is streamlined enough to chase prey at 40–50 km/h

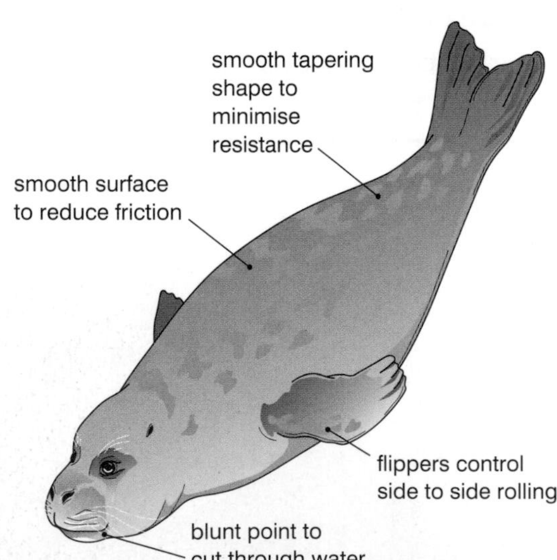

How a seal is adapted to move through the water

Fish use their gills to absorb oxygen from the water but air-breathing animals who swim have to take air supplies with them when they go under water. They return to the surface to breathe.

Water plants grow best near the surface. This is because light is absorbed as it passes down through water. Deep down it is too dark for plant growth.

Life in the air

Flying animals have to be light. They usually have a small body. Birds have hollow bones with bony struts. Their feathers are light and make a smooth surface for the air to flow over. Feathers are good insulators.

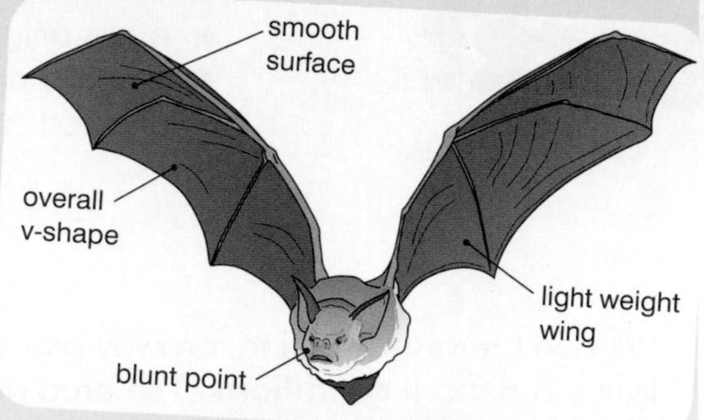

Bats are fast fliers

Life in the desert

The Sun's heat dries out moisture from animals and plants. Plants have thick greyish waxy or hairy surfaces and small leaves. This reduces the amount of water evaporating from inside the plant. The Fennec fox's large ears helps it lose heat. Animals stay under stones and in burrows during the day. It is cooler and moister below ground.

This plant's compact shape helps it lose less water

ICT CHALLENGE

Moles live in underground tunnels. Use the Internet to find out about their shape and how they move through the soil? How do they navigate and find food in the darkness? How do they get enough air to breathe?

LINK UP TO PHYSICS

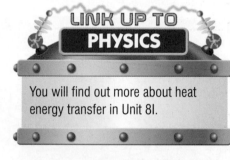

You will find out more about heat energy transfer in Unit 8I.

Smooth movers

- Use modelling materials to make model animal shapes. Drop them down a long cylinder of water. What is the most streamlined shape?

SUMMARY QUESTIONS

1. ☆ Look at the barracuda in the photograph opposite. Which features can you see that adapt it to its life as a predator in the sea?
2. ☆ Give two examples of a physical factor and two examples of an adaptation.
3. ☆☆ Why do you think that animals that feed on water plants spend most of their time near the top while predators and animals that feed on dead remains can live lower down?
4. ☆☆ Cacti don't usually have leaves, but make foods in their stems instead. How does this help them survive in the desert?
5. ☆☆☆ Why do you think good insulation is important for birds with a small body?

Key words

adapted
environment
streamlined

What's it like out there?

Learn about
- measuring environmental factors
- how competition affects plant growth

We don't have to travel to faraway places to find animals and plants living in difficult **conditions**. The area around your school poses plenty of problems for the animals and plants living there.

What is it like round the school?

The school buildings cast shade and make a 'rain shadow' where they prevent rain reaching the ground. Rainwater can't pass through tarmac or concrete either. This makes the soil dry and it has few minerals. The sports pitch has plenty of light (and rain!) but plants are heavily trampled. Buildings block the wind and create sheltered corners. These are warmer too because buildings hold the Sun's warmth.

Q1 List the environmental conditions that can affect living things mentioned in the paragraph you have just read.

You do not need a wildlife area to have animals and plants living at school. They live in lawns, flower beds, trees and hedges and neglected corners. Plants sprout at the bases of walls, in gutters and on the roof. Birds and animals drink from puddles – on flat roofs, for example. Each of these places is a **habitat** that can support a **community** of animals and plants.

Use datalogging equipment to monitor physical factors around your school.

What plants grow near your school?

There are likely to be many wild plants growing in the grounds. These have grown from seeds that arrived from the surrounding area.

Q2 Suggest as many ways as you can how seeds get into your school grounds?

You are most likely to find plants that make huge numbers of seeds. They make so many seeds that some are sure to find somewhere to germinate. Plants have adaptations that help them colonise an empty spot.

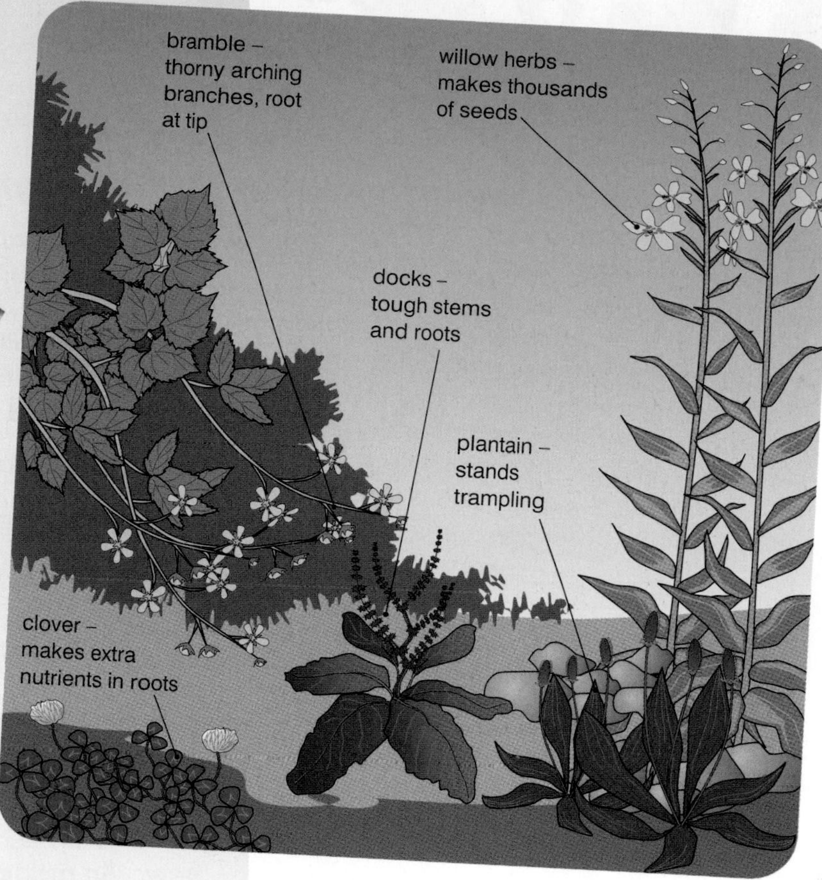

Activities

- Measure and record the physical **factors** in your school grounds.
  The important factors to investigate around your school are:
  a) how much light is available
  b) moisture in the soil
  c) humidity
  d) the air and ground temperature
  e) whether the soil is acid or alkaline
  f) how windy it is.
- Investigate how changing a physical factor affects the behaviour of a small animal. You could try woodlice with moist or dry conditions, or brine shrimps in the light and in darker conditions.
- Identify the plants growing in a sunny place and in a shady place. Are there any differences in plant populations? Can you explain the differences?

SUMMARY QUESTIONS

1 ☆ What word is used to describe a group of plants and animals living together in an area?

2 ☆☆ Select from the list below which instruments you would use to measure **a)** rainfall, **b)** wind speed **c)** air temperature?

pH meter, thermometer, light meter, rain gauge, anemometer

Key words

community
conditions
factors
habitat

78 Daily changes

Learn about

- how animals are adapted to daily changes

As night follows day

Animals and plants change their activity over the course of a 24-hour day. There is plenty of light for animals looking for food during the day. During the day plants make food using sunlight. Their flowers open for pollinating insects. Birds and squirrels look for crumbs round the waste bins. It is easy for **predators** to see their **prey** in daylight and their prey to see them.

The wood mouse does not even go out in strong moonlight, to avoid predators

Plants cannot make food at night when there is no light. Their flowers close because the pollinating insects are not active at night. Flowers that are pollinated by night-flying moths usually attract them with a strong smell instead of colour. Some animals are **nocturnal** and are only active when it is dark.

It is hard for nocturnal predators such as cats or owls to see their prey. Nocturnal hunters have large eyes to cope with the low light levels. They often rely on their other senses. A cat's large eyes are good at spotting movement, their large ears move when they hear rustling in vegetation, and they have a good sense of smell.

Q1 An owl is a predatory bird that hunts mice at night. Which of these features would NOT be helpful?

sharp talons quiet feathers
large eyes eyes at the side of the head

Activities

- Investigate the animals that live in your school grounds.
- Set a pitfall trap to monitor the small animals living in weedy areas.
- Examine the leaves and stems of bushes and leaf litter carefully for insects and other invertebrates.
- Record visiting birds and look for signs of larger animals such as tracks and gnawed food items.
- Find out about the way of life of the animals you have identified.
- Enter your data on a database.

Explore further afield by carrying out a virtual field study using the Internet.

Tides

Along the coast there is a different sort of daily change. The shoreline is exposed to the air twice daily at low tides. It is covered in sea water twice a day at high tide.

Animals and plants living in the **tidal zone** must be protected against drying out at low tide. The slippery coating on seaweed helps prevent water evaporating from its fronds. Animals bury themselves in the sand or hide under rocks. Seabirds and other land predators probe for prey animals hidden in the sand or under rocks and seaweed.

At high tide the waves buffet animals on rocks and seaweed. They could be washed away if they are not firmly attached to something solid.

Q2 Summarise the effects of tides on living creatures.

CHALLENGE

Set up a video-cam to monitor animal life at night in one of the quieter but well-lit areas of the grounds.
Set up a database of animals and plants found in school grounds and information about what they eat.

Crabs and other sea creatures wedge themselves into crevices in the rock to avoid the force of the waves

SUMMARY QUESTIONS

1 A pitfall trap is used to capture beetles and other small animals. Small animals fall in as they walk over it. A pitfall trap was set up in a wild part of the school grounds one evening and emptied the next morning. Nicola and Shreeya identified and counted the animals that had fallen in. They noticed that they had more carnivores than herbivores in their trap. Suggest an explanation for this.

A pitfall trap

2 Look at the owl. Which of its features indicate that this owl is a predator that hunts at night?

An owl

Key words

nocturnal
predators
prey
tidal zone

Seasons

LEARN ABOUT

- how animals are adapted for changing seasons
- migration and hibernation

How the environment changes

The environment changes with the seasons. It is warmer in the summer and there is less rain. Plants grow more quickly and so there is more food for the animals that eat plants. Many animals have their young in summer when there is plenty of food for them. In winter it is colder, windier and wetter than the summer. The temperature may be low enough for ice to form. The days are shorter and there is less light. Plants cannot make much food by photosynthesis and they cannot absorb water from frozen ground. Their growth slows down.

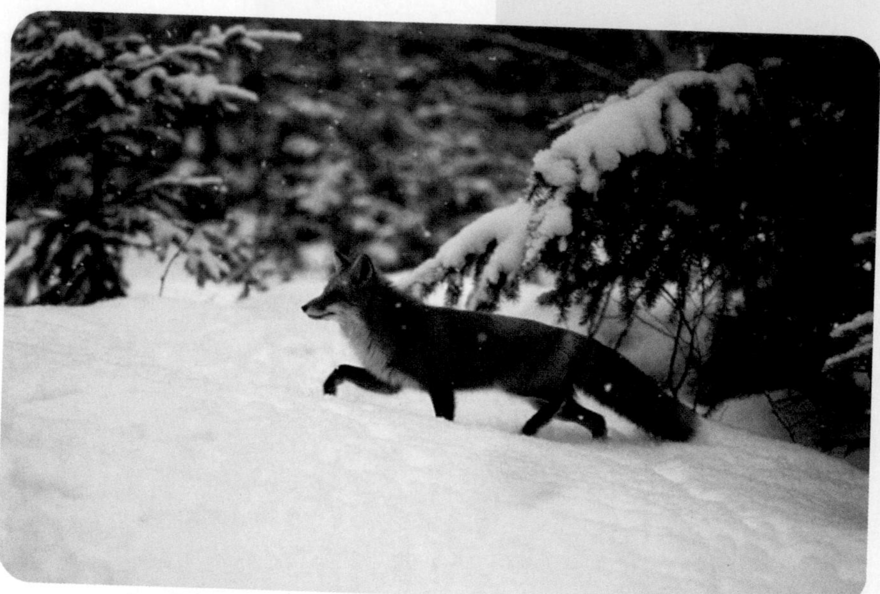

Animals in winter

Frogs and lizards are not very active in winter because their body temperature is too low. Mammals and birds keep a warm body temperature so they can be active when it is cold. Finding enough food to supply the energy to keep warm is hard. Mammals grow thicker layers of fur that insulate the body. They also store fat in the summer and autumn. Fat is an energy store and helps to insulate the body.

Thick fur traps a layer of warm air next to the skin

Bats feed on insects. They hibernate during the winter when there are few insects to eat.

Migration and hibernation

Migration is one way to avoid harsh conditions. Swallows can't find enough insects to eat in winter so they fly further south where there is more food.

Q1 Think of an animal that migrates to the UK in the winter from further north.

Bears survive cold winters by **hibernating**. Hibernating animals find a secure, sheltered place to spend the winter. They slow their body's activity to the minimum needed to stay alive. They survive on fat stores. They are roused by better weather in the spring.

Dormancy

Many plants survive the winter underground. In its first year a carrot plant stores food in its main root, the carrot. In the autumn the leaves die and the carrot becomes **dormant**. It survives on stored food but does not grow. When the ground warms up a carrot grows new leaves using its stored food.

In the autumn many trees withdraw useful materials from their leaves and store them in their roots. Their buds become dormant, then the leaves drop from the trees.

Carrots, potatoes, parsnips and onions are winter survival structures. They store food used for growth the following spring.

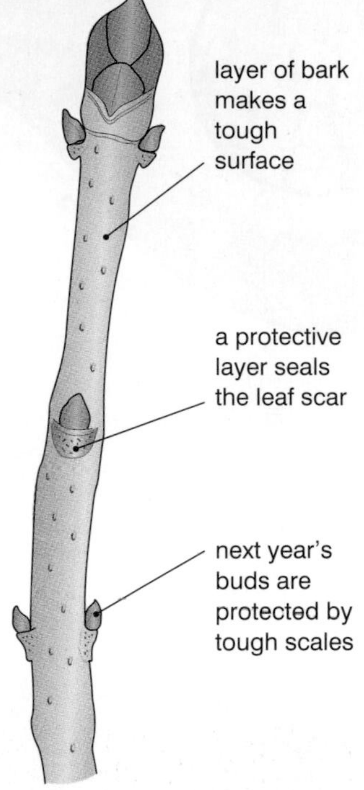
layer of bark makes a tough surface
a protective layer seals the leaf scar
next year's buds are protected by tough scales

Trees protect their twigs during the winter

Surviving the seasons

- Find some items linked to the ways in which animals and plants survive winter. Explain how each is adapted to help the animal or plant survive.
- Investigate how well wool and feathers insulate a flask of hot water. Animals have a layer of oil on their hair or feathers. This stops water wetting them. Find out what happens to insulating materials when they are wet.
- Think about the plants you have identified in the school grounds. How do they change in the winter?
- Name an animal that migrates south in winter.
- Write a definition of migrate.

AMAZING SCIENCE!

A hibernating grizzly bear loses up to half its body-weight in pure fat, over the winter months. No wonder it wakes up starving!

SUMMARY QUESTIONS

1 ☆☆ A stoat hunts rabbits. In north Scotland it grows a white winter coat, called ermine, but in the Midlands it stays dark brown. Can you explain the advantage of this?

2 ☆☆☆ Hibernating animals may die after they have been roused into activity by an unusually warm spell in the winter. Can you explain why?

Key words

dormant
hibernate
migrate

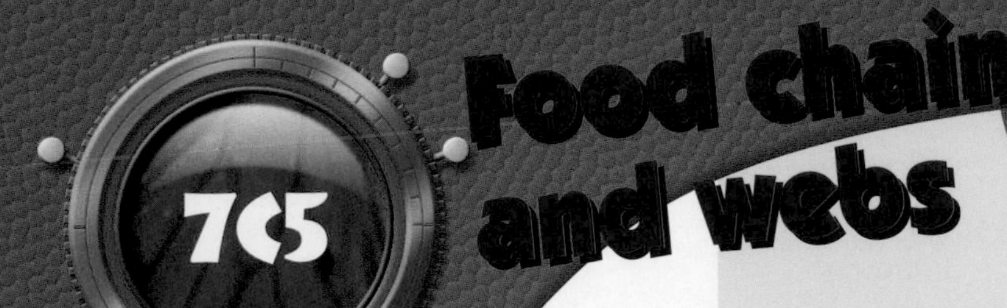

LEARN ABOUT
- why food chains start with plants
- food webs

Food chains

Food chains link animals and plants in a community together. All food chains begin with plants because plants are **producers**. Producers use light energy to make foods. **Consumers** eat plants or animals. Herbivores and predators are consumers.

A food chain is a simple way of showing one possible way the energy can pass from one living thing to another in a habitat. The arrows show the direction in which energy is passing along the chain.

Q1 Do you think bacteria that decay dead organisms are producers or consumers?

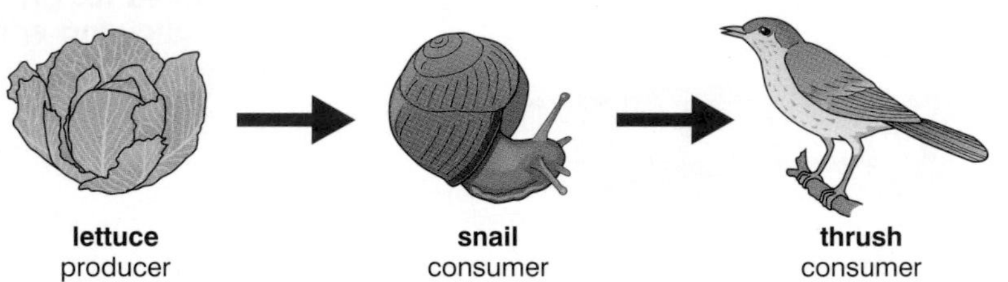

A food chain

Use the database you prepared earlier in section 7C3. You now have the information you need for making a food web.

Food webs

The slugs in your garden are happy to eat cabbages, lettuces, and flowers as well as dead plants. Local foxes eat slugs, worms, apples and mice. A **food chain** showing lettuce → slug → fox is just one of many routes that energy can pass along. Slugs will be in many different food chains. A **food web** is a better way to show the feeding relationships in a community. The woodland food web is made of many interlinking food chains.

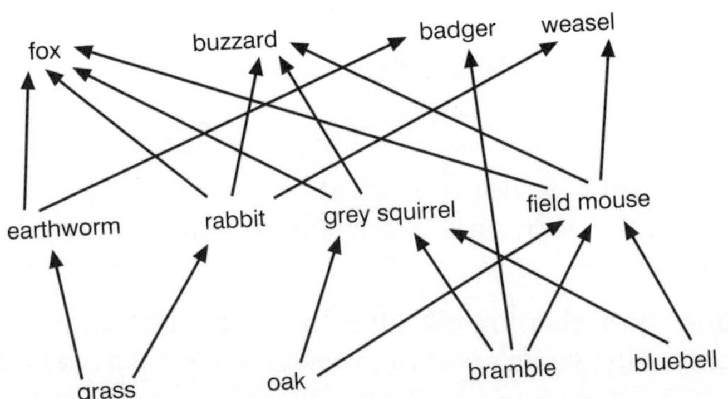

A woodland food web

Q2 Look at the woodland food web – which of these are top carnivores?

oak, rabbit, fox, weasel

Organisms obtaining energy in the same way are placed on the same level of a food web. Plants are producers so they all go at the base. The animals that eat vegetation are on the next level. The level after that consists of smaller predators eating smaller herbivores. At the top are the predators that do not have many natural enemies, the top carnivores.

A large oak tree can support up to 200 different types of organism from the food materials in its leaves, buds, acorns and bark.

Activities

- Use the information you found out about the animals and plants in your school grounds to link them together in food webs.
- Use any observations you made which could help to identify a food source. For example you might have found a housefly in a spider's web.
- Try to explain any missing links.

SUMMARY QUESTIONS

1 ☆ Look at the woodland food web on the previous page.
  a) Pick out three food chains from the food web.
  b) Identify the producers, a consumer, a herbivore and a carnivore in the food web.

2 ☆☆ Write definitions of the following terms:
  producer **consumer** **predator**

3 ☆☆☆ Di and Mike wanted to construct a food web of animals and plants that live in a pond. They found some information in a book. Copy the food web frame into your book. Use the information they found to place each organism on the correct level. Link them with arrows to show the direction of energy flow.
Larvae (singular: larva) and nymphs are young insects.

great diving beetles eat tadpoles, midge larvae and stonefly nymphs
algae are eaten by midge larvae, blackfly larvae and tadpoles
great diving beetles eat dragonfly nymphs
dragonfly nymphs eat tadpoles, midge larvae and caddis fly larvae
caddis fly larvae eat algae
stonefly nymphs eat blackfly larvae

top carnivores	
smaller predators	
herbivores	
producers	

Key words

consumer
food chain
food web
producer

LEARN ABOUT
- how plants can deter browsers
- predators
- defences against being eaten

Predators

Predators have to be able to find, catch and kill their **prey**. The fish eagle in the photograph feeds on fish swimming just below the surface. Its forward facing eyes have acute vision. From high in the air the eagle can spot the shadowy shapes and estimate the distance accurately. It has long legs to reach under the surface while its body stays above the water. Its feet have large sharp curved talons to hook a slippery fish. Its tail acts as a brake when it has dived down. Its powerful wings lift it clear of the water again. The powerful curved beak helps it to tear meat from the fish.

A fish eagle striking a fish

Q1 Fish eagles ambush their prey. Can you think of another predator that ambushes its prey?

The prey

The fish hunted by fish eagles are hard to spot. They are dark grey on the top which **camouflages** them against the bottom of a lake. Underneath they are silvery white. Predators below them don't see the fish camouflaged against the silvery surface.

Prey animals are adapted for detecting and avoiding predators. The large eyes on the side of a rabbit's head allow it to see in all directions. Even a passing cloud shadow overhead alarms them.

Find out how a zebra's and a tiger's stripes, a ladybird's bright colour, and a hedgehog's spines help them survive.

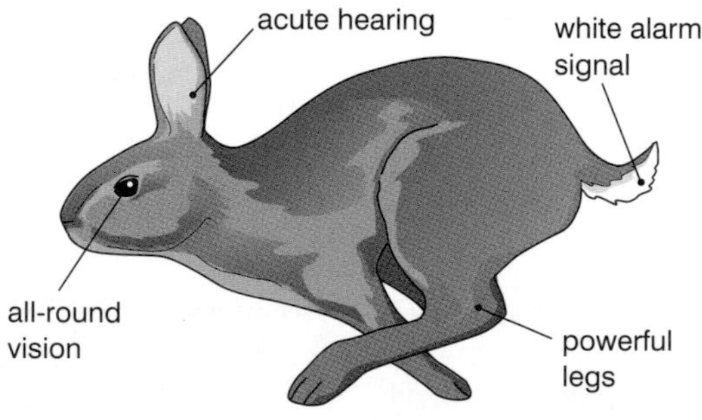

Rabbits are well-adapted to avoid predators

I can't seem to find anyone to help with the dishes.

Prey animals also have large ears with sensitive hearing and a keen sense of smell. They often "freeze" when alarmed. Predators are good at spotting movement but a still rabbit or squirrel merges into the background. If the predator is close, a rabbit runs fast using its powerful back legs. It makes sudden changes of direction to make it harder for the predator to catch it.

Plants

Fine hairs, prickles, thorns or spines protect a plant's leaves from browsing animals. Plants, such as clover, make unpleasant chemicals in their leaves or seeds. Animals quickly learn to avoid them. The nettle's irritant stinging hairs have the same effect.

Herbivores can also damage plants by tugging them out of the ground as they eat, and by trampling on them. Dandelions and docks have long tough roots that resist pulling. Daisies and dandelions keep the growing point close to the ground where they are less likely to be eaten.

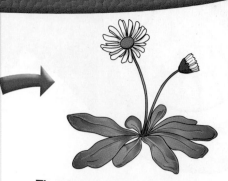

The daisy's hairy leaves are flattened against the ground to avoid browsers

A parrot's beak exerts enough force to break large Brazil nuts

Activities

- Indoors: Cut a caterpillar shape out of paper. Colour it to match the surface of a part of your laboratory. Ask your teacher to fasten it to the surface before the lesson. Test your caterpillar's camouflage by timing how long it takes your classmates to find it.
- Outdoors: Make model caterpillars out of wool or modelling materials. Place them in a particular area of the grounds. Challenge another group to find them.
- Birds that eat sunflower and other large seeds have a big blunt beak shape compared with those that eat small seeds like millet. Use forceps with fine ends or blunt ends as model beaks. Investigate the effect of beak size on picking up bird seed. Test whether a fine point or blunt point beak is better for cracking seeds to get at the kernel inside.

Wild guinea pigs live in long grass. They detect predators by smell and sound. If you have a guinea pig, it can hear and smell you long before it sees you!

SUMMARY QUESTIONS

1 ☆ Continue the table to show the features of predators and prey.

Predators	Prey
Sharp eyes to spot prey at a distance	Good all-round vision

2 ☆☆ Choose an animal and make a spider diagram of the ways in which it is adapted for its life. Think about how it moves, where it lives, how it is adapted for the changes in its environment, what it feeds on, and how it avoids been eaten.

camouflage
predator
prey

LEARN ABOUT

- how changes in one part affects the rest of a food web
- competition in a food web

Competing for food

A hedgehog eats worms, slugs, beetles and small frogs. If frogs are scarce they can eat more beetles. This will affect other animals that also eat beetles. They will find it harder to get what they need. There is more **competition** for beetles. There may not be enough for all the animals to survive and raise their offspring. In the garden food web if the numbers of cabbage white caterpillars decrease then the blue tit and ladybird will compete for greenfly. There will be fewer greenfly, but the roses will grow better.

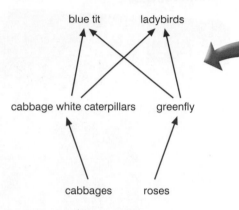

blue tit
ladybirds
cabbage white caterpillars
greenfly
cabbages
roses

A food web in the garden

Q1 What do you think will happen to the cabbages? Better leaves? More chewed leaves?

Why things change

All sorts of events can affect how many animals or plants there are in a community.

Food: The amount of food, or light for plants, is most important. When there is plenty of food the numbers grow. When there isn't very much the numbers decline.

Predators: If there are many predators around the number of prey go down.

Habitat reduction: New roads and housing developments reduce the area for plants to grow and animals to find food. When hedges and trees are removed, safe refuges for animals are lost. They have fewer places to breed or escape from predators. Animals and plants are separated so it is harder for them to breed.

Pollution: Animals and plants are often sensitive to chemicals we use on farms, in factories and in houses. When these get into the environment they can damage animals and plants. Pollution entering a stream may reduce the amount of oxygen in the water. Copper and cadmium compounds in the soil make it hard for plants to grow.

Roads and houses interrupt breeding sites and activity

Winners and Losers

Have you seen a fox or squirrel recently? If so you probably live in a large town. The wild animals and plants we see in towns can exploit new opportunities. They can adapt their behaviour to survive in a different environment. Kestrels nest undisturbed on the top of a block of flats and hunt mice in shop yards and markets. Foxes live under sheds and sleep on garages. They scavenge take-away meals from litter.

Other animals are very particular about their habitat. As marshes and boggy ground are drained to provide farmland, animals like the raft spider almost disappear. Red squirrels survive best in large stretches of conifer woods. We have to protect habitats if we want to **conserve** these species.

Siberian tigers need a large area to hunt away from human activity

Food webs

- Look at the food webs you made of the animals and plants in the school grounds. Work out what will happen if you alter the numbers of some of your organisms.

Find out about conserving tigers, manatees or tamarin monkeys.

SUMMARY QUESTIONS

Use your understanding of food webs to predict what will happen in this food web:

a) ☆ if the farmer uses insecticide to kill the flies.

b) ☆☆ if the farmer decides to remove the hedges to turn three fields into one big field.

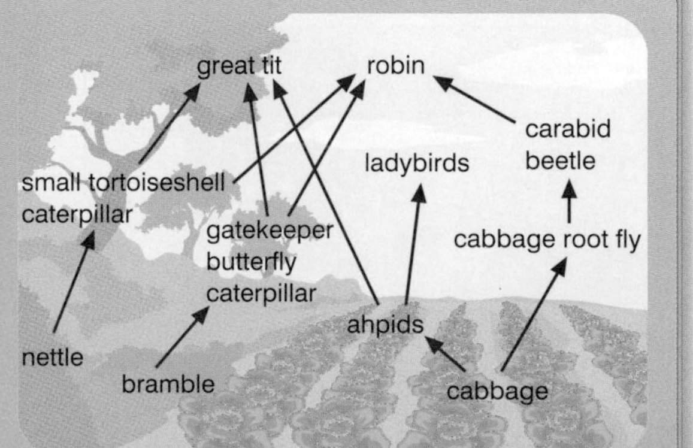

Key words

competition
conserve

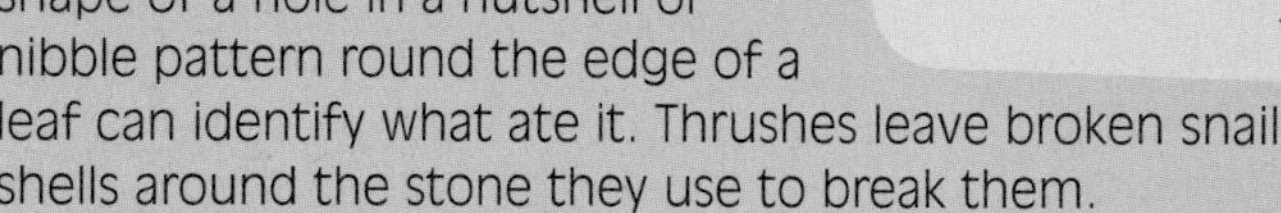

IDEAS AND EVIDENCE

Ecologists are scientists who investigate plant and animal communities. Animals are often very shy. It can be difficult to spot them or to observe exactly what they are eating. Ecologists use different kinds of evidence to identify which animals are present and what they eat. They rely on traces that the animals leave as they go about their business. For example, otters are particularly shy and seldom seen. The presence of their fishy droppings, called spraint, is the main clue that they are around.

Many animals live close to the food they eat. Butterflies lay their eggs on their caterpillars' food plant. Caterpillars are usually eating the plant you found them on. Lots of animals leave distinctive teeth or nibble marks on their food. The shape of a hole in a nutshell or nibble pattern round the edge of a leaf can identify what ate it. Thrushes leave broken snail shells around the stone they use to break them.

Owls cough up owl pellets, which can be found below an owl's roost. An owl pellet contains bones and other indigestible bits of the animals it has eaten. If it is taken apart the remains can be identified and the owl's diet deduced. Scientists also look at the stomach contents of dead animals, for example, sharks that have been caught. They can identify the remains of animals or plants eaten most recently. Not everything in the stomach is food. Sharks have been found to have eaten plastic containers and lifebuoys dropped from ships as well as tin cans.

Otter traces show that they are returning to the edges of cities now that waterways have been cleaned up and fish have returned

SCIENTIFIC PEOPLE

A park ranger manages an area of countryside on the edge of a large town or city. Sutton Park in the Midlands is a lowland heath with lakes and ponds full of wildfowl. Part of it is a Site of Special Scientific Interest (SSSI). This kind of habitat has almost disappeared in Europe and most of what is left is in the UK, so it has to be looked after. At the same time, hundreds of people use it every day for grazing cows, riding horses, walking dogs, cycling, orienteering and other activities.

A team of rangers try to balance the needs of people with the needs of wildlife and manage the area so that its character doesn't change. They look after the woods so that they do not take over the open heath, and keep the ponds and rivers clear. They monitor and encourage the wildlife. They also have play areas and a visitor centre where people can find out about the Park. Most park rangers have a background in estate or countryside management, biological sciences or ecology at university.

• the key physical factors in an environment are temperature, water, oxygen, and light
• organisms are adapted to survive within their environment
• animals are adapted to be active at night and for changing seasons
• animals are adapted for finding their food and avoiding being eaten
• food chains start with plants
• food chains are linked together into food webs
• factors which affect organisms in one part of a food web affect others too.

DANGER! AVOID THESE COMMON ERRORS

The arrows in a food chain show the direction in which energy passes. Energy passes into plants as light energy. Plants use it to make foods. Energy is now stored in plant material. When an animal eats a plant, it gains the energy stored in that plant. Energy passes from a food source to the animal that eats it.

Don't draw your arrows pointing the wrong way, you will be suggesting that lettuces eat slugs and greenfly eat robins!

sun $\xrightarrow{\text{light energy}}$ plant $\xrightarrow{\text{energy stored in the plant}}$ herbivore $\xrightarrow{\text{energy stored in the animal}}$ carnivore

Key words

adapted
ecologist
evidence
food web
ranger

UNIT REVIEW

REVIEW QUESTIONS
Understanding and applying concepts

1 Copy and complete using the words below.

A . . . . . . shows the feeding links between all the animals and . . . in a community. Energy enters as light energy. Plants use light energy to make foods. They are . . . . Animals that eat plants gain the energy they contain. Animals that eat plants are called . . . . Predators are animals that catch and . . . other animals. They are adapted for this. They have keen . . . to detect their prey. The animals they eat often have good . . . and a keen sense of smell to warn them of a predator's approach. Predators in the water, such as sharks, are . . . so they can move quickly . . . hunters have large eyes to make the most of the low light levels.

herbivores, nocturnal, hearing, streamlined, producers, senses, kill, food web, plants

2 The drawing shows a river. Scientists investigated the animals living at three places marked A, B, C.

- **a** Which animals were found in all three samples?
- **b** Which animals were only in the cleanest water?
- **c** Which animals were best adapted for polluted water?
- **d** Which substance, necessary for life, is likely to be plentiful at point A but in short supply at point B?

3 What is the advantage of:

- **a** a red deer growing a longer shaggier coat in the winter?
- **b** blackberry plants having thorns?
- **c** a hoverfly (a harmless predator) having a yellow and black striped abdomen like a wasp?

4 Light is an important physical factor in a plant's environment because the amount limits how much food it can make. List four other important physical factors in the environment.

5 Animals and plants may become scarce because human activity affects their environment. For example there are fewer old barns and church roofs for bats to roost in as people convert them into houses. Similarly work done to prevent rivers flooding has reduced the amount of riverbank habitat. Describe some other ways that human activity has affected habitats.

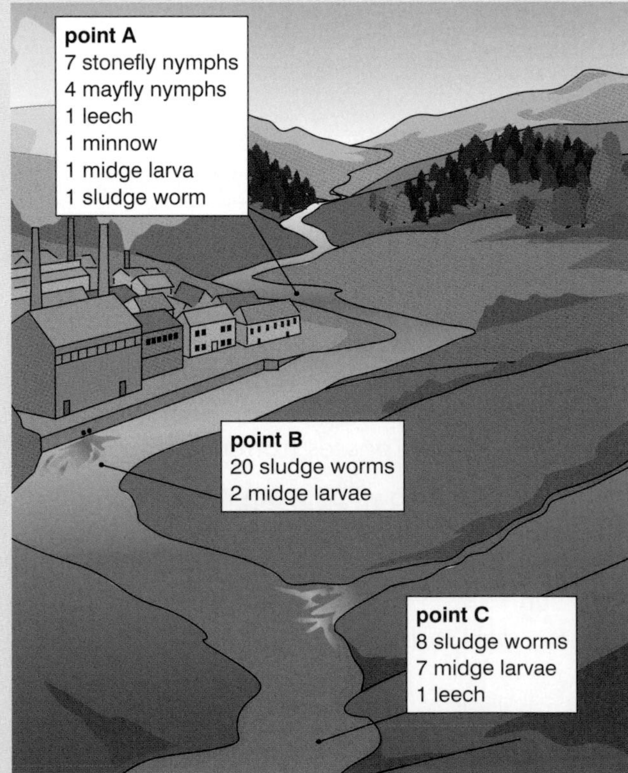

SAT-STYLE QUESTIONS

1 The diagram shows a food web that you might find on a farm.

- **a** Where does the energy for this food web come from? (1)
- **b** One year the population of wood mice almost died out because a small piece of woodland was removed and ploughed. Why would the number of barn owls go down? (1)
- **c** What other effects might there be? (2)

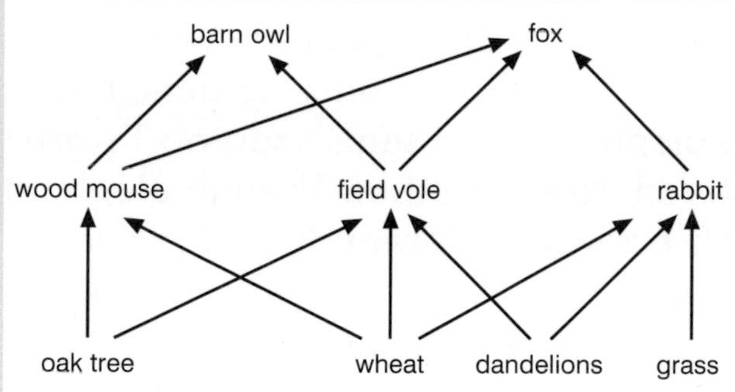

2 Sea turtles are reptiles that spend their lives at sea, eating seaweed and jellyfish. The females come ashore each year to dig a deep hole with their flippers. They lay their eggs in in this hole. What features can you see in the diagram that adapt a turtle for this life? (5)

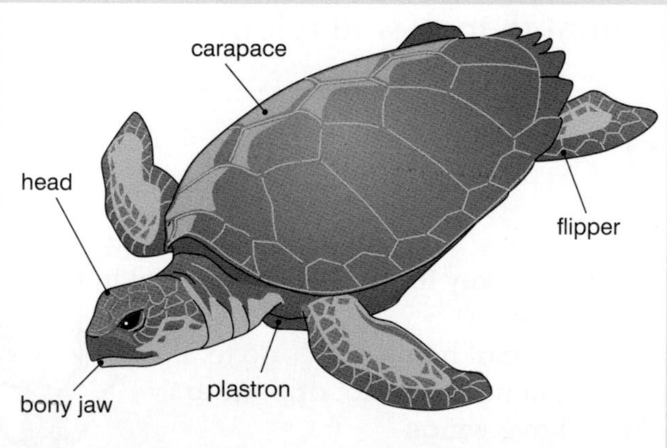

3 Reese and Pip were investigating the animals living in the area behind the Year 7 classrooms. They had found woodlice in a pile of bricks by the fence but there weren't any under a bush nearby. Reese thought that it was not dark enough for woodlice under the branches. They decide to investigate why there were woodlice in one place but not the other. They set up a choice chamber for woodlice as shown below.

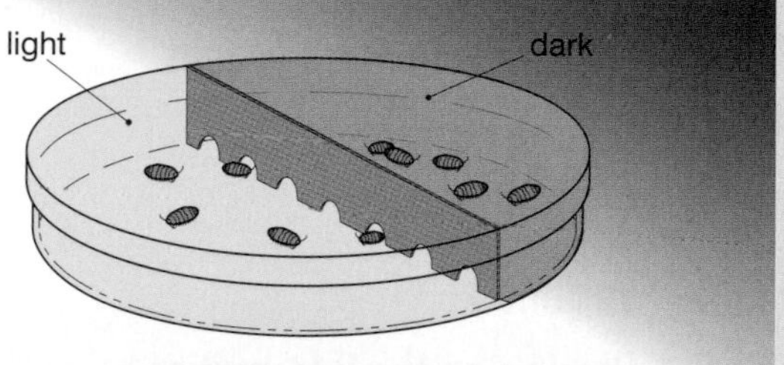

They placed 10 woodlice in the centre of the chamber and left them for 5 minutes. After this time they counted how many woodlice were in each part of the chamber.

- **a** Write down the question the pupils were investigating. (1)
- **b** What would Reese expect to see? This is her prediction. (1)

They found that 7 woodlice were in the dark part and 3 were in the light part.

- **c** Draw a bar chart of the data Reese and Pip collected. (3)
- **d** Do the data support Reese's prediction? (1)

Pip was not certain that they had found out why there were no woodlice under the bush. It was damp under the bricks but very dry under the bush. She thought woodlice need dampness to live because they are crustacea that breathe with gills.

- **e** How could Pip change the apparatus to test her idea? (1)
- **f** Write down a new prediction for Pip's investigation. (1)

Key words

Unscramble these:
nummo city
more scun
mint no never
bait hat
to draper

7D Variation and classification

Coming soon

What's it all about?

Every day you share your life with animals and plants. House plants, spiders, birds, and the elephants and seals seen on TV are very different to each other. Though elephants and seals are very different, they do share some features. For example, both feed their young on milk. Animals that feed their young on milk are called **mammals**. Mammals share other features that other sorts of animals do not have. You will find out more about grouping living organisms together according to the features they share.

Some wild animals and plants have been domesticated by farmers and now look very different to their wild relatives.

What do you remember?

You already know about:

- how plants and animals are adapted to their environment.
- the structure of a plant.
- how to use a key to identify an animal or plant.

1 Which of these is the:

leaf?
root?
stem?
flower?

D
C
A
B

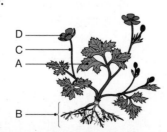

2 Use the key to identify the animal in the picture:

1 animal has wings go to 3
animal does not appear to have wings go to 2

2 animal has a large pair of jaws at the anterior (head) end ... stag beetle
animal has a pair of pincers at the posterior (rear) end ... earwig

3 animal has one pair of wings with legs longer than the body ... crane fly
animal has two pairs of wings with a long ovipositor at the posterior ... horntail

Is it a stag beetle, earwig, crane fly or horntail?

Differences and similarities

What sort of puppy is that?

It's yellow, you could find it in a field and it's not an animal.

Er, a bulldozer?

Ahh, he's got his father's nose...

Don't let it escape!

Hmm... interesting

QUESTIONS

The Scientifica crew are about to find out more about the differences between groups of animals and plants. What can you tell them?

a) Mike doesn't think the puppy is possible because the parents are so different. Is he correct?

b) Pete is trying to guess what Molly's picture is showing. What clues could Molly give Pete to improve his chances?

c) How would Benson explain how the baby looked like its father?

d) How could Pip and Pete find out what the creepy crawly is?

Animal and plant groups

LEARN ABOUT
- sorting living things into groups

What is it?

People have been everywhere; from the bottom of the ocean to tropical rain forests and have found millions of different kinds of living things. Nevertheless, we are still discovering new ones.

How do we know when an **organism** really is new to science? The new organism is carefully observed and a detailed description of its features, or **characteristics**, is written. The description is matched against animals and plants that we already know about. If it does not match in every important characteristic then it could be a new **species**.

Sorting

Animals and plants are sorted into groups for various purposes. A wildflower guide might sort pink flowers into one group and blue into another to speed identification. It could use the month in which the plants flower instead.

Q1 How could you sort birds in a bird guide?

There are between 10 and 30 million species, but no one knows the exact number because new ones are still being found.

Scientists also sort living things into groups. They use clusters of similar characteristics, such as an animal's skeleton and how its young are produced. Plants are sorted using leaf and flower structures, and how they reproduce.

There are five main groups, or **kingdoms**, of living things, shown below. The organisms in a kingdom are divided into smaller groups using the features they share. For example, animals are divided into those which have a backbone and those which do not.

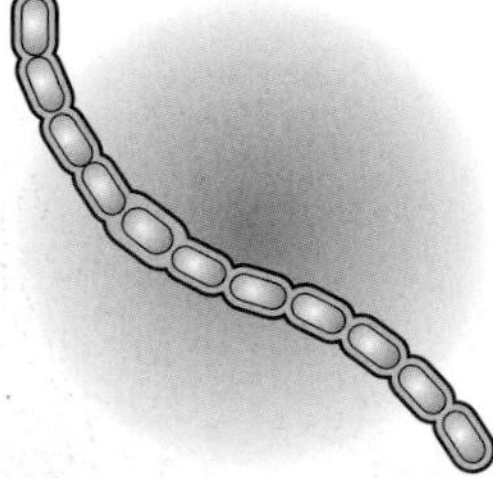

Monera, the single-celled bacteria and relatives

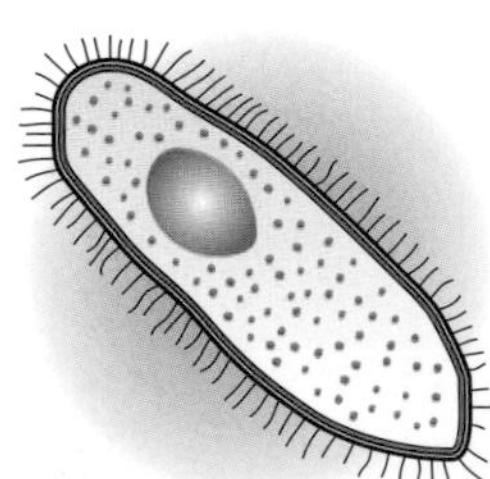

***Protista*,** single-celled organisms, such as *Paramecium*

Fungi, moulds, mushrooms and all their relatives

Animals, organisms that move about and have a nervous system

Plants, organisms that use chlorophyll to make food by photosynthesis

Classification

Classification is the science of sorting organisms into groups. Carolus Linnaeus (1707–1778) started the classification system. It has been modified as we have learnt more about living things. The Linnean system uses physical features to group organisms together. We now know that organisms in a group are similar because they have evolved from shared ancestors millions of years ago. New organisms are fitted into the system. If they are significantly different to other organisms they may become a new group in the system.

What is a species?

Members of the same **species** can freely breed together and produce young. They cannot breed with members of another species even if they look very similar. Each species has a unique scientific name used worldwide. Scientific names avoid confusion. Scientists talking about *Calliphora vomitoria* know exactly which fly they are talking about.

Sorting and describing

- Use pictures of ten organisms to find three different ways of sorting them into groups. Each time you sort them, write down the animals in each group.
  a) What was the reason for sorting each group?
  b) Were any of your animals difficult to place?
  c) Why was that?
- Choose one of your sorts to produce a simple identification guide.
- Carefully examine a specimen provided by your teacher. Use a hand lens or binocular microscope to see small features. Write a description of your specimen. Try to make your description objective (i.e. write down what you see).
- Make a diagrammatic drawing of your specimen and label it. (A diagrammatic drawing is like the one on p.8, where you are not trying to make an artistic exact copy but are picking out key features.)
- Compare your specimen with a different one. Make a table of any important differences between the two specimens.
  d) Do you think they belong to the same species?

SUMMARY QUESTIONS

1 ☆ Why do domestic cats and lions have similar features?
2 ☆ Give an example of one member of each of the five kingdoms.
3 ☆ Find out the scientific names of three animals or plants.
4 ☆☆ Write a definition of 'species'.
5 ☆☆ Why can a poodle and a spaniel breed together, but a chicken cannot breed with a goose?

Key words

characteristic
classification
kingdom
organism
species

7D2 Sorting animals

LEARN ABOUT
- sorting animals into groups

Sorting out the animals

The animal kingdom is a very diverse group ranging from tiny soil mites to huge whales. About 5% of animal species are **vertebrates**. There are five groups of vertebrates. Vertebrates have:

- a bone or cartilage backbone that protects the main part of the nervous system,
- a body that is symmetrical from side-to-side,
- a head and a tail.

The other 95% of animals are called the **invertebrates**. There are eight groups of invertebrates. They are very different to each other. You can see the main features of each vertebrate group and some invertebrate groups on the page opposite.

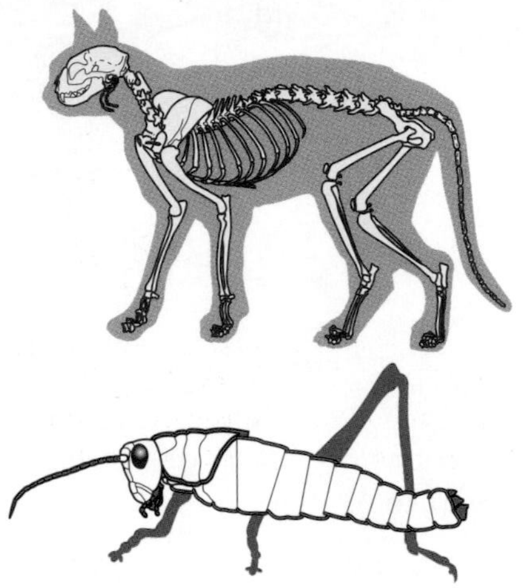

The cat is a vertebrate with a skeleton inside its body. The young locust is an invertebrate which has a hard exoskeleton outside the body.

Once we know some of the characteristics of an animal we can use our knowledge to deduce which group it belongs to and what other features it is likely to have. For example, if it is hairy, four-legged and has warm blood, we can predict that it will probably give birth to live young and suckle them on milk.

Q1 Which group does it belong to?

All human beings, different as we are from each other, belong to the same species, i.e. *Homo sapiens*. We share the general characteristics of mammals.

Sorting and moving

- Look at the animals in the pictures you used for sorting. Use the table of animal groups to decide if each is an invertebrate or vertebrate and the group it belongs to. Give your reasons for your decisions.
- Watch animals from different groups moving. Use your observations to compare the groups.
- Mike was identifying animals in a rock pool. He read this description of an animal he had found. Decide which group it belongs to and explain the reason for your decision.

Animal M

Body up to 10 cm long, transparent or greyish, has head, thorax and abdomen. Abdomen composed of many similar segments, 4 antennae as long as the body. Eyes not on stalks on head, with a pointed extension of the carapace between them (rostrum). Five pairs of legs attached to thorax, first pair has small nippers, second pair longer with larger nippers, abdominal segments have five pairs of appendages called swimmerets, larger in females which may have eggs attached to them. Last pair flattened to form tail fan (telson). Found in shallow sea water and rock pools.

Fish

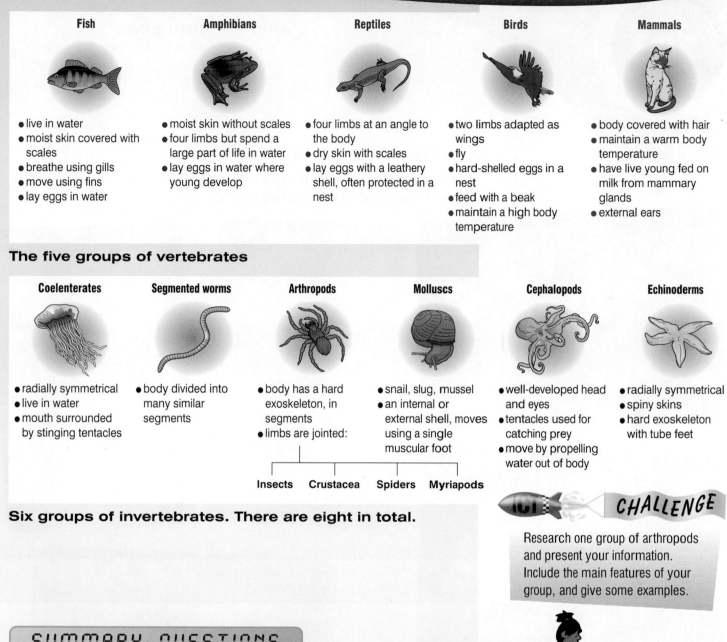

- live in water
- moist skin covered with scales
- breathe using gills
- move using fins
- lay eggs in water

Amphibians

- moist skin without scales
- four limbs but spend a large part of life in water
- lay eggs in water where young develop

Reptiles

- four limbs at an angle to the body
- dry skin with scales
- lay eggs with a leathery shell, often protected in a nest

Birds

- two limbs adapted as wings
- fly
- hard-shelled eggs in a nest
- feed with a beak
- maintain a high body temperature

Mammals

- body covered with hair
- maintain a warm body temperature
- have live young fed on milk from mammary glands
- external ears

The five groups of vertebrates

Coelenterates

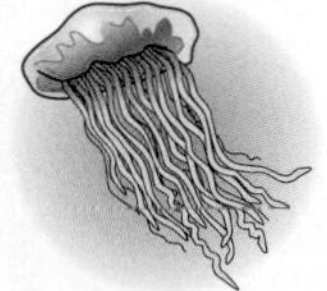

- radially symmetrical
- live in water
- mouth surrounded by stinging tentacles

Segmented worms

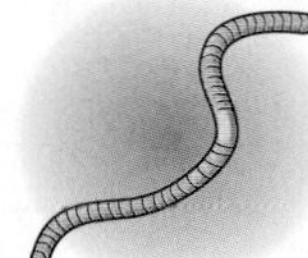

- body divided into many similar segments

Arthropods

- body has a hard exoskeleton, in segments
- limbs are jointed:

Insects | Crustacea | Spiders | Myriapods

Molluscs

- snail, slug, mussel
- an internal or external shell, moves using a single muscular foot

Cephalopods

- well-developed head and eyes
- tentacles used for catching prey
- move by propelling water out of body

Echinoderms

- radially symmetrical
- spiny skins
- hard exoskeleton with tube feet

Six groups of invertebrates. There are eight in total.

Research one group of arthropods and present your information. Include the main features of your group, and give some examples.

SUMMARY QUESTIONS

1 ☆ Which features do all vertebrates share?

2 ☆ Look at the woman with the pushchair. Which group does she belong to?

3 ☆☆ How can you distinguish arthropods from other sorts of invertebrate?

4 ☆☆ You are shown an animal with scales – which groups could it belong to?

5 ☆☆☆ Ants, slugs, snakes and ostriches are all different from the others in their groups, because each has lost one of the typical characteristics of its group. Which groups do they belong to and what is the feature each has lost?

Key words

abdomen
amphibian
arthropod
invertebrate
vertebrate

Sorting plants

Learn about

- the main plant groups

Sorting out the plants

Plants are organisms that make their own food using light energy. This process is called **photosynthesis**.

Plants can be grouped into **flowering** and **non-flowering** types. Flowering plants produce seeds. Most of the plants you see every day are flowering plants. Non-flowering plants, however, reproduce using spores or specialised sex cells. There are several groups of non-flowering plants.

Some important plant groups can be seen on the next page.

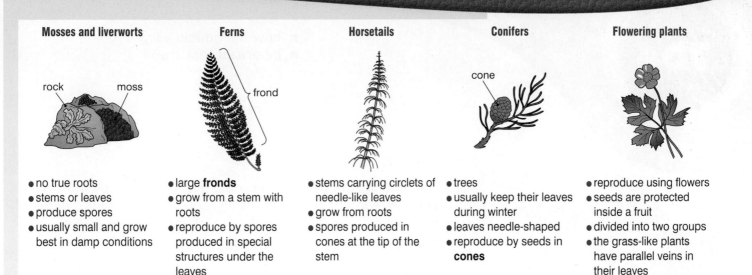

Mosses and liverworts	Ferns	Horsetails	Conifers	Flowering plants
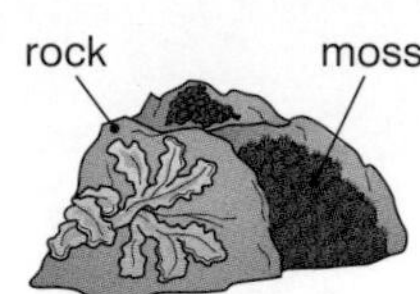	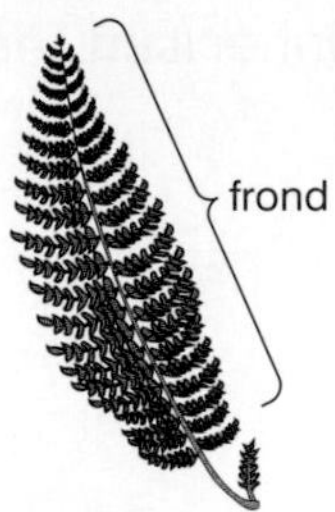			
• no true roots • stems or leaves • produce spores • usually small and grow best in damp conditions	• large **fronds** • grow from a stem with roots • reproduce by spores produced in special structures under the leaves	• stems carrying circlets of needle-like leaves • grow from roots • spores produced in cones at the tip of the stem	• trees • usually keep their leaves during winter • leaves needle-shaped • reproduce by seeds in **cones**	• reproduce using flowers • seeds are protected inside a fruit • divided into two groups • the grass-like plants have parallel veins in their leaves • the other group has branching veins in their leaves

Important plant groups

Sorting and using

- Your teacher will provide you with a plant specimen. Look at it carefully. Use the features listed above to decide to which group the specimen belongs.
- Many plants are useful as food crops, for medicines or as sources of materials. Find out about one important plant, where it grows and what it is used for. Make a poster display of what you have found out. Some examples you could choose from are cotton, potato, papyrus, oak, tea, cocoa, foxglove and lavender.

Some species, such as the dinosaurs and giant ferns, have died out but have left fossilised remains. Find out about an animal or plant that we know about through its fossils.

AMAZING SCIENCE!

The giant redwood tree is the biggest tree in the world, growing to 100 m tall and 24 m round the trunk. One tree, when chopped up, produced almost 150 000 m of planks – enough to build over 20 houses.

SUMMARY QUESTIONS

1 ☆ Look at the photographs (left) and decide which are not flowering plants.

2 ☆☆ Reese read this description in a plant identification guide. Use the features to assign it to a group.
Explain why you decided this was the correct group.

Specimen Z

Common everywhere on heaths and in woodlands. The fronds can grow as high as a man from extensive roots. Young fronds covered in a brown soft scaly and hairy material. Fronds grow vertically with tough channelled stalks. Mature fronds have large triangular blades, each heavily divided into lobes. Tips of lobes folded back on themselves. Spore cases develop in a row under the lobes of the frond. A serious problem in grassland.

Key words

cone
conifer
flowering plant
frond
non-flowering plant
photosynthesis

7D4

Variation

LEARN ABOUT
- how individuals vary
- inherited features

What is it?

Cows all around the world are the same species *Bos taurus*. They are different from each other though, as you can see. They have different length horns, different heights and different body shapes. These differences between members of the same species are **variation**.

Ankole cattle
an African breed

Zebu
a breed found in India

Jersey
bred for a rich creamy milk

Hereford
bred to provide beef

Domestic cattle from around the world

Q1 Can you see any other differences?

Spotting differences

The differences between cattle are easier to spot than between zebra, penguins or the meerkat family seen right.

Meerkats keep a sharp lookout for predators

Meerkats live in groups. Each meerkat can recognise its mate, its parent or offspring, and the boss. They use small differences in voice, smell or appearance to tell each other apart.

Humans are excellent at recognising faces. We can use the smallest differences to identify each other quickly. Identical twins fool us at first, but once we have found a tiny difference between them we never confuse them again.

I wish we were a bit more identical
1
2

Continuous variation

People differ from each other in many ways. We have different eye colours, hair texture, height, sex, and ear shape. Our sex is a simple 'either or' choice, boy or girl. This is **discontinuous variation**.

However, if we measured the height of pupils in Year 7 we would find we had a **range** of values, perhaps from 145 cm to 180 cm. This is **continuous variation**.

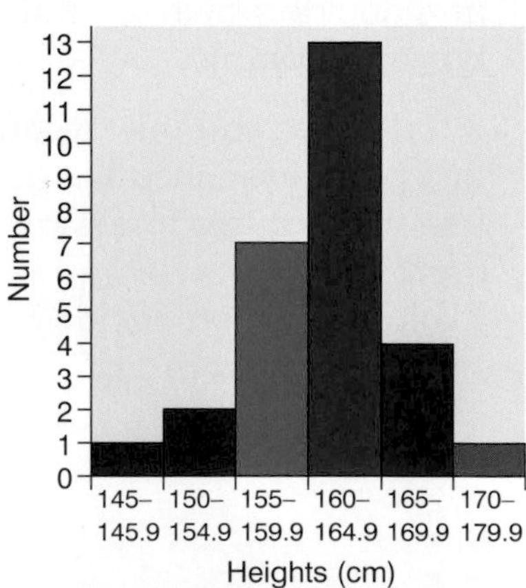

Heights of girls in Year 7

Inheriting features

You **inherit** some features from your parents. Your nose shape, a gap between your front teeth, and your hair type may all be inherited from your parents. All animals and plants inherit features from their parents. The cattle on the previous page have inherited the ability to give large amounts of milk, or to be strong enough to pull a plough.

Individuals that have inherited useful features will cope well with the problems of their environment. This can affect their chances of survival. Arctic animals that have the genes for very thick layers of fur, or a thick layer of waterproofing oil, have a better chance of surviving the harsh winter.

Perfect fruit and vegetables

Supermarkets want their suppliers to provide fruit and vegetables that do not vary. They must be as similar as possible to an ideal standard. Fruit that is marked or different is likely to be left on the shelf.

Unfortunately fruit and vegetables have many features that can be affected by the environment that they grow in. Growers try to make growing conditions as uniform as possible, so that every stick of celery or piece of fruit is the same as the next.

Investigating variation

- Dogs at a dog show belong to the same species. Use pictures of different varieties of dog to describe ways in which the breeds differ from each other.
- Holly leaves on a bush are not all the same. It has been said that leaves nearer the ground have more prickles on them than leaves higher up, because they are more likely to be eaten by herbivores. Plan how you could collect data and display it to test this observation.
- Use your data on plants in your school grounds to find a plant that grows in two different places. Examine the size of the leaves in the two different places. Measure the light intensity in both places. Is there a pattern?

SUMMARY QUESTIONS

1 Look at the photograph below.
  a) List the differences that you can see between the two individuals.
  b) Find two similarities that you think they inherited.
  c) Find two differences that could be affected by the environment.

Brothers

2 Look at the pictures of cattle on the previous page.
  a) Choose features that vary and draw up a table of differences.
  b) Which of these features do you think the cattle inherited from their parents?
  c) Have you enough information to make a key to cattle breeds, or would you need more? How much more?

continuous variation
discontinuous variation
inherit
variation

7D5 Passing on the information

Learn about
- genes
- how we inherit features

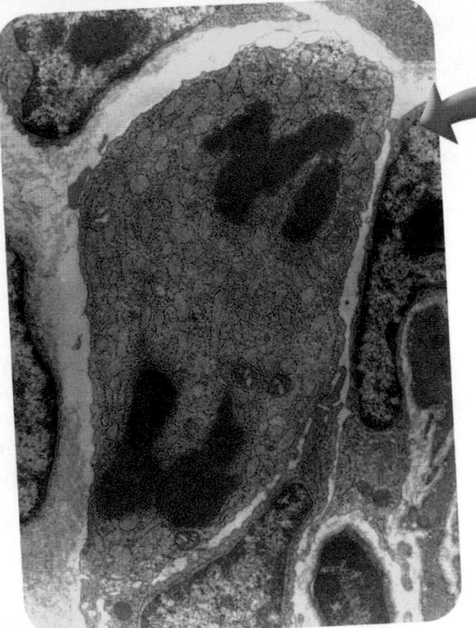

Chromosomes can be seen when a cell is dividing to make two new cells

How is information carried?

The nucleus of a cell carries the information the cell needs to do its job. This information is found as **genes** on structures called **chromosomes**. Chromosomes are made of a substance called **DNA** – **d**eoxyribo**n**ucleic **a**cid. It is the longest molecule found in living things.

What sort of information do genes carry?

Genes are responsible for many of the features that you can see in living organisms. Genes are responsible for the colour of your eyes, the shape of your teeth, and the size of your feet.

Genes affect how an organism's body works and some of its activities. So while genes can determine what colour hair a dog has, they can also affect a cat's hunting behaviour and a peacock's courtship ritual.

Q1 Can you think of a feature in plants that is inherited?

AMAZING SCIENCE!

The largest length of DNA discovered so far is in the tiny *Amoeba dubia,* which is only 0.4 mm long.

My, you've got such beautiful, er . . . eyes

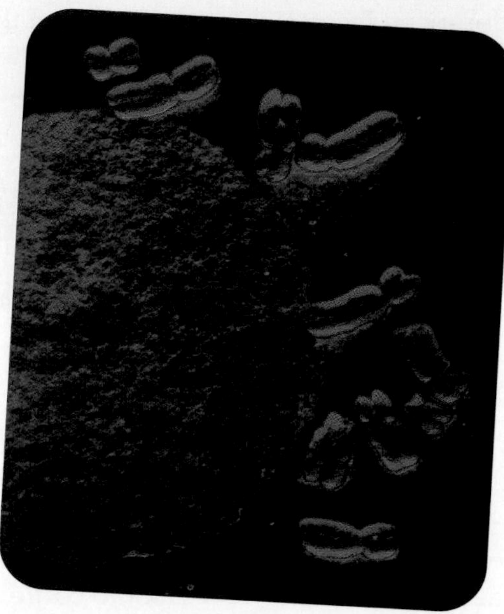

A scanning electron microscope produces a 3-D image of these human chromosomes next to a cell nucleus. We have 46 chromosomes in each cell, as 23 pairs. Each pair has a different shape and size to other pairs so scientists can identify individual chromosomes. Scientists have identified which chromosome carries several of our genes. The picture has been coloured.

How do you get your genes?

Children look like their parents because they have inherited their genes from them. When men and women make sperm and eggs, copies of their genes are passed into them. Plants pass copies of their genes into pollen and ovules.

However, these sex cells do not have copies of all the genes in the parent's cells. They only have copies of half of the genes of each parent. When an egg is fertilised by a sperm, or pollen fertilises an ovule, the two half sets of genes combine to make a full set.

The individual developing from a fertilised egg or ovule has inherited genes from each of its parents. It will not be exactly like either parent, but will have a combination of features from both. Brothers and sisters look similar, because they have inherited similar combinations of genes from their parents.

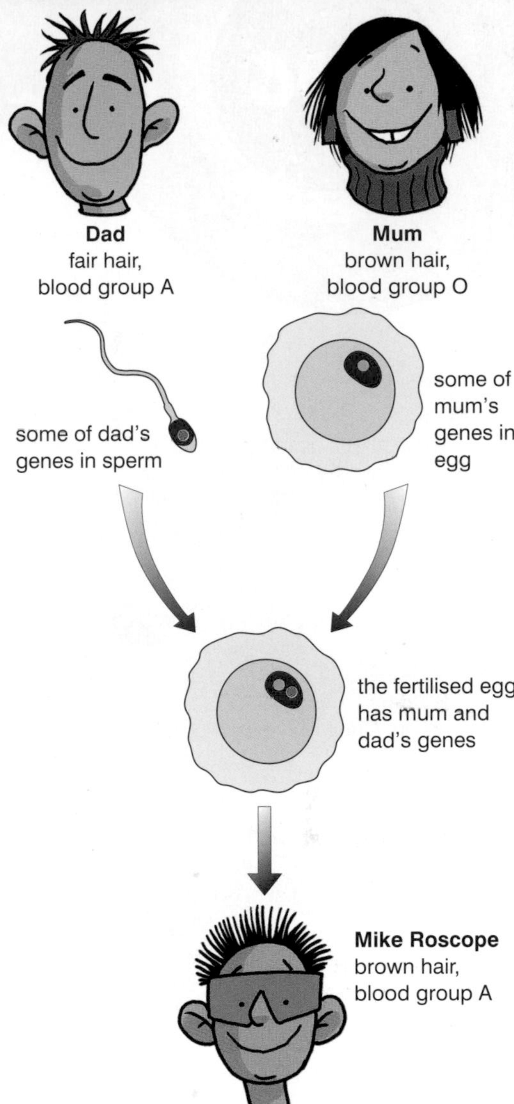

How genes are passed on

Michael Douglas with his father Kirk and his son Cameron. Which features have been inherited?

Studying inheritance

- Look at some family photos, your own or a friend's. Look for features that have been inherited in the family.

SUMMARY QUESTIONS

1 ☆ Look through Units 7D4 and 7D5. Make a list of all the features mentioned which we inherit from our parents.

2 ☆☆ Explain why some people in your group have a different eye colour from you.

3 ☆☆ Think back to the reproduction unit (p.29). Why do identical twins have fewer differences between them than any other pair of brothers or sisters?

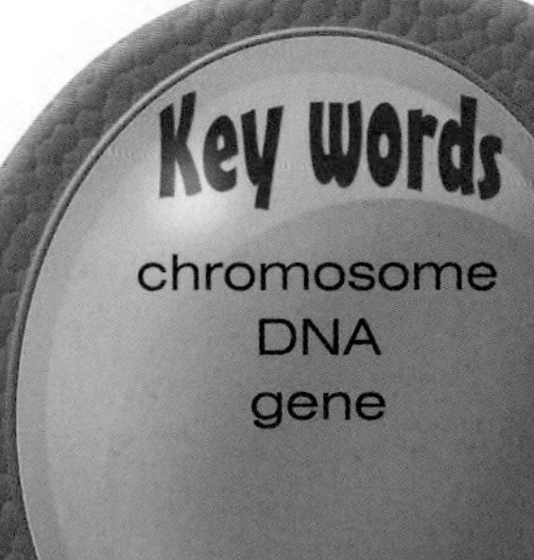

7D6 Making use of genes

LEARN ABOUT
- selective breeding

Wild ancestors

Cattle are descended from wild aurochs that were domesticated about 6000 years ago. Since then farmers have bred them and produced all the different breeds we have today. All the important crops, plants and domesticated animals we know today were bred from wild **ancestors**.

N'Dama
resists African sleeping sickness infection

Highland
survives harsh winters

Texas Longhorn
grows well on poor, dry vegetation

Cattle adapted to different environments

Why do we have different breeds?

We have different varieties of crop plants and animals because they have been bred in different places. Farmers need animals and plants that can cope with their local climate. Their animals must thrive on the local vegetation.

In African countries it can be very hot with many biting insects, but in northern Europe it can get very cold. Plants in these two parts of the world are very different. A cow that thrives in northern Europe is likely to be different from one that is best suited to western Africa.

Q1 What differences might there be between a cow bred in Scotland and one bred in Africa?

Selective breeding

Farmers choose the best of their animals to breed from. They will choose cows that give plenty of milk and chickens that lay plenty of eggs. The best ones will have grown quickly in local conditions and coped with local diseases.

These animals will be the parents of the next generation. Many of these good features are controlled by the animal's **genes**. Their offspring are likely to inherit the good genes and hence have the features. The farmer keeps good individuals to be the parents of the next generation again.

In this way, the farmer's animals are gradually improved. This is **selective breeding**. Over the years, selective breeding has produced cattle that give more milk, are docile and grow much larger than their wild ancestors.

Breeding plants

Crops and flowers have been bred in the same way by keeping bigger or better seeds and fruits for planting instead of eating. Selective breeding has produced wheat from a wild grass, pineapples from a spiky bush, and lemons. The lemon is thought to be the result of breeding two other citrus fruits together around the time of the Romans.

Breeding sweet oranges began in China in the Iron Age. They travelled along caravan routes with limes to Europe. Lemons and grapefruit were bred later.

Farmers would like pea plants with fewer tendrils, so that the plants can put more energy into growing peas. Fruit growers want more saleable fruit from an area of land each season. They also want better colours or flavour, fewer pips, or a more suitable size for school lunch boxes.

Spanish people took oranges to the Caribbean. Now they are the main crop in Florida.

Find out about rare breeds or the ancestry of domesticated animals.

Breeding

- Many children take fruit to school in their lunch box. Work in a group to decide what features the plant breeder should aim for to produce a better lunch box fruit. Plan the breeding programme.
- Use a computer simulation to carry out a breeding experiment.

All the varieties of coat colour in Syrian hamsters are the result of breeding from a single female golden-brown hamster found wild in the 1930s.

SUMMARY QUESTIONS

1 ☆ Explain how the information for good features is carried from parent to offspring.

2 ☆☆ Explain why a fruit grower might want fruits that are quicker to mature, last longer in storage, or are more resistant to pests and diseases.

3 ☆☆ Try to find out the special qualities of these cattle:
Jersey cattle   Hereford cattle   Limousin cattle

Key words

ancestors
genes
selective breeding

IDEAS AND EVIDENCE

Conserving genes

Much of our scientific effort goes into breeding new varieties. Farmers and horticulturalists quickly switch away from older varieties to the new ones, which have fewer problems or develop more quickly. Before long the older varieties become very rare.

Many genes are lost during selective breeding. Flowers may lose their scent, or crops lose their disease-resistance as breeders focus on taller stems. New plant varieties that have bigger yields and better market potential often need fertile soil and the best growing conditions.

Now we recognise that it is vital to keep wild ancestors and traditional varieties going. These varieties have a rich and diverse collection of genes that are not found in newer varieties. The features they carry may become important in the future.

The pressure of a growing human population means that we have to grow crops in drier and poorer soils. Breeders need to use wild varieties and older local varieties as a parent, to regain the genes for growth in poor conditions or pest resistance.

Gene banks have been set up to store seeds of older varieties of plants. Seeds are dried and stored in a deep-freeze at −20 °C. Periodically, some seeds are grown to provide fresh seeds. Similarly rare breeds trusts maintain old varieties of farm animals.

Literacy Word Game

A riddle

Identify the letters that make a word that links the unit.

My first is in vertebrates but not in spine.
My second is in cat but not in feline.
My third is in lizard but not in snake.
My fourth is in conifer but not in rake.
My fifth is in mammal but not in milk.
My sixth is in caterpillar but not in silk.
My seventh is in twin but not in three.
My eighth is in ovule but not in bee.
My last is in gene but have no doubt.
My whole is what this unit's about.

DANGER! AVOID THESE COMMON ERRORS

We can only inherit features that are controlled by genes. We cannot hand on to our children features that we acquire during our lives. For example, if you make a permanent change to your body – having your ears pierced or having a tattoo – your children will not be born with pierced ears or tattoos.

Key words

conserve
gene bank
inheritance
variety

UNIT REVIEW

REVIEW QUESTIONS

Understanding and applying concepts

1 Copy and complete the paragraph using the words below.

Inherited features are carried as . . . They are arranged on . . ., that are found in the . . . of a cell. Everyone is unique, because we have different combinations of inherited features. We inherit our features from our . . . and mother. They pass on these features in sperm and . . .

Farmers choose animals and plants with good features to be the parents of the next generation of offspring. The offspring that have inherited the good features from both . . . are kept. This process is called . . .   .

nucleus eggs genes father parents chromosomes selective breeding

2 a Triturus cristatus is a vertebrate with a moist skin without scales – which group does it belong to?

b Which features would be best to help you decide if an interesting living creature you found was an insect?

c Lacerta agilis is a vertebrate that lays eggs and has a body covered in scales – which group does it belong to?

d Taraxacum officinale has true leaves and roots and produces seeds – which group does it belong to?

e Triturus cristatus, Lacerta agilis and Taraxacum officinale are scientific names. Use a guide to the natural history of Britain to find out what their common names are.

3 Mr Williams loved the fuchsias in his garden. He wanted more, so he chose his best plant and cut off some shoots for cuttings. He planted them in plant pots and put them in a sheltered, shady part of the garden to root and grow. He expected them all to grow the same. Three months later, one was 10 cm tall with four leaves, another 15 cm with six leaves, and one 23 cm tall with seven leaves.

a Why did he expect all his cuttings to be the same?

b Why do you think they were different?

Ways with words

4 We use the Linnean system of classification. Carlus Linnaeus lived in Sweden in the eighteenth century. He developed the system of using a two-part scientific name for each species. Find out about Linnaeus.

Thinking skills

5 The following animals are all arthropods. Sort them into insects, arachnids, myriapods and crustacea.

woodlouse bee ant ladybird wolf spider butterfly centipede scorpion lobster brine shrimp (sea monkey) daddy-longlegs stag beetle house fly crab garden cross spider wasp dragonfly grasshopper mosquito tarantula water skater millipede

Concept map

6 Make a 'concept map' of animal classification; make sure you include these words in your map:

animal vertebrate invertebrate arthropod insect wings

SAT-STYLE QUESTIONS

1 Use the diagrams and your own knowledge to fill in the table below:

Characteristic	Animal A	Animal B	Animal C
number of legs			
number of wings			
body divided into segments			
eyes			
antennae			

(5)

2 Horse racing is a multi-million pound business. Champion racehorses are worth millions because they could pass on their winner's genes to their offspring. Winning horses are fast, but they need other features too. They have to cope with the challenges of races, travelling long distances round the country, and being ridden by several different jockeys.

Think of six features that a breeder might look for when breeding a future winner and explain why they are important. (6)

A winning racehorse is worth millions for its breeding potential

3 Class 7D measured their hand span. They stretched their fingers out and measured the distance from the tip of the thumb to the tip of the little finger.

There were 27 people in school that day; here is the data they collected:

Hand span (cm)

21.0	20.0	17.5	19.5	20.5
19.3	19.0	20.5	18.2	19.5
21.3	20.2	22.3	21.0	20.8
21.9	18.6	19.2	22.8	18.3
19.5	21.4	18.8	18.8	22.0
20.5	20.4			

a Group the data ready to plot a bar chart. Use the class sizes of 17.0–17.9 cm, 18.0–18.9 cm, and so on. (3)

b Plot a bar chart of your data. (5)

c What was the most frequent size of hand span? (1)

d What was the largest hand span? What was the smallest? (2)

e Why do you think there is such a variation? (1)

f Is this continuous or discontinuous variation? (1)

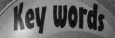

Key words

Unscramble these:

nasic oils facit
frenioc
the rini
escipes
ever trable

7E

Acids and alkalis

COMING SOON

What's it all about?

Acids have a really bad reputation with most people. They only think of acids as dangerous, fuming liquids (the type you see bubbling away on a mad scientist's bench in science fiction or horror movies).

However, we all come across acids every day. Often we don't realise it, and we aren't in danger of having holes burned in our skin! For example, oranges, apples, lemons, yoghurt, tea and vinegar all contain weak acids.

In this unit we will look at a range of **acids**, and their chemical opposites, called **alkalis**. We will find out how they are used and how we can test just how strongly or weakly acidic a solution is.

What do you remember?

You already know that:

- some substances are classified as acids.
- solids can dissolve to form solutions.
- mixing substances together sometimes results in new substances being made.

1 Which word describes a solid that can dissolve in a liquid?

solvable **dissolvable** **soluble** **molten**

2 Which of these substances dissolve in water?

instant coffee **sand** **salt** **sugar**

3 Which of these pairs of substances will form new substances if you mix them together?

vinegar and bicarbonate of soda
milk and water **sand and flour**
sugar and water

4 Which of these is acidic?

soap **washing-up liquid**
pure water **lemon juice**

Ideas about acids

QUESTIONS

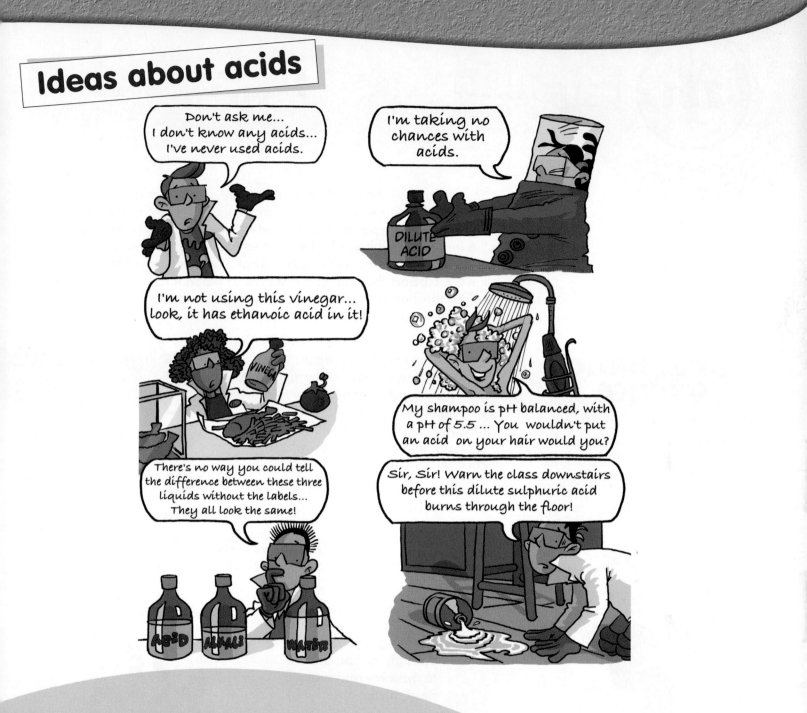

Look at the cartoons above. Pete, Reese, Pip, Molly, Mike and Benson are about to find out more about acids and alkalis. What advice can you give them? Discuss their questions with your partner.

- **a)** Pete does not think he's ever used acids. What do you think?
- **b)** Reese is very careful when she handles any acid. Does she need to take so many precautions?
- **c)** Pip sees that 'vinegar' contains ethanoic acid. Why don't we use acids' chemical names all the time? Should she be worried about ethanoic acid?
- **d)** Should Molly be worried about the shampoo she is using?
- **e)** Mike is wondering how to tell the difference between acids, alkalis and water. Can you suggest some ways he could try?
- **f)** Benson has spilt some acid on the floor. Can you suggest any extra safety precautions he could take? Do you think that the class in the room below are in any danger?

7E1 Acids all around

LEARN ABOUT
- acids that we use at home
- not all acids are hazardous

Acids everywhere!

You've probably heard of acid rain before and, like most people, you might be concerned about pollution. The gases that cause acid rain come from cars, power stations and factories. However, even before the industrial revolution in the nineteenth century, rainwater was naturally **acidic** – but only slightly. That's because one of the gases in the air, **carbon dioxide**, can **dissolve** in water. It forms a weakly acidic **solution** of carbonic acid. Our problem is that pollution has given us 'even-more-acid' rain.

The acids in acid rain are a problem for us, but many acids are useful. Weak solutions of acids have a sharp taste. You will recognise the sharp, tangy taste from vinegar (which contains an acid called **ethanoic acid**) and from fruits, such as oranges, lemons and limes (which contain **citric acid**).

Label from a fizzy drink

The food industry uses acids in many products. Look at the label from a fizzy drink (right):

The 'fizz' in a fizzy drink comes from carbon dioxide gas. A drink has a lot more of the gas dissolved in it than rainwater does!

Q1 Imagine you are a drinks manufacturer. How might you get enough carbon dioxide to dissolve and make a fizzy drink?

Q2 Which other acid is in the cola drink above? How might this harm your body?

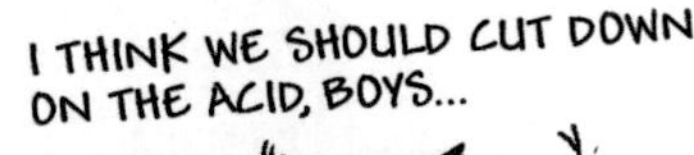

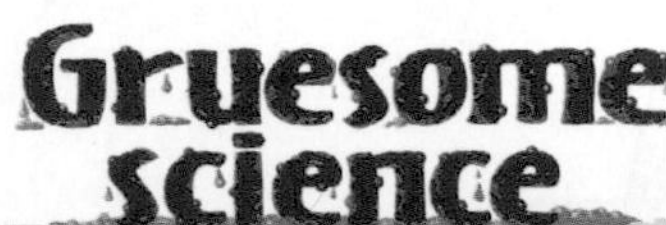

Gruesome science

Supermarkets are studying new techniques to dissolve carbon dioxide gas into fruits to encourage more children to eat them. Tests show that 'fizzy fruits' taste stronger, but bananas unfortunately explode!

How much fizz?

- Design a safe test you could do to work out which of two fizzy drinks had more carbon dioxide dissolved in it. If you can, think of some way to measure the difference.
- Show your plan to your teacher and then try out your test.

Acids in foods

Drinks aren't the only things that have acids added to them before we buy them in shops. Have you noticed the **E numbers** on food packaging? Some of the substances represented by E numbers are acids. For example, E300 is ascorbic acid which you know as Vitamin C. It is often added to foods such as flour and fruit juices.

Acids, such as benzoic acid, also help to preserve foods.

So, although strong acids are hazardous, not all acids are those scary liquids that burn through everything they touch.

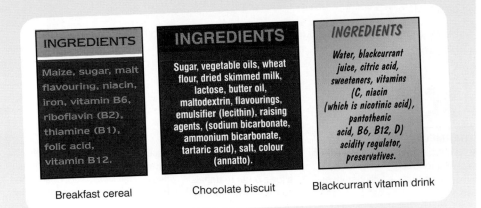

INGREDIENTS
Maize, sugar, malt flavouring, niacin, iron, vitamin B6, riboflavin (B2), thiamine (B1), folic acid, vitamin B12.

Breakfast cereal

INGREDIENTS
Sugar, vegetable oils, wheat flour, dried skimmed milk, lactose, butter oil, maltodextrin, flavourings, emulsifier (lecithin), raising agents, (sodium bicarbonate, ammonium bicarbonate, tartaric acid), salt, colour (annatto).

Chocolate biscuit

INGREDIENTS
Water, blackcurrant juice, citric acid, sweeteners, vitamins (C, niacin (which is nicotinic acid), pantothenic acid, B6, B12, D) acidity regulator, preservatives.

Blackcurrant vitamin drink

Food labels

Food survey

- Do a survey of food and drink labels. Find as many acids as you can.
- Try to find out why the acid has been added.

THE GREAT DEBATE
Why do we add the substances represented by E numbers to foods? What are your views on adding E numbers to foods?

Health: The acid in fizzy drinks attacks the enamel on your teeth. Many also contain lots of sugar, which the bacteria that cause tooth decay can feed on.

Gruesome science

E102 is a yellow colouring called 'tartrazine'. It has been linked to asthma attacks and hyperactivity in children. It is banned in Norway and Austria.

SUMMARY QUESTIONS

1 ☆ Copy these sentences. Complete them by filling in the gaps.
Acids are all around us in everyday life. For example, carbon … gas dissolves in rain to form … acid (a w … acid).
We find acids in many foods, such as … acid in vinegar.
These acids are not haz … .

2 ☆ Make a list of any new acids you have come across on these two pages.

3 ☆☆ Do some research to find out more about one acid that is hazardous. Present your findings as a poster to share with the rest of your class.

Key words

acidic
carbon dioxide
citric acid
dissolve
E numbers
ethanoic acid
solution

7E2 Hazard symbols

LEARN ABOUT
- common hazard symbols
- how to deal with acids or alkalis if they are spilt or splashed on the skin

What are hazard symbols?

Sometimes in Science lessons, you will be using substances that are **hazardous**. You will need to be aware of the dangers and make sure you take proper precautions – your teacher will advise you, of course!

Here are some hazard signs you might come across on the labels of chemicals:

CORROSIVE
These substances attack and destroy living tissues, including eyes and skin

IRRITANT
These substances are not corrosive but can cause reddening or blistering of the skin

HARMFUL
These substances are similar to toxic substances but less dangerous.

HIGHLY FLAMMABLE
These substances catch fire easily

OXIDISING
These substances provide oxygen, which allows other materials to burn more fiercely

TOXIC
These substances can cause death. They may have their poisonous effects when swallowed, or breathed in, or absorbed through the skin

Q1 Chlorine is a poisonous gas. We use it to kill bacteria in water. Draw the hazard symbol you would use on a cylinder of chlorine gas.

Q2 Which hazard symbol do you see on signs at a petrol station?

harmful   highly flammable   corrosive   oxidising agent

Have you ever noticed the hazard warning symbols on the labels of some household products? Look at the examples here:

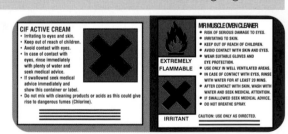

Q3 Which of the following would be most dangerous to get on your skin?

washing-up liquid
oven cleaner
vinegar
lemon juice

Rubber gloves are enough for most people, Mike.

Gruesome science

Derbyshire council is spending £75,000 assessing the damage caused to its lampposts by dog urine. They are worried that acid in the urine could react with and weaken the concrete at the base of streetlights.

Concentrated and dilute acids

- Watch your teacher add some drops of *dilute* sulphuric acid to some sugar in a small beaker.
- Now watch when he/she adds *concentrated* sulphuric acid to sugar.
- Describe the differences you see.
  - **a)** Which of the two bottles of acid is more hazardous to handle and why?
  - **b)** Which word describes concentrated sulphuric acid?

SAFETY

Usually, to make an acidic solution less hazardous we can add water to it. In other words, we **dilute** it down. However, adding water to **concentrated** sulphuric acid is very dangerous. So much heat is given out that the acid spurts out of its container – very nasty! To make dilute sulphuric acid, the concentrated acid is always added to water.

Gruesome science

Accidents with alkalis are often more serious than those with acids of the same concentration. Alkalis attack fats and oils, breaking them down into soapy solutions (that is how soap is made in factories). Unfortunately, alkalis will also do the same to oils and fats in your body tissues and eyes, as well as attacking other substances. The damage can't be reversed.

Transporting hazardous loads

You've probably seen the hazard signs on the back of road tankers. These help the emergency services if there is an accident. The codes tell fire fighters how to deal with the hazards. Look at the hazard sign on a tanker carrying sulphuric acid.

The action code tells a fire fighter at an accident how to deal with the chemical. Look at the code below:

Letter		Details	
P	V	liquid-tight chemical protective clothing	DILUTE SPILLAGE
R			
S	V	breathing apparatus and fire-fighting kit	
T			
W	V	liquid-tight chemical protective clothing	CONTAIN SPILLAGE
X			
Y	V	breathing apparatus and fire-fighting kit	
Z			
E		PUBLIC SAFETY HAZARD	

(V means that a substance can be violently reactive.)

Number	Details
1	coarse spray
2	fine spray
3	foam
4	dry agent

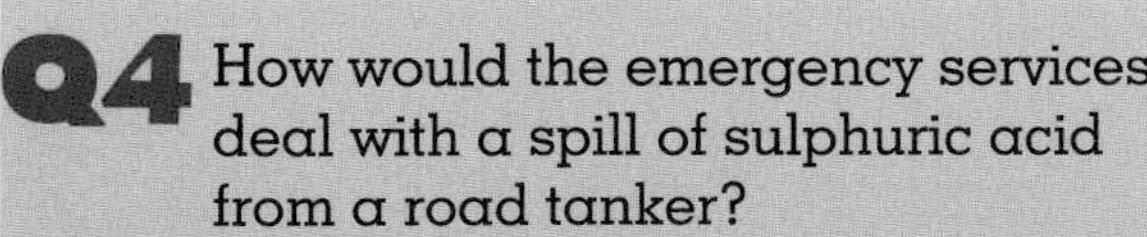

Q4 How would the emergency services deal with a spill of sulphuric acid from a road tanker?

SUMMARY QUESTIONS

1. ☆ What would you do if some acid or alkali spills on a bench. How can they be cleaned up safely?
2. ☆☆ What would you advise fire fighters to do if a road tanker crashes and its hazard sign is marked with the code '2T'?
3. ☆☆ Do a survey of household products and record any hazard symbols you find. Put your results in a table.

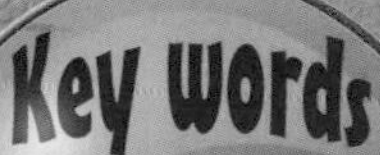

alkali
concentrated
corrosive
dilute
hazardous
irritant

Using indicators

LEARN ABOUT
- making indicators
- classifying solutions as acidic or alkaline
- some common acids and alkalis
- using the pH scale

What are indicators?

Some substances change colour in acid and alkali. These are called **indicators**. Dyes extracted from plants often make good indicators. You can make your own indicator in the next activity.

Making an indicator

STEP 1

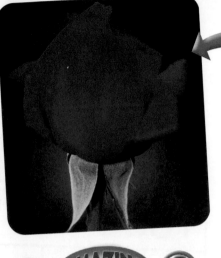

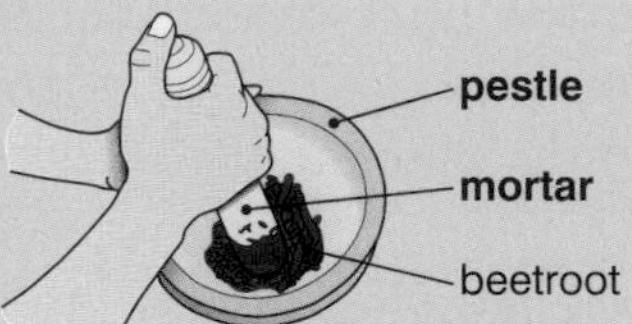

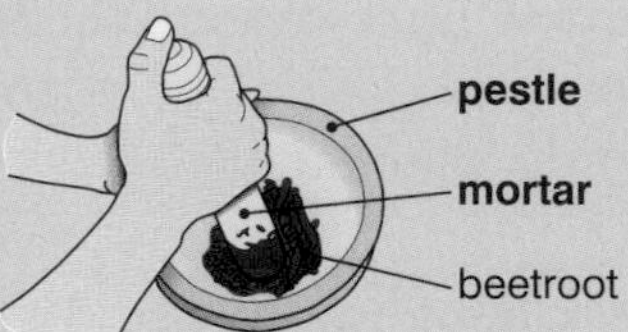

Chop up some red cabbage, or beetroot, and place it in a mortar and pestle. Add a little water, then crush it.

STEP 2

Filter paper stained with beetroot

dropper

Use a dropper to transfer the dye to a piece of filter paper

STEP 3

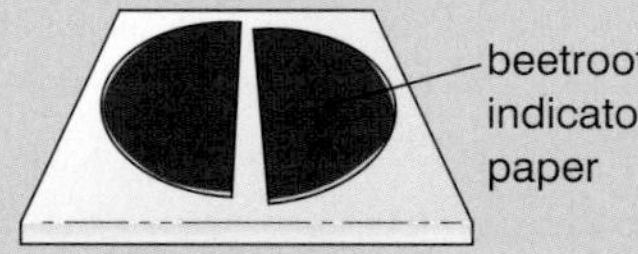

Leave the stained filter paper to dry in a warm place.
Once it has dried, tear it in half and place each half on a white tile.
You have now made indicator paper.

STEP 4

Add a few drops of acid to one half of your indicator paper.
Add a few drops of alkali to the other half.

What colour does your indicator go in i) acid, ii) alkali?

Q1 Think of some other plants that could make a good indicator.

Other indicators

- Test some solutions with a range of different indicators:
- Design a table to put your results in.
- Test the different combinations and record your results.
- Decide which solutions are acidic and which are alkaline.

AMAZING SCIENCE!

Try dipping a red poppy into a solution of washing soda. Then try a blue cornflower in vinegar. Both plants contain the same natural dye. Explain your observations.

Common acids in the lab

sulphuric acid
hydrochloric acid
nitric acid

Common alkalis in the lab

sodium hydroxide solution
potassium hydroxide solution
limewater
(calcium hydroxide solution)

The pH scale

In the last expermient, could you tell which solutions were strongly acidic or just weakly acidic? Was the colour of the indicator the same in all the acidic solutions? How about the alkaline solutions?

Universal indicator can tell us how strongly acidic or alkaline solutions are. It contains a mixture of dyes and so it can turn a whole range of colours. It can even show if a solution is neither acidic nor alkaline. We call these solutions **neutral**. In a neutral solution, universal indicator turns green.

We match the colour of the universal indicator to a **pH number**. This is shown on the **pH scale**:

There must be a way to tell which of these acidic solutions is corrosive, which is irritant and which is so dilute it is harmless.

Q2 Which of these pH numbers indicates the most strongly acidic solution?
1 5 7 14

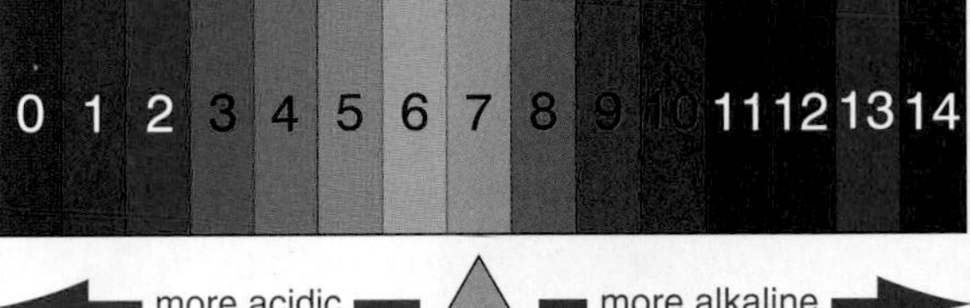

The pH scale

Testing the pH of solutions

- Using the solutions from the last experiment, test their pH by adding a few drops of universal indicator to a small amount in a test tube.
- Design a table that shows the colour of the universal indicator, the pH number of the solution, and what this tells you about the solution.
  a) Which is the most strongly acidic solution you tested?
  b) Which is the most strongly alkaline solution you tested?
  c) Name any solutions you tested that are neutral.
  d) Which solutions are most hazardous to use and which are safest?

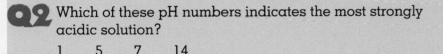

The pH scale is called a logarithmic scale. For each decrease of one unit, a solution becomes 10 times more acidic. That means that a solution with a pH value of 3 is a thousand times more acidic than one with a pH value of 6.

SUMMARY QUESTIONS

1 ☆ What makes a dye a good indicator?

2 ☆☆ **a)** What is special about universal indicator?
b) Arrange these solutions in order, with the most alkaline first:
pH numbers: 2 8 6 3 12 7
c) **i)** Which of the solutions in part b is neutral?
ii) What colour is universal indicator in a neutral solution?

Key words

indicator
mortar
neutral
universal indicator
pestle
pH number
pH scale

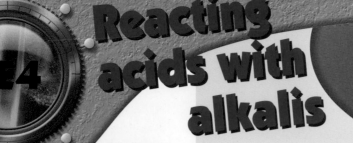

7E4 Reacting acids with alkalis

LEARN ABOUT

- using acids and alkalis
- how pH changes when acid is added to alkali
- reacting acid with alkali

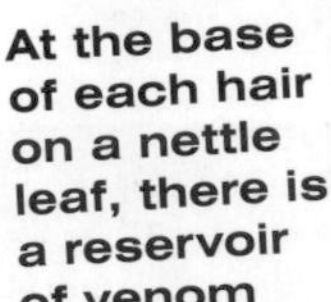

At the base of each hair on a nettle leaf, there is a reservoir of venom

What is a nettle sting?

Have you ever been stung by nettles? Most people have, and they soon recognise that nasty burning feeling on their skin. The leaf of a nettle is covered in very fine hairs. These are like sharp, hollow spikes. When you brush against a nettle, the tip of the hair breaks off and the sting from the base of the spike shoots under your skin.

You can usually find dock leaves growing near nettles. When you rub these on the nettle sting, it soothes the pain. A nettle sting contains **methanoic acid**, as well as other chemicals. One theory says that the dock leaf releases a weak alkali that can 'neutralise' the acid in the sting.

A neutralisation reaction

We can think of acids and alkalis as chemical opposites. They react together, 'cancelling each other out'. When you mix them in equal amounts, they will form a neutral solution. That's why we call the reaction of an acid with an alkali a **neutralisation reaction**.

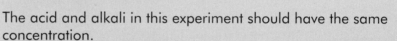

AMAZING SCIENCE!

You might think that being stung by a British nettle is painful enough, but spare a thought for people in Java. A species of nettle on their island has a sting that lasts for months and has even caused the death of some unfortunate victims.

Adding acid to alkali

SAFETY

The acid and alkali in this experiment should have the same concentration.

- Use a dropping pipette and a small measuring cylinder to collect 5 cm^3 of dilute **sodium hydroxide** solution in a test tube. Place the solution in a test tube rack and add a few drops of universal indicator solution.
  a) What is the pH value of the solution?
- Add 4 cm^3 of dilute hydrochloric acid to the same test tube.
  b) What is the pH value of the solution now?
  c) What does this tell you about the solution?
- Now use a dropping pipette to add dilute hydrochloric acid to the test tube, a drop at a time. Try to stop the reaction when the universal indicator turns green. You will have to be very careful to do this successfully.
  d) What is the pH value of the solution when you have added equal quantities of acid and alkali together?
  e) What happens to the pH of the solution if you add too much acid?
- If you add too much acid, you don't have to start the whole experiment again.
  f) How will you make your solution neutral without having to start all over again?

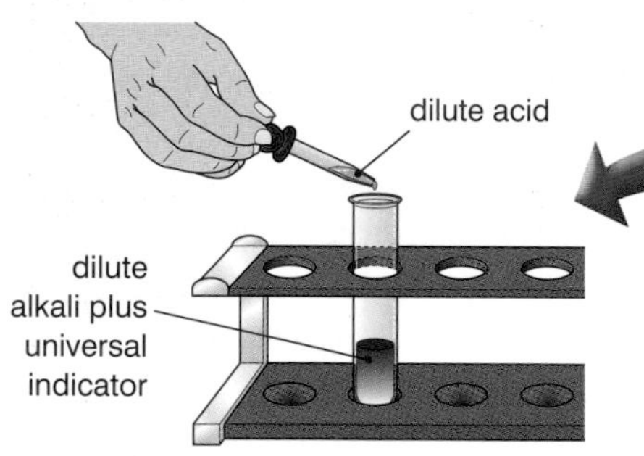

dilute acid
dilute alkali plus universal indicator

Come on, Pete... you must have managed to neutralise that solution by now!

Energy changes

We can get a neutral solution by adding an acid to an alkali. This shows that a chemical reaction has taken place. A new substance or substances must be formed.

If mixed in the right proportions:

acid + alkali → a neutral solution

During chemical reactions, we also get energy given out or taken in. The solution will get hotter or cool down. In the next experiment you can follow the temperature change as the neutralisation reaction happens.

Repeat the experiment opposite but this time use a **temperature sensor** and **data logger** instead of a thermometer. This will monitor the temperature change as the reaction is taking place. Predict the shape of the graph you expect before doing the experiment. Evaluate your prediction after the experiment.

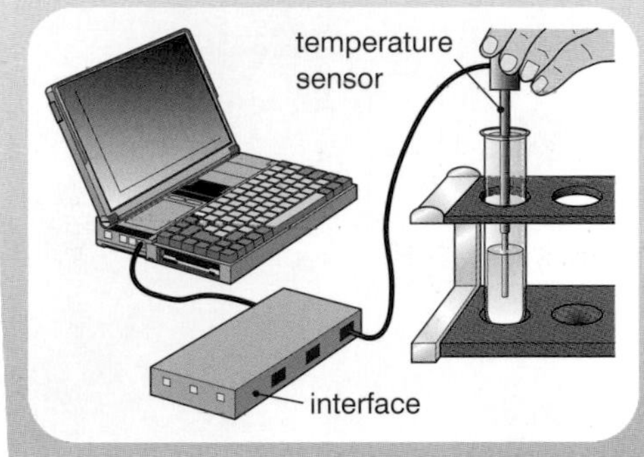

Temperature changes

SAFETY

- Use a thermometer to take the temperature of 5 cm^3 of dilute sodium hydroxide solution in a test tube. Do the same with 5 cm^3 of dilute hydrochloric acid.
- Now pour the acid into the alkali. Record the temperature change.
  - **a)** Does the temperature rise or fall in the neutralisation reaction?
  - **b)** Does the reaction give out energy?

Useful acids and alkalis

- Research acids and alkalis and how we use them. You can use books, videos, leaflets, CD ROMs or the Internet. Here are some key words to help in your search for information:
- Choose one use and present your work as an entry in a class folder entitled 'Uses of acids and alkalis'.

SHAMPOO
SKIN CARE
INDIGESTION
PRESERVING FOOD
TREATING STINGS
SOIL TREATMENT

SUMMARY QUESTIONS

1 ★ Copy these sentences. Complete them by filling in the gaps.

When we add an acid to an alkali, the pH of the solution gets . . . .

When the right amount of acid and alkali . . . together, a . . . solution is formed, with a pH value of . . . .

We call this a . . . reaction.

2 ★★★ When an acid and an alkali react together, a substance called a **salt** is formed, plus water. A salt is a solid substance made of crystals. Many salts are soluble in water.

a) Why do you think that you didn't you see a salt forming in your experiments?

b) How could you get a sample of a salt from the neutral solution formed?

data logger
methanoic acid
neutralisation
sodium hydroxide
temperature sensor

Investigating neutralisation

LEARN ABOUT
- monitoring a reaction
- evaluating indigestion remedies

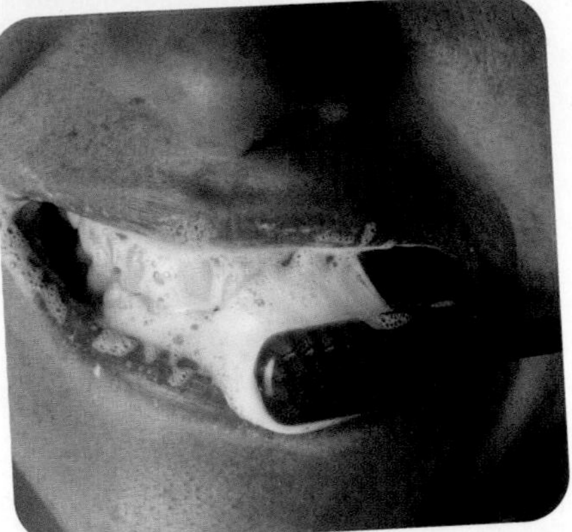

Toothpaste neutralises the acid produced by bacteria in your mouth. Acid attacks the enamel on your teeth causing cavities.

Using neutralisation

You know from the previous lesson that neutralisation is an important reaction. Its uses range from farmers neutralising acidic soil to the use of weakly alkaline toothpastes.

Q1 Why are toothpastes only weakly alkaline?
because strong alkalis are too expensive
because strong alkalis can be corrosive

In the next experiment, you can monitor the pH changes as a strong alkali is added to a strong acid. You, or your teacher, will use a **pH sensor** to monitor the changes. A burette will add precise volumes of alkali to the acid. This technique is called **titration**.

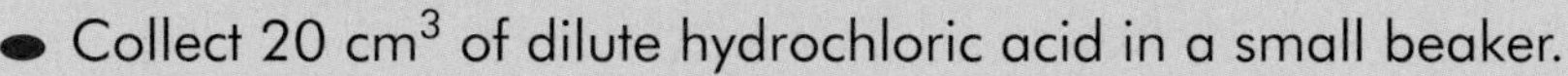

Monitoring pH changes during neutralisation

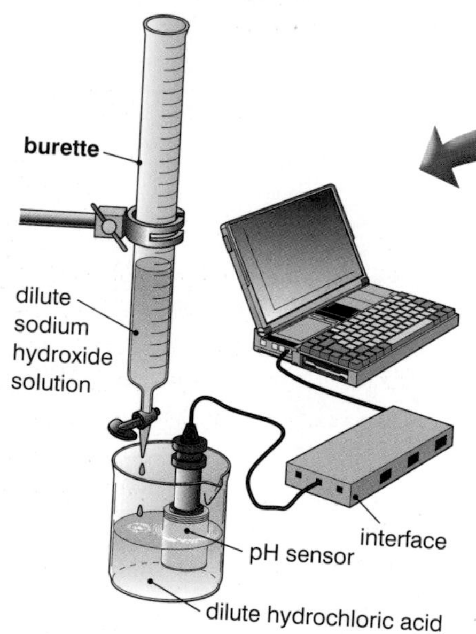

- Collect 20 cm^3 of dilute hydrochloric acid in a small beaker.
- Record its pH using a pH sensor.
- Add dilute sodium hydroxide solution to the burette.
  a) Predict the change of pH you will get as you add the sodium hydroxide to the hydrochloric acid.
  You can sketch a predicted line on axes like the ones below:

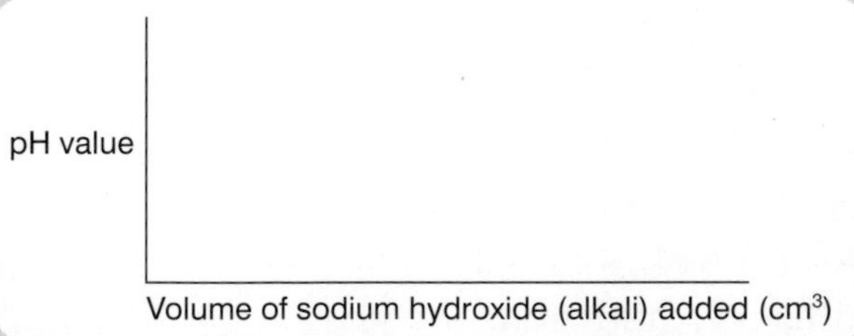

- Now add the sodium hydroxide, 1 cm^3 at a time to the acid. Stir after each addition of alkali and measure the pH of the solution in the beaker. You can record your results in a table and show your data on a graph. Alternatively, use the computer to do the job for you.
  b) Evaluate your prediction.

Gruesome science

When you vomit, you get a burning sensation in your throat. This is because the hydrochloric acid in your stomach has a pH value of between 2 and 3. Mucus lines the wall of your stomach to protect it from attack by the acid.

Indigestion remedies

Did you know that your stomach contains hydrochloric acid? It is used to help break down your food and to kill bacteria.

However, sometimes you eat too much or too quickly. Then you can produce too much acid. That's when you get that burning feeling called **indigestion**. Have you ever had indigestion? If you have, you may well have taken a tablet to relieve the discomfort. These indigestion remedies are called **antacids**.

LINK UP TO BIOLOGY

The process of breaking down our food is called **digestion** and you will learn more about this in Year 8 (Unit 8A).

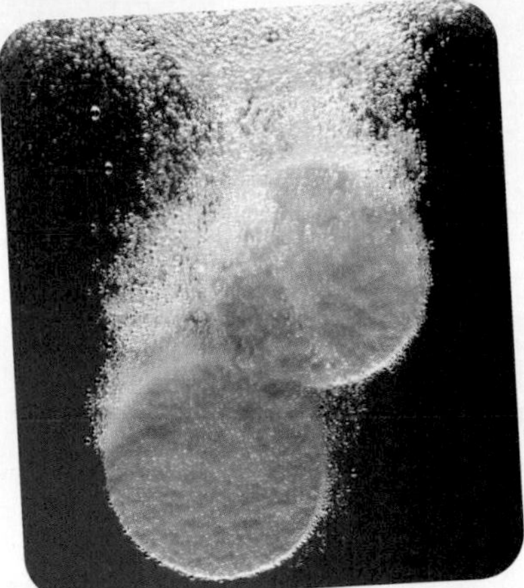

Why don't antacids contain sodium hydroxide?

Ingredients in antacids

- Look at a variety of antacids and write down the names of their active ingredients. The **active ingredients** will react with acids to neutralise them. These are substances called **bases**. These include alkalis, but bases do not necessarily dissolve in water (all alkalis do).

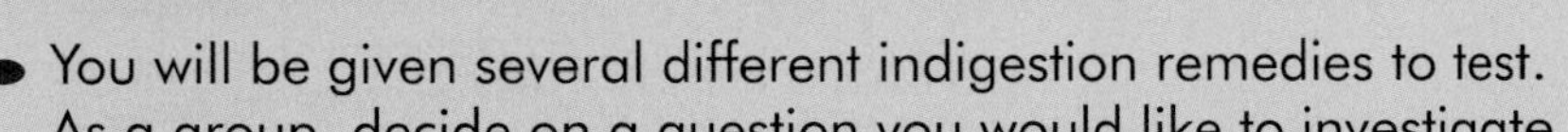

Investigating indigestion remedies

SAFETY

- You will be given several different indigestion remedies to test. As a group, decide on a question you would like to investigate.
- Plan your investigation, remembering to make it a fair and safe test.
- Try out some of your ideas to help you plan how much acid and antacid you will use, and how you will measure the effects.
- Record your question, method, results and conclusion.
- Discuss your investigation with other groups.
- Then evaluate your method, comparing it with those used by other groups.
- Summarise the findings of your class and evaluate the effectiveness of the different remedies.

I don't want to be around when that gas escapes!

LINK UP TO PHSE

Taking too many indigestion tablets can be bad for you. The salts made in the neutralisation can cause a range of problems. For example, calcium and magnesium salts can form kidney stones, aluminium salts can cause bone disease and sodium salts cause high blood pressure.

SUMMARY QUESTIONS

1 ☆ a) Which acid causes indigestion?
b) How do we treat the symptoms of indigestion?

2 ☆☆ Design an advert for the most effective antacid tested in your investigation. Include any scientific data you can quote to persuade people to choose that particular antacid.

Key words

active ingredients
antacid
bases
burette
digestion
indigestion
pH sensor
titration

IDEAS AND EVIDENCE

Acids for health

Have you ever looked at the ingredients on a bottle of vitamin supplements? You will see quite a few different acids listed on the label. The chemical name for Vitamin C is ascorbic acid. In vitamin pills, it is often taken in the form of a salt closely related to ascorbic acid. Why do you think this is a good idea?

You will also find folic acid in most multi-vitamins. This vitamin is essential during pregnancy and can reduce the risk of heart disease. Pantothenic acid, also known as Vitamin B5, is another ingredient in vitamin supplements.

The proteins in your body are made up from amino acids. You need 20 different amino acids to stay healthy. Your body can make 11 of the acids. However, you must take in the other 9 amino acids in your diet. One of these 'essential amino acids' is only needed when you are young.

SCIENTIFIC PEOPLE

The story of aspirin

The ancient Greeks used the leaves and bark of the willow tree to relieve pain. In the nineteenth century scientists found out that it was an acid that caused the pain to go away. They named it salicylic acid (after the Latin word for the willow family, *Salix*). However, the acid caused painful ulcers in the mouth and attacked the lining of the stomach. So a salt made from salicylic acid was tried, and the side effects disappeared. Unfortunately, the salt tasted absolutely horrible so the search for another painkiller went on.

Hippocrates used a 'willow tea' to ease mothers' pain during childbirth

In 1853, a French chemist made the first aspirin. He used salicylic acid as his starting material. He didn't call his new substance aspirin – this is a trade name used by the German chemical company that eventually marketed the drug at the start of the twentieth century.

The latest research on aspirin suggests that its effects go way beyond pain relief. For people over 50 years of age, a small, regular dose appears to reduce their chances of heart disease, certain cancers and strokes. However, around 6% of people still suffer stomach problems as a side effect. Doctors are calling for more research to assess the full benefits of the 'not-so-new' wonder drug.

Well, there's ascorbic acid in oranges, ethanoic acid in vinegar, citric acid in citrus fruit... loads of acids in fact!
So my shampoo is weakly acidic with a pH of 5.5!
Universal Indicator will tell me which is which!

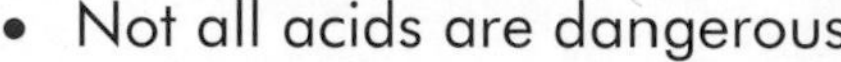

Always behave sensibly and wear eye protection when using acids and you'll be quite safe.
A little vinegar is harmless... the ethanoic acid in it is only a weak acid.

Don't worry! I'll mop it up with plenty of water... it is not concentrated sulphuric acid, but we still have to take care.

- Not all acids are dangerous
- Concentrated acids are corrosive (they attack materials and living tissue)
- The more dilute the acid, the safer it is to use
- Indicators change colour in acids and alkalis
- Universal indicator changes to a range of colours. We can match the colour to a pH value on the pH scale.
- Acids and alkalis react together in a neutralisation reaction.

We use acids and alkalis in everyday life, and most solutions are not corrosive.

You have to take care using the pH scale, as the neutral point (neither acidic nor alkaline) is at pH 7. Below 7, the *lower* the number, the more strongly acidic a solution is. Above 7, the *higher* the pH number, the more strongly alkaline a solution is.

Acids and alkalis react together in a chemical reaction called neutralisation – but you only get a neutral solution if *exactly* the right amounts of acid and alkali are mixed together.

Key words

acid
alkali
corrosive
universal indicator
dilute
neutralisation
pH scale

UNIT REVIEW

REVIEW QUESTIONS

Understanding and applying concepts

1 Jason tested some unknown solutions with universal indicator. He recorded the colours:

Solution tested	Colour of universal indicator
A	green
B	red
C	turquoise (blue/green)
D	orange/yellow
E	purple

a Which solution is:
i) strongly acidic,
ii) weakly acidic,
iii) neutral,
iv) weakly alkaline,
v) strongly alkaline?

b Draw a table showing the pH value of each solution.

c Which solution could have been made from a substance found in some toothpaste?

d Which solution could be a concentrated solution of sodium hydroxide?

e Which solution could be vinegar?

f i) Which of the solutions would react with solution B?
ii) What do we call this type of reaction?

g A solution of B is marked with this hazard sign:

What is this sign?

Mind map

2 Draw a concept map linking these terms together. Don't forget to label your links, explaining what the connection is.

acid alkali strongly acidic weakly acidic strongly alkaline weakly alkaline neutral indicator universal indicator corrosive sour

Ways with words

3 Make up a rhyme to help you remember some important points about the pH scale.

4 Make a table with two columns and list some points 'for' and 'against' adding chemicals with E numbers to foods. Then discuss the statement 'We could not live in today's world without additives in foods'.

Making more of maths

5 We can measure the concentration of solutions in units called 'grams per decimetre cubed' ($g\,dm^{-3}$). One decimetre cubed equals 1000 centimetres cubed (cm^3).

In a solution of sodium hydroxide we have 40 g dissolved in 1 dm^3.

a How many grams of sodium hydroxide would be dissolved in 10 cm^3 of a solution with the same concentration?

b If you have a solution of sodium hydroxide that is twice as concentrated as the original solution, how many grams would be dissolved in 250 cm^3 of solution?

6 For every decrease in pH of one unit, a solution becomes 10 times more acidic.

How many times more acidic is a solution with a pH value of 2 than one with a pH value of 6?

7 A group of students monitored the pH of an acid as they added alkali to it.

Here are their results:

Volume of alkali added (cm^3)	pH value
0	3.9
5	5.1
10	5.8
15	6.0
20	6.4
25	8.8
30	10.1
35	10.9
40	11.1
45	11.2
50	11.3

a Draw a graph of their results.
b Use your graph to find out how much alkali was needed to produce a neutral solution.
c Draw the apparatus the group could have used to gather their data.

Extension questions

8 Make a list of all the acids you have come across in this unit.
Organise them into groups and explain the reasoning behind your decisions.

9 Do some research to find out the products that we can manufacture from sulphuric acid. Present your findings on a poster to display to the rest of your class.

SAT-STYLE QUESTIONS

1 You can try to make your own indicator using some coloured flower petals.
The first step involves crushing and grinding the petals to release the colour into a little water.
a What apparatus would you use to grind up the petals with water? (2)

A group of students made some indicator solution from three different colours of petal. They added their indicator to an acid and an alkali. Here are their results:

Colour of petals and indicator solution in water (pH 7)	Colour in a solution of pH 1	Colour in a solution of pH 14
yellow	yellow	yellow
red	red	green
purple	pink	blue

b What colour would the red petal indicator be in a solution of sulphuric acid? (1)
c What colour would the purple petal indicator be in a solution of salt, which is neutral? (1)
d What colour would the purple petal indicator be in a solution of sodium hydroxide? (1)
e Explain which colour of flower petal would make the best indicator for both acids and alkalis. (2)

2 The table shows the pH values of five solutions whose labels have been lost.

Solution	pH value
A	6.0
B	7.5
C	7.0
D	4.5
E	8.0

a Which solutions are acidic? (2)
b Soap solution is weakly alkaline.
Which of the solutions could be soap solution? (1)
c i) Give two solutions that would react together. (1)
ii) What do we call this type of reaction? (1)
iii) Two new substances are made in the reaction. One is a salt, what is the other substance formed? (1)

3 A group of students monitored the pH of the solution formed as they added acid and alkali together.
Look at their experiment and the graph produced below:

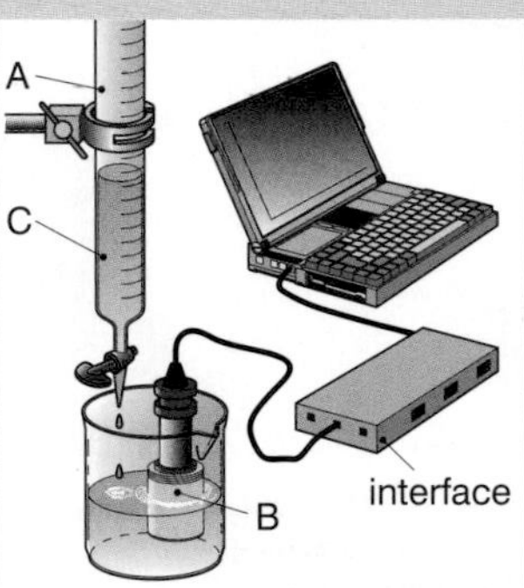

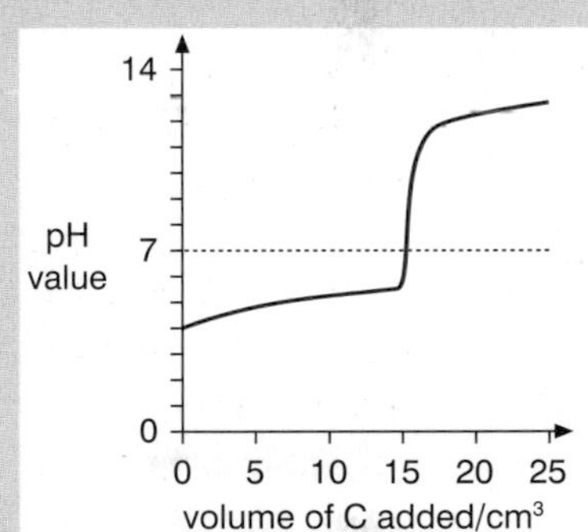

a What do we call the apparatus labelled A? What is its function? (2)
b What do we call the apparatus labelled B? (1)
c Did the students start with an acid or an alkali in the beaker? How can you tell? (1)
d What was the pH of the solution in the beaker when 10 cm^3 of solution C had been added? (1)
e How much of solution C was added to get a neutral solution? (1)
f Name a substance that could be solution C. (1)

Key words

Unscramble these:
icad
rcoorvies
lrnonatiue sait

7F

Simple chemical reactions

Coming soon

Concrete setting is an example of a slow chemical reaction

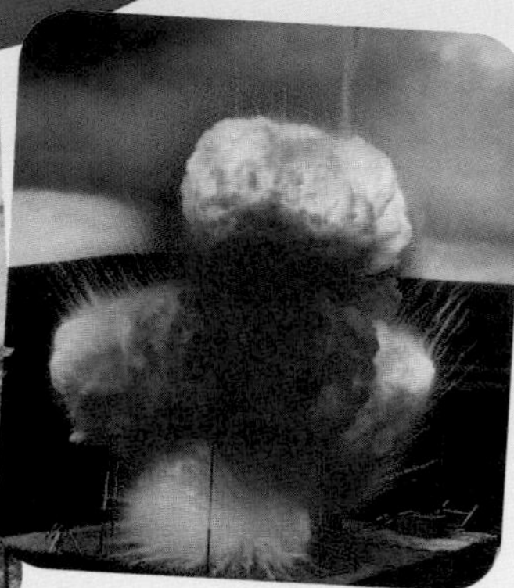

Gunpowder exploding is a fast chemical reaction

What's it all about?

Goalkeepers in football or hockey need fast reactions. They have to change position quickly to save shots. In Science we also have some changes that we call **chemical reactions** – although these aren't always fast.

Our lives depend upon the chemical reactions inside our bodies. These reactions make new materials and also transfer energy to our cells.

In this unit you will learn more about chemical reactions and try some out for yourself. You will find out about:

- recognising chemical reactions
- reactions of acids that make a gas
- burning substances in air or oxygen
- using word equations to describe reactions
- testing gases.

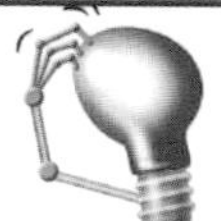

What do you remember?

You already know:

- there are many different gases.
- there are changes in which new materials are formed and which, sometimes, cannot be easily reversed.
- the pH scale is a measure of how strongly acidic or alkaline a solution is.

1 Which one of these substances is a gas at room temperature?

sulphur **hydrogen**
sodium hydroxide **diesel**

2 Which of these changes forms a new substance?

ice melting **alcohol boiling**
paper burning **sugar dissolving**

3 Which of these pH values shows that a solution is alkaline?

1 4 7 11

Ideas about chemical reactions and substances

This must be a chemical reaction because the water has turned to ice.

Chemical reactions in the kitchen? Surely we only do those in a science lab!

This boiling water is giving off a gas... it must be reacting with the air

The pH of this solution is 14. It is a high number so it must be very acidic.

How can gases really be there... They don't weigh anything, do they?

QUESTIONS

Look at the cartoons above and discuss these questions with your partner.

a) Why are Pete, Reese, Molly and Mike wrong when they talk about:
water freezing; making toast; water boiling?

b) What do you think the pH of 14 tells us about a solution?

c) Do you believe gases really exist? Explain why.

7F1 Observing reactions

LEARN ABOUT
- making and interpreting observations
- recognising chemical reactions

What are reactions?

Lots of people enjoy fireworks on bonfire night and at other celebrations.
We can thank **chemical reactions** for all those spectacular effects.
Remember that chemical reactions form new substances.
They also involve energy changes. You often find energy given out as heat, and sometimes as light or sound.

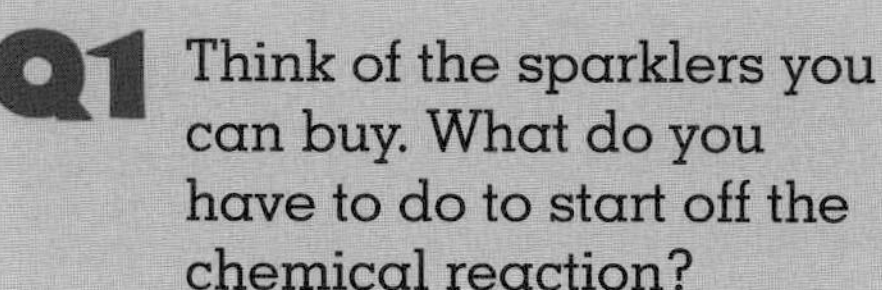

Q1 Think of the sparklers you can buy. What do you have to do to start off the chemical reaction?

Q2 Once the sparkler has finished, can you use it again? Why not?

The sparks from sparklers are tiny pieces of burning iron.
In the next experiment you can burn some iron in a Bunsen flame.

AMAZING SCIENCE!

Tarragona is in Spain, 60 miles south of Barcelona. In 2002 it held its thirteenth fireworks contest. One competitor managed to ignite over 1500 kg of explosives in just one night.

LINK UP TO RE

It is thought that the Chinese were the first people to make fireworks in the sixth century. They used them to ward off evil spirits during religious festivals.

Heating iron wool

SAFETY

- Hold some loosely packed iron wool in a pair of tongs.
- Put the end of the iron wool into a Bunsen flame until it **ignites**.
- Then take it out of the flame and watch the reaction. Make sure you hold the burning iron wool over a heatproof mat.

  a) How can you tell that this chemical reaction gives out energy?

  b) How did you start the reaction?

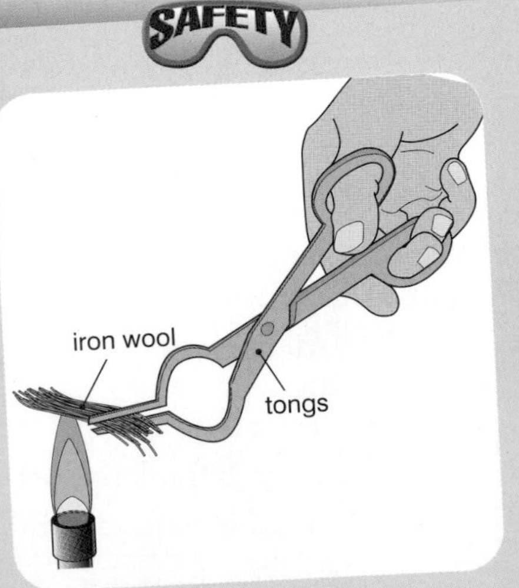

Reactants and products

The new substance made in the reaction when iron wool burns is called iron oxide. It is difficult to see, as it forms as tiny bits of solid. You can learn more about burning reactions on p.102.

The new substances made in chemical reactions are called **products**. The substances we start with are called **reactants**.
So in a chemical reaction:

reactants → products

We read this as 'reactants give products'.

Observing reactions

Mix the following pairs of substances together. Record all your **observations** (include feeling the container) in a table, as below:

- Plaster of Paris and water (in a yoghurt pot and stir with an ice-lolly stick)
- Lemon juice and bicarbonate of soda (in a beaker)
- Baking powder and water (in a beaker)

Reaction between	Observations
plaster of Paris and water	
lemon juice and bicarbonate of soda	
baking powder and water	

a) In which reactions was it easiest to see that a new substance was made?
What made it easy to observe?
b) Which reactions gave out heat and which felt cool?
c) Which reaction was slowest?

LINK UP TO FOOD TECHNOLOGY

Baking powder contains bicarbonate of soda and a weak acid. When the powder gets wet, the acid and the bicarbonate of soda react together. One of the products of the reaction is carbon dioxide gas. This helps cake mixture to rise. Self-raising flour has baking powder already added.

Can you help, I think this reaction has got out of hand!

SUMMARY QUESTIONS

1 ☆ Finish this sentence:
In a chemical reaction new ....

2 ☆ **a)** What do we call the substances that we start with before a chemical reaction takes place?
b) What do we call the substances formed in a chemical reaction?

3 ☆☆ Make a list of chemical reactions that take place in everyday life.

4 ☆☆ On mixing two solutions in a beaker, the temperature increased. What does this tell us about the change taking place?

chemical reaction
ignite
observations
product
reactant

Acids and metals

LEARN ABOUT
- testing for hydrogen gas
- acids reacting with metals

Zinc metal reacts with dilute acid

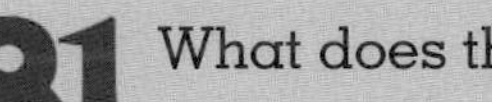

Corroding metals

In Unit 7E we saw how some acids are corrosive. They corrode materials.

Q1 What does the word 'corrode' mean?

Even weak solutions of acids can corrode materials, if given enough time. You will have heard of **acid rain**. It can attack many metals, and other building materials, that are left exposed to the rain.
In the next experiment, you will investigate the chemical reaction between a metal and an acid.

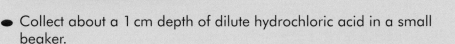

Magnesium plus acid

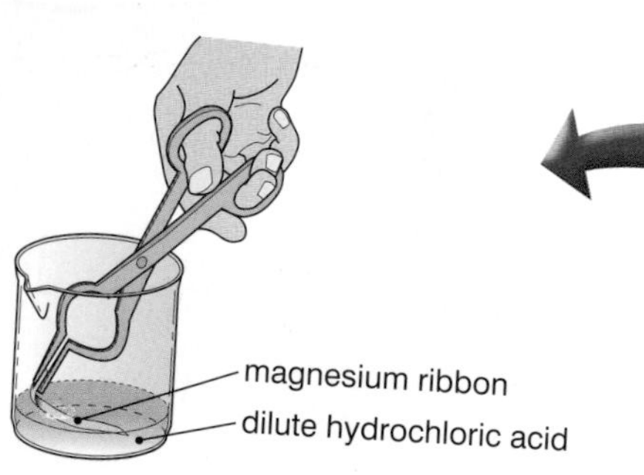

- Collect about a 1 cm depth of dilute hydrochloric acid in a small beaker.
- Hold the end of a strip of magnesium ribbon in a pair of tongs.
- Dip the other end into the acid for a few seconds.
  a) What happens to the size of the magnesium ribbon?
  The acid **corrodes** the magnesium metal.
- Now collect 5 cm^3 of dilute hydrochloric acid in a test tube.
- Measure its temperature with a thermometer.
- Add a 2 cm strip of magnesium ribbon to the acid.
- Take the maximum temperature of the reacting mixture.
  b) How can you tell that a chemical reaction takes place? Include two observations in your answer.
- After the reaction, use a dropping pipette to transfer some of the solution left in the test tube on to a watch glass. Then put about the same volume of dilute hydrochloric acid onto a second watch glass. Label the watch glasses and leave them until the next lesson.
  c) Why did you have to set up *two* watch glasses to see what was formed in solution during the reaction?
  d) What do you see on each watch glass?
  e) What does this tell you about the reaction between magnesium metal and hydrochloric acid?

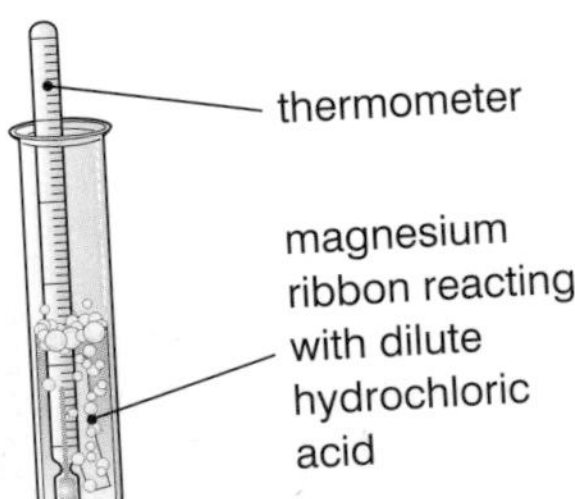

The products formed

The gas we get when magnesium reacts with hydrochloric acid is called **hydrogen**. It is the lightest (least dense) of all gases. It is also highly flammable. (See the story of the Hindenburg on p.106.) We can use this property to test for the gas in the next experiment.
The white solid left on the watch glass is the other product of the reaction. It is dissolved in the solution during the reaction. Its name is **magnesium chloride**.

Hydrogen was used to provide lift for the first balloons

Q2 Name the two reactants in the last experiment above.

Q3 Name the two products in the last experiment above.

Testing for hydrogen gas

- Repeat the reaction between magnesium and dilute hydrochloric acid in the apparatus shown:
- Test the gas collected in the boiling tube as shown:
  a) What happens when the hydrogen is tested with the lighted splint?

*The test for **hydrogen gas**: hydrogen gas burns with a **squeaky pop** when we apply a **lighted splint**.*

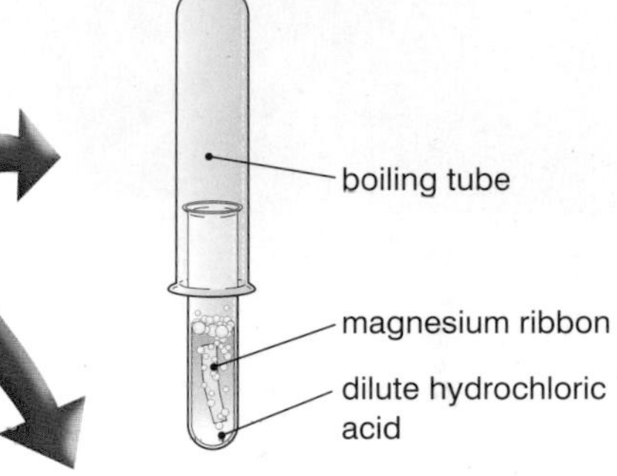

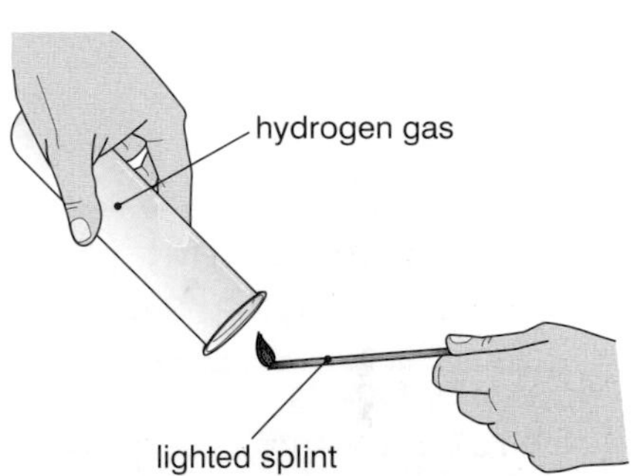

In the next experiment, you can test a range of metals with different acids. Look out for any patterns or **generalisations** you can find.

Investigating metals and acids

You will be able to test the reactions of the following metals:

- Zinc
- Copper
- Iron
- Calcium

SAFETY: Do not touch calcium metal

You will also have these dilute acids:

- Hydrochloric acid
- Sulphuric acid
- Nitric acid
  a) Design a table to record your results in.
- Now try out your tests.
  b) What happens generally when a metal is added to an acid?
  c) Which metal does not fit into the general pattern?

SUMMARY QUESTIONS

1 ☆ Copy the sentence. Complete it by filling in the gaps.
Many metals react with . . . to produce . . . gas.
We can test this gas with a . . . splint. The gas burns with a squeaky . . . .

2 ☆☆☆ Make a fact sheet on hydrogen gas for another Year 7 class.

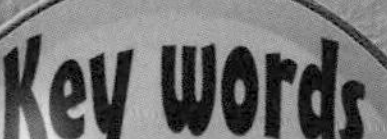

Key words

acid rain
corrode
generalisation
hydrogen
magnesium chloride
nitric acid
sulphuric acid

Acids and carbonates

LEARN ABOUT
- testing for carbon dioxide gas
- uses of carbon dioxide

What is the 'fizz'?

What happens when you open a can of Cola that has been shaken? Do you know which gas puts that 'fizz' in a fizzy drink?
It is the same gas as one of those we breathe out. Fizzy drinks are also known as 'carbonated' drinks. The name comes from the **carbon dioxide** gas dissolved in them.

In the next experiment, you can make some carbon dioxide and test the gas.

Making and testing carbon dioxide

- Set up the apparatus as shown below:

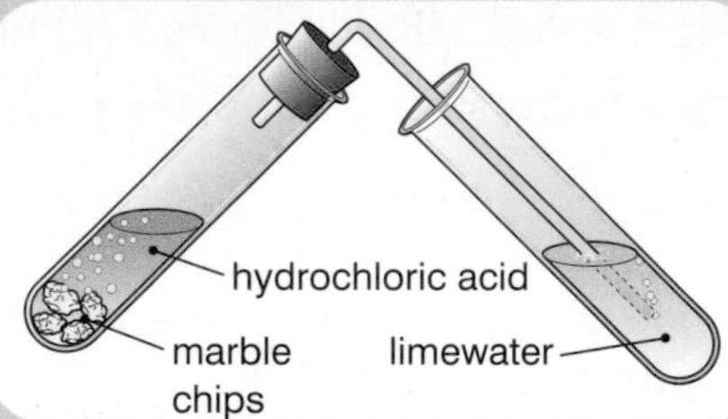

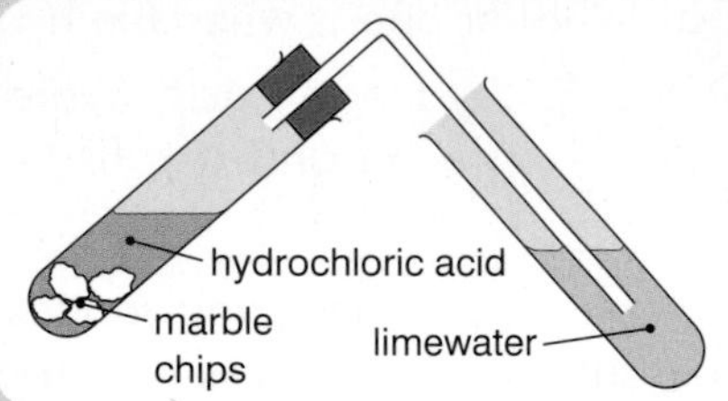

a) How can you tell that the marble chips and acid react together?
b) What happens to the **limewater**?
c) How can you tell when the reaction has finished?

- Now collect some carbon dioxide gas, or watch your teacher do the experiment below:

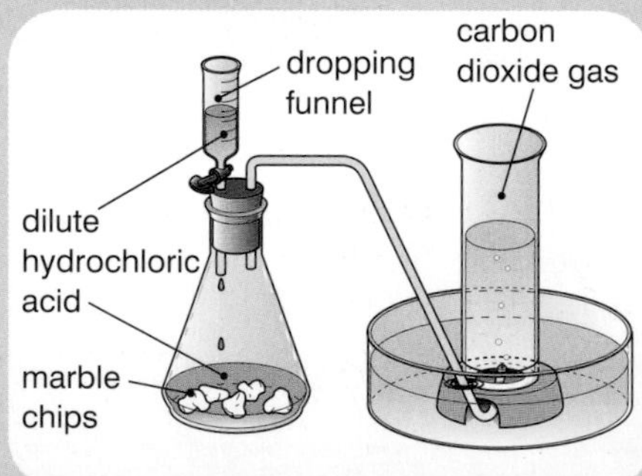

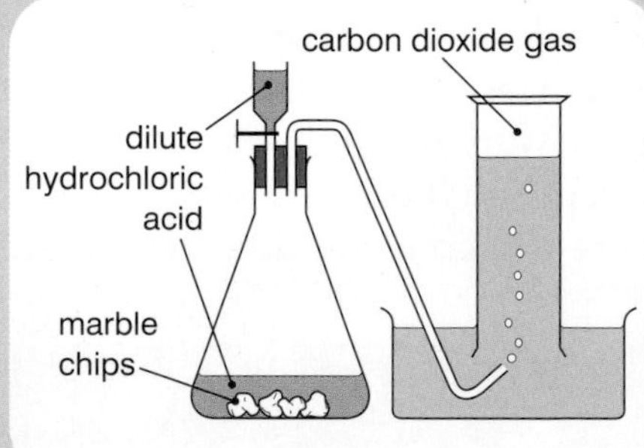

- Add a few drops of universal indicator solution to the gas jar and shake it up.
  d) What does this tell you about carbon dioxide?
- Try 'pouring' a gas jar of carbon dioxide on to a burning nightlight.
  e) What does this tell you about carbon dioxide?

How's that for a diagram?
Well, that's not really what I had in mind.

*The test for **carbon dioxide: limewater** turns milky / cloudy.*

Reacting carbonates

Marble chips are made up mainly of calcium carbonate, as is limestone. There are lots of other **carbonates**. In fact, just think of a metal and add the word carbonate and you have probably named a carbonate. Examples include lead carbonate, zinc carbonate and iron carbonate. *Do all carbonates react with any acid to produce carbon dioxide gas?* You can investigate this question in the next experiment.

These limestone statues are being restored and will then be put back outside Rouen Cathedral. How were they damaged?

Investigating carbonates and acid

SAFETY

- You will be given a range of different carbonates and different acids to test. Think about these questions as you observe each carbonate react with an acid.
  a) Is a gas given off? If so, which gas is it?
  b) How will you test the gas?
  After your investigation, answer these questions:
  c) In what ways are the reactions similar? How do they differ?
  d) Using your evidence, write down a general statement that might be true whenever you add a carbonate to an acid.

Uses of carbon dioxide

We use carbon dioxide in **fire extinguishers**. It is useful on electrical and many chemical fires, where water might make matters worse. Sometimes the carbon dioxide is trapped in foam so that it stays on the fire.

Q1 Why is it a good idea to use foam on an aeroplane fire?

Q2 Explain how the soda-acid fire extinguisher shown works?

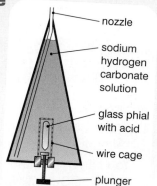

nozzle
sodium hydrogen carbonate solution
glass phial with acid
wire cage
plunger

A soda-acid fire extinguisher. Why wouldn't you use it on an electrical fire?

AMAZING SCIENCE!

The cloudiness you see when testing for carbon dioxide comes from tiny bits of solid **calcium carbonate** formed as the gas reacts with limewater. These tiny white particles are now used in making paper to bulk it up. This means that fewer trees need to be cut down to make the same amount of paper (which is good for the environment).

Gruesome science

In the 1990s, almost two thousand people were mysteriously found dead in the villages on the shores of Lake Nyos in the Cameroon, Africa. Scientists eventually worked out that a cloud of carbon dioxide had killed them. The gas was released from the lake when a landslide stirred up the water. There was no warning, as the colourless, odourless gas raced at about 60 miles per hour across the countryside.

SUMMARY QUESTIONS

1 ☆ Copy these sentences. Complete them by filling in the gaps.
All carbonates react with . . . to produce . . . dioxide gas.
We can test this gas by bubbling it into . . . which turns . . . .

2 ☆☆☆ Make a fact sheet on carbon dioxide gas for another Year 7 class. Include the uses of carbon dioxide. Why wouldn't you use it on an electrical fire?

Key words

calcium carbonate
carbonates
carbon dioxide
fire extinguisher
limewater

7F4 About combustion

LEARN ABOUT
- what is needed for things to burn
- the new substances formed when things burn
- writing word equations

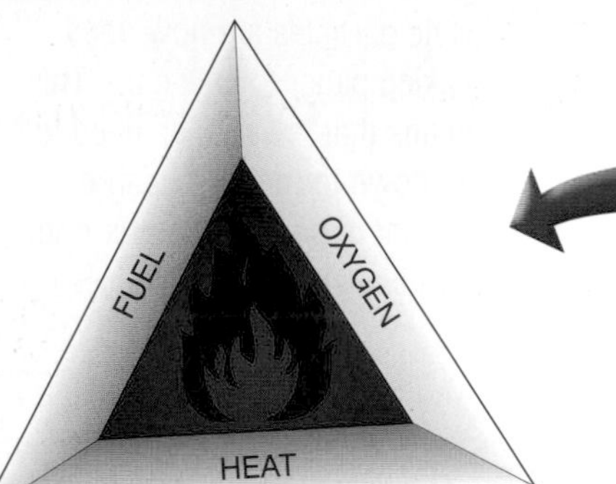

The fire triangle

On the previous page, we saw how carbon dioxide can put out fires. A fire needs three things to keep it burning. We can show these in the **'fire triangle'**. If you can remove one part of the fire triangle, the fire goes out. Carbon dioxide from an extinguisher stops oxygen gas getting to the burning fuel, and so the flames die down.

Combustion

The air around us is a mixture of gases. The two main gases in the air are nitrogen and oxygen. As you have seen from the fire triangle, it is the oxygen that is important in burning. Burning is a chemical reaction. The substance that burns reacts with oxygen. In this chemical reaction, new substances called **oxides** are formed. Energy is also released during the reaction.

Burning is also known as **combustion**. A fuel releases energy, as it reacts with oxygen in a combustion reaction.

The sparks in welding are formed by the combustion of iron

Gruesome science

In 1967, the three crew members of the Apollo 1 spacecraft were killed when practising for their flight. They were in an atmosphere of pure oxygen, when a small electrical fault produced a spark. The resulting flash-fire killed them instantly.

Research into fire-fighting

- Use secondary sources to find information on how to extinguish different types of fire.

  You can use reference books, videos, CD Roms or the Internet.
- Working as a group, produce a leaflet on either:

  'Fire fighting' or 'Preventing fires'

  Make sure that you explain clearly the science involved.

Now you can try out a combustion reaction. The reaction will release a lot of energy, so follow the instructions carefully.

Burning magnesium ribbon

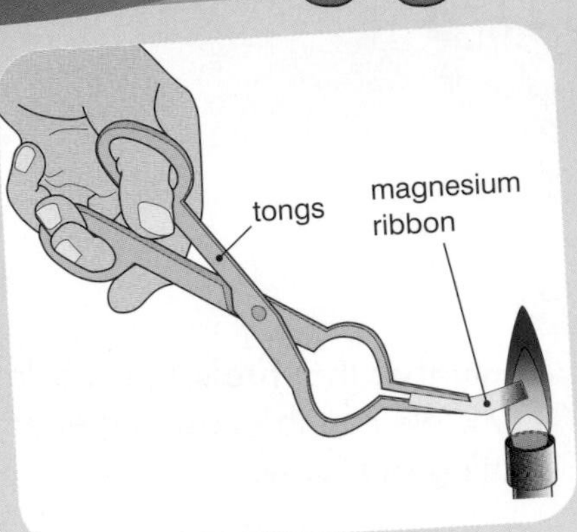

- Hold a small piece of magnesium ribbon at one end in a pair of tongs.
- Ignite the other end in a hot Bunsen flame. Do not look directly at the burning magnesium.
- As soon as the reaction starts, remove the magnesium from the Bunsen flame. Hold the burning magnesium above your heatproof mat. Make sure it is well away from the Bunsen tubing.

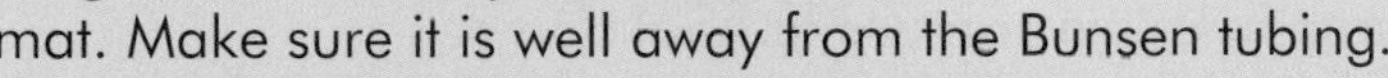

  a) Describe what happens in the reaction.
  b) How does the product differ from the magnesium ribbon you started with?
  c) Which gas in the air did the magnesium react with?

Magnesium powder is used in fireworks

Word equations

We can show the substances involved in a chemical reaction in a **word equation**. A word equation states the reactants we start with and the products we end up with. We can show the combustion of magnesium as:

magnesium + oxygen → magnesium oxide

Q1 Name the reactants and products in the combustion of magnesium.

Q2 Zinc is another metal that reacts with oxygen. Write a word equation to show this.

Q3 You have burned magnesium in air. Remember that air is a mixture of gases; so what do you think will happen if we burn magnesium in pure oxygen gas?

Reactions in pure oxygen

- Watch your teacher demonstrate burning different substances in pure oxygen. Notice the difference between each reaction as it starts off in air and when the burning substance is plunged into the oxygen.
- Your teacher will also test the products with universal indicator.
  a) Design a table to record your observations.
  b) Write a word equation for each reaction.
- You will also see the test we do for oxygen gas.
  c) Describe how we test for oxygen and its result.

SUMMARY QUESTIONS

1 ☆ Copy these sentences. Complete them by filling in the gaps.
The chemical name for burning is . . . .
When things burn, they react with . . . gas in the air.
The products formed are called o. . . .
. . . gas relights a . . . splint.

2 ☆☆☆ **a)** List the safety precautions your teacher took when burning things in pure oxygen.
b) Evaluate the safety measures you took when burning magnesium in air.

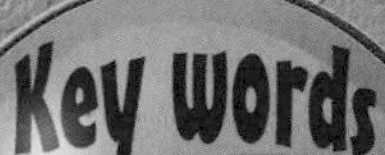

Key words
combustion
fire triangle
magnesium oxide
oxide
oxygen
word equation

Investigating burning

LEARN ABOUT

- the products formed when we burn fuels
- the combustion of methane
- investigating combustion

Fuels

Remember that **fuels** are substances that release energy when we burn them. We can then use the energy to do some useful job, such as heating our home.

Q1 List three fuels we can use to heat homes.

Most of the fuels we use are **fossil fuels** (or are made from fossil fuels).

Examples of fossil fuels are coal, oil and natural gas. These were formed millions of years ago from dead animal and/or plant matter. (See Unit 7I, p.144.) Fossil fuels contain lots of carbon. Can you guess what might be formed when we burn a fossil fuel?

Burning methane

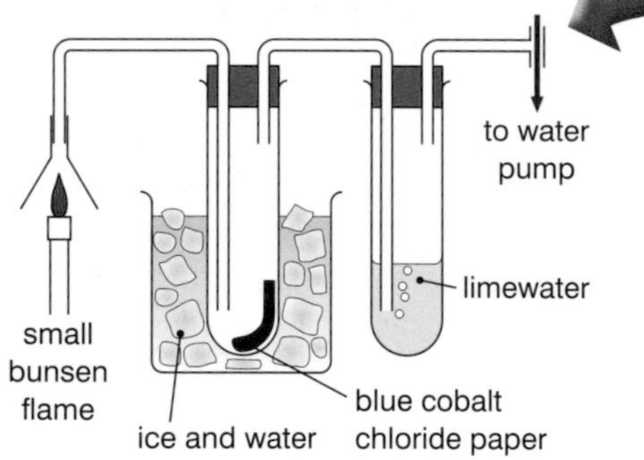

- Watch your teacher carry out the experiment shown:
- You know the test for carbon dioxide. You also need to know the test for water.

  Test for water: *blue cobalt chloride paper turns pink (or white anhydrous copper sulphate turns blue).*

  a) What do you see happen in the experiment?
  b) What are the products formed when methane burns?
  c) Why is the first tube surrounded by ice?

Products of combustion

When a fuel containing carbon burns, the carbon turns to carbon dioxide (as long as there is plenty of oxygen around to react with).

As well as carbon, fossil fuels also contain hydrogen. This reacts with oxygen in the air to form water.

Bunsen burners usually use natural gas as their fuel. Natural gas is made up mainly of a gas called **methane**. Methane contains carbon and hydrogen.

So when methane burns, it produces carbon dioxide and water in its **combustion** reaction.

We can show this information in a **word equation**:

methane + oxygen → carbon dioxide + water

Gruesome science

During the Gulf War, in 1991, many Kuwaiti oil wells were set alight. The smoke was visible from Space and blotted out the Sun in the desert for several days.

Q2 Which of these substances are the **reactants** when methane burns?

methane **oxygen** carbon dioxide water

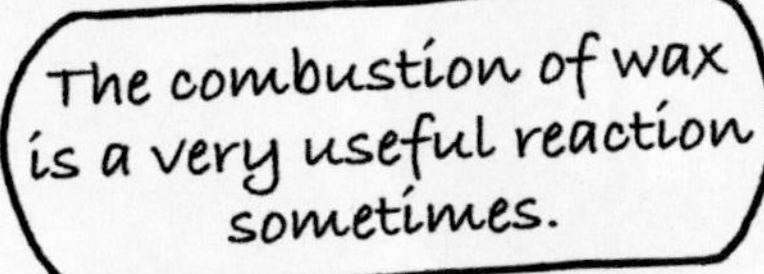

The combustion of wax is a very useful reaction sometimes.

What happens to the air?

We have seen that when substances burn they react with the oxygen in air.

- Watch the experiment and record your observations:
  - **a)** What was in the beaker at the start?
  - **b)** What is made when wax burns? What is in the beaker after the reaction?
  - **c)** Why did the water level rise up the beaker?

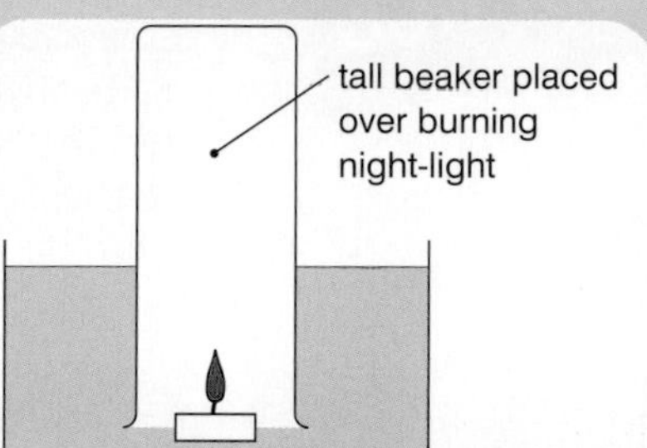

Investigating burning

- Your task is to find out: *How does the volume of air affect the time a night-light burns?*

  You can use a variety of different-sized beakers in your tests.
- Think about these points as you plan and write-up your investigation:
  - **a)** What would you expect a graph of your results to look like?
  - **b)** How will you measure the volume of air in each beaker?
  - **c)** How will you make your results reliable?
  - **d)** How will you record your results and show them on a graph?
  - **e)** What does your graph show? Explain your results.
  - **f)** Evaluate your investigation. How could it be improved?

SUMMARY QUESTIONS

1 ☆ Copy these sentences. Complete them by filling in the gaps.

Fossil fuels contain . . . and hydrogen. When the fuels burn they react with . . . gas releasing e. . .. The products of the c. . . reaction (in plenty of air) are carbon . . . and . . ..

2 ☆☆ Butane is a fuel we get from crude oil. We use it in camping stoves. Butane contains carbon and hydrogen. Write a word equation to show the combustion of butane in plenty of air.

3 ☆☆ Find out the names of some other fuels we get from crude oil.

Key words

combustion
fossil fuel
fuel
methane
oxygen
word equation

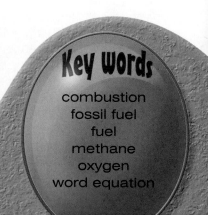

7F
Read all about it!

A modern airship, filled with helium gas

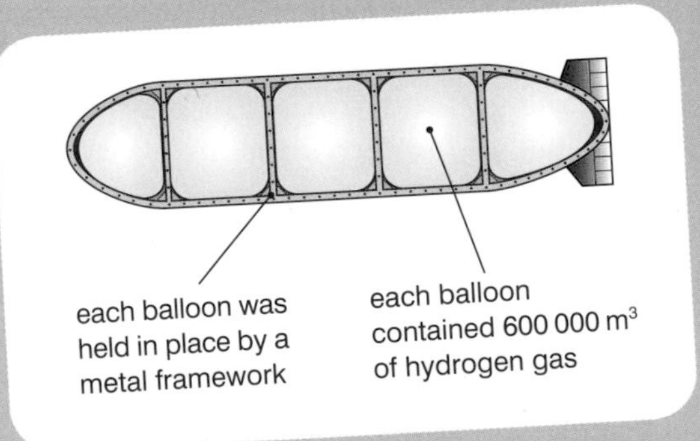
each balloon was held in place by a metal framework
each balloon contained 600 000 m³ of hydrogen gas

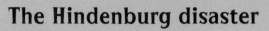

IDEAS AND EVIDENCE

The Hindenburg disaster

Have you seen the airships that sometimes fly over big sporting events? They take those spectacular overhead shots for TV. Modern airships are filled with a gas called helium, and they are a very safe way to travel. However, this was not true of the giant airships built in the 1930s.

Airships are really huge balloons fitted with engines that drive propellers. The Germans were the masters of airship technology. They used them in the First World War to drop bombs on London. After the war in 1918, they continued developing airships for passenger flights. The main manufacturers were the Zeppelin Company. Their biggest airship was the Graf Zeppelin, which was like a fine, flying hotel. It flew right around the world (although it did take three weeks).

The airships were filled with the lightest of all gases, hydrogen (not helium as nowadays). Britain built two large passenger airships too – named the R100 and the R101. But on October 4, 1930, the R101 crashed in France. It was on its way to India and 48 people died. After that experience, travel by airship was left to the Germans.

Around this time, Adolf Hitler became leader of Germany. He used Germany's biggest airship, called the Hindenburg, as a symbol of their technical supremacy. This massive airship could carry 72 passengers in complete luxury. It had everything an ocean liner had, but it went twice as fast and you didn't get seasick! It was so big that it took 200 people to help land it, and three jumbo jets could have fitted inside. It was about three football pitches long!

However, in 1937 disaster struck on its sixty-third voyage. It crashed as it came in to land in New Jersey, USA. It was a stormy day, but crowds had still gathered to see the remarkable airship arrive after flying over the Atlantic. They couldn't believe their eyes as it burst into flames on landing. In just about 30 seconds all that was left was its skeleton.

The hydrogen gas burned fiercely as it reacted with the oxygen in the air:

hydrogen + oxygen → water ***(hydrogen oxide)***

36 people died at the airfield. Remarkably 62 others survived, although some died later of their injuries.

Nobody knows for sure what caused the disaster. Some people think a bomb was planted aboard the airship. Scientists today are still trying to solve the problem.

An American scientist called Addison Bain works for NASA. He thinks that the outer skin could have become charged with static electricity (remember it landed in a storm). It was coated in a type of waterproof paint that is flammable. If this caught fire, the hydrogen would soon explode.

The older Graf Zeppelin provides some evidence that supports this theory. It was coated in a different paint and landed safely many times in similar stormy conditions.

One thing is for sure, hydrogen was just too dangerous to use in airships.The Hindenburg marked the end of the road for giant airships.

The ice is melting and turning back into water so it can't be a chemical reaction... ice is just solid water!
Once you know what to look for, you can see plenty of chemical reactions in the kitchen.
No this gas is still water. Look the vapour has condensed back to liquid water again...no new substances formed here.
Oops! This is strongly alkaline
The air in this balloon must have mass as it's heavier than the empty balloon.

In a chemical reaction, we get new substances formed. The substances we start off with are called the reactants.
The new substances formed are called the products. We can show a chemical reaction by a word equation.
For example:

magnesium + oxygen → magnesium oxide

When substances burn they react with the oxygen gas in the air. The products of these combustion reactions are called oxides.

methane + oxygen → carbon dioxide + water (hydrogen oxide)

DANGER! AVOID THESE COMMON ERRORS

There are two types of change that chemists investigate – **chemical changes** (reactions) and **physical changes** (such as melting and boiling). The main difference is that we get new substances formed in chemical changes, but no new substances form in a physical change.

Key words

carbon dioxide
combustion
hydrogen
oxygen
products
reactants
reaction

UNIT REVIEW

REVIEW QUESTIONS

Understanding and applying concepts

1 When flour burns in a good supply of oxygen, we get carbon dioxide and water (in the form of gas) produced. Inside flour mills there are strict safety measures in place. Any naked flame or spark could cause an explosion because of flour 'dust' in the air.

- **a** What is the scientific word for 'burning'?
- **b** Write a word equation to show flour burning.
- **c** Explain fully how flour 'dust' in a confined space could cause an explosion.
- **d** What hazard signs would you display inside a flour mill?
- **e** What do you think would happen if you dropped a lighted match into a bowl of flour? Explain your answer.

2 Copy and complete the following word equations:

- **a** copper + . . . → copper oxide
- **b** . . . + . . . → sulphur dioxide
- **c** sodium + oxygen → . . .
- **d** methane + oxygen → . . . + . . .

3 Draw a concept map linking these terms together. Don't forget to label your links, explaining what the connection is.

burning **product** **oxides** acid
carbonate **hydrogen** **reactant** oxygen

Ways with words

4 Write a short poem about burning. Make sure you use your knowledge of the fire triangle within your poem.

5 Write your own definitions of the following words:
a fuel **b** oxygen **c** limewater **d** ignite

Making more of maths

6 Crude oil is a source of many different fuels.

a Draw a pie chart that shows the different fuels we get from this sample of crude oil from the North Sea:

Fuel	Approximate percentage
gas	3
petrol	25
kerosene	10
diesel and gas oil	20
fuel oil and residue	42

b The supply of fuels from crude oil does not always match the demand for them. Look at this data:

Fuel	Demand (%)
gas	3
petrol	30
kerosene	7
diesel and gas oil	21
fuel oil and residue	29

i) Think of a way to display visually the data in both tables above, highlighting the differences between the supply and demand of fuels in North Sea oil.

ii) Comment on the differences between the supply and demand of different fuels in North Sea oil.

7 Pete and Pip looked at the reaction between magnesium and dilute sulphuric acid. They measured how much hydrogen gas was given off every 30 seconds. Here are their results:

Time (s)	Volume of gas collected (cm^3)
0	0
30	30
60	45
90	52
120	57
150	60
180	61
210	61.5
240	62
270	62
300	62

a Draw a line graph, using a line (curve) of best fit, to show their results.

b What does your graph tell you about the reaction between magnesium and dilute acid?

c Draw the apparatus that Pete and Pip could have used to carry out their experiment.

d They wanted to find out if cutting the magnesium up into smaller pieces made any difference to the reaction. What variables would they have to control (keep the same) to make sure it was a fair test?

Extension question

8 Find out about the chemical reaction used by brewers to make alcohol, and by bakers to make bread rise. Write an information sheet on the reaction to help shoppers understand that chemical reactions play an important part in everyday life.

SAT-STYLE QUESTIONS

1 Here is a key you can use to identify gases:

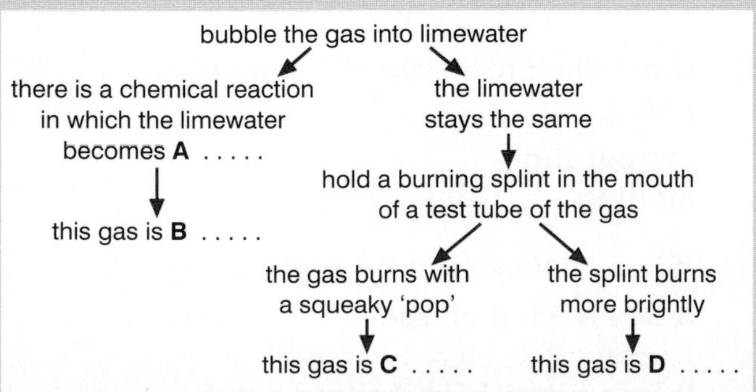

a What are the missing words, A to D? (4)

b i) What would you see if you burned a piece of magnesium ribbon in gas D? (1)

ii) What safety precautions would you (or your teacher) take when doing this experiment? (2)

iii) Write a word equation for the reaction in part b i). (2)

2 A candle is burned under a gas jar in a sand tray:

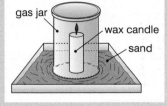

a When the candle burns a chemical reaction takes place.
Name two of the products of this reaction. (2)

b As the candle burns, wax gets used up. Name two other ways in which we can tell that a chemical reaction takes place. (2)

c Explain what you see happen in the experiment above. (2)

d What safety precaution has been taken in the experiment? Why? (2)

3 A group of students were looking at the reaction between calcium carbonate and dilute hydrochloric acid. They decided to take the mass every minute.

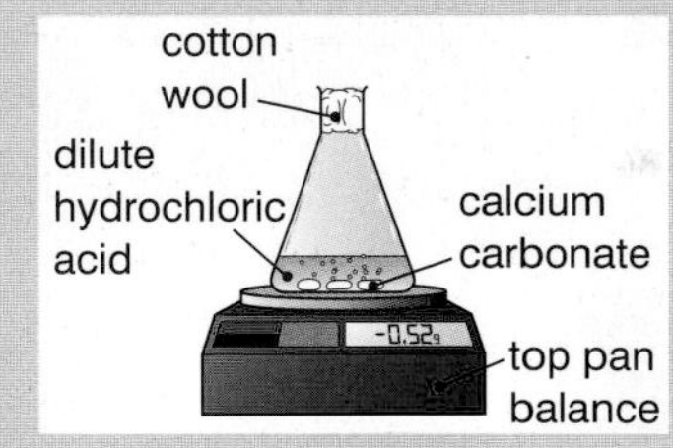

a Which gas is given off in the reaction? (1)

b The students took readings from the balance for 10 minutes, by which time the reaction had been finished for 2 minutes. Use axes like the ones shown to sketch the shape of the graph you would expect. (2)

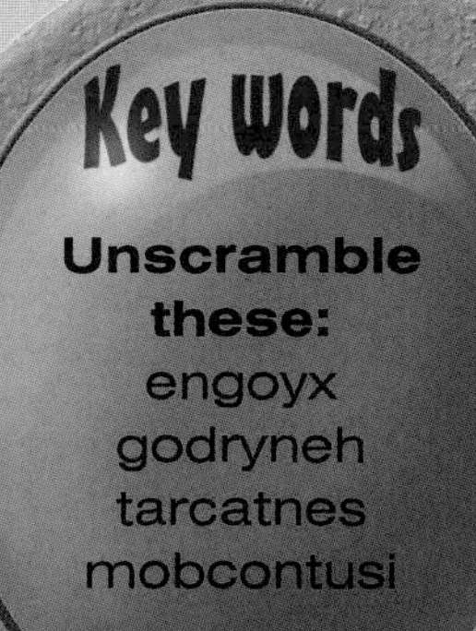

7G The particle model

Coming soon

Point out the solids, liquids and gases in this volcanic eruption

What's it all about?

Throughout history, people have been interested in explaining how the world works. Sorting things into groups, such as solids, liquids and gases, is one way to start making sense of the world.

Thinking more deeply, people also wanted to know *why* some things are solids but others are liquids or gases at room temperature. They also wanted to explain the way materials behave, and that's where the theory of particles comes in.

In this unit, you will have lots of opportunities to look at evidence and to think about explaining your observations.

What do you remember?

You already know:

- the properties of solids, liquids and gases.
- that the same material can exist as a solid, a liquid and a gas.
- that melting and freezing are opposites.
- about evaporation and condensation.

1 Name the process in which a liquid turns to a solid.

boiling **condensing** **freezing** **melting**

2 Name the process in which a gas turns to a liquid.

evaporating **boiling**
melting **condensing**

3 Which of these is a property of a gas?

It has a fixed shape.
It cannot be compressed.
It has a very high boiling point.
It fills the shape of its container.

Ideas about solids, liquids and gases

QUESTIONS

Look at the cartoons above and discuss these questions with your partner.

a) Why do you think some gases float and others don't?

b) Do you believe that everything is made up of particles? Do you believe in anything you've never seen with your own eyes? Try explaining why a piece of elastic stretches when you pull it.

c) What do you think of Benson's idea about the particles in ice, water and steam?

d) Does Pete and Molly's idea about hot materials make sense to you? Why?

7.1

Evidence from experiments

LEARN ABOUT
- classifying materials as solid, liquid or gas
- interpreting and explaining results

Solids, liquids and gases

No, don't shout... she's only experimenting!

You start experimenting to find out the properties of solids, liquids and gases from a very early age. Toddlers soon learn that they can shake their drinking cup upside-down and make a nice puddle in the tray of their highchair – great for splashing their hands in (and much more fun than drinking!). We find out that liquids spread out easily, can flow and don't have a fixed shape.

Table 1 A summary of the properties of solids, liquids and gases

	Does it have its own fixed shape?	Is it easy to compress?	Does it spread out or flow easily?
Solid	yes	no	no
Liquid	no	no	yes
Gas	no	yes	yes

AMAZING SCIENCE!

The Forth Rail Bridge is made of iron. In summer it is about 50 cm longer than it is in the winter.

Q1 Classify the following substances as **solids**, **liquids** or **gases** at 20 °C. Put your answers into a suitable table.

petrol oxygen nitrogen concrete cooking oil iron carbon dioxide Perspex vinegar

Discussing ideas

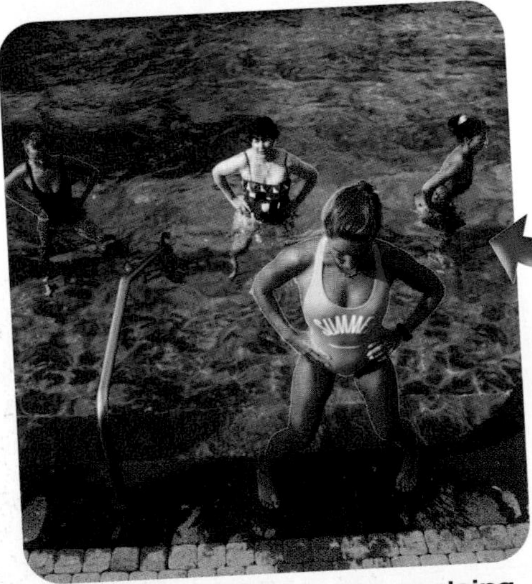

What are the benefits of exercising in water?

Have you ever tried to run through the water in a swimming pool? It's hard work!

a) Why is it so much harder to get through water than it is to move through air?

- Talk about your ideas in pairs. After a few minutes, share your ideas with a neighbouring pair.

b) Do you all agree on the answer to why it is easier to move through air than water?

- Draw a large diagram to display your ideas to the rest of the class.
- Discuss the ideas from the other groups, comparing them with your own.

Investigating solids, liquids and gases

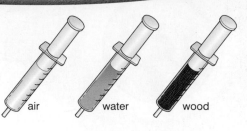

Now you can try a series of experiments to help explain why solids, liquids and gases behave differently.

- Try to push in the plunger of the three sealed syringes.

  a) What do you feel?

  b) Explain your observations.

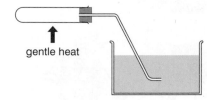

air water wood

- Warm the boiling tube gently using a Bunsen burner.

  c) What do you see at the end of the delivery tube? Remove the end of the delivery tube from the water before you stop heating. Do this by lifting the clamp stand. Why is this important?

  d) Explain your results.

gentle heat

- Try the 'bar and gauge' experiment or the 'ball and ring' experiment.

  e) Explain what happens.

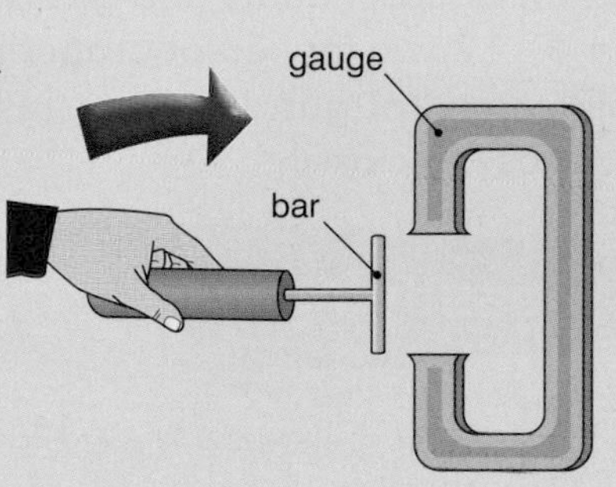

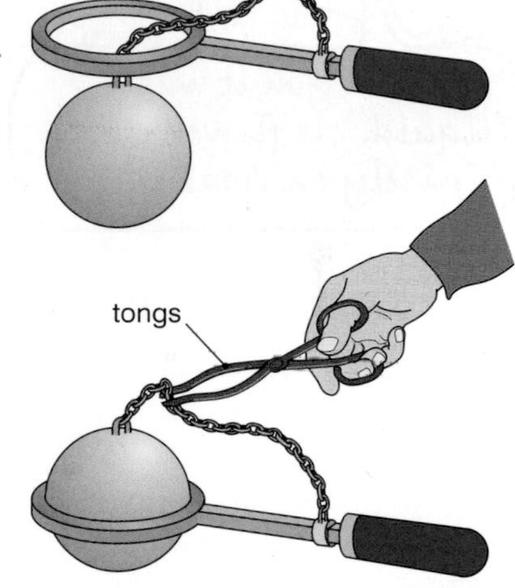

SAFETY: Hot metal!

- Use tweezers to place a coloured crystal at the bottom of a beaker of cold water, and one at the bottom of some hot water.

  f) Explain your observations.

- Compare the masses of blocks of materials that are the same size. Put your results in a table.

  g) Explain your data.

- Suspend an increasing number of masses from an elastic band. Remove the masses after each additional mass.

  h) Explain what you see happen.

- Discuss and evaluate the explanations together as a whole class.

Gold is a very dense metal. A block the size of a large matchbox has a mass of about 4 kg.

SUMMARY QUESTIONS

1 ☆ Copy these sentences. Complete them by filling in the gaps.

Solids and liquids cannot be . . . easily, unlike a gas.

A solid has a fixed . . . whereas liquids and gases take up the . . . of their container.

A gas will . . . out in all directions, but solids . . . in one position.

2 ☆☆☆ Make a list of materials that would be tricky to classify as a solid, a liquid or a gas.

Classifying materials

LEARN ABOUT

- classifying materials as solid, liquid or gas, but realising that some are difficult to classify
- how theories can be based on experimental data

States of matter

I told you it was a liquid... it flowed quite nicely on your face.

Have you ever played with a tub of green slime that you can buy in toy shops?
Maybe you have a younger brother or sister who still annoys you with it.
Would you say the slime was a thick (**viscous**) liquid or a soft solid?

We call solids, liquids and gases the three **states of matter**.
On p.112, we looked at properties of materials and classified them as solid, liquid or gas. However, just like green slime, some things are not that easy to classify.

Classifying tricky materials

- Copy and complete the table for the materials listed below:

Material	I would classify this as a. . . . (solid/liquid/gas)	Explanation

Materials to attempt to classify:
flour sponge hair gel hair mousse whipped cream cling-film glue-stick wallpaper paste hair spray toothpaste (and green slime, of course!)

Models in science

Scientists use **models** to help them explain the way the world works.
A scientist's model can be a **theory**, a mathematical equation or a computer simulation that explains our observations. We can then use the model to make **predictions** in new situations. If the prediction proves to be correct, then the model is more likely to be accepted as a good one by other scientists.
Imagine that you had the most powerful microscope ever invented and could look right inside materials.

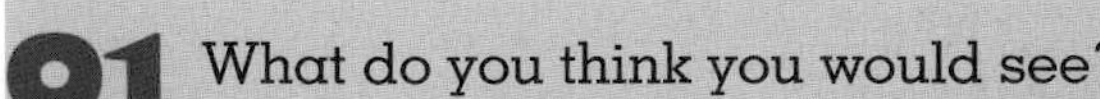

Q1 What do you think you would see?

Q2 How would your model explain the differences we find between solids, liquids and gases?

Share your ideas with others in your class. Discuss how different people have used their **evidence** to support their suggested model.

Scientists also use physical models like this to help explain the world

Changing models

The ancient Greeks were the first people to suggest that everything is made of tiny **particles**. The Greeks were great thinkers about the world they lived in, although they didn't bother much with experiments. A Greek philosopher called Democritus put forward his model to explain the way materials behave. The particles he talked about were so small that you couldn't see them.

Democritus was a wealthy Greek philosopher, born in 460 BC. He has been commemorated on Greek stamps and has a large research institute near Athens named after him.

He imagined that the particles were hard and could not be destroyed. Our word 'atoms' comes from the Greek *atomon*. It means indivisible (or something that can't be broken down).

Democritus explained the properties of materials by saying that their particles were different. For example, he said a runny liquid must be made up of smooth, round particles so that they can slide over each other. On the other hand, he said hard solids must be made up of particles that are sharp and jagged. These particles get stuck in position, so he said that explains why they don't flow and are hard.

This appealed to the logical mind of Democritus, but most people still believed in a model suggested by another, more famous, Greek philosopher called Aristotle. He said that all materials were mixtures of earth, air, fire and water. In this model, all materials differed because they contained different proportions of earth, air, fire or water. This was a powerful theory too, as people could use it to explain many observations.

Eventually, over 2000 years later, scientists developed the theory of particles that is still useful today. We don't think that everything Democritus suggested is correct, but we do believe in particles. Experiments carried out around 1800 played a big part in refining our ideas about particles – not something the ancient Greeks took part in unfortunately.

Devise a branching database that could be used to classify materials as solid, liquid or gas. You will need to think up questions that can be answered 'Yes' or 'No', leading to the word 'Solid', 'Liquid' or 'Gas'.

SUMMARY QUESTIONS

1 ★ Copy these sentences. Complete them by filling in the gaps.
Scientists use . . . to help explain the way materials behave.
The Ancient Greeks were the first to think that everything is made of tiny invisible . . . .

2 ★★★ Write a conversation between Democritus and Aristotle, with each one defending his own theory about what makes up materials.

evidence
model
particles
prediction
theory
viscous

The particle theory

LEARN ABOUT
- using a model based on things we can't see directly
- explaining the differences between solids, liquids and gases using the particle model

Can we see the particles?

Scientists in the 1800s found new evidence that particles exist. In 1805 John Dalton explained chemical reactions in terms of particles. About 20 years later, Robert Brown actually observed the effects of particles when he looked at pollen grains under a microscope. He noticed that pollen grains in water appeared to jiggle about constantly. Their movement was **random** and was eventually explained using particle theory. The pollen grains could be struck by the particles that make up water. We can't see these particles because they are just so small.

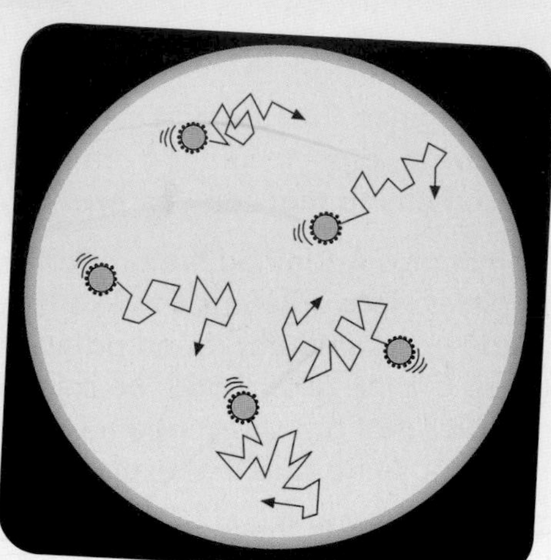

You can see this effect, called **Brownian motion**, by observing smoke. Smoke is made up of tiny pieces of solid.

The smoke cell experiment

- Observe the smoke in the plastic container under the microscope.

  The blobs that you can see lit up are the bits of solid in smoke.

  a) What happens to the smoke? Describe the movement you see.

  b) Try to explain your observations.

The particles we are talking about in this unit are incredibly small. If we could line up a couple of million average-sized particles, they wouldn't even measure 1 mm from one end to the other – that's why we can't see them!

Models of solids, liquids and gases

Solid

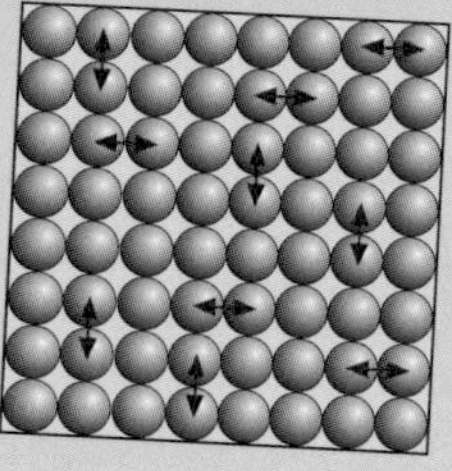

We can think of the particles in a **solid** as being very close together. Each particle is touching its neighbouring particles. They are fixed in position. However, they are not motionless. They **vibrate** constantly.

Q1 What do you think happens to the vibrations of the particles if you heat a solid?

Gas

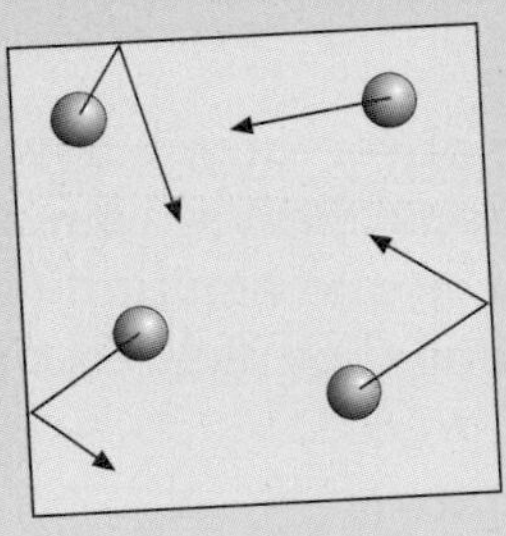

The particles in a gas are free to zoom around in any direction. On average, there is plenty of space between the particles. They collide frequently with other particles in the gas and with the walls of their container.

Q3 How does this model explain why it is easy to move through a gas?

Liquid

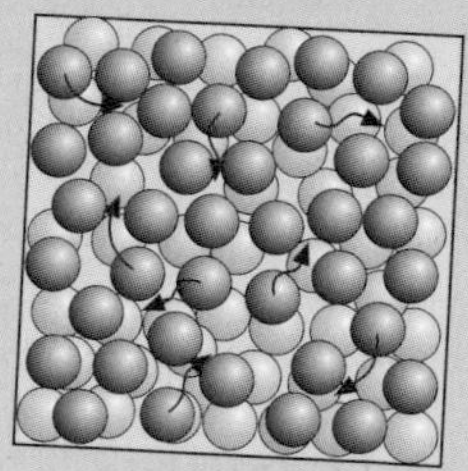

The particles in a **liquid** are still very close together. You can imagine the particles rather like a bunch of grapes. They touch each other, but there is no regular arrangement. Unlike the particles in a solid, they are *not* fixed in position. They are free to slip and slide over and around each other. This motion is completely random.

Q2 How does this particle model explain how you can pour a liquid?

Now I know how the particles in a liquid feel!

It's just like being inside a solid... we all have our position, but there's plenty of jiggling about!

SUMMARY QUESTIONS

1 ☆ Copy these sentences. Complete them by filling in the gaps.

The . . . in a solid are packed . . . together.

They are . . . in position but they do v. . ..

In liquids, the particles are . . . together, but can slip and . . . over each other.

In a gas, the particles . . . around, bashing against other . . . and the . . . of their container.

2 ☆☆ Imagine that the people in your class are particles. You can use them to demonstrate the arrangement and movement of particles in a solid, liquid and gas. Think up a set of instructions for this modelling activity.

Key words

Brownian motion
gas
liquid
random
solid
vibrate

Applying particle theory

LEARN ABOUT
- using the particle theory to explain observations
- diffusion
- gas pressure

Can you believe it?

A world made up of tiny particles too small to actually see might be difficult to imagine at first. However, when you start using this particle theory to explain things, you'll find it is easier to believe.

On the previous two pages we saw how particles are arranged in solids, liquids and gases. We also looked at the way the particles move in each state of matter. As we heat up a material, we transfer energy to its particles. This makes their movement more vigorous.

Q1 Use the particle theory to explain what happens when you heat butter gently in a pan.

Think back to the experiments on p.113.

Q2 Explain your observations now using the particle theory. Have your ideas changed since the start of this unit? Discuss any differences and similarities between your original ideas and the accepted particle theory with your group.

Gruesome science

One of the foulest smelling substances on Earth is ethyl mercaptan. Its smell has been described as a combination of garlic, onions, rotting cabbage and sewer gas – Yuk!

Diffusion

Do you like the smell of freshly baked bread? You can thank a process called **diffusion** for spreading the particles from the bread, through the air and into your nose.

Diffusion happens when substances mingle and pass through each other. It happens without us having to stir the substances up.

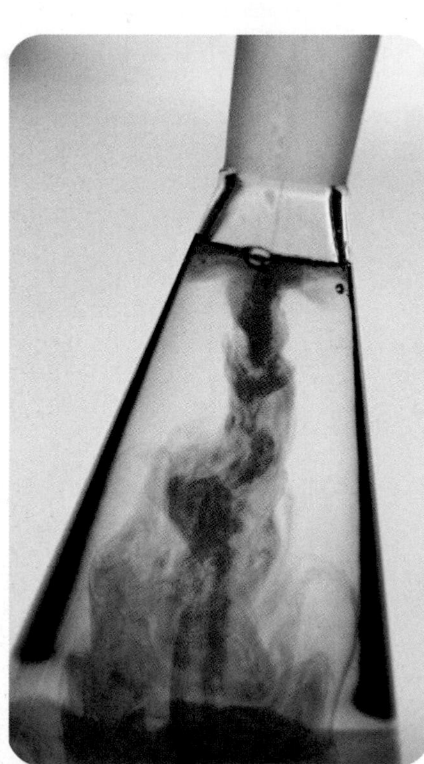

This green dye is diffusing through water

I must get some of that new body spray!

Looking at diffusion

Now use the particle theory to explain the following experiments.

- Use tweezers to place a few crystals of potassium manganate(VII) in a Petri dish of agar gel.

  Record and explain your observations next lesson.

- Bromine is a dark brown liquid that evaporates easily at room temperature. The gas (or vapour) given off is dark orange. The gas is much more dense than air.

  Your teacher will place a little bromine in the bottom of a gas jar, then place a second gas jar on top of it.

  a) What do you think will happen?
  b) Why is the experiment done in a fume-cupboard?

Gas pressure

Do you feel like you are being constantly **bombarded** by particles of the gases in air? Of course, we don't feel these **collisions** but they are happening.

...and we are constantly being struck by gas particles.
I knew I felt under pressure!

As you know, the particles in a gas whizz around at fast speeds.

They collide with each other and anything else they bump into, including the walls of their container. Each collision will result in a tiny force being applied. This force causes gas pressure.

Gas pressure is a measure of the force exerted per unit area by the particles of gas.

The average speed of the particles of nitrogen gas in the air (at 20 °C) is about 500 m/s – that's fast! It explains why they collide over a thousand million times every second!

SUMMARY QUESTIONS

1 ☆ Copy these sentences. Complete them by filling in the gaps.

When substances mix automatically, without us having to . . . them, we call it . . .. This happens because particles in liquids and . . . are free to . . . around in a random manner.

When the . . . of a gas collide with the walls of their . . .. they produce a . . . that causes gas . . ..

2 ☆☆☆ Explain why the sides of a sealed steel can collapse inwards when the air is sucked out of it by a vacuum pump.

 SCIENTIFIC PEOPLE 

Otto von Guericke and his amazing scientific demonstrations

The name of Otto von Guericke will always be linked to his beloved city of Magdeburg in Germany. His wealthy family had lived there for three centuries before Otto was born on 20 November, 1602. He went to university at the age of 15, and finally studied law at the Dutch university of Leiden for three years until he was 23. Whilst at Leiden, he also studied engineering and was especially interested in building fortresses.

His fortunes changed when Magdeburg was ransacked in the Thirty Years War, and he left Germany to work as an engineer in Sweden. However, he was able to return to Magdeburg in 1632, putting his engineering knowledge to good use in helping to rebuild the city. He became mayor of the city for over 25 years.

However, he will be best remembered for his famous demonstrations involving air pressure. Having invented the air pump in 1650, Otto was able to create a vacuum. He could remove the air from a container and show the great force that air pressure can produce. Otto really knew how to impress people; look at one of his experiments above:

In this experiment 20 men, using a pulley, tried to pull a piston upwards, as one man moved it downwards by sucking air out of the cylinder. People were amazed when the 'one man' (plus the help of air pressure) won the tug of war.

Then he organised an even more spectacular tug of war between two teams of six pack-horses.

Otto had two halves of a copper sphere made so that they fitted together perfectly. He had the local blacksmith, and some helpers, use a pump to suck the air out of the sphere. On his signal, the two teams of horses pulled and pulled, but could not separate the two halves of the sphere. The crowd of curious onlookers cheered. They were even more impressed when the horses had stopped and Otto returned to the copper sphere. He asked for silence as he released a valve and a hissing sound could be heard. As the air rushed back inside the sphere, it suddenly fell in two. Cue rapturous applause from the astounded crowd. What a demonstration!

Otto's demonstrations continued to be a great success as he toured around Europe, performing at several royal courts.

This technician is about to coat the silicon disc in a material that will form a tiny electrical circuit. The material used is heated in a vacuum, so that it evaporates easily. Then it condenses and coats the disc.

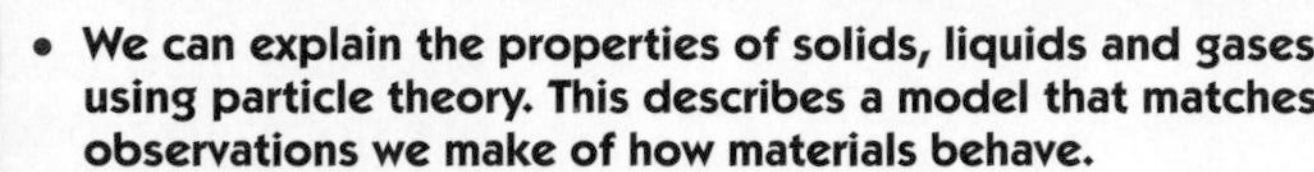

- We can explain the properties of solids, liquids and gases using particle theory. This describes a model that matches observations we make of how materials behave.
- In a solid, the particles are lined up next to each other, very close together.

  They are fixed in position but do vibrate.
  As we heat a solid, its particles vibrate more and more vigorously.
- In a liquid, the particles are still very close together, but can slip and slide over each other.
- In a gas, the particles whizz around and there is lots of space within the gas.

  As the particles in a gas collide with the walls of their container, they produce a force that causes gas pressure.
- Diffusion is when substances mix without us stirring them up. This happens automatically in liquids and gases because their particles are free to move around.

Even Helium gas has mass... It's just very light. There's a lot of space between the particles of gas in both balloons but the actual particles in my balloon are lighter than yours.
He
CO_2
This particle model we've used really can explain a lot of stuff, you know.
It's just the arrangement and movement of the particles that change when a material melts or boils... The particles themselves don't change... That would only happen in a chemical reaction.
The particles vibrate more when they get hot so the gaps between them get a bit bigger...That's why a hot solid takes up more space than when it's cold.

DANGER! AVOID THESE COMMON ERRORS

We can compress gases a lot, but liquids are very difficult to compress because their particles are very close together – there are no large spaces between them, as there are in gases. The particles in a liquid and a gas can both move around randomly, but the particles in a gas move a lot more quickly.

When we heat a solid, its particles gain energy and vibrate more vigorously. In liquids and gases, heating causes the particles to move about more quickly. This extra movement means that substances expand as they get hotter.

Gas pressure is not a force – it is the force per unit area. So the total force of colliding particles can be large, but if the particles are spread over a large area, the gas pressure will be low.

Key words

diffusion
gas
gas pressure
liquid
particles
solid

UNIT REVIEW

REVIEW QUESTIONS

Understanding and applying concepts

1 Using particle theory, explain Otto von Guericke's experiment with the copper sphere, described on p.120.

2 When bromine gas diffuses through a vacuum, the orange colour spreads through a flask in a split second. When the same flask is full of air, it takes an hour for the orange colour to spread evenly throughout the flask.
Explain these observations.

3 On motorway bridges, the concrete sections are slotted together using expansion joints like the ones shown in this photo:

Explain why tar is used in these expansion joints.

4 If your job was fitting new telephone wires between poles, what difficulties would changes of temperature cause you? How would you plan to overcome these problems?

5 Give three ways in which you could increase the pressure of a gas in a container.
Explain how each change you suggest increases the gas pressure in the container.

6 Draw a concept map linking these terms together. Don't forget to label your links, explaining what the connection is:

solid liquid gas particles diffusion

Ways with words

7 Write the instructions for a Year 7 class who are going to model solids, liquids and gases using marbles and the lid of a shoe box.

8 Write a short story, or cartoon strip, about a water particle that starts off in an ice cube in a freezer and ends up in a drop of water on the inside of the kitchen window.

Making more of maths

9 If the particles in a sample of gas collide 8 000 000 000 times each second, how many collisions would there be in one hour?

10 On average, the volume of a material increases by about 4% when the solid melts to form a liquid. Assuming expansion of 4%, what is the volume of liquid formed from 550 cm^3 of solid when it melts?

Thinking skills

11 The particles that make up rubber are long and thin.
- a Think up a model that will explain why a rubber band stretches when you pull it, then springs back to its original length when you let go.
- b Using your model, explain why a rubber band snaps if you stretch it too far.

Extension question

12 We can find the density of a substance using the equation:

density = mass/volume

- a Work out the density of theses two substances (one is a solid and one is a gas):
  Substance A: 2.6 cm^3 of A of mass 50 g
  Substance B: 10 000 cm^3 of B of mass 30 g
- b Which substance is the gas and which is the solid? Explain your answer using particle theory.
- c Using the information in question 10, work out the density of the liquid formed when the solid identified in part **b** melts.

d Most liquids contract when they freeze, but water is an exception.
i) Find out why water is an exception.
ii) Give one disadvantage that arises from this property of water.

SAT-STYLE QUESTIONS

1 Solid, liquid and gas are called the **three states of matter.**

The particles in a solid, liquid and gas are shown below.

The arrows represent changes of state:

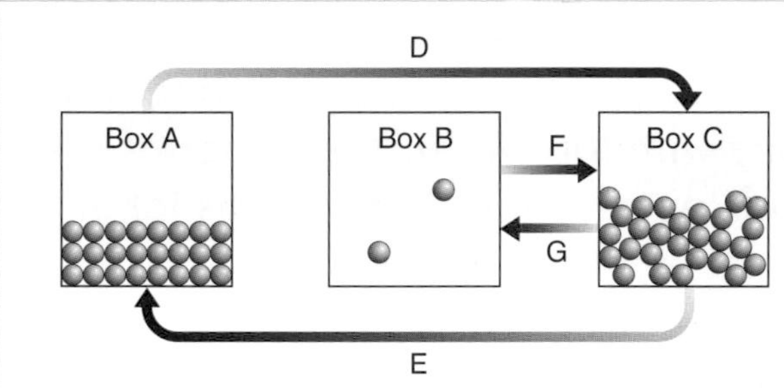

a Which box contains:
i) a solid, ii) a liquid, iii) a gas? (1)

b Which state of matter is most easily compressed? (1)

c i) Identify the changes of state labelled D, E, F and G. (4)
ii) Which changes of state require cooling down to take place? (2)

d Pip wanted to see how easily sulphur powder melts.
Sulphur burns in air to form toxic sulphur dioxide gas.
Give two safety precautions that Pip should take in her experiment. (2)

2 Mike and Pete are investigating diffusion.

In Test 1, they plan to time how long it takes a coloured gas to diffuse throughout a gas jar of air.

In Test 2, they want to fill the gas jar with water and time how long a coloured crystal takes to diffuse through the liquid.

a What measuring instrument will they need to judge which test is quicker? (1)

b Predict which test will happen more quickly. (1)

c Explain your answer to part **b** using particle theory. (2)

3 Benson and Molly were testing four metals (A, B, C and D). They set up the apparatus below and timed how long it took for each drawing pin to drop off the different metals:

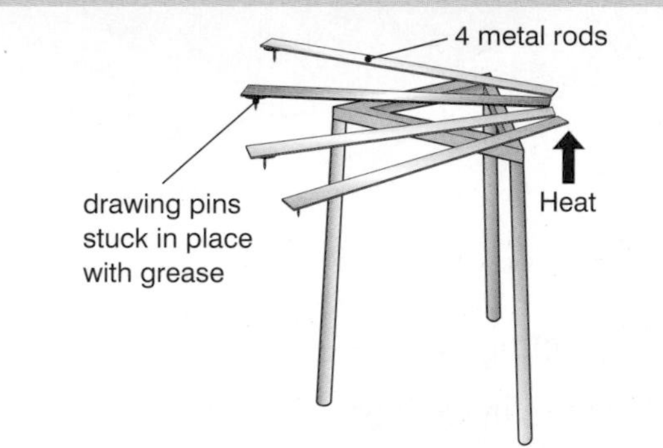

Here are their results:

Metal	Time for drawing pin to fall (s)
A	550
B	470
C	360
D	545

a Finish off the question that Benson and Molly were investigating.
Which metal is the best . . .? (1)

b How can they make their results more reliable? For which two metals is this particularly important? Why? (2)

c Give two ways in which Molly and Benson tried to make their investigation a fair test? (2)

d Benson wanted to display their results on a graph.
i) What type of graph should he choose? (1)
ii) Sketch the axes he should use. (1)

e Before their tests, Benson and Molly felt the metals.
Molly predicted 'I think metal C will be best, because it feels coldest.'
Do their results support her prediction?
Explain your answer. (1)

f Use particle theory to explain what happens to the length of each rod in this investigation. (2)

Unscramble these:
dilos
riplatesc
offsinudi

7H

Solutions

Coming soon

What's it all about?

We all need water to stay alive and doctors encourage us to drink plenty each day. Some people like bottled mineral water, others are happy with tap water. Are either of these liquids pure water? Look at this label from a bottle of mineral water.

Sometimes, we want solids to dissolve in liquids – for example, when we make a cup of tea or coffee. At other times, we want to separate a liquid from any dissolved solids – for example, in dry countries where they turn sea water into drinking water.

In this unit you can find out more about dissolving solids to make mixtures, and also about separating these mixtures. You will have a chance to use the particles theory from Unit 7G to help explain your experiments.

What do you remember?

You already know:

- that some solids dissolve and others do not.
- how to separate mixtures of solids and liquids.
- that not all liquids contain water.
- that all materials are made up of very small particles.

1 Which one of these solids does *not* dissolve in water?

sugar **salt** **chalk** **copper sulphate**

2 How would you separate the solid bits from a mixture of soil and water?

evaporation **filtration**
condensation **freezing**

3 Which one of the following does *not* contain water?

petrol **milk** **cola** **vinegar**

Ideas about solutions

QUESTIONS

Look at the cartoons above and discuss these questions with your partner.

a) What do you think has happened to the salt in the pan?

b) Do you think you can purify any sample of water, no matter how dirty it is? How would you try it?

c) Explain the trouble Pete is having trying to get the dissolved blue solid back again.

d) Will Molly and Pete succeed in making the sweetest drink ever? Why?

e) Is it true that if a substance won't dissolve in water, it won't dissolve in any liquid? How would you help Mike get rid of the stain?

f) Is melting the same as dissolving? Explain your answer.

LEARN ABOUT
- finding out which liquids are pure and which are mixtures
- separating salt from rock salt

Pure water?

Some people think that rainwater is the purest water you can get. Others might say that the purest water is the water from a mountain stream. But lots of substances, including some gases, dissolve in water. Even rain falling through pollution-free air will be a mixture by the time it reaches the ground. Some carbon dioxide gas will have dissolved in it. The water in streams also contains dissolved gases as well as any soluble solids it has passed over. Look back to the mineral water label on p.124 to see what's dissolved in it.

Q1 Why do you think tap water has been treated with chlorine before it arrives at your home?

Pure substance or a mixture?

- You will be given five unknown liquids, labelled A to E.
- Your task is to devise a safe way to test if the liquids are pure or if they are mixtures.
- How can you find out if there are any solids dissolved in them?
- Show your plans to your teacher before starting any tests.
- Describe and explain the tests you carry out.

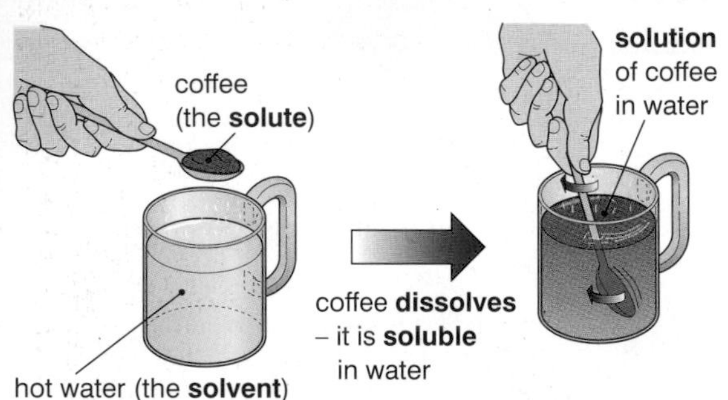

When we look at substances dissolving, there are certain words we need to know. Look at the list of definitions below:

Soluble – describes a substance that dissolves in a particular liquid
Insoluble – describes a substance that does not dissolve in a particular liquid
Solvent – the liquid that does the dissolving
Solute – the substance that has dissolved in the liquid (solvent)
Solution – the mixture of solvent and solute

Rock salt

Do you add salt to your food? The salt that we sprinkle on food is called **sodium chloride**. As you know, sodium chloride is soluble in water. We find it in nature as seams of rock salt under the ground or as the main solid dissolved in seawater. The sodium chloride in rock salt is mixed with sandy bits of rock that are insoluble in water. Rock salt is mined from underground seams by large cutting machines. Much of it is used in this impure form to grit the roads in winter.

How much salt in rock salt?

You can separate pure salt (sodium chloride) from rock salt.

- Plan a series of steps to arrive at a pure sample of salt.
- You also have to work out the percentage of salt that was in the rock salt you started with.
- Show your plans to your teacher before you start your practical work.
- After your experiment, compare your results with the results of the other groups in your class.
- Think of some reasons why different groups arrived at different percentages of salt in rock salt.

CHALLENGE

Doctors are worried that people are eating too much salt. Find out which foods have large amounts of salt in them and what problems excess salt in your diet causes.

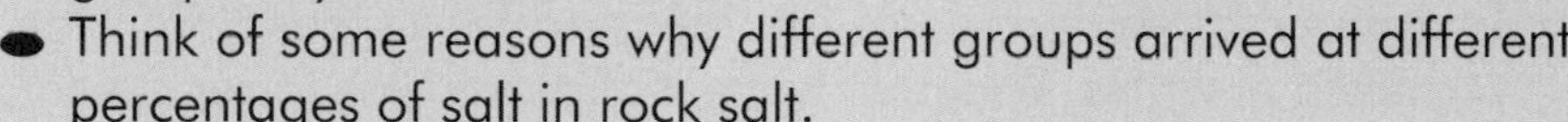

Solution mining

Here's another way to get the salt from a seam of rock salt to the surface. This works because sodium chloride dissolves in water. Look at the diagram below:

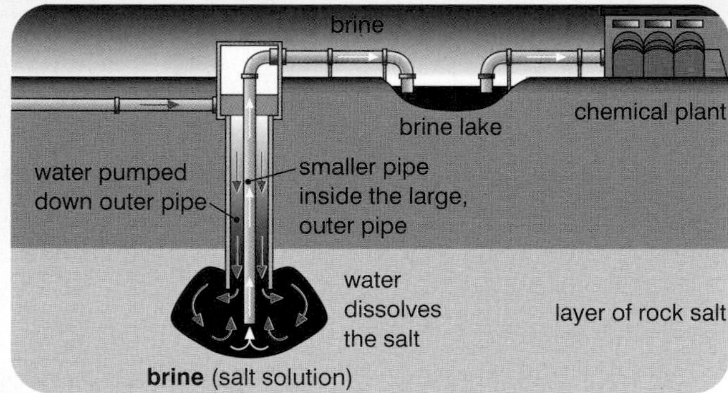

Hot water is pumped down the outer pipe and salt solution, called brine, is forced up to the surface through the inner pipe. The brine is stored in a reservoir until the chemical factory needs it. Many useful substances are made from the substances we get from brine.

AMAZING SCIENCE!

There is a 12 room hotel in Bolivia, South America, that is made from salt bricks. The bricks were cut from the salt flats left behind when an inland sea evaporated. Perhaps not surprisingly, the hotel has no showers!

Q2 Why are the impurities in rock salt left underground when we mine salt in this way?

SUMMARY QUESTIONS

1 ☆ Copy these sentences. Complete them by filling in the gaps.
A soluble solid will . . . in a liquid to form a . . . .
The soluble solid is called the . . . and the liquid is called the . . . .

2 ☆☆ Do some research to find out the useful substances we can make using sodium chloride as the starting material.

Key words

brine
insoluble
sodium chloride
soluble
solute
solution
solvent

7H2 Particles in solution

LEARN ABOUT
- conservation of mass
- using particle theory to explain dissolving

Using the particle theory

You have already seen how we can explain observations using particle theory in Unit 7G. You know about the arrangement and movement of particles in solids and liquids, so how can we use this model to explain dissolving?

Q1 Imagine that you have lots of blue marbles representing the particles of water. You also have white marbles to represent the particles in a solid. A shoe box could represent a beaker. Using this model, describe what you think happens when a solid dissolves in water.

What happens to the mass?

- Using your model of dissolving from Q1, predict what will happen to the mass of salt and water before and after we stir them together. Will the total mass increase, decrease or stay the same?
- Plan a safe experiment to test your prediction.
- Show your plan to your teacher before trying it out.
- Name the solute and solvent in your experiment.
- Did your results support your prediction? Did the experiment provide evidence for your model of dissolving? Explain your answers.

The solid before it dissolves

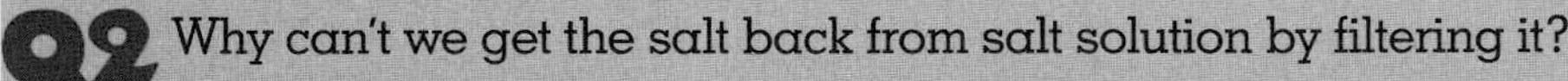

Q2 Why can't we get the salt back from salt solution by filtering it?

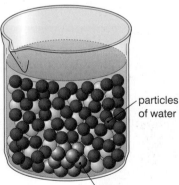

Explaining how solids dissolve

This series of diagrams use particle theory to explain our observations of a solid forming a solution.

As the solid is added to the solvent, its particles are still in their usual regular arrangement.

For a solid to dissolve in a solvent there must be quite strong **forces of attraction** between the particles in the solute and those in the solvent.

The solvent particles 'pull' the particles of the solute from their neighbouring particles in the solid. Each one gets surrounded by solvent particles.

The process of dissolving begins

As you know, the particles in a liquid are constantly moving around, slipping and sliding over each other. This random motion of the particles in the liquid means that the dissolved particles get spread evenly throughout the solution formed. The particles of the solute and the solvent **intermingle**.

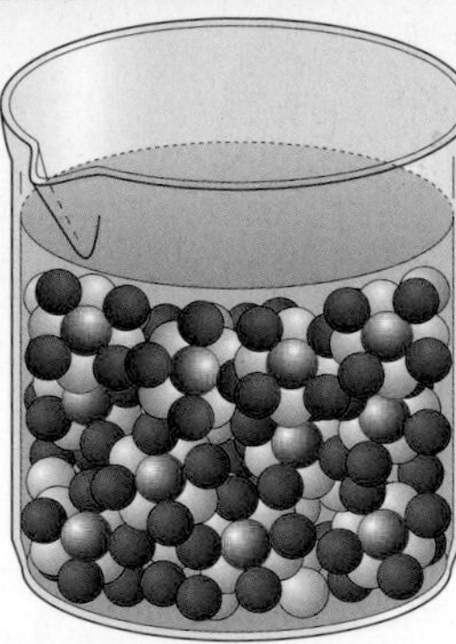

The solid has dissolved to form a solution

Investigating the rate of dissolving

You can now apply the particle theory to explain and investigate one of the factors that affect how quickly a solid dissolves. You can use copper sulphate as the solute and water as the solvent.

- List the factors that might affect how quickly the copper sulphate dissolves.
- Choose one factor to investigate. This is your **independent variable**. You can choose which values it has in your investigation.
- How will you find out how quickly the copper sulphate dissolves? This is your **dependent variable**. (Its value depends on the values you choose for the independent variable.)
- Write down the question you will investigate and make a prediction. Explain your prediction using the particle theory.
  a) How will you make it a fair test? These are your **control variables**.
  b) How will you make your results reliable?
- When you have planned what to do, let your teacher check it before you start.
- Record your results in a suitable table and display the data on a graph.
  c) Comment on your data and check if it supports your prediction or not.
  d) Evaluate your method. Comment on the quality of the data you have collected.

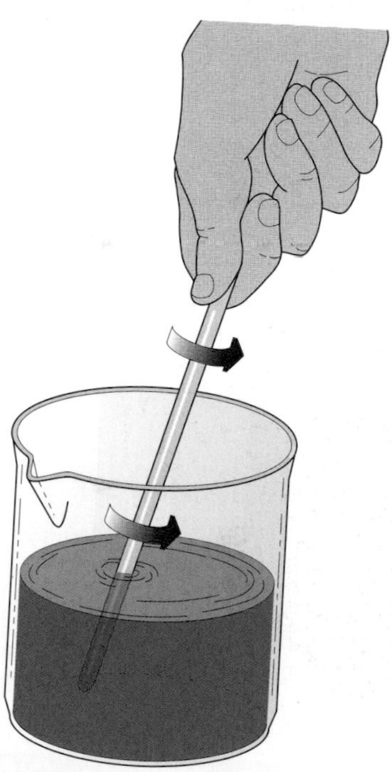

SUMMARY QUESTIONS

1 ☆ Copy these sentences. Complete them by filling in the gaps.

There are quite strong . . . of attraction between the . . . in a solute and a solvent. The particles of . . . get 'dragged from' the other particles in the solid and are surrounded by particles of . . . .

The movement of the . . . particles results in the solute getting . . . throughout the solution.

2 ☆☆☆ Sand is insoluble in water.

Use the particle theory to try to explain why.

control variables
dependent variable
forces of attraction
independent variable
intermingle

Distilling mixtures

LEARN ABOUT

- separating a solution by distillation
- explaining how distillation works

Uses of distillation

We use perfumes to create nice smells. Scientists can make new pleasant smelling substances in chemical reactions. However, long before this, people found ways to extract perfumes from plants.

Have you ever brushed against a lavender bush? It smells wonderful. You can find its scent used in aromatherapy treatments to help people relax. Cosmetic scientists use a process called **distillation** to extract the perfume from the lavender bush.

Scientists have identified over 280 different substances in the aroma produced by strawberries. That's the reason why food scientists have struggled to make a really good synthetic strawberry flavouring.

A lavender field

When we distil a solution we can separate off and collect the liquid. To do this, we heat the solution so that the liquid boils. The gas given off is then cooled down and it condenses. The pure liquid can now be collected. Any substances dissolved in the liquid remain in the heated flask.

Distillation is the separation of a liquid from a solution by boiling it and then condensing the gas given off.

Separating water from a solution

Try this experiment to see if you can separate water from a solution.

- Add a few drops of food colouring to 20 cm^3 of water in a boiling tube.
- Set up the apparatus shown.
- Then heat the mixture *very gently*. You don't want the coloured mixture to shoot through the delivery tube.
  a) What collects in the receiving tube?
  b) Explain how your experiment worked, using the words **evaporated**, **condensed** and **particles**.

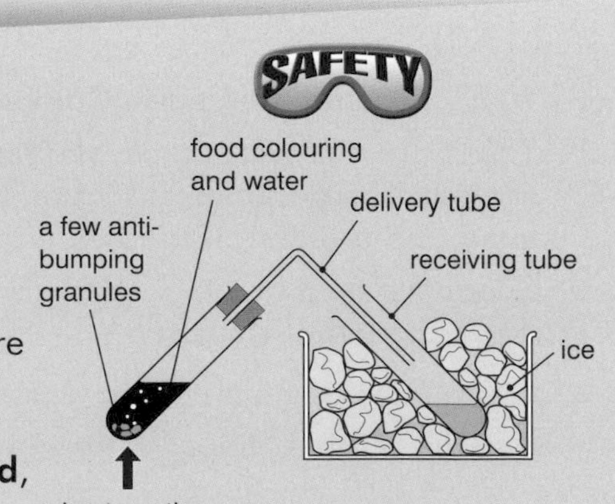

History of distillation

Hundreds of years ago, Arabian chemists were the first to make apparatus that could distil solutions effectively. Look at the pictures of early apparatus below.

Distillation apparatus used by alchemists

Here is the apparatus we use to do a simple distillation nowadays:

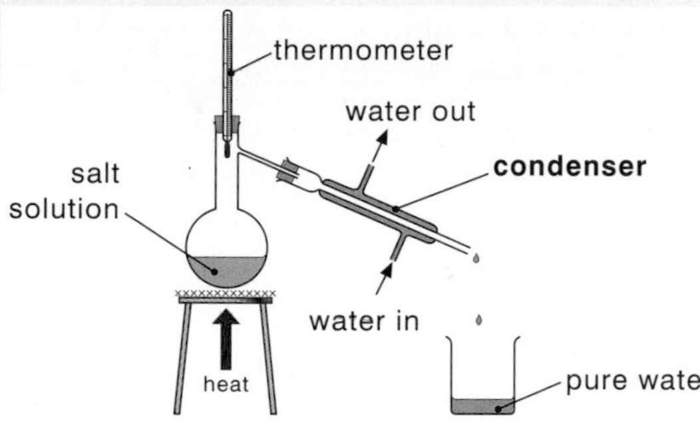

The chemists of the Middle Ages were known as 'alchemists'. Alchemy was a strange mix of science and magic.

The alchemists spent their time looking for the elixir of life and trying to turn metals like lead into gold – but they never did succeed.

Q1 Collect a copy of a diagram of the distillation apparatus. Draw water particles as blue spheres and salt particles as white spheres on the diagram. Then explain distillation using the particle model.

Q2 Explain how the condenser works.

SUMMARY QUESTIONS

1 ☆☆ If you found yourself stranded on a desert island, how could you get pure water from seawater? Draw a diagram and explain the method you would use.

2 ☆☆☆ Imagine the problems that a country with very little fresh water will face.
  a) If the country has a large coastline, it has plenty of seawater available. Why can't it use this water directly for most purposes?
  b) How do you think the country could purify the seawater?
  c) Find out which countries obtain supplies of fresh water from seawater.
  d) Find out and describe how a desalination plant works.

3 ☆☆☆ Find out more about the Arabian chemists who first developed apparatus for distilling mixtures.

Key words

condense
distillation
evaporate
particles

7H4 Chromatography revealed

LEARN ABOUT
- separating solutes by chromatography
- interpreting chromatograms

Separating solutes

Do you know what you are eating when you suck on a coloured sweet? How do the manufacturers make those bright colours? Do they have a single dye for each colour or is each colour made by mixing different dyes? Chromatography can help us to find the answers. You can use chromatography to separate two or more solutes that are dissolved in a solvent.

Dyes in inks

- Set up the experiment opposite:
  Let the water soak up the wick and spread out onto the filter paper.
- You can try different coloured water-soluble inks.
  a) Why do the inks have to be water soluble?
  b) Which inks are made from only one dye?
  c) Which inks were mixtures? Which colours are mixed to make each ink?
  The pieces of paper left at the end of the experiment are called **chromatograms**.
  d) Explain how the pattern on a chromatogram is formed.
  Try the same experiment with a permanent marker pen. Explain what happens.

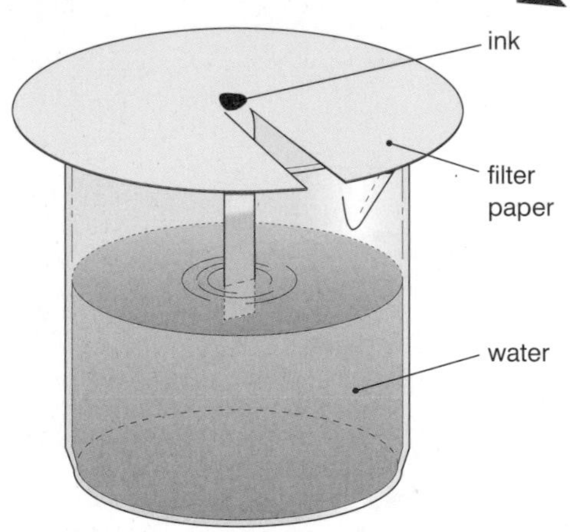
ink
filter paper
water

You can also make chromatograms by letting the solvent run up absorbent paper.

In this case you dip the paper into the solvent. The different solutes are carried up the paper different distances in a given time. Look at the example below:

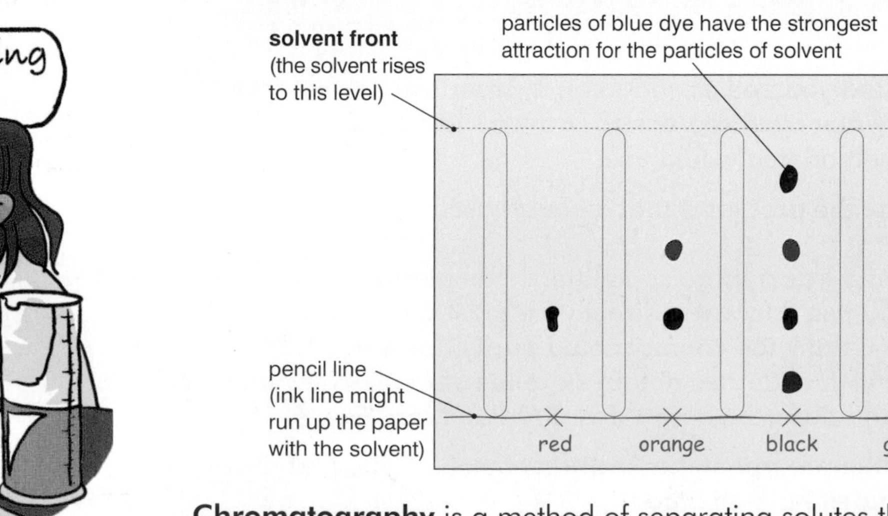
solvent front
(the solvent rises to this level)
particles of blue dye have the strongest attraction for the particles of solvent
pencil line
(ink line might run up the paper with the solvent)
red
orange
black
green

Chromatography is a method of separating solutes that are soluble in a particular solvent.

Stop it - you're eating our experiment

Testing sweets

In this experiment you can test the dyes we use to colour sweets.

- To make a good chromatogram you need to start with small, concentrated dots of each colour.
- Make sure the water level starts below your coloured spots.
  - **a)** Summarise the results on your chromatogram in a labelled diagram.
  - **b)** What conclusions can you draw from your chromatogram?
  - **c)** Explain why different dyes were carried up the paper to different heights.

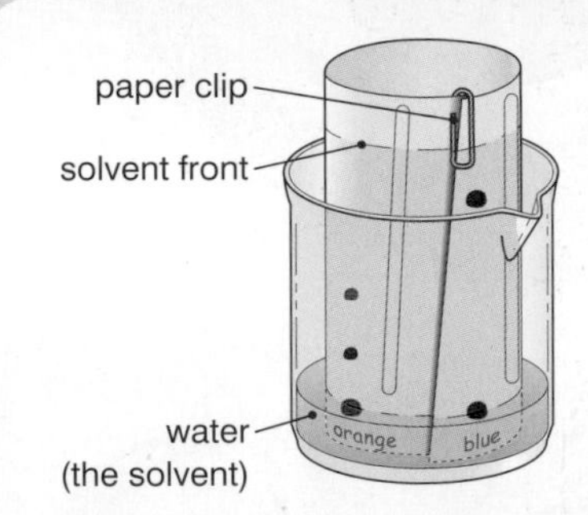

Using chromatography

We can use a chromatogram to identify unknown substances. You can compare the spots produced by the unknown substance with the spots from substances you do know. You then compare the spots and see which match up. The same substance will be carried up the paper the same distance in identical conditions.

Some substances do not appear as coloured dots on a chromatogram. However, they will appear when sprayed with a stain. For example, doctors might be analysing the amino acids in a patient's urine. The spots only show up when the chromatogram has been sprayed with a substance called ninhydrin. Forensic scientists also use chromatography to identify unknown substances found at the scene of a crime.

The forensic scientist is using a technique called High Pressure Liquid Chromatography to identify a drug

Scientists now often use gas chromatography to separate mixtures. Instead of using water and paper, the heated sample is carried by gases through a column containing a resin. The substances coming from the end of the column are identified by complex instruments.
Gas chromatography can help detect illegal drugs in race horses and athletes.

Scientists can separate the solutes in urine, then test for illegal substances

SUMMARY QUESTIONS

1 ★★ Copy these sentences. Complete them by filling in the gaps.
. . . is used to . . . a mixture of solutes. You use a . . . in which the solutes will dissolve. There will be different forces of . . . between the particles of the . . . and the particles of solute. The solutes with the strongest . . . will be carried along . . . by the solvent.

2 ★★ Draw a flow diagram that describes how to set up a chromatogram.

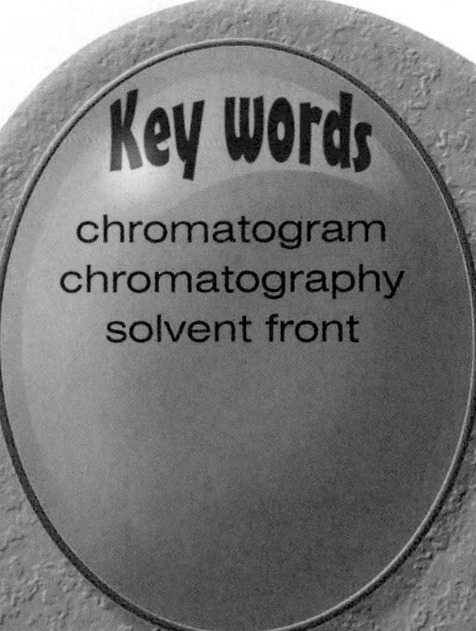

Key words

chromatogram
chromatography
solvent front

7H5 Finding solubility

LEARN ABOUT
- solubility in different solvents
- solubility curves

Other solvents

Have you ever helped to decorate a room? If you have painted a door, you probably used gloss paint. At the end of the job you have to clean the paint off your brush. Gloss paint is an oil-based paint so water can't dissolve it. As you probably know, oil and water do not mix. You have to wash your brush in white spirit – a liquid that does dissolve oil. We can say that water and white spirit are both good solvents, but for different substances.

Which colour would you choose for your bedroom?

Looking at different solvents

You will be given two solvents to investigate – water and **ethanol**. Your task is to find out how much solid will dissolve in each solvent. The solids you can use are sodium chloride, sodium hydrogen carbonate and potassium nitrate.

- Weigh a small amount of solid (the end of a spatula-full). Then add it to 10 cm^3 of solvent in a boiling tube. Stopper the tube and shake. Continue this until no more solid will dissolve.
- Record your results and conclusion.

SAFETY: Ethanol is highly flammable so make sure there are no Bunsen burners lit when you use it.

Saturated solutions

From the previous experiment you will see that only a certain amount of solute can dissolve in a particular solvent. This amount varies from solute to solute. A **saturated solution** is a solution in which no more solute will dissolve at a given temperature.

Q1 How could you test whether a solution is saturated or not?

We can describe how well a solute dissolves in water by its **solubility**. The solubility of a substance tells us how many grams of it will dissolve in 100 g of water at a certain temperature. For example, the solubility of sodium chloride is 36 g per 100 g of water at 25 °C.

Q2 Why do you think we must state the temperature when we give the solubility of a substance?

We can find the solubility of a solid at different temperatures by observing when crystals first appear from a cooling solution.

At this point of crystallisation, the solution is saturated.

When we have several results, we can plot a graph showing how the solubility changes with temperature. This is called a **solubility curve**.

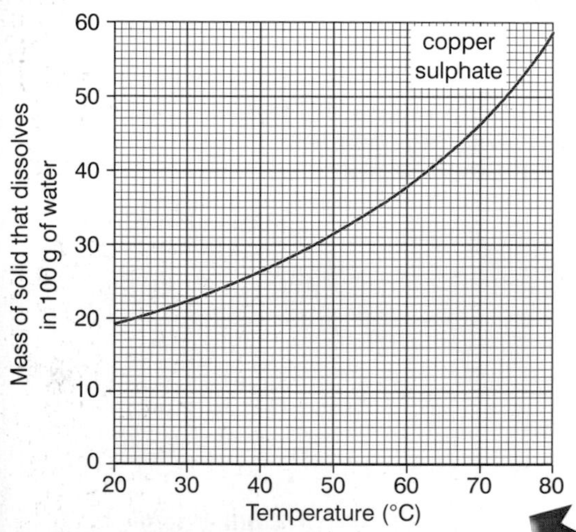

The solubility curve of copper sulphate

Solubility curve of potassium nitrate

- Measure out 10 g of potassium nitrate.
- Heat some water to 70 °C in a small beaker.
- Use a graduated pipette to transfer 10 cm^3 of the hot water to a boiling tube.
- Now add the 10 g of potassium nitrate to the boiling tube. Put a bung in the boiling tube and shake it. This should form a solution that is almost saturated.
- Let the boiling tube cool down and note the temperature when the first crystals appear.
  a) At what temperature does the solution become saturated?
  b) Copy and complete using your answer to part a).
  At . . . °C, 10 g of potassium nitrate dissolve in 10 g of water.

Therefore the solubility of potassium nitrate at . . . °C is 100 g/100 g of water.

- Now add another 5 cm^3 of water to the boiling tube to make the volume up to 15 cm^3. Shake the solution again so that the potassium nitrate redissolves.
- Warm the tube gently if necessary.
- Again, let the tube cool and record the temperature at which the solid appears.
- Repeat for total volumes of 20 cm^3, 25 cm^3 and 30 cm^3 of water.
- Record your results and solubilities in a table.
  c) How will you convert your results into solublities per 100 g of water? (You could use a spreadsheet to do these calculations for you.)

Think about how to make your results as reliable as possible.

Once you have converted your results to solubilities per 100 g of water, draw a solubility curve for potassium nitrate.

d) How does the solubility of potassium nitrate vary with temperature?
e) Use your solubility curve to find the solubility of potassium nitrate at 40 °C.

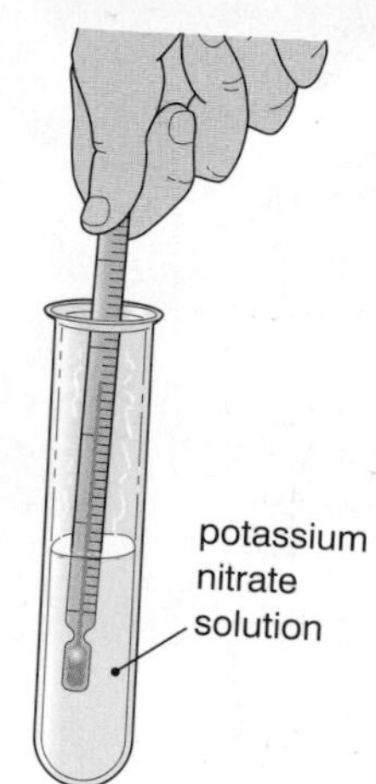

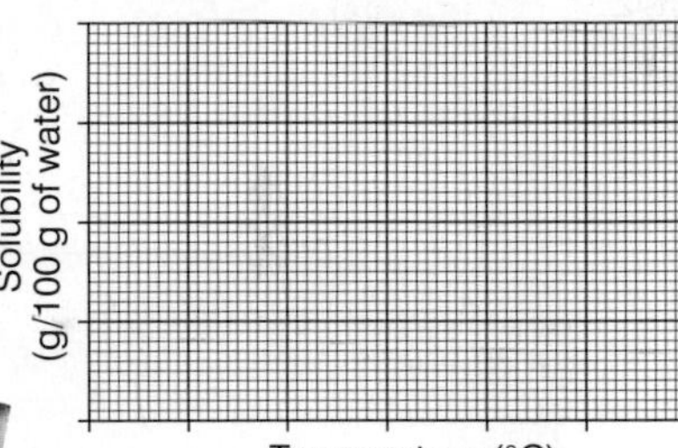

SUMMARY QUESTIONS

1 ☆ Copy these sentences. Complete them by filling in the gaps.
The . . . . . . of different solutes will vary in different solvents.
T. . . . . .. also affects the . . . . of solutes. We quote the solubility of a solute in g/100 g of . . . . . at a certain temperature.
We can show how solubility varies with temperature on a solubility . . . . .

2 ☆☆☆ The solubility of potassium sulphate in water increases as the temperature rises.

a) Sort out these data into a table and draw the solubility curve of potassium sulphate. All measurements were taken in 100 g of water. At 90 °C 22.9 g dissolve; at 50 °C 16.5 g dissolve; at 70 °C 19.8 g dissolve; at 10 °C 9.3 g dissolve; at 30 °C 13 g dissolve.
b) Use your curve to find the solubility of potassium sulphate at 20 °C.
c) How much potassium sulphate will dissolve in 25 g of water at 60 °C?

The Dead Sea contains about 350 g of dissolved salts in every litre compared to about 40 g in normal seawater. Its waters are so dense that it is very easy to float in it.

ethanol
saturated solution
solubility
solubility curve

IDEAS AND EVIDENCE

Dopey horses

Horse racing is a multi-million pound industry. With so much money at stake, there are people who are willing to break the rules of the sport. One way to 'fix' the results of a race is to give a horse some kind of drug.

Some drugs act as stimulants that help a horse run faster. Others 'dope' a horse and have the opposite effect on it. In this way, criminals gamble on a race and try to make sure their bet wins.

Trainers of an injured horse might be tempted to give it painkilling injections so it can run in a big race. This could damage the horse permanently.

That's why we need scientists to check that horses are free from drugs. As mentioned on p.133, this involves gas chromatography to separate the drug from natural substances in the horse's urine or blood.

In this process, a gas carries the different substances through a long tube containing a solid resin. The substances with the weakest attraction for the resin will get through the tube first. A detector draws peaks when the different substances arrive at the end of the tube. Look at the machine below:

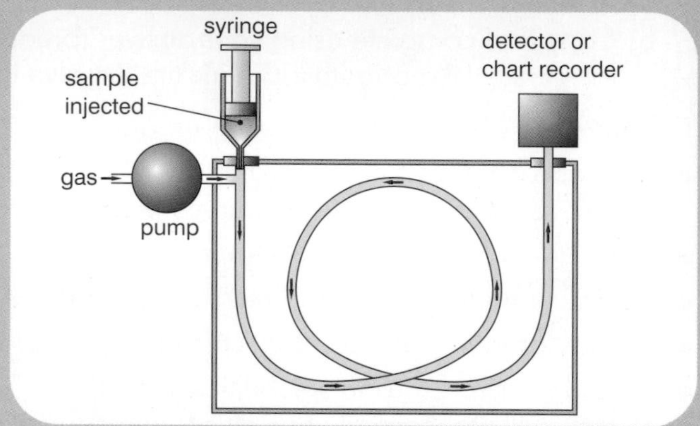

The scientist will then also test some water, a sample of normal horse urine, and a solution of the suspected drug in the same way. Look at the results:

Q1 Can you explain how these results could be used at an inquiry investigating the results of a race?

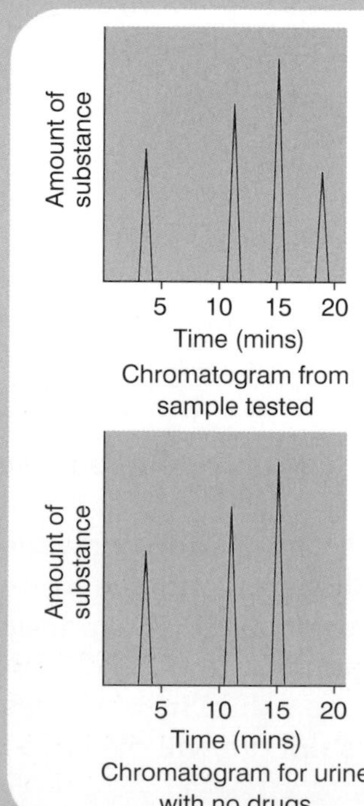

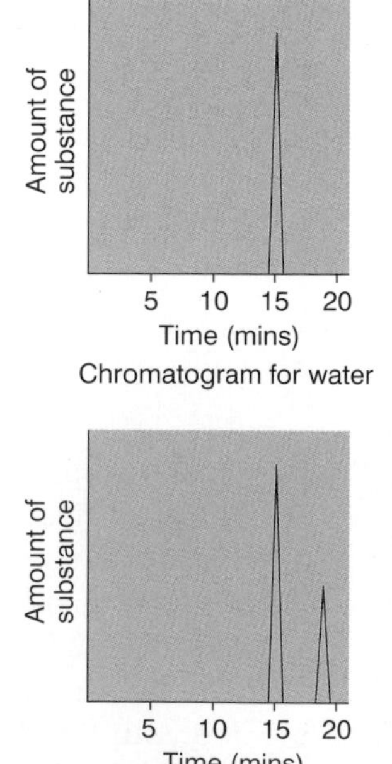

- When solids dissolve in a liquid their particles become intermingled.
- The solid is called the **solute**, the liquid is the **solvent** and the resulting mixture is a **solution**.
- We can collect the solvent (liquid) from the solution by **distillation**.
- If a solvent contains two or more solutes, we can separate the solutes by **chromatography**.
- A solution that will not dissolve any more solid at a particular temperature is called a **saturated** solution.
- The **solubility** of a substance varies with temperature. We can show this on a graph called a **solubility curve**.
- We measure solubility by the number of grams of solute that will dissolve in 100 g of water (g/100 g of water) at a certain temperature.

DANGER! AVOID THESE COMMON ERRORS

When a solute dissolves, it only *appears* to disappear – its particles are still there, but they intermingle with the particles of the solvent. Just because a solute is soluble in a solvent, it does not mean that you can add more and it will just keep dissolving. The solute will dissolve only until the solution becomes **saturated** at that particular temperature.

Key words

chromatography
distillation
saturated
solubility
solute
solution
solvent

UNIT REVIEW

REVIEW QUESTIONS
Understanding and applying concepts

1 Explain the following observations using the particle theory:
- a Sugar dissolves in water when making a cup of coffee.
- b Two dyes in an ink are separated using paper chromatography in a forensic laboratory investigating a forged cheque.
- c Pure water is collected from seawater by distilling the mixture.

2 Customs officers at an airport are suspicious about a flask carried by a passenger.
It contains a colourless liquid which they suspect might have an illegal drug dissolved in it. The flask is taken off to their forensic laboratory for tests.
- a How could they test to see if a solid is dissolved in the liquid?
- b Draw the apparatus they could use if they wanted to collect the solvent to test separately.
- c How might they test the original liquid to see if it contains more than one substance dissolved in it?

3 Food scientists test a new type of orange squash to see if it contains a banned substance. The scientists have three banned dyes that they think might be used to colour the squash and two other dyes that are safe to use. Look at their paper chromatogram.

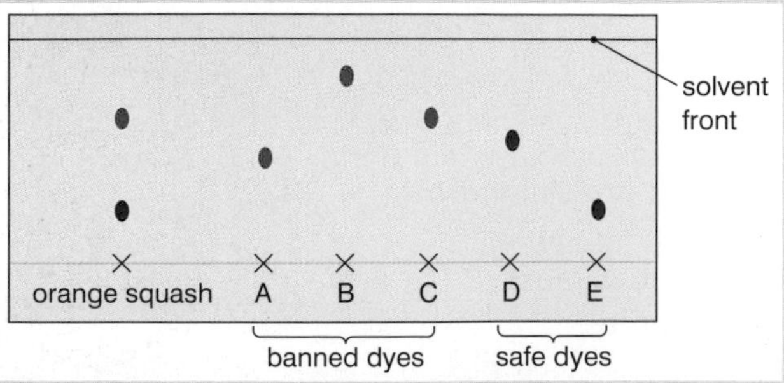

- a Make as many deductions as you can about the new squash.
- b Which dye has the strongest attraction for the particles in the solvent?

4 Draw a concept map linking these terms together. Don't forget to label your links, explaining what the connection is.

water **sodium chloride** **distillation** **rock salt** **filtration**

Making more of maths

5 A group of students did a series of tests to find the solubility curve of copper sulphate.
Here are their results:

Temperature (°C)	Solubility (g/100g of water)
20	20.5
30	25.0
40	28.5
50	33.5
60	40.0
70	47.0
80	55.0
90	64.0

- a Plot a graph of these results, extending the horizontal axis from 0 °C to 100 °C.
- b Use your graph to predict the solubility of copper sulphate at:
  i) 55 °C ii) 5 °C iii) 100 °C
- c How much copper sulphate would you need to dissolve in 100 g of water to form a saturated solution at 25 °C?
- d You dissolve 45 g of copper sulphate in 100 g of water at 80 °C. What mass of copper sulphate will crystallise out of solution if you cool it down to 25 °C?

Thinking skills

6 The solubility of potassium chlorate at 20 °C is 7.5 g/100g of water.

a How much potassium chlorate will dissolve in 20 g of water at 20 °C?

b A student added 15 g of potassium chlorate to 50 g of water at 20 °C. How much potassium chlorate remained undissolved after stirring?

7 If a maximum of 9 g of sodium chloride dissolve in 25 g of water at 20 °C, what is the solubility of sodium chloride?

SAT-STYLE QUESTIONS

1 The apparatus shown here is used to separate pure water from impure water.

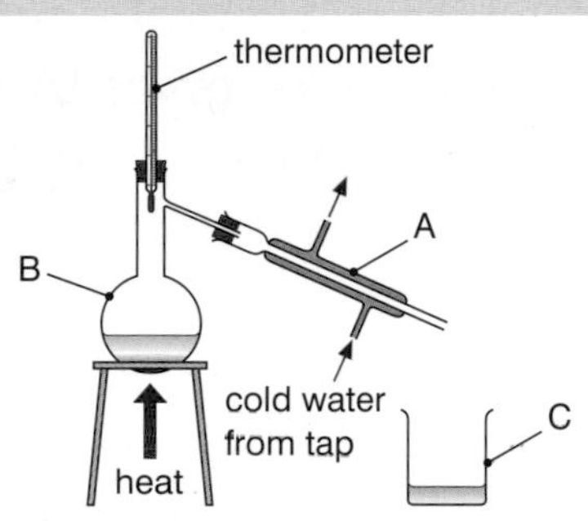

a What would be the temperature on the thermometer? (1)

b Where would you place the impure water in the apparatus? (1)

c Where would you get the pure water collecting? (1)

d What is the function of A? (1)

e What do we call this process? (1)

2 Mike made a chromatogram showing four different felt-tipped pens. His chromatogaram shown below:

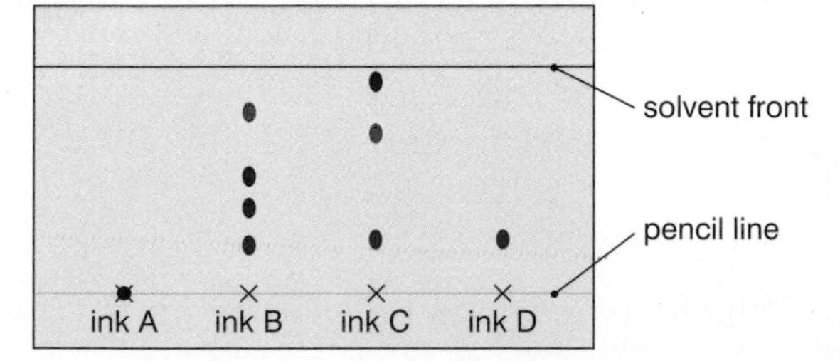

a Why did Mike use a pencil, and not ink, to draw a line across the bottom of the paper? (1)

b Which ink was a mixture of four dyes? (1)

c Which ink definitely contained only one coloured dye? (1)

d Which ink has the weakest attraction for the solvent? (1)

e Which ink contained the dye that has the strongest attraction for water? (1)

3 The graph below shows how the solubility of two salts varies with temperature as shown by the results of two different groups. A line has been drawn through the points for sodium chloride:

a What is the solubility of sodium chloride at 50 °C? (2)

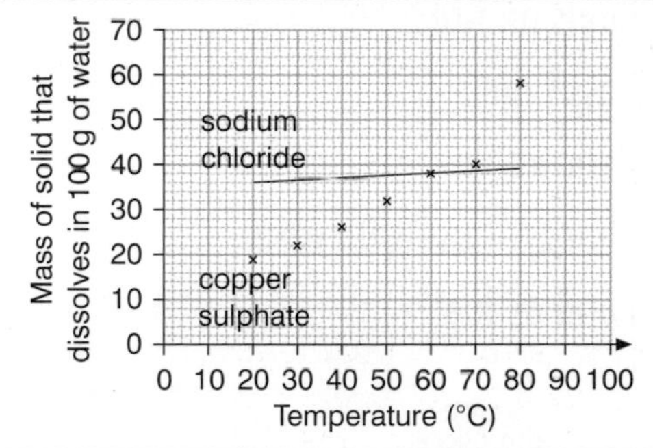

b i) The group investigating copper sulphate had one anomalous result (a result that appears to be wrong). At which temperature did the group get their anomalous result? (1)

ii) Use the graph to predict a more likely value for the solubility of copper sulphate at this temperature. (1)

iii) Explain what could have produced this anomalous result. (2)

c Describe the shape of the line you would draw through the points for copper sulphate. (1)

d i) How much copper sulphate can dissolve in 50 g of water at 30 °C? (1)

ii) What do we call a solution in which no more solid will dissolve at a given temperature? (1)

e At which temperature do the two salts have the same solubility. (1)

f Describe how temperature affects the solubility of copper sulphate.) (2)

Key words

Unscramble these:

tosuel
velnots
tidlis
gotromachmar

71 Energy

Coming soon

What's it all about?

Have you ever climbed a mountain, or swum a mile? It's tiring doing things like this, and you soon run out of energy. You can renew your energy reserves by eating food. **Energy** is something you need whenever you are doing something. Even sitting and thinking takes energy.

Human beings have learned lots of ways of making use of energy. It must have been exciting when people first learned to ride wild horses. On horseback, you can travel quickly making use of the energy of the horse. Today, a big car may have a 100 horsepower engine – it is like riding 100 horses!

Scientists often use the idea of energy when they are talking about different activities. In this unit, you can find out about the scientific idea of energy. You will use this idea to think about how we use energy resources, and why we may soon have to change some of the things we do.

What do you remember?

You already know about:

- how plants grow.
- materials that burn.
- keeping things warm.

1 Which of these things does a green plant need if it is to grow?

light **water** **warmth** **air**

2 Which of these can be used as fuel?

air **water** **oil** **sunlight**

3 Name some materials that can be burned. What substance from the air is needed for burning? Is burning a reversible process?

4 What do we call a material that is good at keeping heat in? Give some examples.

Young technologists

As the car moves along, the air turns the windmill.

That generates electricity.

Electric motors turn the wheels.

We added these solar panels to make electricity from sunlight.

Red cars go really fast!

But somehow we still can't get it to start!

QUESTIONS

Lots of scientists and technologists are working to design better cars – cars that are easier to drive, that go faster, that use less fuel. Some are trying to design cars that don't use any fuel at all.

a) What fuels do most cars use?

b) A few cars run on electricity. Where do they get their electricity?

c) Look at the car in the picture above. It doesn't use fuel. So what different things are supposed to make it go? Do you think a car like this could ever work?

d) Why would it be good to design a car that runs on sunlight? Would the car have any disadvantages?

Fuels on fire

LEARN ABOUT
- burning fuels
- energy from fuels

Burning bright

Around the world, many millions of people use wood or charcoal as their **fuel** for cooking and heating. Fuel is important. It's often the job of children to gather wood, and they may spend several hours a day at this work.

If you have wood fires at home, you may have a stack of wood ready to use in the winter. It's convenient – just prepare the fire, apply a match, and heat the house. **Burning** releases the **energy** stored in the fuel.

Food can taste really good if you cook it out of doors, on a barbecue. The fuel is charcoal or gas.

Q1 What other ways do we have for heating houses?

What is a fuel?

From these examples, you can see what we mean by 'fuels'. A **fuel** is a material that we burn in order to release the energy that it stores. There are many different fuels in use. There are even power stations that burn household rubbish, including waste paper and used plastic, to generate electricity.

Q2 Think about what we mean by a 'fuel'. Name some fuels that are used for cooking. Can you name some other methods of cooking that don't use fuels?

Testing Bunsen flames

Have you learned how to use a Bunsen burner safely? You can use a Bunsen burner to find out about the energy released when gas is burned.

- With the air hole closed, the flame is yellow and smoky.
- With the air hole open, the flame is blue and roaring.
- You can adjust the air hole between these two positions. Try heating some water in a glass beaker. Use a thermometer to see the temperature rise.

a) Which flame releases energy most quickly?

You may not be able to try different flames. You will need to compare your results with other people.

b) How can you be sure that your comparison is as fair as possible?

Always wear eye protection when using a Bunsen burner.

Useful fuels

We use fuels because they are useful – the energy they release allows us to do things. So what do we mean by 'energy'?

- A candle is made of wax, which is a fuel. When it burns, it gives out light.
- A central heating boiler may use coal, oil or gas. When the fuel burns, it gives out heat.
- Cars and other vehicles run on petrol or diesel fuel, and they allow us to move around. The energy from the fuel gives us movement.
- Some cars have fuel cells instead of petrol engines. The fuel goes into a sort of battery that releases electricity to drive the wheels.

You can't **see** the energy stored in a fuel, but you can certainly tell when the energy is released. You get light, heat, movement or electricity. We can think of all of these as 'energy on the move'.

This bike uses petrol as its fuel. When the energy of the petrol is released, it can make the bike move very quickly.

More fuels

Here are some more examples of fuels at work:

- a petrol-engine lawnmower
- a bonfire
- a gas lamp, used for camping

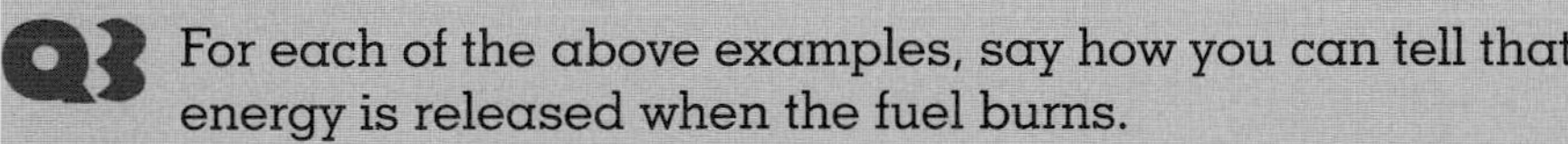

Q3 For each of the above examples, say how you can tell that energy is released when the fuel burns.

CHALLENGE

Does petrol really 'burn' in a car engine? Use the Internet or a CD-ROM encyclopaedia to find an animation of how petrol is used in a car engine.

SUMMARY QUESTIONS

1 ☆ Skim through these two pages. As you do so, list all the different fuels that are mentioned.

2 ☆ What do we have to do to release the energy of a fuel?

3 ☆☆ Find out which fuels are used in these different situations:

camping stoves **aircraft** **hot air balloons**
heating the water in a swimming pool

712 Fossil fuels

LEARN ABOUT
- using fossil fuels
- how they are formed

Much of the gas used in Britain for cooking and heating comes from under the seas that surround us. A giant network of pipes carries it around the country.

Going up in smoke

Coal, oil and natural gas – these are **fossil fuels**. They are extracted from underground. Coal is mined; oil and gas are usually found together, and are brought to the surface through pipes. Oil is usually brought ashore in tankers.

Generating electricity

Sometimes, we use the energy from fossil fuels without even thinking about it. Most of the electricity we use in the UK comes from fossil fuels. Coal and gas are burned in **power stations**. The heat they release is used to boil water to make high-pressure steam, and the steam turns an electricity generator. In a year, it takes about a tonne (t) of coal and gas to generate the electricity used by the average person in the UK.

That's not all. Each of us uses another 3 t of oil and gas for transport and heating, and for the industry that keeps us working. So a family of four would get through about 16 t of fossil fuels in a year. Fortunately, you don't have to burn it all at home.

This big power station has a giant stock of coal. It needs a trainload to be delivered every hour if it is to keep generating at full power.

Q1 Explain how oil is important for transport.

The story of fossil fuels

Once upon a time, 300 million years or so ago, Britain was rather different. The climate was warm, and swampy forests grew in river deltas. There were ferns and mosses, but no flowering plants. There were reptiles and amphibians, but no mammals.

When plants died, they fell into the swamps. At first, they rotted away to become peat; then they became buried deeper. Heat and pressure compressed the plant remains until they eventually became coal.

Oil and gas formed in a similar way, but from plant and animal remains in the sea.

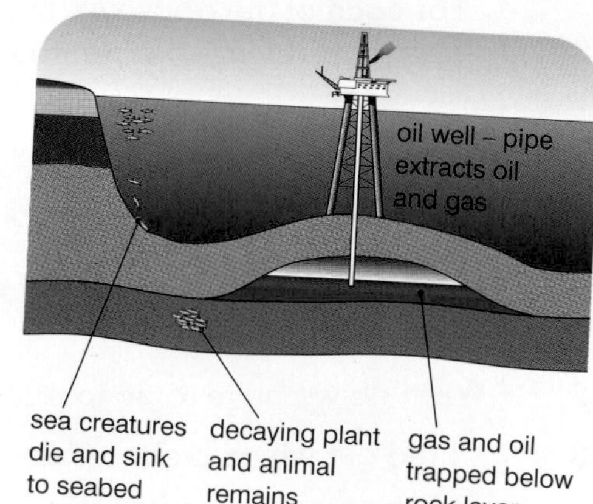

Oil and gas try to rise up from underground, but they get trapped by solid rock

Running low

- Once fossil fuels have been burned, they are gone forever. Remember, they formed hundreds of millions of years ago, and no one wants to wait that long for petrol when their car has run out!
  a) List some everyday activities that make use of fossil fuels. For each one, suggest how we might be able to continue with the activity without using fossil fuels.

Big problems

Fossil fuels are very useful to us. They give us the energy we need to do all sorts of things that make our lives easier, more comfortable and more enjoyable. However, there are problems.

How would you feel if your neighbour spent his time burning dead fish and rotting vegetation in his back yard? It wouldn't be very nice, but that is almost what we do when we burn fossil fuels. Most fuels produce carbon dioxide when they are burned. They may also produce hazardous waste gases that can poison the environment.

Power stations have tall chimneys to carry the waste gases high into the atmosphere, so that they don't affect people close by. They still cause problems.

- Increasing carbon dioxide in the atmosphere is causing **climate change** – most scientists agree about this now.
- Other waste gases cause **acid rain**, which makes soil and water acid and kills plants and fishes.

Every litre of petrol that is used by a car produces about 3 kg of carbon dioxide.

Q2 How is climate change likely to affect the temperature of the Earth? What other problems have you heard of that might be caused by climate change?

Peat is another fossil fuel. In Ireland, there is a power station that burns nothing but peat.

Discuss how individuals, companies and governments can reduce the damage they do to the environment by their energy use.

SUMMARY QUESTIONS

1 ☆ Name as many fossil fuels as you can.

2 ☆☆ Explain why wood is a fuel, but not a fossil fuel.

3 ☆☆ Some people hope that hydrogen can be used as a fuel in future, in place of fossil fuels. When hydrogen is burned, an important substance, H_2O, is produced. Why do you think this will be less harmful to the environment?

4 ☆☆☆ Draw a chart to show how the energy we get from burning coal came originally from plants living millions of years ago.

acid rain
climate change
fossil fuel
power stations

7B Renewables

LEARN ABOUT
- renewable energy resources

Biomass energy

Eventually, we will run out of fossil fuels. We need to find other **energy resources**. An energy resource is anything from which we can get energy. Perhaps wood will be part of the answer.

Wood from trees is an example of a **biomass** fuel. In the UK, farmers are experimenting with fast-growing willow and poplar trees. After a few years, these are cut down and used as fuel in power stations.

Another example is bio diesel. This is made from soya beans or maize, and used as fuel in buses.

Unfortunately, we use energy at such a rate that biomass can only be part of the solution.

Learning from history

The Anasazi people lived in southwest USA for over a thousand years. Their main fuel was wood. Unfortunately, they cut down trees faster than they grew. Eventually their lands turned to desert and, by 1300, they had to abandon their villages.

This farmer in Oxfordshire is growing willow trees as a renewable energy resource

We can learn from this environmental disaster. We need to find energy resources that can be replaced as quickly as we use them up – they must be **renewable** energy resources. Trees are renewable, because we can grow new ones to replace the ones we cut down. (The Anasazi people didn't do this.)

We describe fossil fuels as **non-renewable** energy resources. Once coal, oil and gas are burned, we can never get them back again – unless we can wait for a few hundred million years.

Q1 Is bio diesel a renewable or non-renewable energy resource? Explain your answer.

A supermarket in south Wales sold out of vegetable oil because people were using it as a cheap fuel in their cars!

Electricity from renewables

- Try out some model systems that show how electricity can be generated from sunlight, moving water and moving air.
- For each model, suggest how a full-size version can be used for generating electricity.

Cleaner electricity

You can sense the energy of the water gushing from this hydroelectric dam in Canada

Electricity is a clean and convenient way of transferring energy from place to place, and we use a lot of it. So it's important to find ways of generating electricity from renewable resources. Here are some:

- **Hydroelectric power** – electricity generated using moving water. Usually, the water is stored behind a dam. Most hydroelectric schemes are in mountainous, rainy places.
- **Wind power** – electricity generated using moving air. Perhaps you have seen a wind farm, with several turbines held high up to catch the wind.
- **Wave power** – electricity generated from the movement of waves on the sea. This has not been properly developed yet, which is a shame, because the UK is surrounded by wavy seas.
- **Solar power** – electricity generated from sunlight, using solar cells.
- **Geothermal power** – electricity generated from hot rocks inside the Earth.

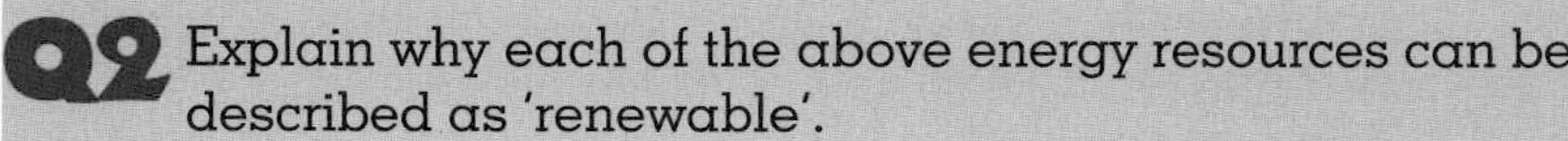

Q2 Explain why each of the above energy resources can be described as 'renewable'.

I guess they're called wind generators because they're used to generate wind.

No harm done?

Renewable energy resources sound good, but they're not perfect. Each comes with its own problems. They don't produce gases that damage the atmosphere, but they are generally expensive.

For example, a hydroelectric dam floods land, and people may have to move out. Wind farms may be noisy, and some people think they are ugly.

Q3 Can we rely on electricity from renewables? Discuss what would happen on a day without wind or sunshine.

How do we decide where to build a new power station? You will find out in Geography.

SUMMARY QUESTIONS

1. ☆ Skim through these two pages. As you do so, list all the different renewable energy resources that are mentioned.
2. ☆☆ Is natural gas a renewable or non-renewable energy resource? Explain your answer.
3. ☆☆ Most spacecraft use solar cells to generate electricity. Explain why this is a good choice.
4. ☆☆ About 20% of the UK's electricity is generated in nuclear power stations. Their fuel is uranium. Uranium is mined in a few places around the world. Is this a renewable or non-renewable energy resource?

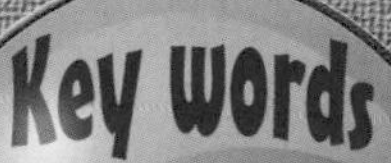

biomass
energy resource
non-renewable
renewable

7I4 Energy – use with care!

LEARN ABOUT
- conserving energy resources

Buildings old and new

Many blocks of flats like this have had new double-glazed windows fitted, to help save energy

Many old buildings were built when we weren't very concerned about energy. Fuel was cheap, and people didn't realise that they were damaging the environment by burning fossil fuels.

The flats in this photo have very thin walls, and lots of big windows. When the flats were built, the windows were single-glazed. That made it very easy for heat to escape.

Today, it would be against the law to build flats like this. There are regulations that ensure that all new buildings have well-insulated walls, floors and roofs. Their windows must be double-glazed. It adds a bit to the cost of the building, but it saves energy. In the long run, it's cheaper, and better for the environment.

Better by design

You could live comfortably in a place like this, and it is good for the environment

Look at the building in this photo. It is a residence for university students in Glasgow. It has been carefully designed to use less energy. The walls are made of a special insulating material; it lets light through, but keeps heat in.

There are other ways that architects and builders can save energy:

- Have big windows facing south, to catch the energy of the Sun's rays – it is free!
- Have smaller windows facing north (the cold side of the building), so that less heat escapes through them.

People power

People release energy too. We are all warm, and heat leaves our bodies. This is important when designing buildings.

A class of 30 pupils is equivalent to a large electric heater, so that saves the school a lot of money. Perhaps you should start charging for the energy you supply!

Q1 Think about your own home or school. Has it been well designed to save energy? Could it be improved in any way?

Conserving energy

You can see that architects and builders have to think carefully about energy resources. Energy is expensive, we are running out of fossil fuels, and we are harming the environment. We need to **conserve** our energy resources – use them carefully, wasting as little as possible.

Capturing sunshine

Crete is a sunny place, so it is a good idea to use the sunshine to heat water. You can see the pipes that take the hot water indoors.

Sunlight is a wonderful energy resource – there's a lot of it, and it's free. There are two ways of capturing the energy of sunlight:

- **Solar cells** change sunlight into electricity.
- **Solar panels** use sunlight to heat water.

Solar panels are like radiators in reverse. When sunlight falls on a panel, the water inside gets hot and is then pumped around the house. Hot water is useful for washing, and it also stores energy that can be used at night, for heating.

Q2 Why is it useful to be able to store energy from sunlight?

If you have solar cells on your roof, you can make money by selling any spare electricity to the supply company!

Designing solar panels

What makes a good solar panel? The water inside it should heat up quickly when sunlight falls on it. Try an experiment to investigate some of the factors involved.

- Use an aluminium food tray, or something similar. Put water in it, and place it in the Sun.
- Use a thermometer to find out how quickly the temperature of the water rises.
- What can you change? Think about the shape, size and colour of the tray, and the amount of water. How about stretching clingfilm over the top of the tray?

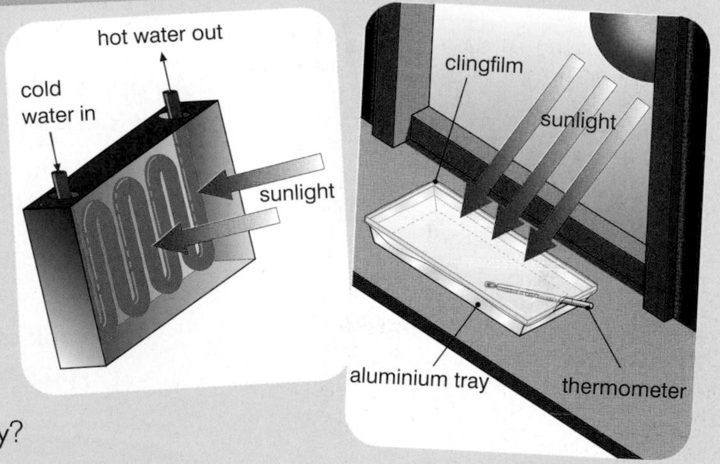

SUMMARY QUESTIONS

1 ★★ Give as many reasons as you can why we should conserve our energy resources.

2 ★★ How can houses be better designed to use sunlight as an energy resource?

3 ★★★ Fossil fuels are expensive, but the wind is free. However, electricity from a wind farm is more expensive than electricity made by burning fossil fuels. Suggest some reasons for this.

Food as fuel

LEARN ABOUT
- energy from food
- the Sun as an energy source

Energy for activity

We need energy all the time. Our bodies need energy just to keep going. We need energy at a faster rate if we are being especially active. Play a tough game of hockey or tennis and your body tells you that you need more energy, quickly – you feel hungry. **Food** is our energy resource.

Most packaged foods have a label to tell you how much energy they supply. It tells you in two ways:

- in **calories** (kcal) – the old scientific unit of energy
- in **kilojoules** (kJ) – a more modern scientific unit, equal to 1000 J (joules)

Energy is stored in the carbohydrates, fats and proteins that make up food.

People concerned with their diet tend to think of food energy in calories; scientists think in kilojoules

Joules

The scientific unit of energy is the **joule**. This is sometimes written as J. It is a small unit. To get an idea of just how small it is, picture this:

An apple is lying on a table. You pick it up and lift it 1 m into the air. That takes a little energy – about 1 J, in fact.

Now imagine eating the apple. That will give you about 400 000 J of energy – enough to lift 400 000 apples 1 m into the air.

In a day, we need about ten million joules of energy from our food.

Q1 Look at the food label in the picture. How much energy do you get from eating 100 g of baked beans?

Diet cola contains virtually no energy. You use more energy in opening the can and lifting it to your mouth than you get from the drink.

Burning food

When food technologists invent a new kind of food, they have to find out how much energy it contains. They do this by burning it in a special closed container, to see how much energy it releases. It's rather like the experiment on p.142, to find the energy released by a Bunsen flame.

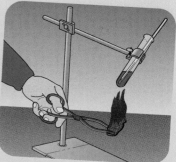

- Devise a safe experiment to compare the energy resource in foods. The easiest things to burn are dry foods, like breakfast cereals and crisp breads.

Plant food

Some animals eat plants, but where do most plants get their food? The answer is, they make it themselves. Here's the recipe they use:

- Take carbon dioxide from the air and water from the ground.
- Add lots of sunlight, and the result is **sugar**.
- To do this, the plants must be green. They need to contain the special green substance called **chlorophyll**, which is needed for the chemical reaction to happen.

The sugar that is made contains some of the energy of the sunlight. It is converted to starch if it has to be stored for a while.

These green leaves are trying to capture as much sunlight as possible

Q2 Look at the photo of the toothwort plant. Why is it white? What does this tell you about how it gets its food?

Energy from the Sun

Plants get their energy from the Sun. In fact, most of our energy originates in sunlight:

- Coal – energy from plants that grew long ago.
- Wind power – energy from wind, caused by the Sun heating the air.
- Energy from moving water – sunlight evaporates water, which later falls as rain.

Q3 Explain how the energy of oil and natural gas came originally from the Sun.

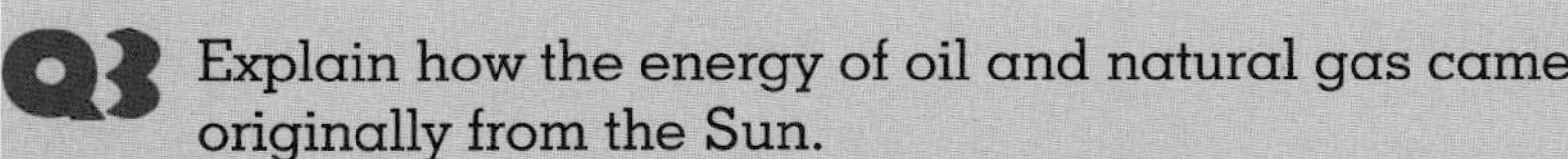

SUMMARY QUESTIONS

1 ☆ What is the scientific unit of energy?

2 ☆☆ Why do green plants have chlorophyll in their leaves?

3 ☆☆☆ Draw a cartoon strip to show how the energy we get by burning coal came originally from the Sun.

Gruesome science

Scientists have found ways of injecting water into mass-produced chicken, so that each kilogram contains fewer joules of energy than it used to.

This toothwort plant is a 'cheat'. It gets its food by sending its roots into another plant and robbing it.

Key words

calories
chlorophyll
food
joule (J)
kilojoules
sugar

SCIENTIFIC PEOPLE

IDEAS AND EVIDENCE

Fair shares for all?

Some people use more energy than others. The diagram shows this. People in developed countries (North America and Europe) use much more energy than those in developing countries. Just look at how little energy the average African person uses, compared to someone in North America.

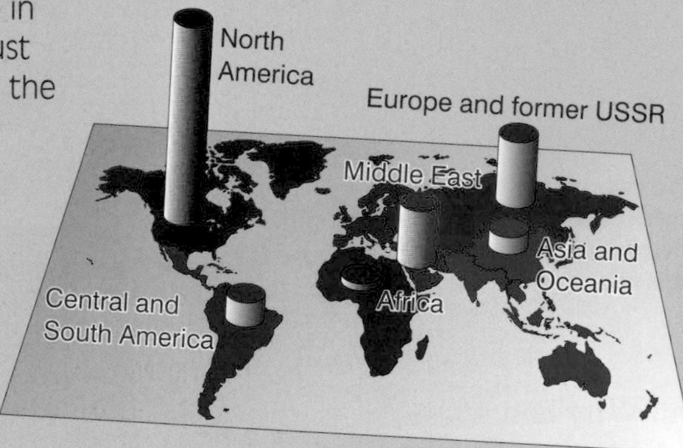

People in developed countries use more energy, so they do more damage to the environment. We need energy, because it allows us to do things – it gives us a high standard of living. However, we must find ways of using energy resources that don't harm our environment.

Going under?

People on the Pacific islands of Tuvalu are very concerned. The sea is rising, and their islands are in danger of being swamped. They blame climatic changes, caused by our use of fossil fuels.

As the Earth's temperature rises, two effects cause sea levels to rise:

- The water in the oceans expands.
- Ice from the polar ice caps melt.

The 11 000 Tuvalu islanders, who don't use much fossil fuel, feel that they are paying the price for everyone else's thoughtless energy consumption.

A tropical paradise under threat from climate change

Predicting climate change

The Earth's temperature is increasing – it's official. The United Nations set up the IPCC, an international panel of scientists, with the task of deciding whether our climate really was changing.

At first, not everyone agreed. However, as new scientific evidence was gathered during the 1990s, it gradually became clear that temperatures were rising, and that the culprit was probably carbon dioxide, released when fossil fuels are burned. That's how science works – someone has an idea, evidence is gathered, and the idea is accepted, modified or rejected.

The graph shows how the panel expect temperatures to rise over the next decades. There are two lines, because we cannot be sure about this. Scientists are rarely 100% certain about the future!

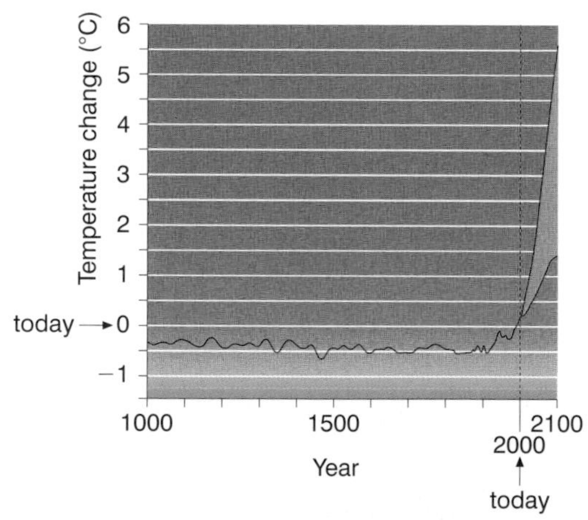

- energy allows us to do things.
- an energy resource is anything from which we can get energy.
- fuels are energy resources; they are materials we burn to release energy.
- renewable energy resources can be replaced as quickly as we use them.
- our use of energy resources can harm the environment.

DANGER! AVOID THESE COMMON ERRORS

How do you think of energy? It's something we need whenever we want to be active. We can get energy from lots of different places – from food and fuels, from wind and moving water, and so on. Those are our energy resources.

However, be careful! Coal isn't energy. Wood and water aren't energy. Energy isn't 'stuff'.

Think about burning some wood. There is a chemical reaction as the wood combines with oxygen from the air. We get heat and light; but the atoms that made up the wood and the oxygen haven't changed into heat and light. They still exist, but they have been rearranged.

You should be getting an idea of how to recognise energy resources. Water flowing downhill has more energy than when it reaches the foot of the hill. You can get that energy out by making the water turn an electricity generator. Petrol is an energy resource, because you can burn it in a car's engine and make the car move.

Look out for energy resources all around you. It's the energy we get from them that allows us to be active!

Key words

climate change
energy
energy resources

UNIT REVIEW

REVIEW QUESTIONS

Understanding and applying concepts

1 We need energy to be active. What energy resources are made use of by each of the following? (There may be more than one answer in each case.)

a a rabbit **b** a car
c a train **d** a solar cell

2 We need to conserve energy resources. Draw and label a picture to show a situation where lots of energy resources are being wasted. Choose from one of the following situations (or think of one of your own):

- in the kitchen
- a teenager's bedroom
- going to school
- the city centre

Ways with words

3 When we talk about 'conserving' energy resources, we mean that we should not waste them. Other people might use the word 'conserving' or 'conservation'. How might the following people use these words?

a a museum keeper
b a wildlife ranger
c an athlete

Making more of maths

4 The photo shows a solar-powered car. It needs a lot of solar cells to make it go.

Tests on an experimental car gave these results:

- energy of sunlight falling on solar cells = 1000 J
- energy carried by electricity from solar cells to storage battery = 200 J
- energy supplied by battery to electric motors = 150 J
- energy supplied by motors to wheels = 100 J

You can see that, at each stage, some energy is lost.

a Find a way to show this information as a diagram.
b Technologists have found ways of making better solar cells. How do you think your diagram would change if the test car were fitted with these new solar cells?

Thinking skills

5 Here are some examples of energy resources:

coal wood running water sunlight wind

a Add some more to the list.
b Make a mind map that shows:

- Some energy resources come from living material.
- Some energy resources are renewable; others are non-renewable.

Extension question

6 The diagram shows the different energy resources that contribute to the UK's energy supply.

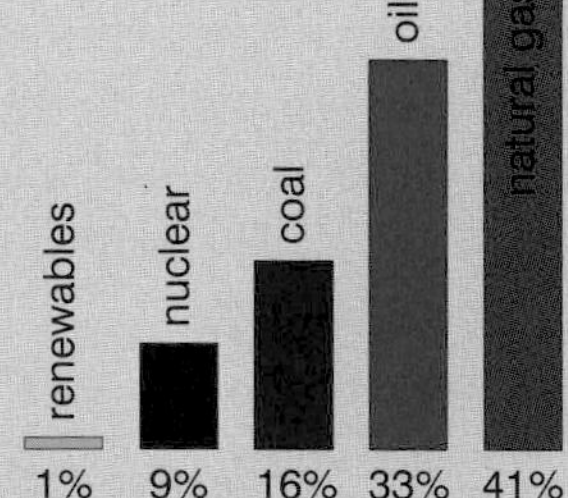

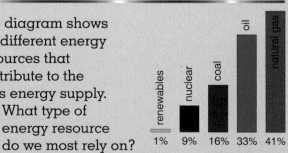

a What type of energy resource do we most rely on?
b It is hoped that, by 2010, one-tenth of our energy will come from renewable sources. How will this change the diagram? Why is it important for us to make this change?
c Imagine that you were alive in 2200. How do you think this picture of our energy resources would have changed?

SAT-STYLE QUESTIONS

1 Pip's house is on a remote island. Her parents have installed solar cells on the roof, and a wind turbine. These generate electricity.

The house also has a diesel generator that can generate electricity when the solar cells and wind turbine are not working.

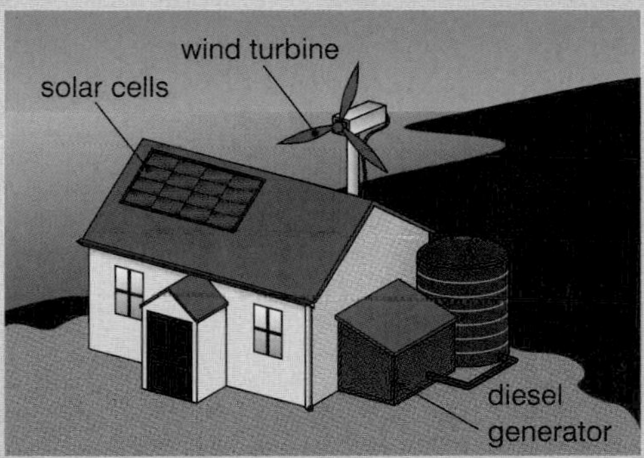

a For each method of generating electricity, draw a line to the energy resource which it makes use of: (3)

Method	**Energy resource**
diesel generator	sunlight
solar cells	running water
wind turbine	chemicals
	moving air

b The solar cells do not work at night. Explain why not. (1)

c The wind turbine does not always supply electricity. Explain why not. (1)

d Explain why it is important for Pips family to have a petrol generator. (1)

2 Year 7 have been studying energy resources. They have made a list of different resources, which their teacher shows on the whiteboard:

geothermal **biomass** **oil** **coal**
moving air **tidal** **running water**
nuclear **solar** **natural gas**

a From the list, name three fossil fuels. (3)

b From the list, name three renewable energy resources. (3)

c The class has been reading about a new tidal power station to be built near their town. The local newspaper published this picture of how it will work:

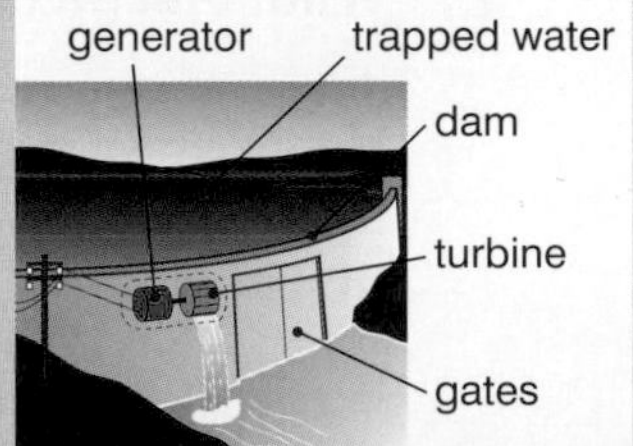

The boxes below show the stages in generating electricity.

A The generator produces electricity.

B The gates shut, trapping the water.

C Water flows out past the turbine, making it turn.

D As the tide comes in, the water level behind the dam rises.

E The turbine turns the generator.

Put the boxes in the correct order. The first one has been done for you.

D				

(4)

3 Reese and Pete are investigating a small electric heater. They are using it to heat 200 cm^3 of water in a beaker. They measure the temperature of the water every minute.

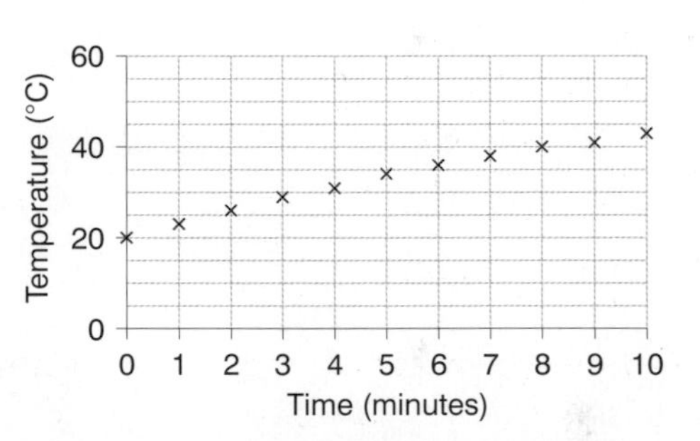

The graph shows their results.

a Explain why Reese stirred the water each time before taking its temperature. (1)

b Pete wrote this prediction:
'If we wait twice as long, the temperature of the water will go up twice as much.' (2)

Do the results of the experiment support Pete's prediction?

c Copy the graph. Add a line to show the results you would expect if the experiment were repeated with 400 cm^3 of water in the beaker. (2)

Unscramble these:
greeny
correuse
near belew
nescover
metalic ganche

7J

Electrical circuits

Coming soon

It's made with electric currants.

What's it all about?

We make use of electricity every day – it's one of our most important technologies. It allows us to do all sorts of things at the flick of a switch. Think of computers, music systems, TVs, cars, kitchen appliances – they all depend on electricity.

Electricity can be natural, too. There's electricity in the nerves of our bodies, and in every lightning flash.

You should already know quite a lot about electric circuits – how to connect them up, perhaps how to draw a circuit diagram. In this unit, you will learn to connect up more complex circuits. You will also learn how to think about electricity, and use these ideas to explain how circuits work.

What do you remember?

You already know about:

- materials that conduct electricity, and materials that don't.
- simple electric circuits.

1 Which of these materials are good at conducting electricity?

copper **plastic** **wood** **steel**

2 What electrical symbols do you know?

3 How can you change the brightness of a bulb in a circuit? Give as many ways as you can think of.

4 If you look at an electric circuit (or a diagram), how can you tell if it will work?

Young electricians

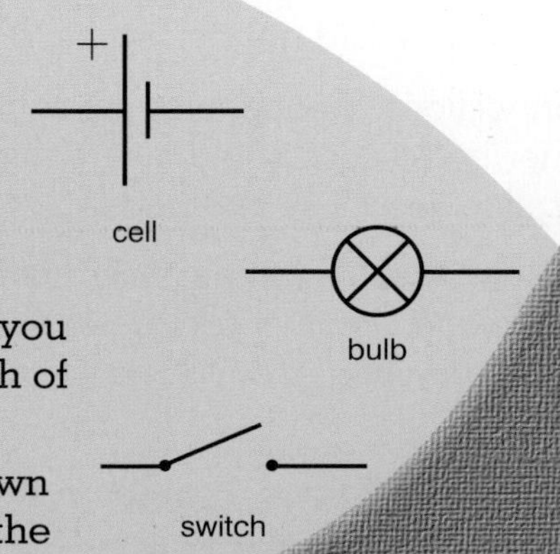

QUESTIONS

If this lot were in charge of rewiring your home, you'd be in trouble!

a) Who has made a complete circuit?

b) Who has made a dangerous circuit?

c) Does it matter what colour the wires are?

d) How does electricity flow through a glass bulb?

Sometimes it's easier to see a problem with a circuit if you have a diagram of it. Standard symbols represent each of the components in the circuit.

e) Can you draw diagrams for each of the circuits shown above? Use your diagrams to explain why some of the bulbs won't light up.

+

cell

bulb

switch

Complete circuits

LEARN ABOUT
- tracing a complete circuit
- circuit symbols
- conductors and insulators

Why won't it work?

It can be annoying if you have a torch that won't work. Perhaps chemicals have leaked out of the batteries. Perhaps they are 'dead'. The metal inside the torch may have gone rusty, or the bulb may be dead. Lots of things can go wrong to stop the electricity from getting to the bulb.

A torch has cells, a switch and a bulb. (In science, a single battery is called a **cell**.) There must be a complete circuit of metal from one end of the cells, through the switch and the bulb, and back to the other end of the cells.

The lines show how the different chips are connected together in this computer circuit

Q1 Why must the circuit be metal?

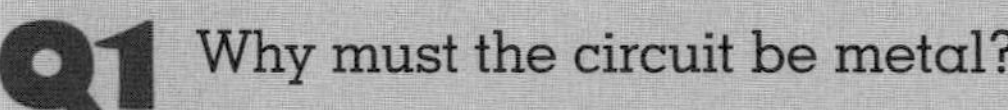

Getting the picture

Scientists and engineers draw circuit diagrams to represent electric circuits. They use standard symbols for the components, and join them with lines to show the wires.

The circuit diagram shows the order in which the components are connected. It also shows that there is a complete circuit.

Look at the circuit diagram for the torch. Use your finger to trace round the complete circuit, starting at the positive (+) end of the cells.

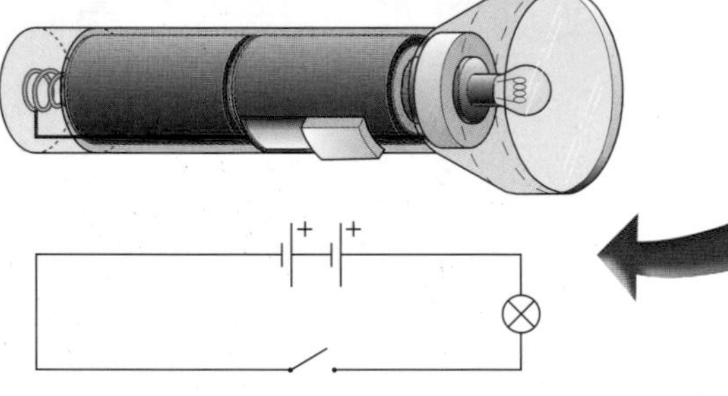

Q2 Draw the symbol for a switch. Explain how it shows the way a switch works.

Ways in, ways out

- When you wire up a circuit, each component must have *two* connections. Otherwise, the electricity would not be able to get through, and the circuit would not be complete.
- A cell has *two* connections. At one end, the shiny knob is labelled + (positive). The other end is also shiny metal; this is the negative (−) end. Examine a cell to see these two parts.
- Look closely at a bulb. Inside is a thin wire, called the **filament**, which lights up when the circuit is complete. You can't see, but the ends of the filament are connected to two metal parts on the outside of the bulb.
- When the bulb is put in its holder, it can be connected into the circuit.
  a) Explain how the bulb connects to its holder.

Electricity needs a way in and a way out. This bulb has a metal screw part, and a metal base.

A look at wires

The connecting wires you use at school are plastic-covered. This is **insulation**, material that prevents you from accidentally touching electricity because it doesn't conduct. If one wire accidentally touches another, electricity can't jump between them. If the insulation gets in the way when you make a connection, the electricity may not get through.

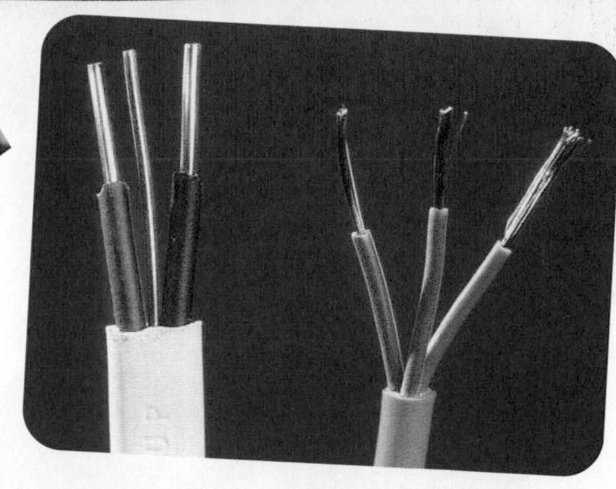

Inside, the wires are made of metal – usually strands of copper, a good conductor. They are quite thick to make it easy for electricity to pass through.

Electrical appliances such as lamps and heaters are connected to the supply using a flex or cable. This has two or three separate wires inside it. Each wire has a different colour of insulation.

Q3 Why does each wire in the flex have a different colour?

Circuit challenge

- Design and construct a circuit using cells, switches and bulbs.
- Draw a circuit diagram to match your circuit.
- Put your circuit with the others from the class.
- When your turn comes, display your diagram and see who can match it to the correct circuit.
- When the diagrams are matched to the circuits, predict what will happen when the switches are closed in each circuit.

In Technology, you will learn to connect up control circuits and to solder wires.

SUMMARY QUESTIONS

1. ★ Copy the circuit diagram for the torch on the opposite page. Label each component with its name.
2. ★★ Copy the circuit shown here. Add another wire to the diagram to complete the circuit.

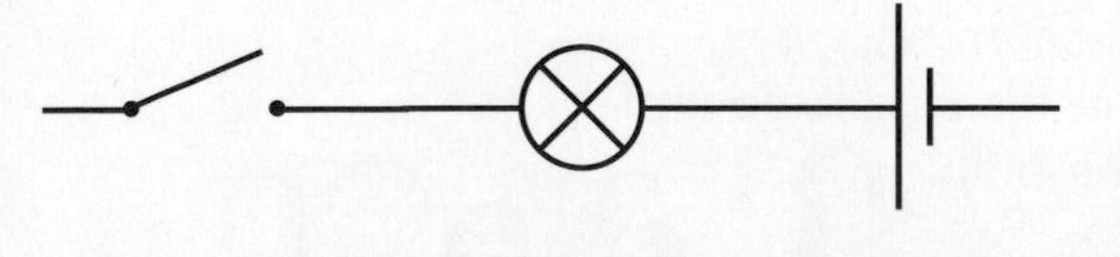

3. ★★ After a Science lesson, the pupils complain that some of the bulbs don't work. Design a simple way for the technician to test the bulbs.
4. ★★★ Give as many reasons as you can why it is a good idea to have standard symbols to represent electrical components.

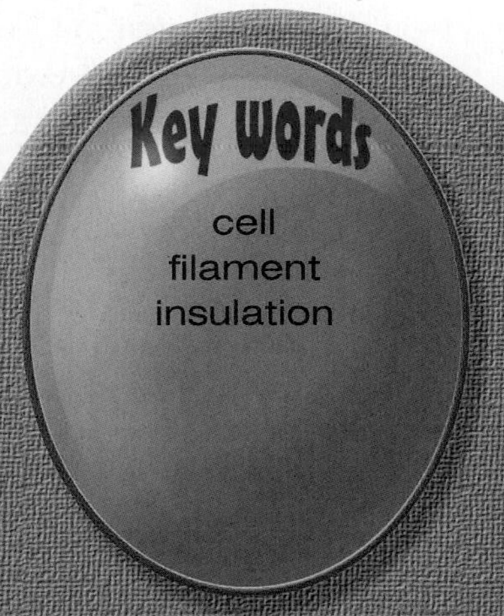

Electric current

LEARN ABOUT
- electric current
- using an ammeter
- electrical resistance

What is it?

How do you think about electricity? Is it something that flashes, like lightning? What's going on in the wires when you switch on the light?

In fact, 'electricity' is not a very helpful word. It doesn't really describe what's going on. Scientists talk about **electric current**, which flows in the wires. (It's a bit like a current of water, flowing in a river.) So, when you close a switch, the circuit is complete and electric current flows.

Lightning is a very violent form of electricity

Ideas of current

When current flows in this circuit, it makes the bulb light up. How do you picture the current?

- Does it simply flow from the + of the cell to the bulb, along the red wire?
- Does it flow out along the two wires, red and black, so that two currents meet at the bulb?
- Does it flow from the + of the cell, gradually getting used up as it flows round the circuit?
- Or does it flow all the way round, and back to the – of the cell?

These are four different possible ways of imagining electric current, but only one is right! You are going to find out which of these **models** is correct. In Science, a model is something that helps you to understand your observations.

Q1 The circuit wouldn't work if the black wire was missing. This suggests that one of the ideas of current is wrong. Which one?

Using an ammeter

We need some way of showing us what current is flowing at different points in a circuit. We use a meter called an **ammeter** (because it measures current in amps). This circuit has an ammeter to measure the current flowing *into* the bulb.

- Set up a circuit like this, and then measure the current.
- Now, move the ammeter to a different point in the circuit, so that you can measure the current flowing *out* of the bulb.
- Before you connect up, make a prediction:
  - **a)** What will the ammeter read now?
  - **b)** Will the current be more than before, less than before, or just the same?
  - **c)** Also, think about the four models of electric current listed above. Think about what each one would predict.
- Connect up and find the answer.

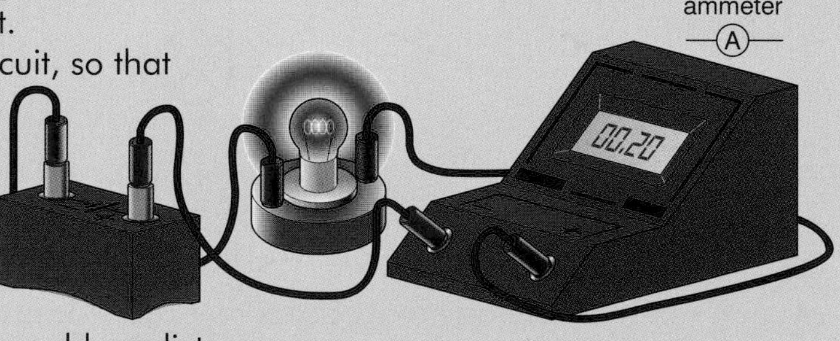

From positive to negative

Electric current flows all the way round a circuit, without getting used up. We imagine it in the wires, flowing steadily round a circuit. It flows out of the positive end of the cell, and back in at the negative end.

Current can't escape from wires, because it needs to stay inside a conductor. It can't leak out through the insulation.

It's hard to picture electric current. Even if you had a very powerful microscope, you wouldn't be able to see an electric current in a wire. This is because the current is actually made up of vast numbers of tiny particles, even smaller than atoms, called **electrons**. Particles can't just disappear, so they flow all the way round the circuit.

Q2 Look at the picture of the garden fountain. In what ways is it similar to an electric circuit? What is its 'current' made of? What is its 'cell'?

water intake

Some gardens have fountains like this. The pump makes water flow round and round, like current going around a circuit. This elastic pump is specially designed to work under water.

Changing current

What happens if you connect two bulbs in a circuit, one after the other? You don't need an ammeter to tell you. The bulbs are equally bright, because each has the same current flowing through it. The bulbs are dimmer than before, showing that the current is less. Why is this?

With two bulbs, it is harder for current to flow around the circuit. It has to push its way through one bulb, and then through the other. We say that there is more **resistance** in the circuit.

Resistance is a bit like friction. Friction is a force that makes it difficult for things to move past each other. Resistance makes it difficult for electric current to flow.

The volume control on this radio works by changing the resistance in an electric circuit

SUMMARY QUESTIONS

1 ☆ Copy these sentences. Complete them by filling in the gaps.

Electric . . . flows all the way round a circuit.

Current flows from . . . to . . . .

Current is measured using an . . . .

If there is more resistance in a circuit, the current flowing will be . . . .

2 ☆☆ Two light bulbs are connected, one after the other, to a cell. They both light up. An ammeter shows that a current of 1 amp is flowing into the first bulb. How much current flows out of the first bulb, into the second one? How much flows out of the second bulb?

3 ☆☆☆ Use the idea of 'resistance' to explain how you could control the speed of an electric motor.

ammeter
electric current
electrons
model
resistance

Cells and batteries

LEARN ABOUT
- voltage
- connecting cells

Which battery do I need?

Sometimes you get given presents that need **batteries** to work. It can be very annoying if you don't have the right batteries. What makes one battery right and another one wrong? The battery must be the right size and shape, of course; but it must also be the correct voltage.

Cells and batteries come in all shapes and sizes. There are tiny ones to fit in hearing aids, and big, heavy ones to go in cars and lorries. They are all marked with their voltages. The letter V stands for 'volt'.

Q1 Look at the batteries in the photograph. What are their voltages? What do you notice about these values?

Cell + cell = battery

A 1.5 V 'battery', such as an AA or AAA type, is really a single cell. You may need two or more of these to make something work. For example, a Walkman usually needs 3 V, so you have to put in two 1.5 V cells.

You can probably guess what's inside a 6 V battery. There are four cells, each giving 1.5 V. In Science, a single 'battery' is a cell.

Q2 How many 1.5 V cells are needed to make a 4.5 V battery?

Gruesome science

An electric eel can zap you with up to 800 V.

The 'push' of cells

You already know that a cell is needed to make a circuit work. The cell 'pushes' the electric current around the circuit.

- Try out some different cells and batteries. Connect them, one at a time, in a circuit to light up a bulb. See how brightly the bulb lights up.
- Put your observations in a table, and draw a conclusion.

Take care! Don't connect too many cells to a bulb. If the voltage is too great, the current will be too big. The filament in the bulb will heat up too much, and melt. That's the end of that bulb.

Cell or battery	Voltage	Observation
AA	1.5 V	Bulb not very bright

The meaning of voltage

The **voltage** of a cell or battery tells you about the push it can give, to make current flow around a circuit. The greater the voltage, the greater the push. A 3 V battery gives twice as much 'push' as a 1.5 V cell. We can use this idea to understand how to connect cells together to make a battery from separate cells.

To make a battery, the cells must be connected the right way round. Inside some appliances, such as torches and radios, there is often a picture to show the correct way to put the cells. They go end-to-end, with the positive of one cell connecting to the negative of the next one, and so on. Then their voltages will add up.

When components in a circuit are connected end-to-end, we say they are connected **in series**.

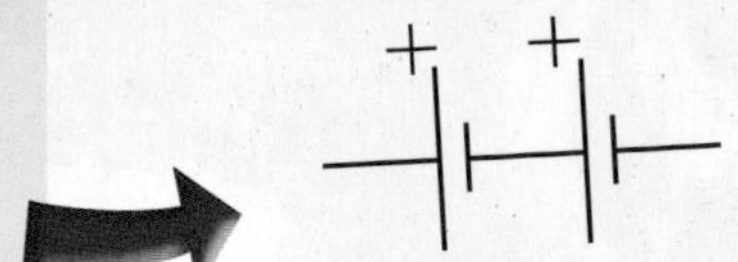

Two cells connected in series give twice the push of a single cell

Adding up, cancelling out

Here are the rules for cells connected in series:

- Two cells are connected positive to negative: their voltages add up.
- Two cells are connected positive to positive: their voltages cancel out.

a) Devise a method of checking these rules. Check your method with your teacher, and try it out.
b) Make a prediction: If you have three 1.5 V cells connected in series, but one is the wrong way round, what voltage will they provide? Test your prediction.

SUMMARY QUESTIONS

1 ★★ Copy these sentences. Complete them by filling in the gaps.
The voltage of a cell tells you the . . . it gives to make a . . . flow in the circuit.
To make a . . ., connect cells together in . . . .

2 ★★ Look at the diagrams. Work out the voltage provided by each combination of cells. (Each cell provides 1.5 V.)

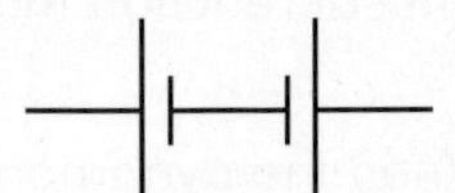

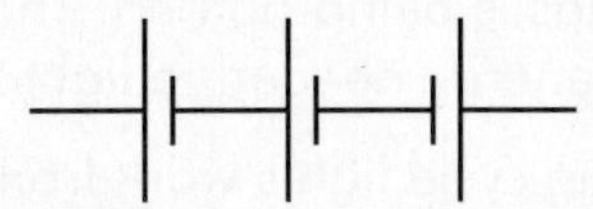

3 ★★★ Find some electrical items that need more than one cell, for example, a Walkman or battery-powered radio, a cycle lamp, a TV remote control. Look in the battery compartment. Work out which way the batteries go, and how they are connected in series.

7J4 Electricity from Chemistry

LEARN ABOUT
- energy from a cell
- the difference between current and voltage

What's going on?

Batteries are an expensive way of buying electricity. We buy them because they are convenient, but they soon run out. Worse than that, they sometimes leak chemicals, which can cause damage to the appliance they are being used in.

Inside a cell, there are chemicals. When you connect the cell into a complete circuit, the chemicals start to react with each other, and this pushes the current around the circuit. Disconnect the circuit and the reaction stops.

Because the chemicals used in a cell are hazardous, you should not open one up. If the chemicals leak, wipe them up and throw away the cell. Don't get the chemicals on your hands.

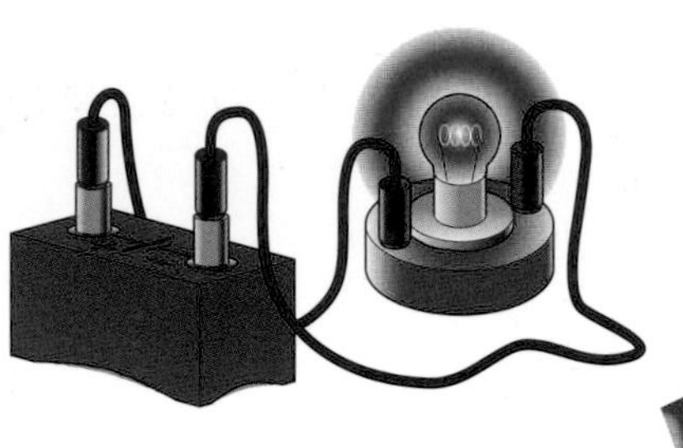

Running down

Look at the picture of the circuit. How can we describe what's going on?

There is a chemical reaction going on in the cell. At the same time, the bulb is giving out light. We can describe this by thinking about **energy**. We say that the chemicals in the cell are a store of energy; when the circuit is complete, the energy from the chemicals is transferred to the bulb, and comes out as light.

Eventually, the chemicals run out, and the battery is 'dead'. Its store of energy has been used up, and the bulb won't shine.

Q1 An AA cell is bigger than an AAA cell. Both have a voltage of 1.5 V. Use the idea of 'energy' to explain why the AA cell will keep a bulb lit for longer. Why is the bulb the same brightness whichever cell is used?

There are other ways to light a bulb. You could plug a reading lamp into the mains. Electricity is coming from a power station, where coal or gas is being burned. That's another chemical reaction that provides the energy needed to light the bulb.

Some cycle lights work from a **dynamo**. When the dynamo is working, you have to pedal a little harder. You are providing the energy needed to light the bulb.

Q2 Explain why the lights go out when the bicycle stops. Some lights keep shining for a while after the cycle stops. How can this happen?

Current and voltage

It is easy to get confused about the difference between current and voltage. Here are the things to remember:

- Current travels all the way round a circuit (its unit is amps, A).
- Voltage tells you about the push of a cell or battery (its unit is volts, V).
- While a cell is pushing current round a circuit, it is providing energy for the components in the circuit.

Look at the circuit on the opposite page. If you make a break in the circuit, the current can't get through. The light goes out, because it is no longer getting energy from the cell.

This tells us why current is important: it carries the energy from the cell to the bulb. Once it has reached the bulb, it gives up the energy, and returns to the cell.

Q3 In a circuit like the one on the opposite page, it doesn't matter if the switch comes before or after the bulb. Why not?

AMAZING SCIENCE!

A large power station supplies electricity at half a million volts. The current leaving it may be over 1000 A.

The water model

One way to think about current and voltage is to use a model. In this case, the model is an actual object – a water circuit. The pump pushes water through the pipes. It can make a wheel turn round.

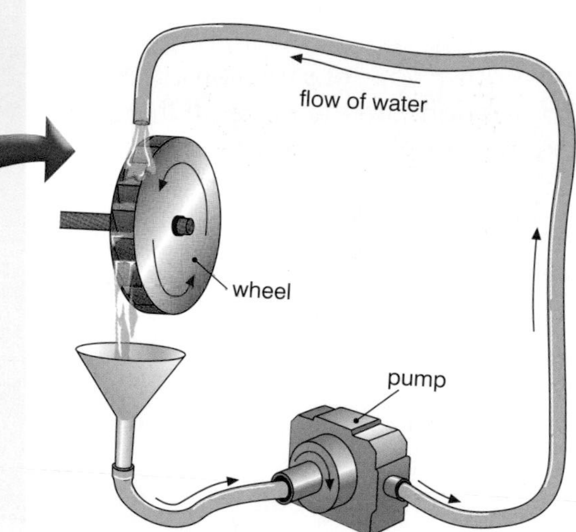

Q4 Think about this model. What does the flowing water represent? Which part of an electric circuit does the pump represent? How is energy transferred from the pump to the wheel?

With this model, you can make changes. For example, use thinner pipes. The water flows more slowly because it finds it hard to get through thin pipes. This is like having more **resistance** in an electric circuit.

SUMMARY QUESTIONS

1 ☆ Copy the table. In each box of the first column, write 'current', 'voltage' or 'energy'.

	Measured with an ammeter.
	Tells you the push of a cell.
	Stored in the chemicals of a cell.
	Carried by current part way round a circuit.
	Flows all the way round a circuit.

2 ☆☆ Here's another model which someone thought up to represent an electric circuit:

In a school, a pupil has to be the messenger. She collects a pile of messages from the office, and then runs round all the classrooms, delivering the messages. Then she goes back to the office to see if there is anything more to deliver.

a) What represents the electric current?
b) What represents the cell?
c) What represents the energy which is being transferred?

7J5 Series and parallel

LEARN ABOUT
- series and parallel circuits

What is it?

If you connect up a circuit with two or three bulbs in series, together with a switch, you can switch the bulbs on and off. They always go on and off together.

Q1 Explain why the switch controls all the bulbs.

Your lights at home don't work like this. If you switch one light off, the others stay on. Sometimes two switches control one light! It would be a great nuisance if you had no choice – all the lights in the house on, or all the lights off.

They must be connected up in a different way from a simple series circuit. In fact, there are two different ways of connecting two bulbs in a circuit with a cell. They can be connected:

- in series (end-to-end),
- or in parallel (side-by-side).

Here are two bulbs connected **in parallel** with a cell:

Getting wired

The more bulbs you connect in series, the dimmer they get. If you connect bulbs in parallel, they stay just as bright. You can probably guess that the lights in a house are connected in parallel; otherwise, the more you switched on, the dimmer they would get.

Christmas tree lights are different. They are often connected in series. If one bulb fails, the whole lot may go out. There is a break in the circuit and the current can't get through.

Q2 Sometimes you see a car with just one headlight working. Does this tell you that the two headlights are connected in series or in parallel?

Connecting up

Try setting up these circuits. Draw circuit diagrams for each, and note down your observations. (How bright are the bulbs? If there are two, are they both the same brightness?)

- A single bulb and a single cell.
- Two bulbs in series with a single cell.
- Two bulbs in parallel with a single cell.
  - **a)** In the circuits with two bulbs, what happens if you unscrew one bulb?
- Now try adding switches to the parallel circuit.
  - **b)** Can you arrange to switch only one bulb off? Where would you connect a single switch to control both bulbs?
  - **c)** Think about how the current flows in your circuits. Be prepared to discuss your ideas with the rest of the class.

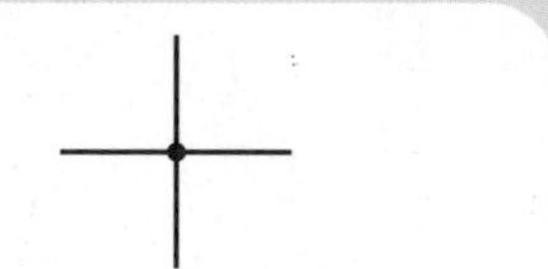

When two wires meet, add a blob to the diagram to show how they are connected together

How the current flows

Think about how the current flows around the parallel circuit. Try tracing around the circuit, starting from the + end of the cell. What happens when you get to point A? The current can go two ways. So half goes through one bulb, and half through the other.

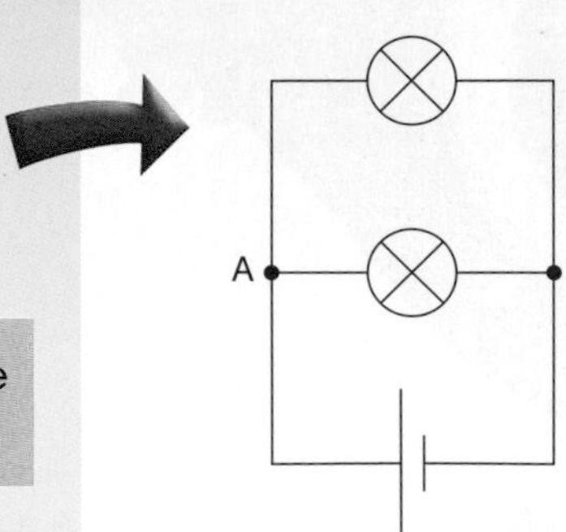

 How do you know that each bulb gets an equal share of the current?

In fact, you can imagine *two* lots of current flowing round the circuit, one through each bulb. (Try tracing the circuit with two fingers.) In a parallel circuit like this, each bulb feels the full push of the cell, so each is as bright as if there was only one bulb.

It is easier for current to flow round a parallel circuit than a series circuit, because it has two possible routes to flow along. It's a bit like an obstacle race. Imagine that your whole class had to run a race. The course goes through two long pipes. If the pipes are arranged end-to-end (in series), it is much harder to get everyone through than if they are arranged side-by-side (in parallel). With pipes in parallel, half the class can go through one and half through the other.

Home electrics

Here's how a building such as a house is wired up. Two wires run all round the house. One has red insulation, the other has black. They are like the positive and negative ends of a cell.

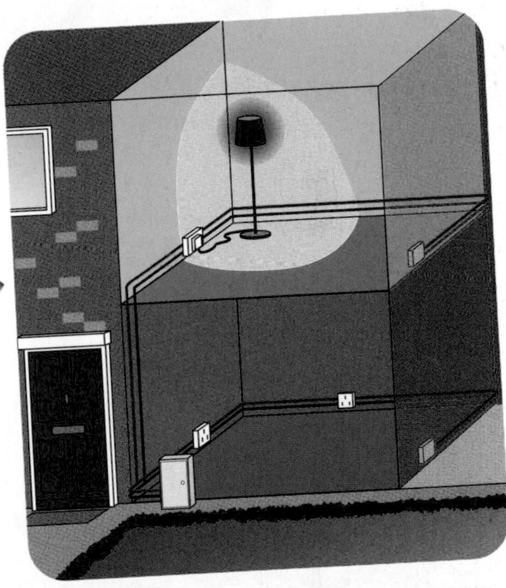

When you plug an **appliance** into a socket, the two short pins on the plug connect the appliance to the two wires. Now current can flow from the red wire, through the appliance, and out to the black wire. So all the electrical appliances in a house are connected in parallel, and each feels the full push of the mains voltage.

SUMMARY QUESTIONS

1 ★★ Copy the table; write 'series' or 'parallel' in each box in the first column.

	The same current flows through each **component**.
	There is more than one route around the circuit.
	The current splits as it travels around the circuit.
	Components can be separately controlled.

2 ★★★ Invent a circuit, and draw a circuit diagram to represent it. Your circuit must have at least two cells, two bulbs and one switch. It can also include any other components you know about.

At least two components must be connected in parallel with each other.

Write a sentence or two to explain what happens when the switch or switches are operated.

7J6 Keeping safe

LEARN ABOUT
- how to use electricity safely

What is it?

Electricity can kill. We know this because occasionally people get killed by lightning, or if they touch the mains electricity. The mains voltage is 230 V, and that can push a much bigger current through you than a 1.5 V cell.

Perhaps you have been nervous about connecting up some of the circuits you have made in this unit. Have you been careful not to touch the metal plugs? Of course, you would come to no harm, but it is wise to be cautious!

Domestic appliances are designed so that you cannot easily get at the high voltages inside.

This hazard symbol warns you of electrical dangers

Fuse protection

There are lots of safety devices used in electrical systems. Here's one – a **fuse**. A bulb will blow if too big a current flows through it. The circuit in the diagram shows how to investigate this.

- You have to use a power supply, so that you can gradually increase the voltage. The power supply can give more volts than a cell. Keep it switched off until the circuit is set up.
- The fuse wire is connected in series with the bulb. Set the power supply to 0 V, and switch it on. Slowly increase the voltage. Watch the bulb and the fuse wire. What happens?

Fuse wire is cheap and easy to replace.

a) Explain how the fuse wire protects the bulb.

b) What would have happened if you had used thicker fuse wire?

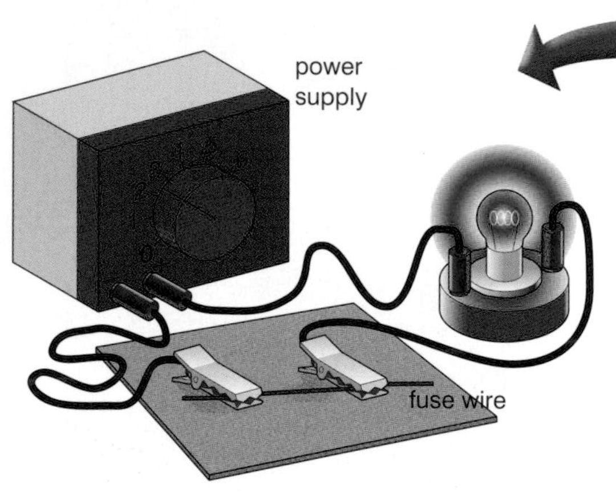

More safety

Fuses make sure that the current flowing in a circuit doesn't get too big. A big current might cause the wiring or components in the circuit to get hot, so that they are damaged. Hot wires can even set a home on fire. The fuse wire melts so that the circuit is broken. Some circuits have **trip switches**, which automatically break the circuit when the current gets too big. They can be reset as soon as the problem has been sorted out – that's much easier than replacing fuse wire or a cartridge fuse. Look for the 'RESET' button on the front of a lab power supply.

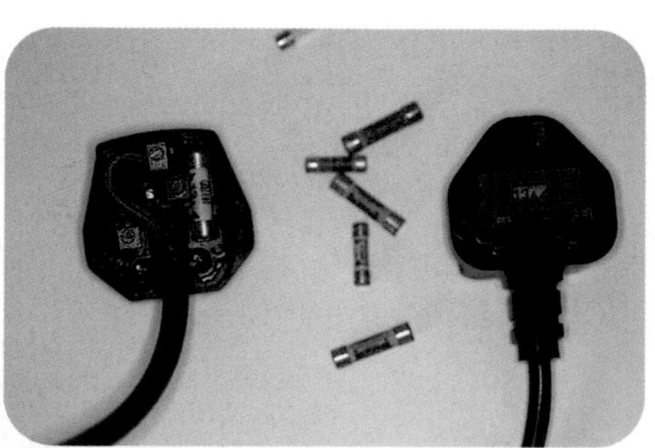

There is a small cartridge fuse inside every mains plug. Inside is a thin piece of fuse wire.

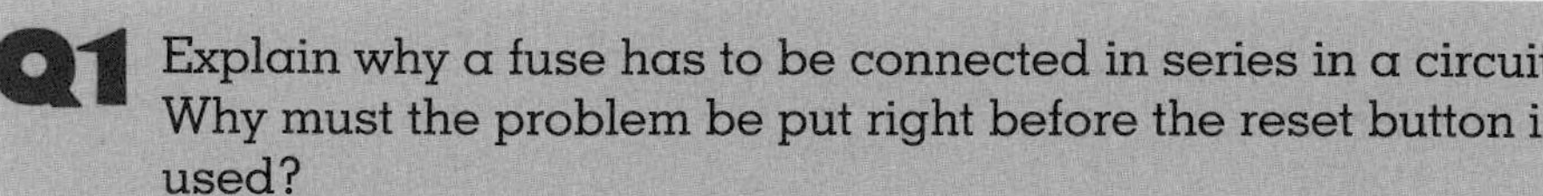

Q1 Explain why a fuse has to be connected in series in a circuit. Why must the problem be put right before the reset button is used?

Staying alive

It doesn't take much electric current to kill a person – much less than 1 A. So we need to be protected from currents flowing through our bodies. There's another type of safety device that does this. Your science lab will have one.

Suppose you are working in the lab and you accidentally get a shock from a power supply. A small current flows through your body, but almost instantly there is a 'click' and the power is switched off by the **circuit breaker** on the wall.

This type of circuit breaker looks to see if there is any electric current escaping from the circuits in the lab. It does this by comparing the current flowing into the lab with the current flowing out. Remember that electric current can't simply disappear. So if less current is leaving the lab than is coming in, some must be disappearing somewhere, and that spells danger! You might feel a bit of a shock, but it won't last long enough for you come to any harm.

It is sensible to use a circuit breaker with an electric hedge-trimmer. If you accidentally cut through the power cable, you will be protected from getting a shock.

Q2 You have to be careful to avoid touching electrical equipment with wet hands. Why is this?

Current and voltage (again)

It can take less than 0.1 A to kill you. In some of the circuits you have made, the current is much bigger than this. However, you have not been in danger. The cells don't have a big enough voltage to push this much current through you.

Q3 Which is bigger, the resistance of your body or the resistance of a bulb? Explain how you know.

Gruesome science

Each year in the UK, about 40 eleven-year-olds die in accidents with electricity. Don't let it happen to you!

SUMMARY QUESTIONS

1 ☆☆ A light bulb will blow if a current of 8 A flows through it. In normal use, a current of 4 A flows through it. What fuse should be used to protect it? Choose from 2 A, 5 A, 10 A. Explain your choice.

2 ☆☆☆ In most houses, there is one circuit for the upstairs lighting, and one for the downstairs lighting. There are circuits to the power sockets upstairs and downstairs, and a separate circuit for a cooker. Each has its own fuse. Explain why this is better than having a single fuse for everything.

Key words

circuit breaker
fuse
trip switch

Read all about it!

IDEAS AND EVIDENCE

Nervous about electricity?

Our nerves work by electricity. Tiny currents flow along them, allowing the brain to control our various organs. The connection between bodies and electricity was first discovered by an Italian scientist called Luigi Galvani. He made simple electric circuits with frogs' legs in them, and saw the legs twitch when he completed the circuit. At first he didn't understand what was going on, but his work soon led to the invention of cells and batteries.

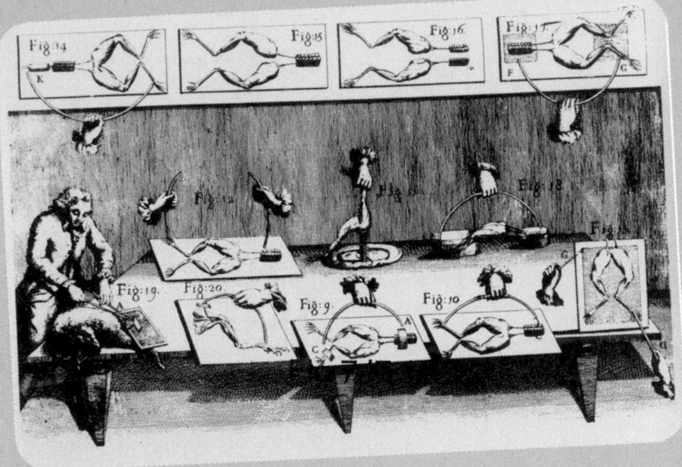

The picture comes from a book that Galvani wrote, and which was published in 1791. You can see some of the different arrangements he tried out. It's a bit surprising to discover that nerves and muscles still work when an animal has died. Many scientists came to believe that it was 'animal electricity' that kept us alive, and that made the difference between animals and other living things.

Shocking stuff

Here is another connection between animals and electricity. This horse brake was invented in the 1880s. There is a battery beside the driver; when he pulls the lever, it sends a current through the reins to the horse's mouth. The horse gets a shock, and pulls up in a hurry.

The horse brake seems cruel to us today. Animals soon learn to avoid electricity. An electric fence will give a mild shock to any animal (or person) that touches it. Watch out! To save energy, the fence is only live every few seconds. You may think a fence is off, and then get a nasty shock!

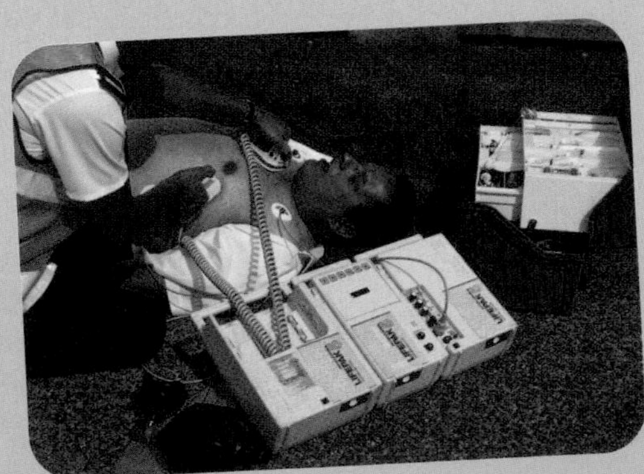

If you have a heart attack, the nerves to your heart may not be able to control it. An electric shock from a defibrillator may restart its regular rhythm. The ambulance man in the photograph is giving a patient a shock – you have probably seen scenes like this in TV dramas.

A complete circuit is needed to make a current flow.
The current flows through one component after another in a series circuit... it doesn't get used up.

1·5V
The voltage of a cell tells you how much push it gives a current.

Current is measured with an ammeter.
A

Current divides in a parallel circuit.

The current carries energy from the cell to the components in the circuit.
ENERGY RELEASED
ENERGY STORED

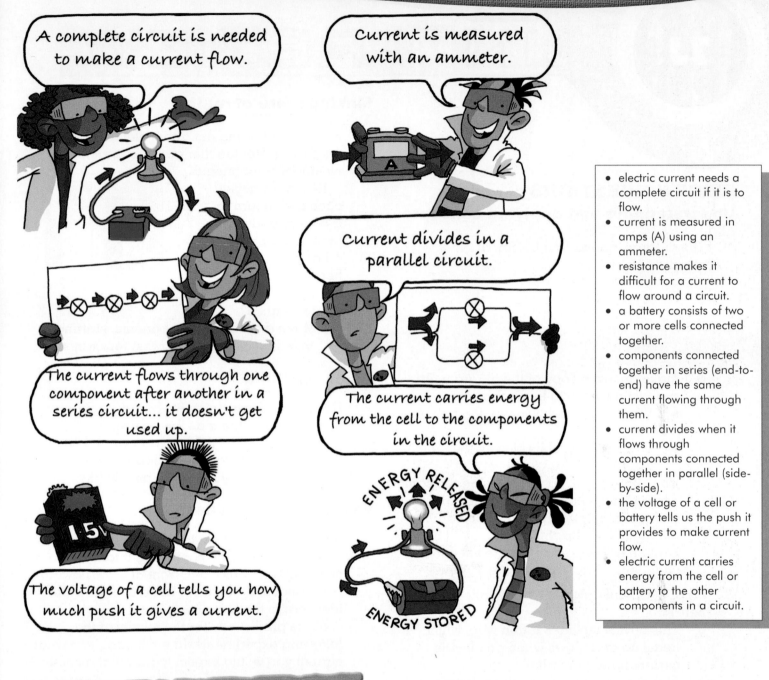

- electric current needs a complete circuit if it is to flow.
- current is measured in amps (A) using an ammeter.
- resistance makes it difficult for a current to flow around a circuit.
- a battery consists of two or more cells connected together.
- components connected together in series (end-to-end) have the same current flowing through them.
- current divides when it flows through components connected together in parallel (side-by-side).
- the voltage of a cell or battery tells us the push it provides to make current flow.
- electric current carries energy from the cell or battery to the other components in a circuit.

DANGER! AVOID THESE COMMON ERRORS

It can take a while to understand the difference between voltage and current. Voltage is the push; current is what gets pushed around the circuit. Current flows; voltage doesn't go anywhere.

In this unit, you will have thought about some models to represent electric circuits, such as the water circuit model. However, we have to be careful about models; they can be very useful for showing us ideas, and for suggesting new ideas. They can give us ways of thinking about things; however, you should remember that a model cannot represent everything about, say, electric circuits. Don't forget that models have their limitations.

Key words

current
electric circuit
model
voltage

UNIT REVIEW

REVIEW QUESTIONS

Understanding and applying concepts

1 The diagram shows four electrical components.

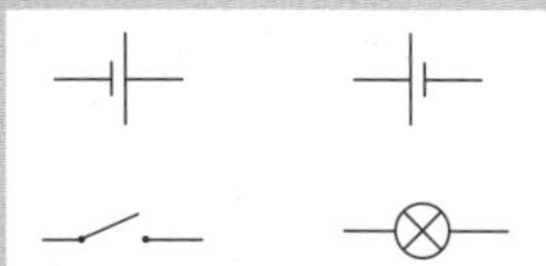

a Make an exact copy of the diagram. Add connecting wires to make this circuit:
- When the switch is open, the bulb is off.
- When the switch is closed, the bulb is on.

b Now draw a second circuit using the same components and an extra switch. By changing the switches, the bulb can be off, dimly lit or brightly lit.
Explain how the switches are used to change the brightness of the bulb.

2 What electrical devices are described here?

a This device includes a thin wire, which heats up and glows when an electric current flows through it.

b This device has two positions. In one, it allows an electric current to flow through it.

Ways with words

3 A fuse protects an electric circuit. If a high current flows, we say that the fuse 'blows'. Which of the following words is a better description of what happens to the fuse? Explain your choice.

The fuse:

explodes **breaks** **melts** **blows up**

Making more of maths

4 Reese was finding out about electrical resistance. Her teacher gave her several electrical components.

Reese connected each one in turn to a battery and an ammeter. She made a bar chart to show her results.

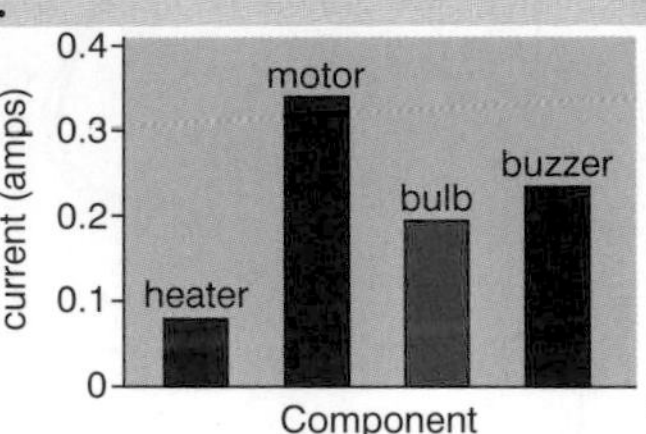

a Which component had the lowest resistance?

b Make a list of the components, starting with the one with the lowest resistance.

Thinking skills

5 Devise an 'electric circuits' board game. Use snakes and ladders as the basic idea.

What will be the snakes, and what will be the ladders? Explain your choices.

Describe briefly how the game works.

Extension questions

6 Molly was measuring the current flowing through a bulb. She connected it to a single cell, and found that a current of 0.2 A flowed.

Her teacher then gave her a second bulb, identical to the first one.

Make predictions for the results of the following experiments. In each case, say what current you would expect to flow in the circuit, and why.

a Molly connected the second bulb to a single cell.

b Molly connected the two bulbs in parallel, and then connected them to a single cell.

c Molly connected the two bulbs in series, and then connected them to a single cell.

7 Benjamin Franklin was an American scientist who did some pioneering experiments on electricity. Find out why he flew a kite in a thunderstorm. Why was this experiment dangerous, and what did he do to make it safer? How did this lead to the invention of lightning conductors?

SAT-STYLE QUESTIONS

1 Mike set up the circuit shown. He had three bulbs to test. Each gave a different reading on the ammeter.

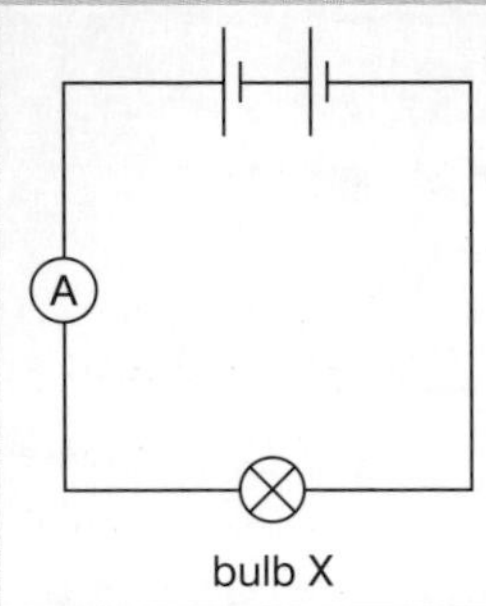

Bulb X	Ammeter reading = 0.4 A
Bulb Y	Ammeter reading = 0.2 A
Bulb Z	Ammeter reading = 0.6 A

a Which bulb has the least resistance? (1)

Mike then set up a circuit with two bulbs connected to the same battery as before.

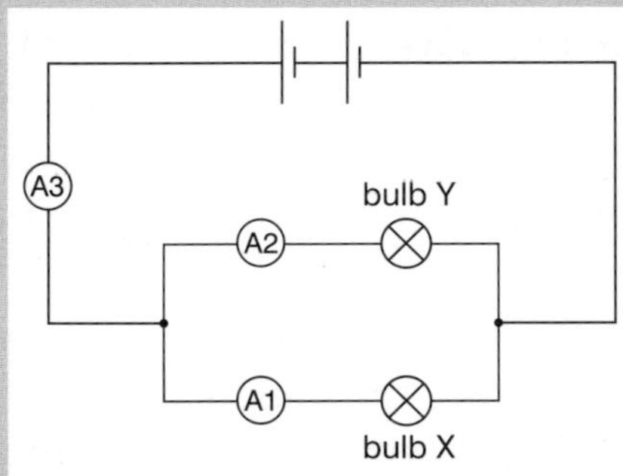

b Are the bulbs connected in series or in parallel? (1)

c What readings would you expect to see on the ammeters A1 and A2? (2)

d What reading would you expect to see on the ammeter A3? (1)

e Suggest two changes you could make to the circuit to increase the reading on ammeter A3. (2)

2 Pete's teacher gave him an electrical 'black box' to investigate. Pete connected the black box to a cell. He included an ammeter in the circuit to measure the current flowing through the black box.

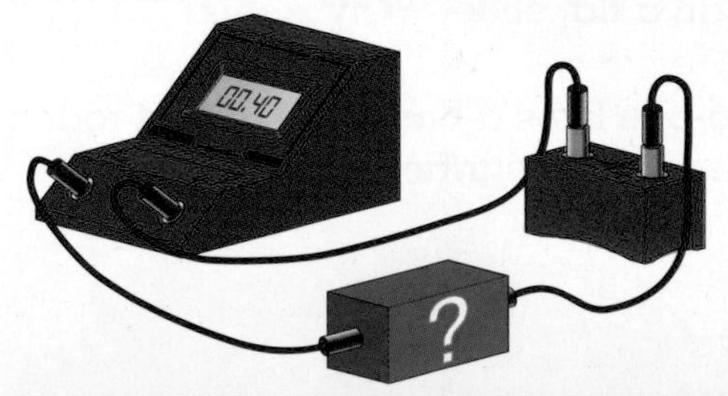

Pete added more cells, and recorded the current each time. The table shows his results.

Number of cells	Current flowing (A)
1	0.40
2	0.80
3	1.40
4	1.60

a When the teacher looked at Pete's results, she suggested he might have made a mistake with one of them. Which one? (1)

b Draw a graph of Pete's results. Draw a line through his correct results. Use your graph to make a prediction: what current would flow if the black box was connected to 5 cells? (3)

3 Pip went camping. She forgot to turn her new torch off when she went to sleep. It shone brightly for several hours, then grew dim and faded out.

a Which graph might represent how the current flowing from the battery changed during the night? (1)

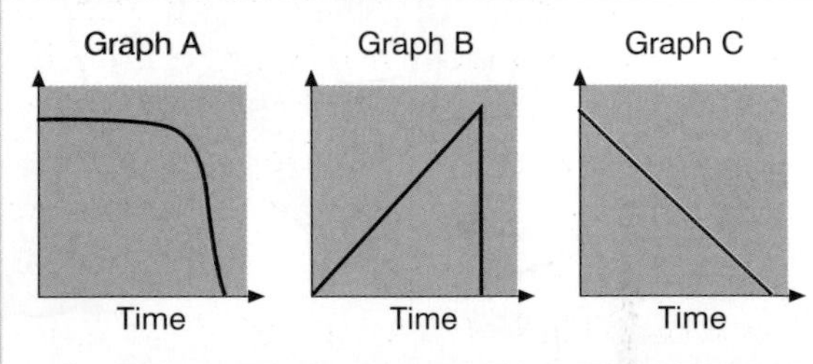

b Which graph might represent how the energy stored in the battery changed during the night? (1)

Key words

Unscramble these:
taterby
unlatinors
cruciti
restainces
temmera
galvote

7K Forces and their effects

Coming soon

What's it all about?

You already know quite a lot about forces. But think back a few years – to before you were born. Then, you floated around in your mother's womb, and you probably didn't have to concern yourself much with forces. Perhaps you moved your arms and legs around, getting ready for the big wide world.

Then you were born. It probably took you about a year to learn to walk, and you must have learned about gravity by falling over. Gradually, you will have learned about different forces and how to make use of them.

That was all without thinking consciously about forces. It's different for scientists and engineers. They need to have very clear ideas about forces if they are going to understand the world, or make things such as cars, bridges and boats. In this unit, you are going to learn more about the way scientists think about forces.

What do you remember?

You already know:

- weight is a force, measured in newtons.
- a forcemeter is used to measure forces.

1 What force pushes up on us when we are swimming?

gravity **flotation**
upthrust **water resistance**

2 What force pulls down on us when we are swimming?

gravity **flotation**
upthrust **water resistance**

3 What unit is used for force?

kilogram **newton**
archimedes **forcemeter**

4 A crumpled sheet of paper falls more quickly than a flat sheet. Why is this?

5 No-one likes a bumpy road, but roads must have rough surfaces. Why is this?

Gravity and Bounce!

QUESTIONS

The Scientifica crew have studied forces, but they seem to have forgotten almost everything they learned.

a) Which forces have they named?

b) Can you name any forces they have forgotten about?

Pete would like their teacher to organise a trip to a fun park on the Moon.

c) What would it be like to be on the Moon? Do you agree with his ideas?

Go on – force yourself!

LEARN ABOUT
- measuring forces
- representing forces

The effects of forces

Forces can change the shapes of things, and how they move – as these unfortunate drivers discovered

You stub your toe; you bump your head on a low branch; you trip over the dog. Life can be painful. Our bodies are covered with nerve endings; some of these can detect forces that act on us. If the force is too big, we may experience pain.

Forces are not something we can see, but we may be able to see their effects. If you hit a tennis ball, your racket exerts a force on the ball and you see how the ball speeds off in a different direction. Stretch a piece of chewing gum and the forces you exert on it make it change shape.

Give another example of a force changing movement, and of a force changing the shape of something.

Measuring forces

We show up a force when we measure it. Forces are measured using **forcemeters** (sometimes called newton-meters). A forcemeter has something springy inside. When a force pushes or pulls the spring, it is squashed or stretched and you can read off the size of the force from the scale.

The **newton** is the scientific unit of force.

The meter shows the size of the force in **newtons**. We usually write N for newton. One newton (1 N) is roughly equal to the weight of an apple.

I'm using this newton-meter to measure some Newtons.

The four engines of a jumbo jet provide a force of one million newtons.

The big push

School labs have bathroom scales which show forces in newtons.

- Try one out. Try pushing on it with your arms, and with your legs.
  a) What is the biggest force you can exert?

Picturing forces

We can't see forces, but we can work out where they are, and show them on diagrams. We draw an arrow to represent a force. We use arrows because they can show the direction in which the force acts.

It's important to know the direction of a force. For example, the Earth's gravity pulls downwards on all of us. That's what keeps us on the Earth. If gravity acted upwards, we would all be pushed upwards, and we would fly off into space.

The drawings show some force arrows. It is important to label them, too, so that everyone knows what each arrow represents. The label tells us:

- what kind of force it is – push, pull etc.
- what causes the force
- what the force is acting on

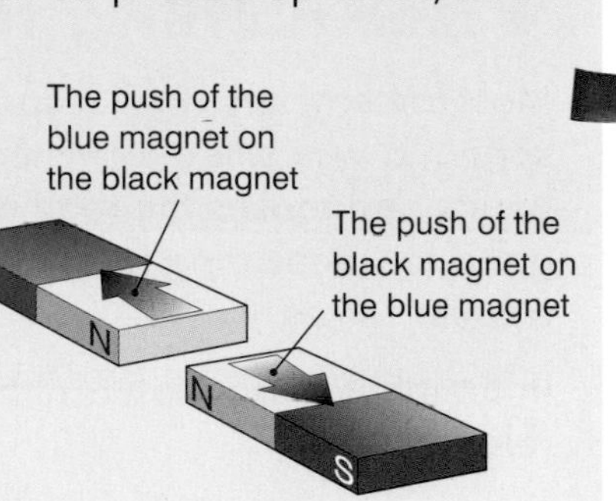

Q2 Make a drawing of someone pushing a shopping trolley. Use an arrow to show their pushing force, and label it.

Magnetic attraction

A magnet can attract a piece of iron – but did you know that the iron also attracts the magnet?

- Devise an experiment to find out about these forces.
- Can you answer the question:
  Which force is bigger, the pull of the magnet on the iron or the pull of the iron on the magnet?

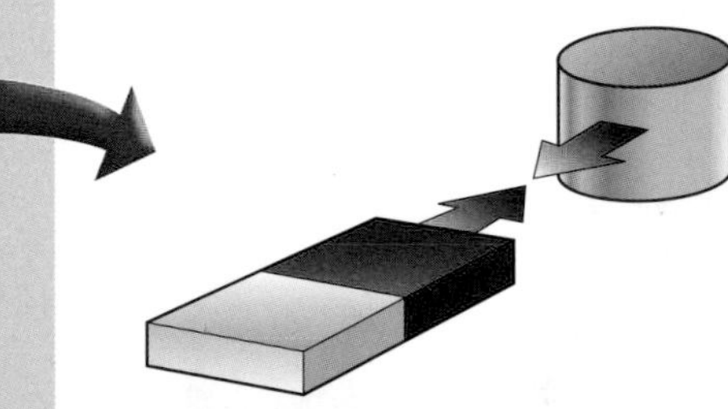

SUMMARY QUESTIONS

1 ☆ Copy these sentences. Complete them by filling in the gaps.

Forces are measured using a . . . . The scientific unit of force is the . . . (symbol . . .).

On diagrams, forces are represented by . . . , because it is important to know the . . . of a force.

2 ☆ Draw a diagram to show a foot kicking a ball. Show the force of the foot on the ball.

3 ☆☆☆ Here are the results from an experiment. Seven children took it in turn to weigh a brick. Look at the results and use them to decide: what was the weight of the brick? Explain how you came to your answer.

Alex: 24 N Bruce: 24.3 N Cath: 24 N Dee: 24.3 N
Eric: 28 N Farah: 24.2 N Gail: 24.3 N

7K2 Bend and stretch

LEARN ABOUT
- weight
- stretching springs

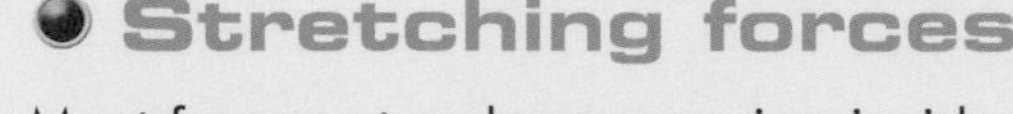

Stretching forces

Most forcemeters have a spring inside. Even bathroom scales have a spring, a very stiff one. When you stand on the scales, the spring bends and makes the reading on the scale change. A stiff spring is good for measuring large forces, and a less stiff spring is good for smaller forces.

In the photograph, an ornithologist is weighing a swallow before releasing it.

Q1 Look at the forcemeter in the picture. What can you say about its spring – how stiff is it?

Weight and gravity

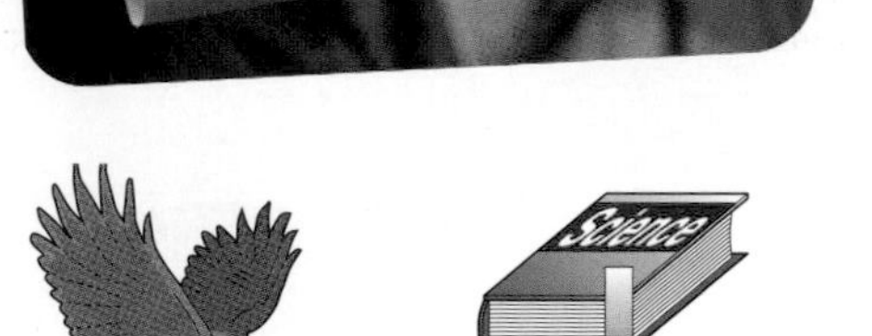

A small bird doesn't weigh much – its **weight** is small, perhaps one-tenth of a newton. Your weight is much greater – perhaps 500 N. 'Weight' is the name we give to the pull of the Earth's **gravity** on us, or on any other object. The Earth is a very large object, and it attracts things to it with the **force of gravity**.

We represent the force of weight by an arrow pointing downwards, because we are attracted downwards, towards the centre of the Earth. If there was a hole all the way to the centre of the Earth and you fell into it, you would be pulled all the way to the bottom.

Investigating a spring

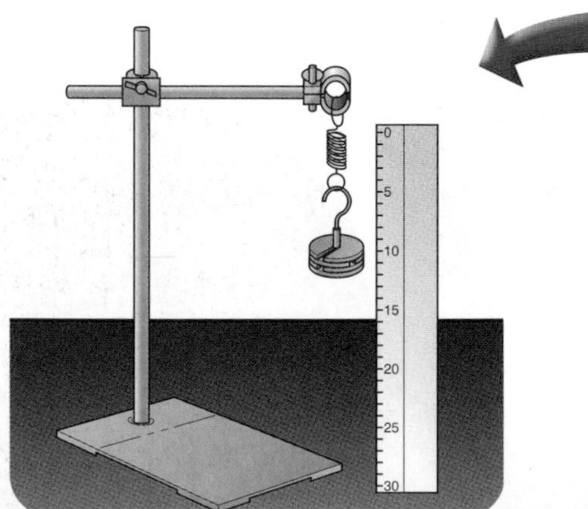

You can investigate the effect of forces on a spring using the apparatus shown. The top end of the spring is fixed firmly. When you hang weights on the end, their weight provides the force to stretch the spring.

When you try this experiment, see if you can answer these questions:

a) What pattern is there in the way the length of the spring changes, as you increase the force stretching it?

b) If your teacher gives you a pebble, how can you use your measurements to find its weight?

c) Why is a spring a good thing to use for making a forcemeter?

Take care! Don't overload your spring or it will be stretched permanently and it won't be any good as a weighing machine.

SAFETY: Take care that heavy weights don't drop on your fingers or toes.

Hooke and springs

Robert Hooke was the first scientist to work out the rule about how springs stretch, in the seventeenth century. He wanted to prove that he had done it, without anyone else actually knowing the rule.

So he wrote an anagram: ceiiinosssttuv. Later, when challenged, he untangled this as: *Ut tensio, sic vis*, which is Latin for 'the extension increases as the force increases'.

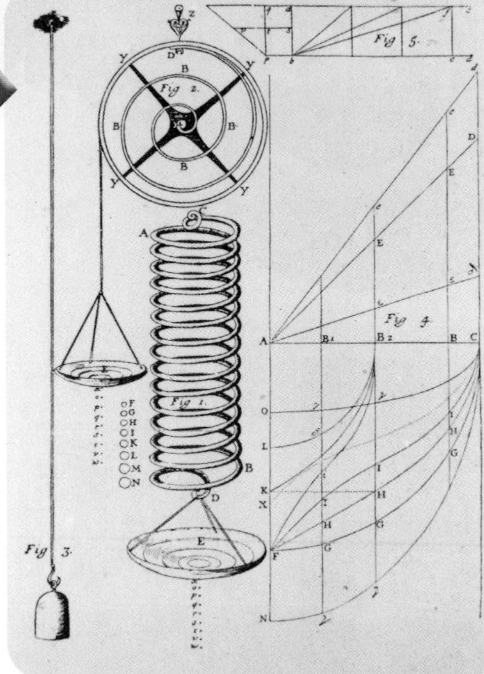

This is Robert Hooke's drawing of his experiment on springs. He was an inventor as well as a scientist, so he investigated spiral springs which he wanted to use in a new type of watch.

Bending a ruler

A ruler is bendy. You can make a weighing machine by clamping one end of a ruler, and hanging things on the other end. The heavier the object, the more the ruler bends.

- You need to devise a way of measuring how much the ruler bends when you add different weights. It will help to make repeat measurements.
- Show your measurements as a graph. Then you can hang another object on the end of the ruler and use your graph to find its weight.

Q2 How would you design a weighing machine like this that you could use to find the weight of small objects?

Your weight is a little less if you climb a mountain – because you are further from the centre of the Earth.

SUMMARY QUESTIONS

1 ☆ Copy these sentences. Complete them by filling in the gaps.
The . . . of an object is the . . . of the Earth's . . . on it.

2 ☆ What units do we measure weight in? Why do we use these units?

3 ☆☆ Why do we use an arrow to represent the weight of an object? Which direction does the arrow point in?

4 ☆☆☆ When you float in water, it is as if you are weightless. Some people imagine that this is because water blocks gravity. Suggest how you could convince them that they are wrong.

LEARN ABOUT

- the difference between mass and weight

Getting started

In a comedy film, Charlie Chaplin is walking down the street. He kicks an old hat that is lying on the ground – and hurts his toe. Someone has hidden a brick under the hat.

Charlie was expecting to kick something with a small **mass**, but the brick has a much larger mass than a hat. A small mass is easy to start moving, but a large mass is much harder.

The mass of an object is measured in **kilograms** (kg). When you buy fruit and vegetables at the market or supermarket, the price is given 'per kilogram'. The more kilograms you buy, the greater the mass you will have to carry home. If you fill the car up with lots of shopping, the driver will notice that it is harder to get going, and also harder to stop – they will have to press harder on the brake.

Q1 It is much easier to catch a fast-moving tennis ball than a cricket ball or hockey ball that is moving at the same speed. Use the idea of 'mass' to explain why.

Thinking about mass

The mass of something tells us about how much **matter** it is made of. A tennis ball has less mass than a cricket ball because it is hollow. The air inside it has very little mass.

Matter is made of tiny particles – atoms – and every atom has mass. Iron atoms have a lot of mass, and they are packed close together. That's why, in the Middle Ages, people chose iron to make their cannon balls.

They didn't make cannon balls out of expanded polystyrene, because the atoms in polystyrene don't have much mass, and they are spread out. And, it hadn't been invented.

My mum says I was a ten pound baby...
...I'm sure I cost more than that!
PHOTOS

Getting confused

Do you know what your mass is? How many kilograms? Your mass is probably more now than when you were five years old. The idea of mass sounds a lot like the idea of weight. We talk about weighing ourselves, but the answer comes out in kilograms, so we have really found our mass. Try to remember these important differences:

- **Mass** in kilograms tells us how much **matter** something is made of.
- **Weight** in newtons is a force; it tells us about the **pull of gravity** on something.

The mass-weight connection

We use forcemeters to measure weight, because weight is a force. Find some objects that have their mass marked on them – for example, a packet of rice.

- Weigh the objects to find their weight.
- Make a table to show the mass and weight of each object, and use it to draw a graph.
- Can you work out the relationship between mass and weight?

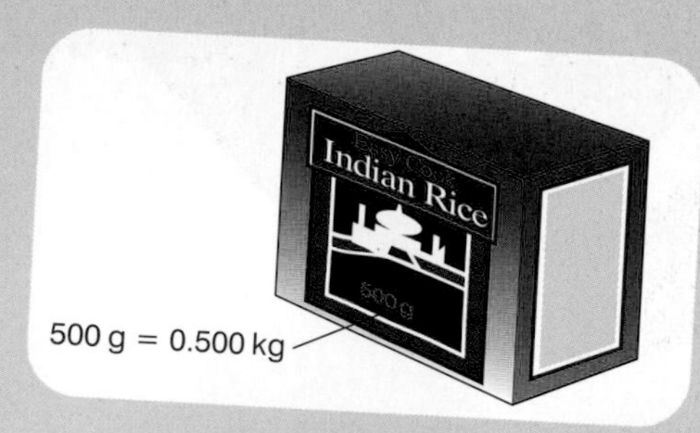

To the Moon

If you went to the Moon, you would find things were very different there compared to here on Earth. You would be able to jump much higher, and throw a ball much farther. This is because the Moon's gravity is much less than the Earth's, and so the weight of everything is less – about one-sixth of its weight on Earth. You would weigh fewer newtons on the Moon.

But that doesn't mean that your mass would be less than on Earth. You would still be made of just as much matter, so your mass would be the same number of kilograms.

The pull of the Moon's gravity is less than the Earth's because it is a much smaller object than the Earth. If you could go far out into empty space, a long way from the Earth or any other planet, you would be completely weightless, but you would still have exactly the same mass as before.

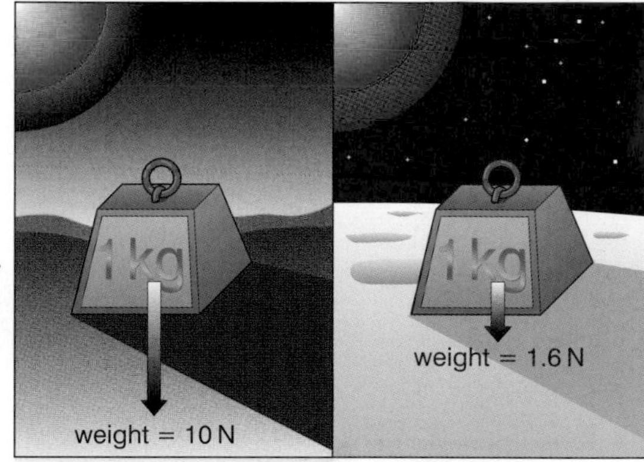

A 1 kg mass has a weight of 10 N on Earth, but only 1.6 N on the Moon

Q2 A girl has a mass of 60 kg. What is her mass on the Moon?

SUMMARY QUESTIONS

1 ☆ Copy the table. Complete it by filling in the gaps.

Mass	the amount of . . . in an object	measured in . . . (kg)
. . .	the	measured in . . . (. . .)

2 ☆ A 1 kg mass has a weight of 10 N on Earth. What is the weight of a 50 kg mass?

3 ☆ A box has a weight of 1000 N on Earth. Draw a diagram of the box, and add a labelled arrow to represent its weight. Label the box with its mass.

4 ☆☆ Jupiter is a giant planet, so its force of gravity is much stronger than the Earth's. How would your weight change if you went to Jupiter? How would your mass change?

5 ☆☆☆ The members of a slimmers' club are thinking of taking a trip to the Moon, because they have heard that people weigh less up there. What advice would you give them?

Try e-mailing these questions to three or four people, including at least one adult.

a) What would you notice if you dropped a stone on the Moon?

b) Why is the Moon's gravity different from the Earth's?

Compare what you find with the results of other people in the class.

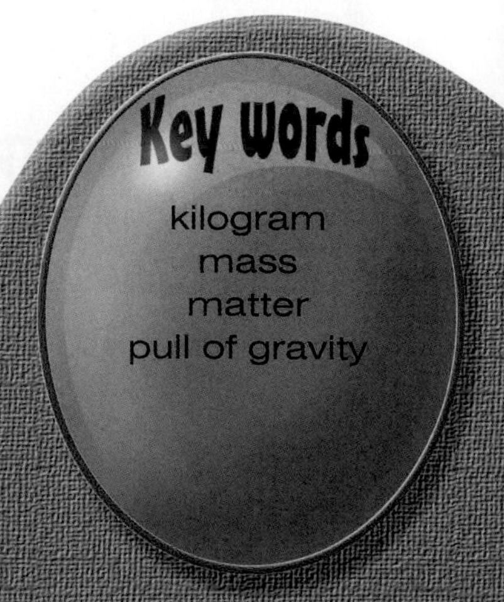

Key words
kilogram
mass
matter
pull of gravity

Floating and sinking

LEARN ABOUT
- forces in water
- balanced forces
- measuring and calculating density

Going under

At the swimming pool, a small child is nervously holding onto the edge. He's sure that, if he lets go, he will sink to the bottom. Up at the deep end, show-offs are diving in from the high board. As they plunge towards the bottom of the pool, the water pushes upwards on them so that they quickly return to the surface. It's very difficult to stay completely underwater (unless you fill your pockets with lead weights). But the nervous boy still thinks that he might sink, and he's sure that the deeper the water, the more easily he would sink.

There are two forces involved in a dive: your weight (caused by the Earth's gravity), and the **upthrust** of the water. These forces change during a dive:

- As you fall through the air, your weight makes you go faster and faster.
- When you are under the water, its upthrust is slightly more than your weight, so it wins out – it pushes you back up to the surface.
- When you reach the surface, there is less of you under water, so the upthrust is less. In fact, the upthrust pushing you upwards equals your weight pulling you downwards.

When two equal forces act in opposite directions like this, they cancel each other out. We say they are **balanced**.

Staying still

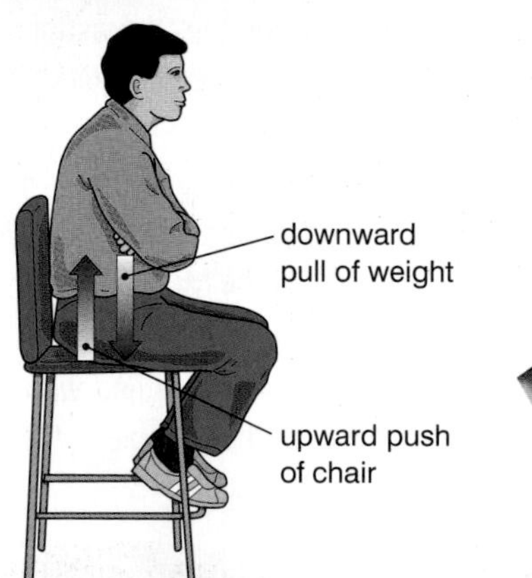

If an object isn't moving, we know that the forces acting on it are balanced. For example, if you sit on a chair, there are two forces acting on you:

- Your weight pulls you downwards.
- In response, the chair pushes upwards.

If the chair wasn't strong enough to produce that upwards push, you would fall through it, and land on the floor.

Q1 Draw a diagram to show the forces which act on a ball lying on the ground. What extra, unbalanced force could make the ball move? Add it to your diagram.

A man who survived the wreck of the Titanic fell into a puddle, knocked himself unconscious and was drowned.

Measuring upthrust

It's tricky to measure the upthrust force. Here's one way to do it:

- Weigh a heavy object, using a forcemeter. This tells you its weight.
- Weigh it again, submerged in water. It weighs less, because the water is pushing upwards on it.
- Find the difference between your two measurements.

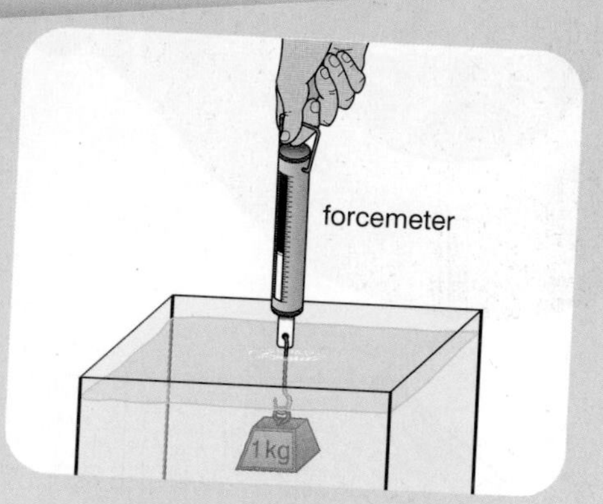

Q2 Explain why this tells you the upthrust on the object. Include a diagram to help your explanation.

Why do we float?

Some things float in water, but others sink. What's the difference? It depends what material things are made of. 'Heavy' materials sink, 'light' materials float. A scientist can predict if a material will float by finding out its **density**. There are three steps in this:

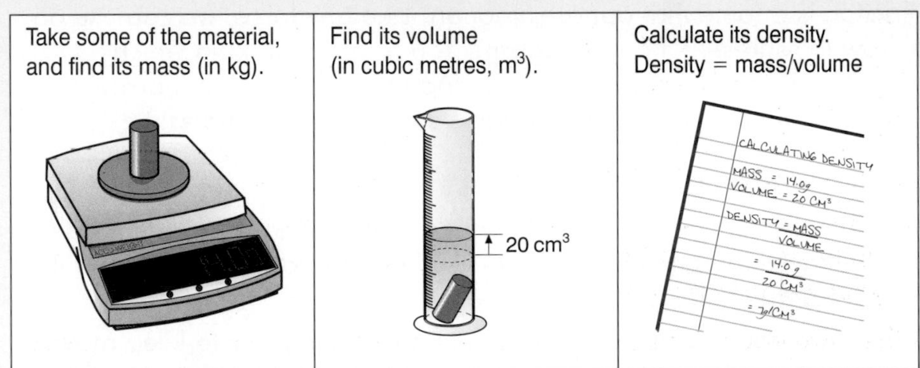

Take some of the material, and find its mass (in kg).
Find its volume (in cubic metres, m³).
20 cm³
Calculate its density. Density = mass/volume
CALCULATING DENSITY
MASS = 14.0g
VOLUME = 20 CM³
DENSITY = MASS / VOLUME
= 14.0 g / 20 CM³

It is better to talk about a 'dense' material than a 'heavy' material. A dense material has a lot of mass squashed into a small volume. If its density is greater than the density of water, it will sink. Fortunately, people are a little less dense than water, so we float. The upthrust of the water is enough to balance our weight.

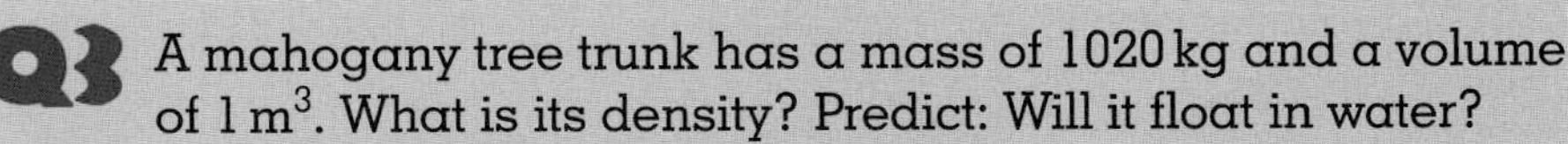

Q3 A mahogany tree trunk has a mass of 1020 kg and a volume of 1 m^3. What is its density? Predict: Will it float in water?

Mercury is a very dense liquid. If the sea was full of mercury, we would float with less than one-tenth of our bodies submerged.

SUMMARY QUESTIONS

1 ☆ A duck floats on the surface of a pond. Draw a diagram to show the two forces which are acting on it. Are the forces balanced or unbalanced?

2 ☆☆ Calculate the density of paraffin wax. A wax block of volume 2.0 m^3 has a mass of 1800 kg. Would the block float in water?

3 ☆☆ A helium balloon will float in the air. There are two ways to explain this.
   a) Use the idea of density to give one explanation.
   b) Use the idea of forces to give another explanation.

All about friction

LEARN ABOUT

- friction, drag and air resistance
- lubrication

Smooth talking

Friction can be a nuisance, but it can also be enormously useful to us.

- Suppose you want to push a heavy object along the ground. The force of **friction** makes this difficult. You can use rollers, or make the ground smoother, to reduce the friction.
- Imagine walking on an ice rink. It's almost impossible, because there's hardly any friction.

You can see that friction is an important force. We make use of it all the time. Think of what you do when you start to run, perhaps at the start of a race. Your foot pushes *backwards* on the ground as you launch yourself *forwards*. You are trying to make your foot go backwards, but friction stops it. If the ground is slippery, you're in trouble. (Even when you are walking, you are making use of friction like this.)

Friction is a force that opposes motion. Like any force, we can use an arrow to represent it on a diagram. You have to think: in which direction is the object moving, or trying to move? Then the arrow is in the opposite direction. The diagrams show some examples.

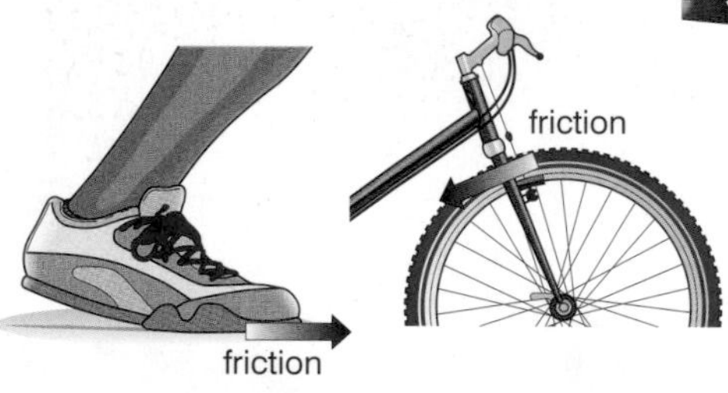

Opposing friction

Friction appears whenever one surface tries to slide over another. The two surfaces rub against each other – they tend to wear away and they may even get hot.

Because friction can make it difficult to move things, or to keep moving, we have to find ways to overcome it. Smooth, polished surfaces are good. Alternatively, we can add a **lubricant**. That's why car owners have to put oil into their car engines from time to time. Then the metal parts can slide smoothly over each other.

Q1 Look at the cartoon above of the children on the slide. What lubricant is at work here? What would it be like without this lubricant?

Investigating friction

Here's one way to find out about friction. Place a block of wood on one end of a plank. Gradually raise that end of the plank. Eventually, the block will slide down to the other end. The greater the angle of slope, the greater the friction between the block and the plank.

Use this idea, or one of your own, to plan an investigation into friction. Try to answer this question:

- What factors affect the amount of friction between two surfaces?

Ask your teacher to check your plan before you carry it out.

Movement through water

Friction isn't the only force that opposes motion. Ships and submarines are slowed down by the force of **drag** as they move through the water. This is partly because they have to push the water aside to get through it, and partly because there is friction as the water rubs past the surface of the boat.

Marine engineers try to overcome this. They design boats to be a good shape for cutting through the water, and they paint the hull with a lubricant. You may have been on a catamaran-style fast ferry. These rise up out of the water when they are moving quickly.

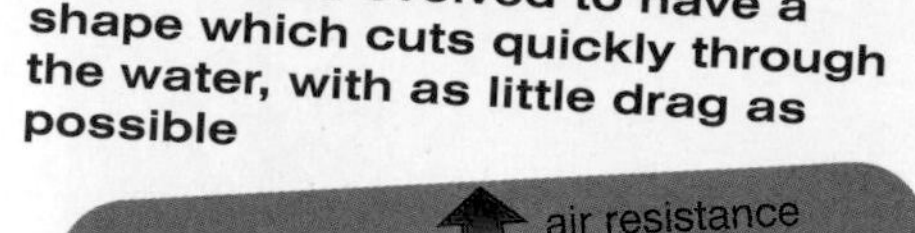

Sharks have evolved to have a shape which cuts quickly through the water, with as little drag as possible

Explain why there is less drag on a fast ferry when it is moving quickly.

Through the air

There is drag in air, too, but it's called **air resistance**. Because air is much less dense than water, there is less drag and it is possible to travel much faster. That's why it's possible to have supersonic aircraft but not supersonic submarines.

Parachutists make use of air resistance. Their chute has a large area to give a lot of resistance, so that they slow down to a safe speed before hitting the ground.

Car designers need to understand air resistance. If they want a car to have a higher top speed, they have a choice: they can give it a more powerful engine, or they can give it a more streamlined shape.

Sketch the outline shapes of two cars. Give one a much more streamlined shape than the other.

SUMMARY QUESTIONS

1 ☆ Copy and complete these sentences by filling in the gaps:
Friction is a force which . . . motion when two . . . try to slide over one another.
Friction can be reduced by using a . . . .

2 ☆☆ Draw a diagram to show a child moving down a slide. Using one colour, draw a labelled arrow to show the direction of her movement. Using a different colour, draw a second arrow to show the force of friction acting on the child.

3 ☆☆☆ Picture a book lying on a table. Imagine that you had a powerful microscope, so that you could see the rough surfaces of the book and the table. Draw a diagram to show what you think this would look like. Explain why this roughness gives rise to friction if you try to slide the book across the table. Draw a second diagram to show how a lubricant could reduce this friction.

Submarines have an outer coating designed to imitate the skin of dolphins, which gives as little drag as possible.

Key words

air resistance
drag
friction
lubricant

7K6 Graphs that tell stories

LEARN ABOUT
- speed and its units
- distance-time graphs

Drivers tend to slow down when they see traffic police at work

Quantity	Units
Distance travelled	metres, kilometres, miles
Time taken	seconds, hours
Speed	m/s, km/h, m.p.h., etc.

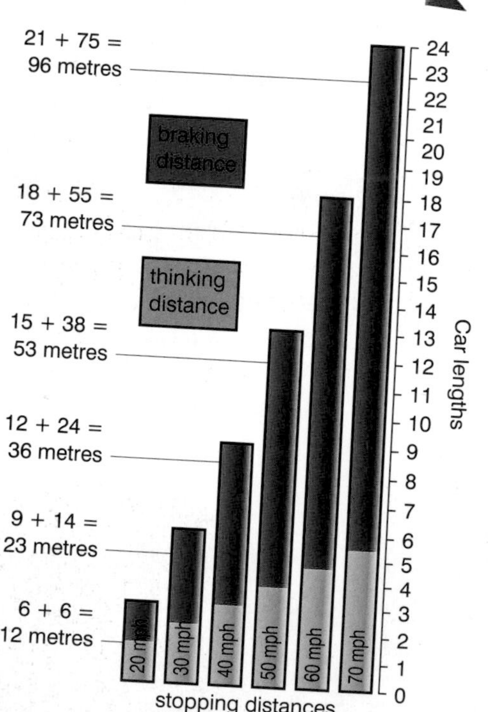

Top speed

What is the fastest you have ever travelled? On motorways in the UK, the highest permitted speed is 70 m.p.h. (112 km/h), though many people drive faster than that. In Germany, there is no motorway speed limit and people often travel at 200 km/h.

A jumbo jet needs to reach 340 km/h before it can take off, and its cruising speed is about 1000 km/h. Spacecraft orbiting the Earth travel at about 8 km every second! That's about 250 times the UK speed limit.

We use different units for **speed**,depending on the units we are using for measuring distance and time.

Q1 Why do you think we write 'm.p.h.' for miles per hour, rather than 'm/h'?

Braking hard

Drivers have to think ahead. They must be ready to stop as they approach a junction, or traffic lights. If they are travelling too fast, they may not be able to stop in time. If you ride a bike, you will know the dangers of not being able to stop in time at a junction.

The chart in the *Highway Code* shows how far a car, moving at different speeds, will travel before it comes to a halt. This is its '**stopping distance**'.

Q2 Use the chart to answer these questions:

a) If a car is travelling at 30 m.p.h., what is its stopping distance?

b) If a car is travelling twice as fast (60 m.p.h.), is its stopping distance twice as much?

Some cars are more difficult to stop than others. People carriers are popular family cars, but they may need a bigger distance to stop in. This is because they have a large mass, and the brakes may not provide a big enough force to stop the car in a short distance. If the driver brakes too hard, the car may skid out of control. That's why drivers have to 'read the road ahead'.

The Great Debate

Every year, there are over 3000 deaths on the UK's roads. Many of those killed and injured are pedestrians or cyclists. The numbers would be reduced if people drove more slowly, so that they could stop in time, or cause less damage when they hit someone.

How could we use our scientific knowledge to reduce the numbers of deaths and injuries on the road?

Going up

The graph shows someone's journey in a lift to the top of a tall building. Make sure you read the labels on the axes of the graph.

The lift started off slowly, then rose at a steady speed for a while. It slowed down as it came to a halt at the top.

What happened half-way up?

From the graph, we can find out various things about the ride in the lift. The building was 100 m high, and the complete journey took 50 s.

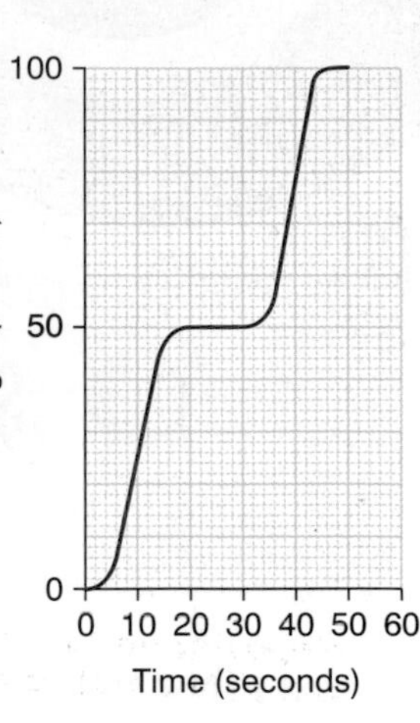

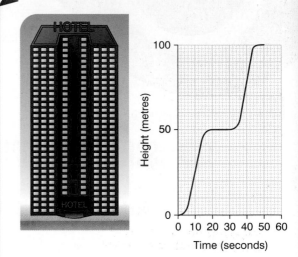

Along the road

The next graph shows this journey:

'I walked along the road, and waited at the bus stop. The bus took me all the way to school without stopping.'

You can see the three parts of the journey on the graph. The line slopes up when I was walking. It is horizontal when I was at the bus stop, not moving. Then it slopes up again; it is steeper, because the bus was faster than my walking.

Graph challenge

- On a piece of paper, draw a **distance-time graph** for a journey. It doesn't need to have accurate figures on it.
- Next, in a small group, put all your graphs on display.
- Then, take it in turns to describe your journeys. Everyone has to guess which is the correct graph.

You will have developed useful skills for interpreting and drawing graphs in your studies of maths.

SUMMARY QUESTIONS

1 ☆ Which of the following is not a unit of speed:

m/s m.p.h. km/h s/km

2 ☆☆ Look at the second graph above. How can you tell the bus didn't stop?

3 ☆☆ Draw a graph to represent this journey:

'I was walking to school. Then I suddenly realised I was going to be late, so I ran all the rest of the way. I had to sit down on the steps when I got there.'

Key words
distance-time graph
speed
stopping distance

 SCIENTIFIC PEOPLE 

Archimedes and Galileo

You probably know the story of Archimedes in his bath. King Hiero had ordered a new gold crown, in the shape of a wreath of leaves. He suspected that the jeweller had cheated him by mixing silver with the gold. Could Archimedes find a way of checking the crown without damaging it?

Archimedes was in his bath when he thought of the solution. As everyone knows, when you get in the bath, the water level rises because your body displaces some of the water. Archimedes, seeing how he could put this to use, leapt from the bath and ran down the street shouting 'Eureka!'. That means 'I have it!'

Here is how the Roman historian Vitruvius described Archimedes' test of the crown.

The solution which occurred when he stepped into his bath and caused it to overflow was to put a weight of gold equal to the crown, and known to be pure, into a bowl which was filled with water to the brim. Then the gold would be removed and the king's crown put in, in its place. An alloy of lighter silver would increase the bulk of the crown and cause the bowl to overflow.

Archimedes was using the fact that gold is denser than silver, so it takes up less space. He found that the new crown was indeed a cheat, and the jeweller was punished.

Galileo lived 19 centuries after Archimedes, but he was able to read about his work. He investigated the force of **upthrust**, and realised he could go one step further than Archimedes. He invented a special type of weighing scales for finding out the amount of silver which had been added to gold. (Most jewellery is made from a mixture of gold and silver.)

The method was to hang a 'gold' object from the scales to weigh it in air. Then it was weighed again, hanging in water. The scales showed a smaller reading, because of the upthrust of the water. If there was more silver in the gold, there would be more upthrust, and so the reading would be smaller. Goldsmiths could quickly check the materials they were working with.

Archimedes and Galileo were both interested in the ideas of science, but they were also great inventors – the technologists of their times.

DANGER! AVOID THESE COMMON ERRORS

In this unit, you have learned about some forces – weight, upthrust, friction and so on. You know that forces can do two things – they can change the way something is **moving**, and they can change the **shape** of something.

If something isn't moving, the forces on it must be balanced. The danger is that we may think that there are no forces at work, because we can't see them. It is important to realise that there may be forces there, but their effects are **cancelling out**.

Floating in water is an example. There are two forces at work, weight and upthrust. They are equal in size but pushing in opposite directions.

Standing on a frozen pond is another example. Your weight pulls you down, and the ice pushes up on you. If the ice isn't strong enough to give the necessary balancing force, you will fall through it.

Key words

technologists
upthrust
weight

UNIT REVIEW

REVIEW QUESTIONS

Understanding and applying concepts

1 The pictures show an experimental rocket, and the forces acting on it. It is designed to carry a heavy load high into the sky.

A: Standing on the ground

B: Just above the ground

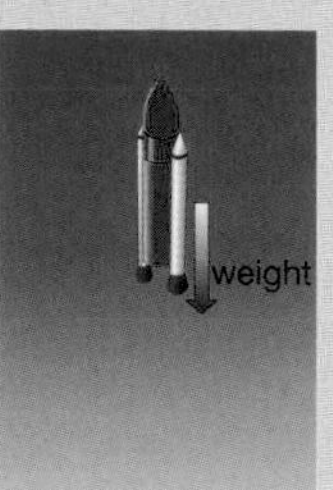

C: High above the ground, all fuel burned

- **a** Look at picture A. Are the forces on the rocket balanced? Will it begin to move?
- **b** Look at Picture B. Use the idea of forces to explain why the rocket rises in the air.
- **c** In Picture C, the rocket has burned all its fuel. Use the idea of forces to predict what will happen next.
- **d** Suggest two ways the rocket could be altered to make it go higher.

2 Benson accompanied his grandmother to the post office. They walked slowly along the road, and then sat on a bench for a few minutes. Then they walked the rest of the way. They had to stand in a queue before they were served.

Draw a graph of distance against time to represent this journey.

Ways with words

3 The newton is the unit of force. It is named after Isaac Newton. Here are two more units, named after scientists.

joule **watt**

Find out about these scientists. What did they study? When did they do their work? What quantities are measured in these units?

Making more of maths

4 We can represent forces by drawing arrows. Each diagram shows the same object, but with different forces acting on it.

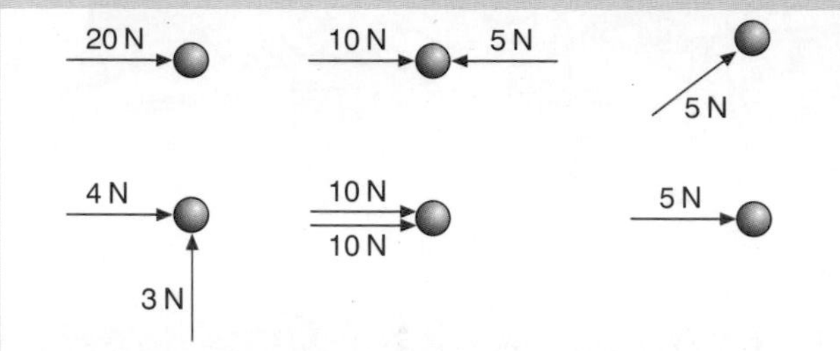

Put the diagrams in pairs. Explain your reasons for pairing them off in this way.

5 Mike and Pete were investigating mass and weight. They had three objects marked with their masses. Mike weighed each one, and shouted out the results. Pete wrote down the results on a scrap of paper.

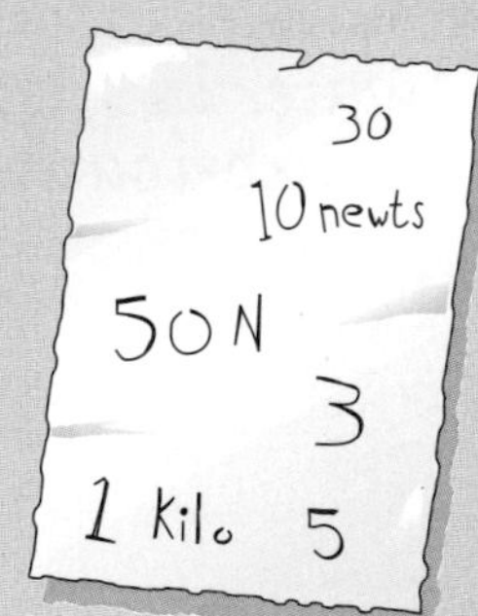

As you can see, Pete didn't do a very good job of this. Can you rescue him by putting the results in a table, with a heading at the top of each column?

Thinking skills

6 These questions are about some objects (A, B, C etc.).

- **a** A and B have the same mass. B has a smaller volume than A. Which is more dense, A or B?
- **b** C has a bigger mass than D. C has a smaller volume than D. How do their densities compare?
- **c** E is denser than F, but it has the same mass. Which has the greater volume, E or F?

Extension questions

7 You can use a newton-meter to weigh a block of wood). The block floats on water. Now if you use the newton-meter, its reading is zero.

Does this mean that the weight of the block is zero when it is floating? Does this experiment prove that gravity doesn't work through water?

8 There is friction when one rough surface tries to slide over another. Imagine that you had a very powerful microscope, and that you could look at the two surfaces. Draw an illustration of what you think you would see.

A lubricant such as oil or water can help to reduce friction. Draw another illustration to show your idea of how this works.

SAT-STYLE QUESTIONS

1 In an experiment to investigate how a spring stretches, Mike and Molly hung weights on the end of the spring and measured its length.

Mike said, 'Every time we increase the weight, the spring will get longer.'

Molly said, 'If we double the weight on the spring, it will get twice as long.'

The table shows their results.

Weight (N)	Length of spring (mm)	Increase in length (mm)
0	40	0
1	46	6
2	52	12
3	58	
4	64	
5	70	

a Study Mike's prediction, and look at the table of results. Was Mike's prediction supported by the results? (1)

b Copy the table, and complete the final column. (1)

c Draw a graph to show the results. (2)

d Use your graph, or the table of results, to find out how much the spring stretched for every newton of load. (1)

e Molly tried to make a better prediction than Mike. What she said is not quite right. Write down a better conclusion, based on the results they obtained. (1)

2 Emil is coming down a water slide.

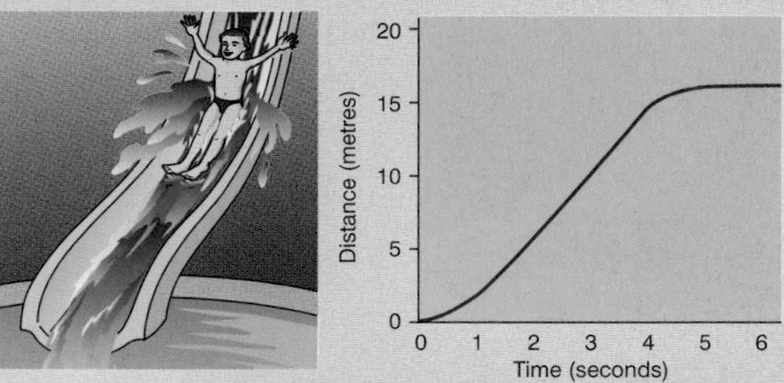

a Name two forces acting on Emil when he is part way down the slide. (2)

b The graph shows Emil's journey down the slide. Describe his motion between 1 and 4 seconds. (1)

c Describe his motion between 5 and 6 seconds. (1)

3 Reese carried out an experiment to investigate floating and sinking. She had a wooden ruler. She weighed a lump of Plasticine, and then attached it to one end of the ruler. Then she floated the ruler in water, and recorded the length of the ruler sticking out of the water.

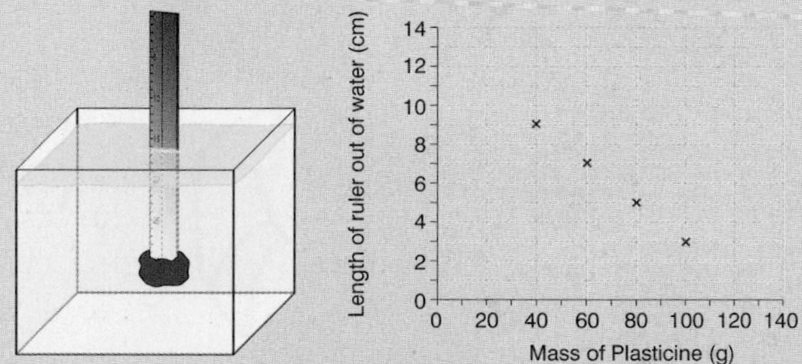

Study the graph of Reese's results.

a Use the graph to predict: what mass of Plasticine is needed to make the ruler sink? (1)

b If there was no Plasticine, what length of the ruler would stick out of the water? (1)

c Put these materials in order, starting with the most dense:

water, wood, Plasticine. (3)

d Reese says, 'As the ruler gets heavier, the upthrust of the water gets less, so eventually the ruler sinks.' Explain why Reese is wrong. (2)

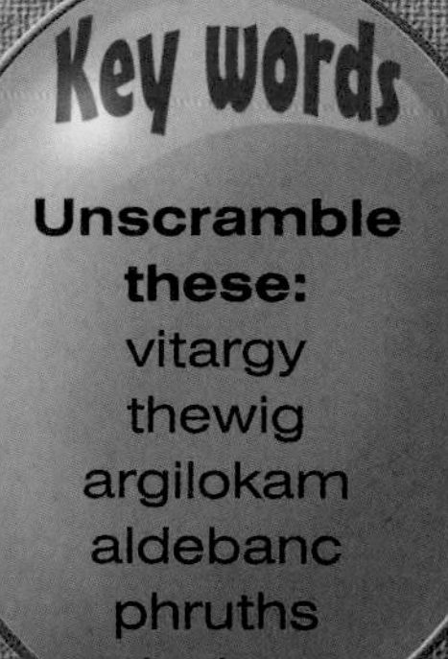

Key words
Unscramble these:
vitargy
thewig
argilokam
aldebanc
phruths
dyehns

7L The solar system – and beyond

Coming soon

What's it all about?

Space – it's all around us and it's vast. You could fly off at the speed of light and, even in a million lifetimes, you wouldn't reach the end of it.

Today we know that the Earth and the other planets travel around our star, the Sun. The solar system is just one tiny corner of an ordinary galaxy. In the Middle Ages, however, they had a very different idea. They thought that the Earth was at the centre of everything, with the Sun, Moon and planets travelling around us. They thought the stars were just beyond Jupiter, the most distant planet they knew of.

In this unit, you will learn about the scientific explanations behind our observations of the solar system, and a little of what lies beyond.

What do you remember?

You already know about:

- the Earth, the Sun and the Moon.
- how we see things.
- how shadows are formed.

1 What shape are the Sun, Earth and Moon?

2 Which is biggest?

Earth **Moon** **Jupiter** **Sun**

Which is smallest?

Earth **Moon** **Jupiter** **Sun**

3 Why does the Sun appear to move across the sky every day?

4 How long does it take the Earth to spin once?

1 hour **1 day** **1 month** **1 year**

How long does it take the Earth to orbit the Sun?

1 hour **1 day** **1 month** **1 year**

5 Describe how shadows change during the course of a day.

Observing and explaining

QUESTIONS

Some people have funny ideas about space! In science, we **observe** things and we try to **explain** them. Sometimes our observations mislead us, and we come up with the wrong explanations.

Look at the amateur astronomers above. Some of their observations are incorrect, and some of their explanations are really terrible.

a) Can you find anyone to agree with?

b) Can you put the others right?

7L1 Light from the Sun

Learn about

- the luminous Sun

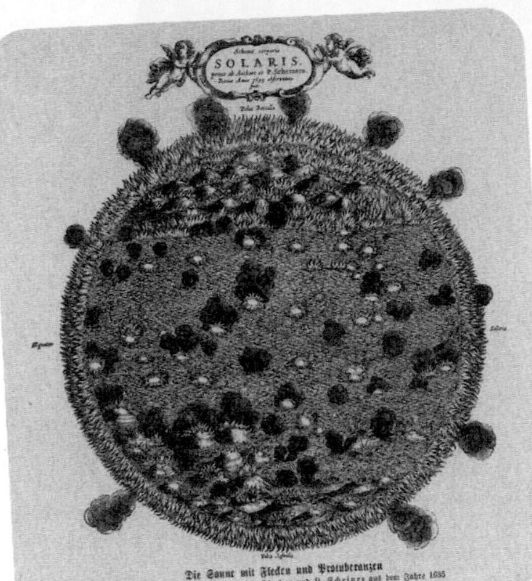

In Victorian times, scientists tried to understand how the Sun could continue to 'burn' for millions of years. They thought it might be made of burning coal. Others thought it might be covered with volcanoes, as shown in this picture. Now we know that the Sun doesn't 'burn' at all. It releases energy by converting hydrogen atoms into helium atoms.

The Sun

The Sun is our star. We get heat and light from the Sun. This keeps the Earth at a comfortable temperature, suitable for life.

The Sun is a boiling, roiling sphere of hot gas, mostly hydrogen and helium. It is a **luminous** object, and without it, the Earth would be a cold, dark lump of rock, drifting in space.

The rays of the Sun's light travel through empty space to reach the Earth, 150 million kilometres away. They take about 8 minutes to get here. It takes the Sun's rays much longer – almost 6 hours – to reach Pluto, the most distant planet in the solar system.

Daytime and night-time

When our side of the Earth faces the Sun, it's daytime and the temperature rises. When the Earth turns so that we are facing away from the Sun, it's night-time. Heat radiates out into space and the temperature drops.

It's fortunate for us that the Earth spins. Imagine living on the side of the Earth always facing the Sun. It would get very hot, much hotter than a hot tropical day. If you lived on the side that was permanently dark, it would be very, very cold – more than 200 degrees below freezing.

Seeing the Sun

It is exceedingly dangerous to try to look directly at the Sun. You could permanently damage your eyes – you could even blind yourself. Fortunately, we have an automatic reflex which makes us look away from the bright Sun.

- The picture shows a safe way to look at the Sun. Your teacher will set this up for you. If you are lucky, you may be able to see sunspots – cool patches on the Sun's surface.

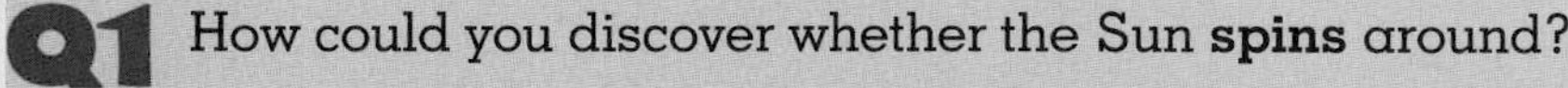

Q1 How could you discover whether the Sun **spins** around?

SAFETY: Never look directly at the Sun, either with the naked eye or through binoculars or a telescope; this could result in eye damage or blindness.

Q2 In which direction does the Sun rise? In which direction does it set?

Your answers will help you to say in which direction the Earth spins on its axis.

The temperature of the Sun's surface is about 5500 °C – that's hot! However it is much hotter inside, about 14 million degrees!

Seeing stars

Stars are powerful sources of light. They come in different colours. The coolest ones are dull red. Others, like the Sun, are hotter and glow bright yellow. Others are hotter still, and give out a bluish-white light. You might be able to spot stars of different colours in the night sky.

When the Moon is full, it looks quite bright, but don't be deceived! Full moonlight is only about one-millionth of the brightness of full sunlight.

The Moon is cold and rocky. It is a bit colder than the Earth. Unlike the Sun, it does not give out its own light.

We see the Moon because it **reflects** sunlight towards us. Rays of light from the Sun bounce off the Moon's surface and travel into our eyes.

(You see this book in just the same way. Look around you. Light rays are falling on the book, and some of them reflect into your eyes.)

Sun's light rays go in all directions

Sun's rays reflected by Moon

this reflected ray reaches Earth

Q3 Draw a diagram to show how light from a lamp can help you read a book.

Coloured planets

Why do the planets have different colours? The Earth is blue and Mars is red, but they are not hot, glowing objects like the Sun. Instead, they reflect the Sun's light, and we see the reflected light. The Earth's blue colour comes from its sky, reflected in its oceans, while Mars is covered in rusty red rocks.

Q4 Pluto is a small planet, which is far from the Sun. Give two reasons why it is very difficult to see Pluto.

Gruesome science

We have a natural reflex that stops us looking directly at the Sun. Some illegal drugs stop this reflex from working, and people have gone blind as a result.

SUMMARY QUESTIONS

1 ☆ Copy these sentences. Complete them by filling in the gaps.

The Sun is a . . . . We see the Sun because it is a source of . . . .

The Moon and planets do not give out their own light; they are not . . . . We see them because they . . . light from the Sun.

LEARN ABOUT
- the Moon's orbit
- phases of the Moon

The Moon: our neighbour

Have you ever looked at the Moon through binoculars or a telescope? You might see mountain ranges and giant craters. You might also see flat areas, known as 'seas', though they are as dry as dust. The Moon may look flat, but remember that you are looking at a giant ball of rock.

Some people imagine that you can only see the Moon at night. In fact, you can often see it during the daytime, too. It looks pale against the blue of the sky, and by midday the sky is too bright to see the Moon.

Moon watching

If you keep an eye on the Moon, you can make some useful observations. In this section, you will learn about these observations and how to explain them.

- **First observation**: The Moon rises in the east and sets in the west, just like the Sun, and it follows a similar path across the sky.
- **Explanation**: Each day, the Earth rotates, from west to east, so that the Moon *appears* to move from east to west.
- **Second observation**: Each day, the Moon rises a little later than the day before – roughly 50 minutes later. Suppose you observe the Moon rising at 6 p.m. one day. The next evening, it will rise shortly before 7 p.m. After about a month, it will rise again at 6 p.m.
- **Explanation**: The Moon orbits the Earth, quite slowly. It takes about 28 days to complete one orbit and return to the same place in the sky. It travels from west to east.

We say that the Moon is the Earth's **satellite**. A satellite is a smaller object travelling around a larger object. The Moon moves steadily along its **orbit**, at a distance of about 400 000 km from the Earth.

If you observe the Moon at the same time each night, you will see that its position in the sky changes. This is because it is orbiting the Earth.

Q1 The Earth is a satellite. What object does it travel around?

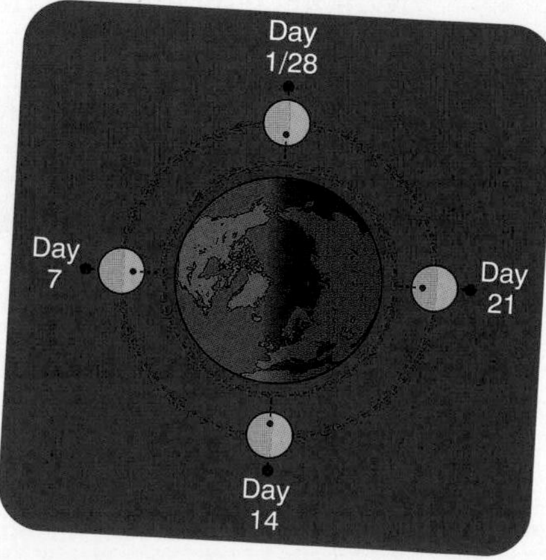

The Moon orbits the Earth every 28 days or so. It also turns on its axis once every 28 days, so that it always has the same side facing the Earth.

Phases of the Moon

There is a third observation we have to explain. The *shape* of the Moon changes during a month. Sometimes we see a round, full Moon; sometimes we see a half Moon. Sometimes, when the Moon is 'new', we see a thin crescent Moon, close to the horizon at sunset. These are the **phases** of the Moon.

The Moon is cold – a few degrees colder than the Earth, because it has no atmosphere to keep it warm. It does not give out its own light, so we describe it as **non-luminous**. We see it because it reflects rays of sunlight. The diagram shows how the Sun's rays light up one side of the Moon, and are reflected towards the Earth.

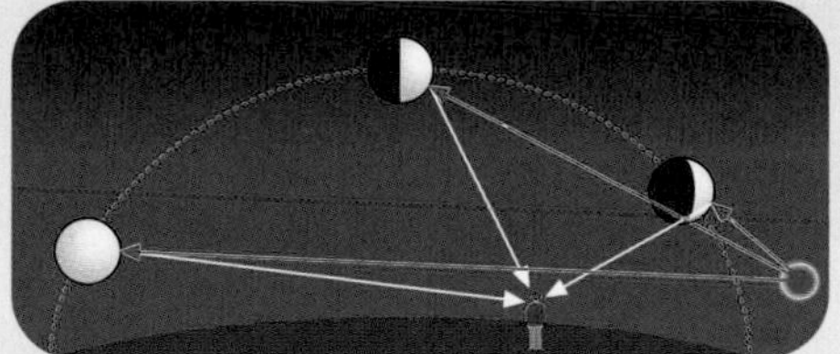

We see the Moon because it reflects sunlight. When the Moon is opposite the Sun in our sky, we see a full Moon. When it is in the same direction as the Sun, we see only the crescent-shaped edge of the side that is illuminated.

Bird's eye view

We are used to seeing the Moon from the Earth. However, to understand our observations completely, we need to leave the Earth and look down on it from above. The diagram shows what we could see from high above the North Pole:

- The Earth turns on its axis, once each day.
- The Moon orbits the Earth, once each month.
- The Earth and Moon each have one side lit up by the Sun.

You have to imagine standing on the Earth and looking towards the Moon. What would you see at each of its positions? The small diagrams in boxes show the views you would get as the Moon travels round the Earth.

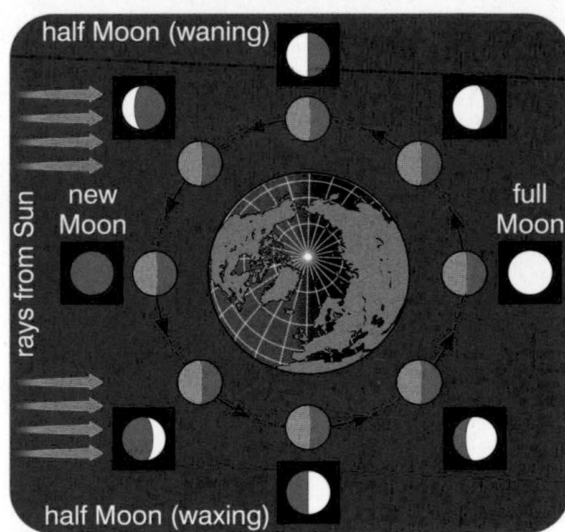

The Earth and Moon, seen from above. The square boxes show the phase of the Moon at each position around its orbit.

Travel to the Moon

Astronauts have visited the Moon, and looked back at the Earth. They saw 'phases of the Earth', just as we see phases of the Moon.

- Imagine that you were visiting the Moon, and you met some puzzled Moon-creatures. You have to explain to them that your home planet doesn't really change shape.
- Devise a way of showing your explanation. You could use diagrams, or make a model using balls of different sizes to represent the Sun, Earth and Moon.

SUMMARY QUESTIONS

1 ☆ Copy these sentences. Complete them by filling in the gaps.
The Moon is non-luminous; we see it by . . . light.
The Moon travels around the Earth; it is our . . . .
We see different . . . of the Moon, according to its position in its . . . .

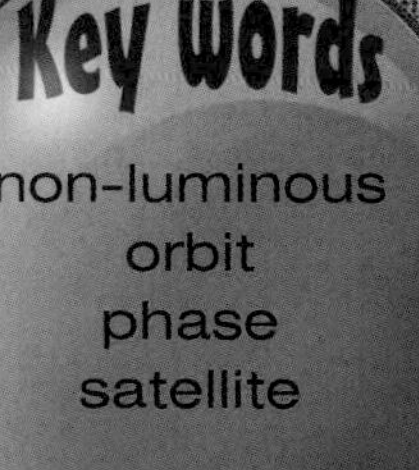

Key words
non-luminous
orbit
phase
satellite

Four seasons – or two?

LEARN ABOUT
- the Earth's tilted axis
- why we have seasons

Seasons

In the UK, we experience *four* **seasons** in the year: spring, summer, autumn, winter. In summer, the days are long and the Sun rises high in the sky. In winter, the days are much shorter and the midday Sun is low in the sky.

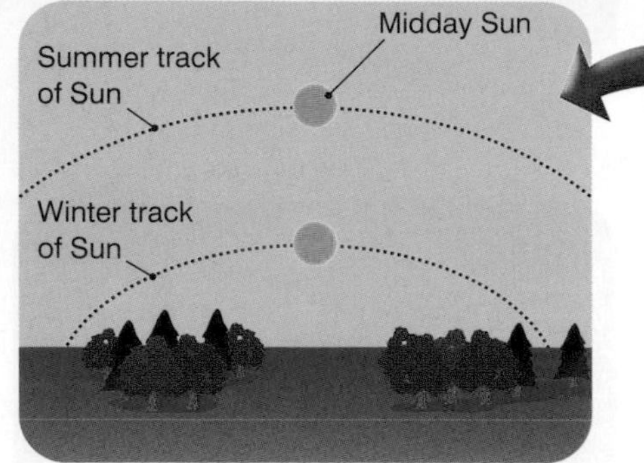

Not everyone experiences four seasons in the year. If you lived in the tropics, you would probably have *two* seasons: wet and dry.

Around the Sun

To understand why we have seasons, we have to think about how the Earth moves around the Sun. It takes $365\frac{1}{4}$ days to complete one **orbit** of the Sun – that's a year.

The Earth spins on its **axis**. Its axis is **tilted**, and this has an important effect. During summer in the UK, the northern hemisphere is tilted towards the Sun. This means that the Sun's path is high in the sky, and the days are longer.

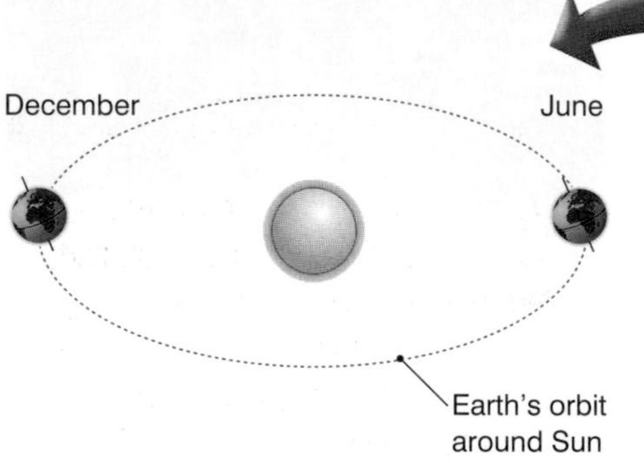

During the winter, the Earth has travelled round to the other end of its orbit. Its axis is still tilted in the same direction, but now our hemisphere is tilted away from the Sun. The Sun stays low in the sky, and days are short.

Q1 Which hemisphere is tilted towards the Sun in December?

In winter, we are tilted away from the Sun. In summer, we are tilted towards the Sun. In June, the Arctic remains in daylight as the Earth turns. It becomes 'the land of the midnight Sun'.

Sloping rays

There are two reasons why it's colder in winter than in summer.

Firstly, in winter, the Sun is in the sky for a shorter time, so our part of the Earth has less time to warm up. Nights are long, and this gives plenty of time for heat to escape into space.

Secondly, in winter, the Sun is low in the sky. From the following diagram, you can see that its rays are spread out over a larger area. (If you have ever been in the tropics, you will know how it feels to have the Sun high overhead. Its rays are concentrated on a smaller area, so it gets much hotter.)

The tilt of the Earth has a major effect on our **climate**. You will learn more about what affects our climate in Geography.

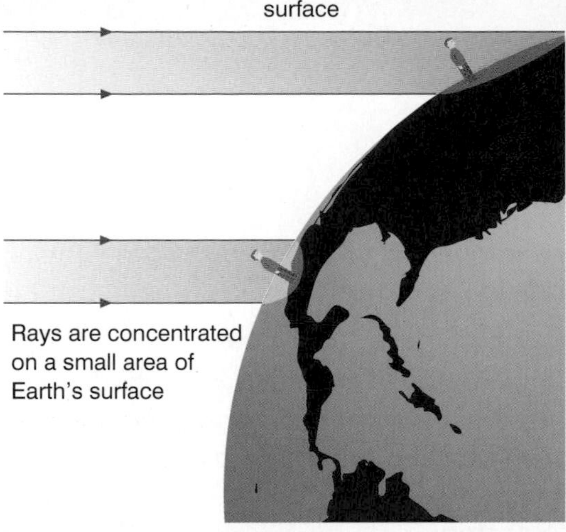

In northern latitudes, the Sun's rays are oblique, the person has a long shadow

In the tropics, the Sun's rays are almost vertical, the shadows are short

Gruesome science

A year on Mars is longer than an Earth year, so its seasons are longer. In winter, the temperature at the poles can drop to –130 °C; that's cold!

Q2 Explain why your shadow is shorter at midday in the summer than in the winter.

You can find graphs like this in holiday brochures. They compare a resort's temperature and hours of sunshine with those of London. They don't show that, in the summer, London has longer days and shorter nights than a resort that is further south – even if it is less sunny.

ICT CHALLENGE

Make a model system to represent the Sun and the Earth. Use light and temperature sensors to make measurements at different points on the surface of your model Earth. Can you use your model to explain why it's hotter in summer than in winter, and why it's hotter in the tropics than near the poles?

SUMMARY QUESTIONS

1 ☆ Copy these sentences. Complete them by filling in the gaps.

The Earth travels in its … around the Sun. Its … is tilted.

In … our part of the world is tilted towards the Sun. In …, it is tilted away from the Sun.

2 ☆☆ In summer, the midday Sun is higher in the sky than in winter.
a) How does this affect the length of shadows?
b) Why does this make the temperature higher?
Draw diagrams to support your answers.

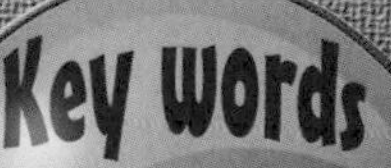

Key words

axis
climate
orbit
seasons
tilted

LEARN ABOUT
- eclipses of the Sun and Moon

Eclipses of the Sun

Eclipses of the Sun occur quite frequently, up to three times a year. However, you are not very likely to see one. You have to be in just the right place on the Earth.

This is what you see: at first, the Sun looks normal – a bright disc in the sky. Gradually, it becomes dimmer. If you look through special filters, you see that its surface has been blocked off. Eventually, it is completely blocked off and the sky goes dark for just a few minutes. Then the Sun slowly returns to normal.

These young people are waiting for an eclipse of the Sun to happen. They are wearing glasses with special filters to protect their eyes from the Sun's rays.

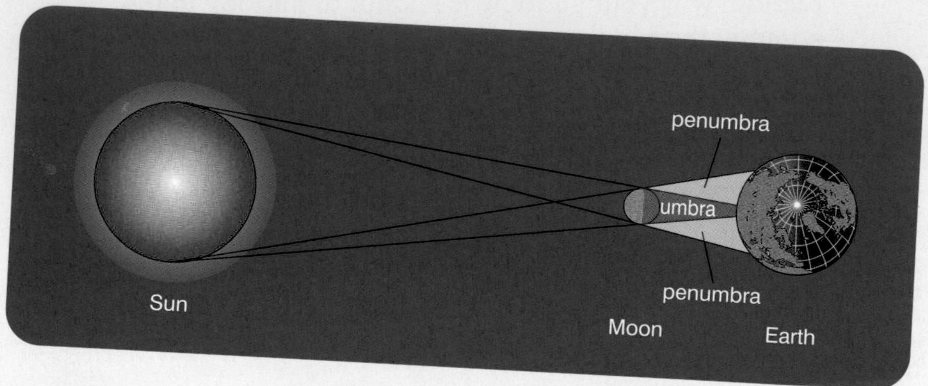

An eclipse of the Sun (a **solar eclipse**) happens when the Moon passes directly between the Sun and the Earth. The Moon's shadow falls on the Earth, and the Sun's light is blocked off for a few minutes.

The shadows of the Moon and the Earth are in two parts:

- the full shadow (the **umbra**), where there are no rays from the Sun,
- the partial shadow (the **penumbra**), where some of the Sun's rays are blocked off.

During an eclipse of the Sun, the Moon's umbra just reaches the surface of the Earth. If you stand at this point, you will see a total eclipse of the Sun. If you stand where the Moon's penumbra touches the Earth, you will see a partial eclipse. A chunk of the Sun is blocked off by the Moon.

Q1 Imagine that you were standing on the Moon, looking at the Earth, when there was an eclipse of the Sun. What would you notice about the Earth? Would it become completely dark?

Gruesome science

During an eclipse of the Sun in 1999, some people insisted that pregnant women should stay indoors because they feared 'harmful rays' could affect an unborn child.

Eclipses of the Moon

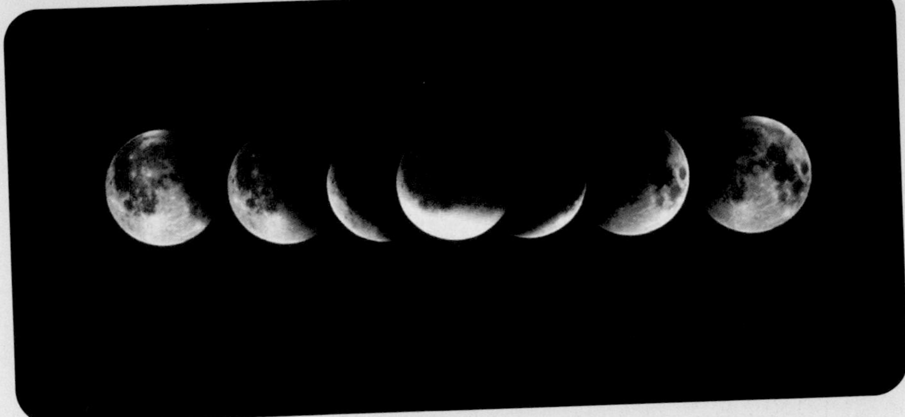

These photos show the Moon as it passes through the Earth's shadow during an eclipse

Every now and then – perhaps once or twice a year – there is an eclipse of the Moon. The full Moon gradually darkens until it becomes very dim; then it gradually lightens up again.

This happens when the Moon's orbit takes it into the Earth's shadow, so that it is no longer lit up by the Sun. If you are anywhere on the dark side of the Earth, you will see the eclipse of the Moon (a **lunar eclipse**).

The Moon travels behind the Earth every month, but we don't have an eclipse every month. This is because the orbit of the Moon is tilted slightly, so it usually passes above or below the Earth's shadow.

A lunar eclipse happens when the Moon passes through the Earth's shadow

Q2 Why do we only see an eclipse of the Moon at night?

Eclipse explanations

- When an eclipse of the Moon happens, many people can see it.
- When there is a total eclipse of the Sun, fewer people can see it. Many people travel to be somewhere on the track of the eclipse.
  - **a)** Why is this? Make a model to answer this question. You could use suitable balls to represent the Earth and the Moon. What will you use for the Sun?
  - **b)** Script a conversation with a younger friend in which you explain why eclipses occur, and why you are less likely to see a solar eclipse than a lunar eclipse.

During an eclipse, the Moon never goes completely dark. Some light from the Sun is bent by the Earth's atmosphere so that it reaches the Moon, colouring it deep red.

SUMMARY QUESTIONS

1 ⭑ Copy these sentences. Complete them by filling in the gaps.
The Moon is eclipsed when it travels into the Earth's . . . .
A total . . . of the Sun occurs when the Moon's . . . falls on the Earth.

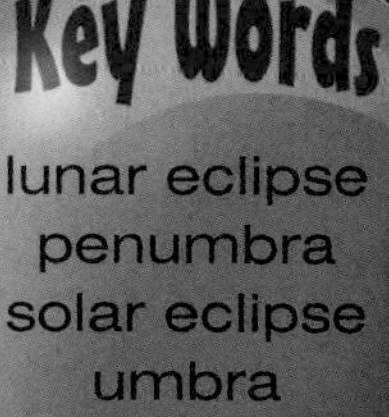

Key words

lunar eclipse
penumbra
solar eclipse
umbra

Solar system

7L5

LEARN ABOUT
- the objects that make up the solar system
- the composition of the planets and their atmospheres

Journey into space

Strap yourself in; make sure the oxygen supply is working, ready for launch. . . . We have lift-off! You're off on a journey of discovery, exploring the solar system.

Look out of the window. What do you see? As you go higher, the blue sky is getting darker. Soon the sky is almost black. It's the middle of the day, and the sunlit Earth looks blue down below, but you can see stars above. What's going on?

You are travelling upwards through the Earth's **atmosphere**, and it's getting thinner and thinner. The atmosphere is the layer of gas around any planet. We need our atmosphere because it's the air we breathe. 10 km up, you wouldn't be able to breathe outside. That's why jet airliners must be pressurised inside. Beyond the Earth's atmosphere, you are out in space. Keep a look out for planets.

Head for the Sun

Imagine you are 400 000 km from Earth, and flying past the Moon. The closer you get to the Sun, the hotter you get. The planets close to the Sun are hot, too.

- Mercury is closest. Its average temperature is 120 °C.
- Venus is farther out, but hotter – a scalding 460 °C! It has a dense atmosphere of carbon dioxide which holds the heat in.

Out past Mars

Mars is farther than Earth from the Sun, so its average temperature is lower. NASA plans to build a base on Mars, the first space station on another planet. Astronauts living there will have to wrap up well!

Mars is the next planet beyond Earth, as you travel out from the Sun. It looks red because its surface is covered with reddish sand. It has a very thin atmosphere, made mostly of carbon dioxide. Mars is the last of the rocky planets.

Take care as you travel through the asteroid belt. An **asteroid** is a lump of rock in space, and many thousands of them lie in the asteroid belt between Mars and Jupiter.

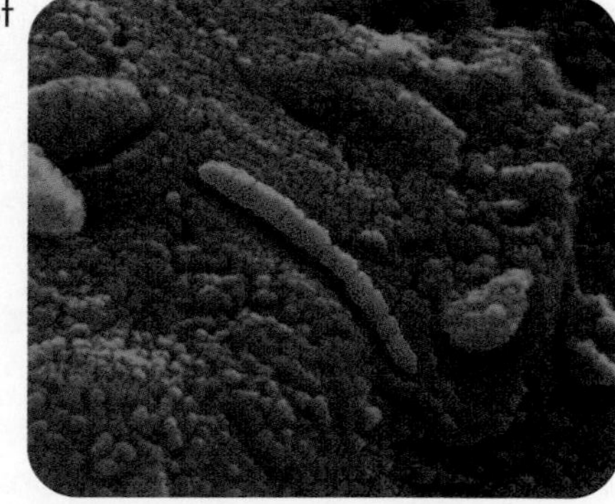

These blobby objects were found in a rock from Mars. Could they be fossilised bacteria? Does this prove that there was once life on Mars?

Q1 How many rocky planets are there in the solar system?

The gas giants

Jupiter and Saturn are two gas giant planets. They are made mostly of liquid hydrogen, but each has a core of solid rock, rather like the Earth. It's as if the Earth was trapped inside a thick, frozen atmosphere of hydrogen.

It's cold where these planets orbit, far from the Sun. That's why gases such as hydrogen and nitrogen are liquid or even solid here.

Beyond these gas giants are three more planets: Uranus, Neptune and Pluto. They are made of water, methane and carbon dioxide, all frozen solid.

Jupiter is famous for its Great Red Spot, a giant storm which has been raging in its atmosphere for hundreds of years

Many moons, cool comets

There are two types of satellite:

- **Natural satellites** are natural objects, such as our Moon; other planets also have moons orbiting them – Saturn holds the record at present, with over 30 known moons.
- **Artificial satellites** are spacecraft we have sent into orbit around the Earth, such as the ones that broadcast satellite TV programmes, and others that carry space telescopes.

Every now and then, a **comet** appears in the sky. It may be visible for a few days. You should see its long tail, pointing away from the Sun.

Planets have orbits that are almost circular. A comet's orbit is elongated – it is an ellipse.

A comet is a ball of dust and ice. As its orbit brings it close to the Sun, it starts to thaw. Material evaporates into space to make the tail. When it has passed the Sun and is disappearing back into the cold depths of the solar system, it refreezes.

This is not a giant pizza. It's Io, one of Jupiter's moons. It orbits Jupiter in less than two days.

Is a comet a satellite? Explain your answer.

Choose one of the following:

- moons
- asteroids
- comets

Make an electronic scrapbook of photographs, collected from the Internet or from CD ROMs. You could scan some photos from books. Write a caption for each of your images. You could use PowerPoint to turn your scrapbook into a slideshow.

SUMMARY QUESTIONS

1 ☆ Copy these sentences. Complete them by filling in the gaps.
The Moon is a natural ... of the Earth.
The ... of a planet is almost circular; a ... follows a more elongated path.
We use ... and ... to find out more about the solar system.

2 ☆☆ a) Name the four rocky planets.
b) Name two gas giant planets.

3 ☆☆ Why would it be difficult for people to live: a) on Mars,
b) on Jupiter?

Beyond the solar system

LEARN ABOUT
- the Sun and other stars
- the night sky

Different religions have different stories to explain how the Universe was created.

The sky at night

There are billions of billions of stars in the Universe. We can only see a few hundreds with the naked eye, but telescopes reveal many more. On a clear night, try looking up at the stars. Think about these questions.

- What is a star?
- Why can't we see the stars during the day?
- Just where do you imagine the stars are?
- Can you see any patterns in how the stars are arranged?

The Hubble space telescope took this picture of some of the most distant galaxies (clusters of stars) in the Universe. It shows them as they were formed, not long after the Universe came into existence.

Seeing stars

The Sun is a star. We know this because, when astronomers study the light of stars, they find it is the same as sunlight. There are billions and billions of stars, and each one is a glowing ball of hot gas, like the Sun.

At night, the stars are distant, twinkling specks of light. If you step out of a brightly lit room, it will take a while for your eyes to adapt to the darkness so that you can see the stars. During the daytime, our sky is brightly lit up by the light from the Sun. Starlight is too faint to be seen against this background. At dusk, the sunlight fades and the brightest stars begin to appear.

It is our **atmosphere** that scatters sunlight and makes the sky blue. If you travel above the atmosphere, the sky is black, even during the daytime.

A close look at the hot surface of a star – the Sun

Q1 Explain why streetlights make it difficult for us to see the stars.

Going around

If you watch the stars at night, you may notice that their positions gradually change. They move across the sky at a steady rate, just as the Sun does during the day – and for the same reason. It's because the Earth is turning. The photo shows how the stars move during a period of 75 minutes.

You may be familiar with the patterns of some **constellations,** i.e. groups of stars that look as if they are close together. In fact, one star may be much farther away than its neighbour. As the year passes by, we see different constellations. This is because the Earth is moving around its orbit, and we get a different view of the sky at night.

Knowing the constellations can be useful for finding your way around. People have **navigated** by the stars for thousands of years. Some birds fly at night, guided by the stars.

Q2 Draw a diagram to show why we see different stars in the winter than in the summer.

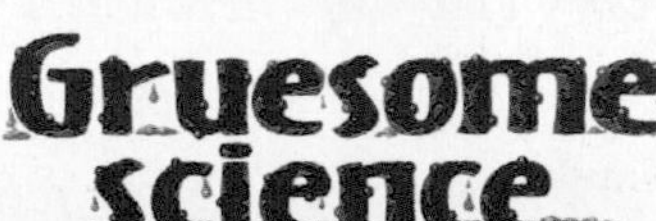

In 1600, an Italian monk called Giordano Bruno was burned at the stake because he claimed that other planets, beyond the solar system, might be home to intelligent beings.

Far out

- This picture was drawn in the fifteenth century. The person who drew it thought the Earth was at the centre of the Universe. The Sun, Moon, planets and stars orbit the Earth.
- Study the picture. The words are in Latin, but you can probably work it out.
  a) Where is the Moon (*Lune*)?
  b) Where is the Sun (*Sol*)?
  c) Is the order of the planets correct?
  d) Where are the stars?
  e) Try to explain why it was reasonable for people to imagine that the Universe was like this.

SUMMARY QUESTIONS

1 ☆ Copy these sentences. Complete them by filling in the gaps.
We see . . . because they reflect sunlight; . . . produce their own light. Light from the . . . makes it impossible to see the stars during the . . .. The stars can be seen to move across the sky at . . . because the . . . is rotating.

2 ☆☆ If you visit the Moon, you will discover that the sky is black during the daytime, and you can see stars. Explain why this is.

Key words
atmosphere
constellation
navigate

SCIENTIFIC PEOPLE

Eclipses now

Francisco Diego is an astronomer from Mexico. He travels the world to see solar eclipses, and to study them. Astronomers can learn a lot more about the Sun during an eclipse, because its intense radiation is blocked off by the Moon.

'To witness a total solar eclipse is a unique experience in your life. The day of a total solar eclipse starts the same as any other day, but you will be waiting for the event.

The Moon and the Sun look the same size in the sky. In fact, the Sun is 400 times as big as the Moon, but it is 400 times as far away. That's why the Moon exactly blocks the Sun during a total eclipse.

Exactly at the predicted time, the Moon will meet the Sun. For some time, you will not notice anything happening around you. Half an hour later, looking at the Sun through your safety filters, you see that more than half the Sun is covered. Then you notice changes. The Sun is not hot enough any more. The landscape takes on a silvery appearance – something is really happening.

Towards the west, the dark shadow of the Moon is rushing towards you at twice the speed of sound, or even faster. Now only a thin crescent of the Sun is left. The darkness increases minute by minute, and you can see planets appear in the sky near the Sun. Then you see the shadow of the Moon, almost on top of you.

This is the diamond ring effect which appears when there is only a tiny part of the Sun which can still be seen beyond the Moon

Looking at the Sun, you see the magical Diamond Ring effect. When it is safe to remove your filters, you see the Sun's beautiful corona. You are inside the shadow of the Moon, and you see twilight around you in all directions. What you see, you will never forget – the solar corona, floating away from the Sun, all white, beautiful in the deep blue sky.'

SAFETY: Never look directly at the Sun, either with the naked eye or through binoculars or a telescope; this could result in eye damage or blindness.

IDEAS AND EVIDENCE

An eclipse then

'On Wednesday, when two nights remained to the completion of the month Jumada, two hours after daybreak, the sun was eclipsed totally. There was darkness and the birds fell whilst flying. The astrologers claimed that one-sixth of the Sun should have remained uneclipsed but nothing of it did so. The Sun reappeared after four hours and a fraction. The eclipse was not in the whole of the Sun in places other than Baghdad and its provinces.'

This description is of a solar eclipse, which was observed in Iraq on 20 June 1061. Astronomers find these reports useful for checking their calculations of ancient eclipses. However, we have to be careful with all such reports – it is most unlikely that an eclipse would cause birds to fall from the sky! It is remarkable that, at that time, astronomers were able to predict eclipses with great accuracy. They were world-leaders in mathematics.

Even today, people can be alarmed by eclipses. They may stay indoors, believing that harmful rays may be coming from the Sun. This picture shows people in the eighteenth century making a lot of noise to try to bring back the Sun. Of course, it worked.

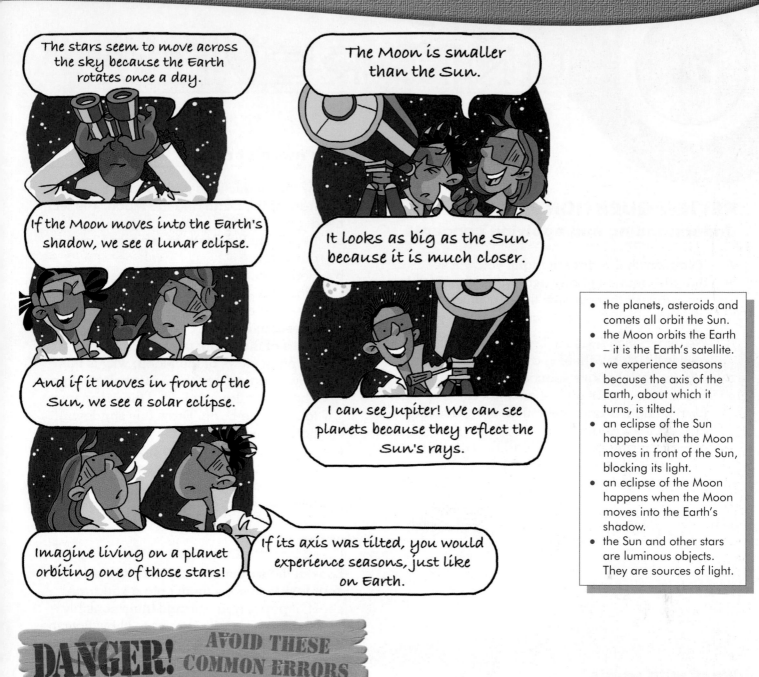

- the planets, asteroids and comets all orbit the Sun.
- the Moon orbits the Earth – it is the Earth's satellite.
- we experience seasons because the axis of the Earth, about which it turns, is tilted.
- an eclipse of the Sun happens when the Moon moves in front of the Sun, blocking its light.
- an eclipse of the Moon happens when the Moon moves into the Earth's shadow.
- the Sun and other stars are luminous objects. They are sources of light.

DANGER! AVOID THESE COMMON ERRORS

It can be tricky to get your head around some of the scientific ideas about the solar system. We feel as if the Earth is stationary, and it looks as though the Sun and Moon go round the Earth every day.

You have to be able to imagine the Earth from a different viewpoint. Try floating in space, high above the North Pole. You will see the Earth turning as it orbits the Sun. You will see the Moon orbiting around the Earth, once a month. Perhaps you have looked at an animation to help with this.

Don't forget the tilt of the Earth's axis: it stays tilted in the same direction; it doesn't tilt back and forth during the year.

If you could see the Earth's orbit, you might just make out that it is not quite circular. It is only very slightly squashed so that we don't notice getting closer to the Sun, or further away. That's why the Sun seems to be the same size in the sky every day.

Key words

eclipse
predict
radiation
shadow

UNIT REVIEW

REVIEW QUESTIONS

Understanding and applying concepts

1 If you watch the stars at night, you will see that they move steadily across the sky. Why do they appear to move like this? In which direction would you expect to see them move?

2 We experience seasons because the Earth's axis is tilted; but there is another reason why a planet might have seasons. Our orbit around the Sun is almost circular. Another planet might have an elliptical orbit, like the one in the diagram.

Explain why this would lead to seasons on the planet. How would these seasons be different from our own?

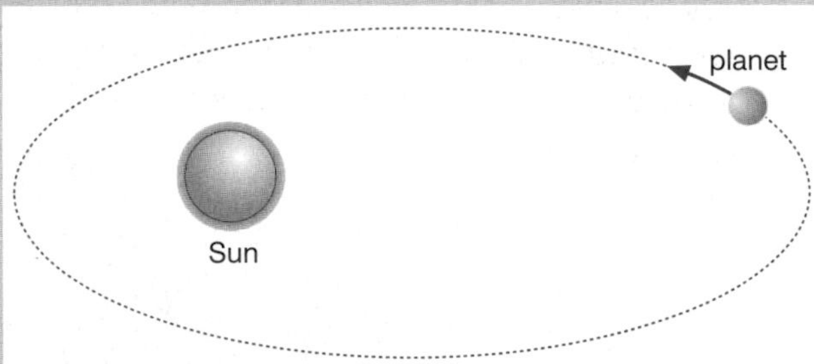

Ways with words

3 A solar eclipse happens when the Moon blocks the Sun's rays. Write another sentence, nothing to do with eclipses, using the word solar.

4 A mnemonic is a way of remembering something. Make up a mnemonic that will help you to recall the names of the planets in the correct order (they are: Mercury, Venus, Earth, Mars, Jupiter, Saturn, Uranus, Neptune, Pluto).

Making more of maths

5 Follow the instructions to draw a scale diagram of the Earth and the Moon. You will need a big sheet of paper.

- **a** Represent the Earth by a circle 12 mm in diameter.
- **b** Represent the Moon by a circle 3 mm in diameter, 36 cm from the Earth.
- **c** Use your drawing to help you answer this question: If two people stand at opposite sides of the Earth, they see slightly different views of the Moon; why is this?
- **d** Now imagine that there is a solar eclipse. The triangular shadow of the Moon just touches the Earth. Draw this shadow; notice how long and thin it is.
- **e** Use your drawing to help you answer this question: How would an eclipse of the Sun be different if the Moon was a little further away from the Earth?

Thinking skills

6 Look at the statements in the boxes below. Your task is to copy them onto a separate sheet of paper and arrange them sensibly, connecting them with arrows to show how they help to explain the following:

- Day follows night; night follows day.
- The Moon's appearance changes from one day to the next.
- The Moon is occasionally eclipsed.

The Earth turns on its axis.
The Sun is a luminous object.
The Earth and Moon have shadows.
The Moon orbits the Earth.
The Earth orbits the Sun.
The Moon is a non-luminous object.

Extension question

7 This is an unusual photograph. It shows both the Earth and the Moon, and was taken from the Voyager 1 spacecraft.

a Imagine looking downwards on the Earth and Moon. Draw a diagram to show the relative positions of the Earth, Moon, Sun and spacecraft at the time this photograph was taken.

b Show the parts of the sides of the Earth and Moon which are lit up by the Sun.

c Explain how your diagram relates to the photograph. Why do both the Earth and the Moon appear as crescent shapes?

SAT-STYLE QUESTIONS

1 Every day, the Sun appears to travel across the sky. The picture shows the path of the Sun across the sky during a winter's day.

a The picture shows the position of the Sun at mid-day. Explain how you can tell from the picture that it is mid-day. (1)

b Copy the diagram and add arrows to show how the Sun moves along its path from dawn to dusk. (1)

c Draw another line on the diagram to show the path of the Sun across the sky on a summer's day. (1)

2 During 2003, an eclipse of the Sun was visible from the north of Scotland. Mike wore his special safety glasses to protect his eyes when he watched the eclipse.

Mike said: 'You must wear safety glasses because the Sun is a luminous object. You don't need to wear them for an eclipse of the Moon, because the Moon is a non-luminous object.'

a Mike said that the Sun is a luminous object. Was he correct? (1)

b Mike was not correct in giving the reason why safety glasses must be worn when looking at the Sun. Give the correct reason. (1)

c The diagram shows the positions of the Sun, Moon and Earth a few days before the eclipse. Copy the diagram and show how light from the Sun allows us to see the Moon. (2)

3 The drawing shows the Earth with the Sun's rays shining on it. Give reasons to support your answers to the questions that follow.

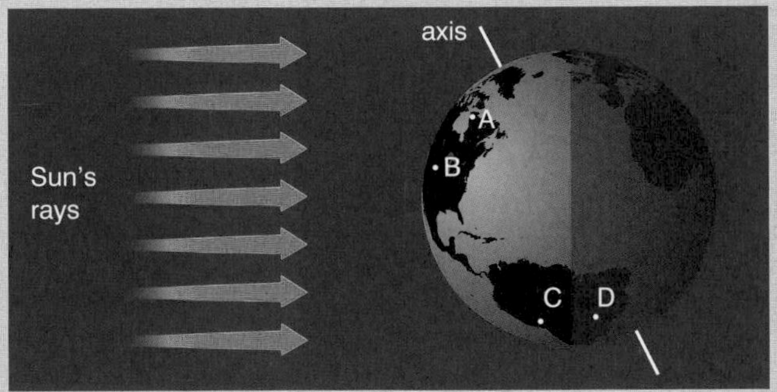

a At which point is it night-time? (2)

b At which point is the Sun highest in the sky? (2)

c At which points is it winter? (3)

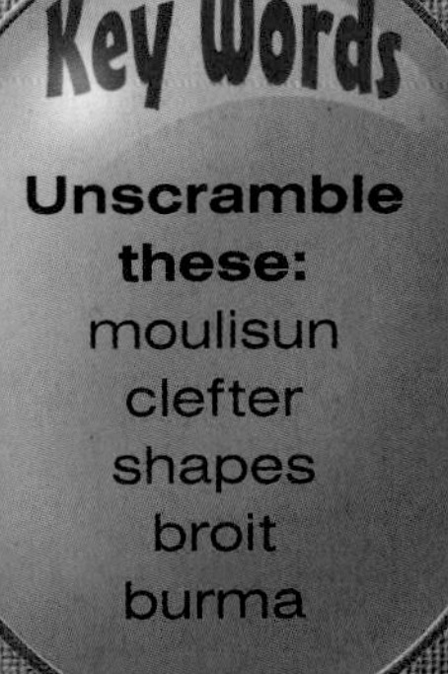

Back in Year 6, Molly and Benson investigated dissolving. You may have carried out a similar investigation. Look at what Molly and Benson did – do you think they made the most of their investigation?

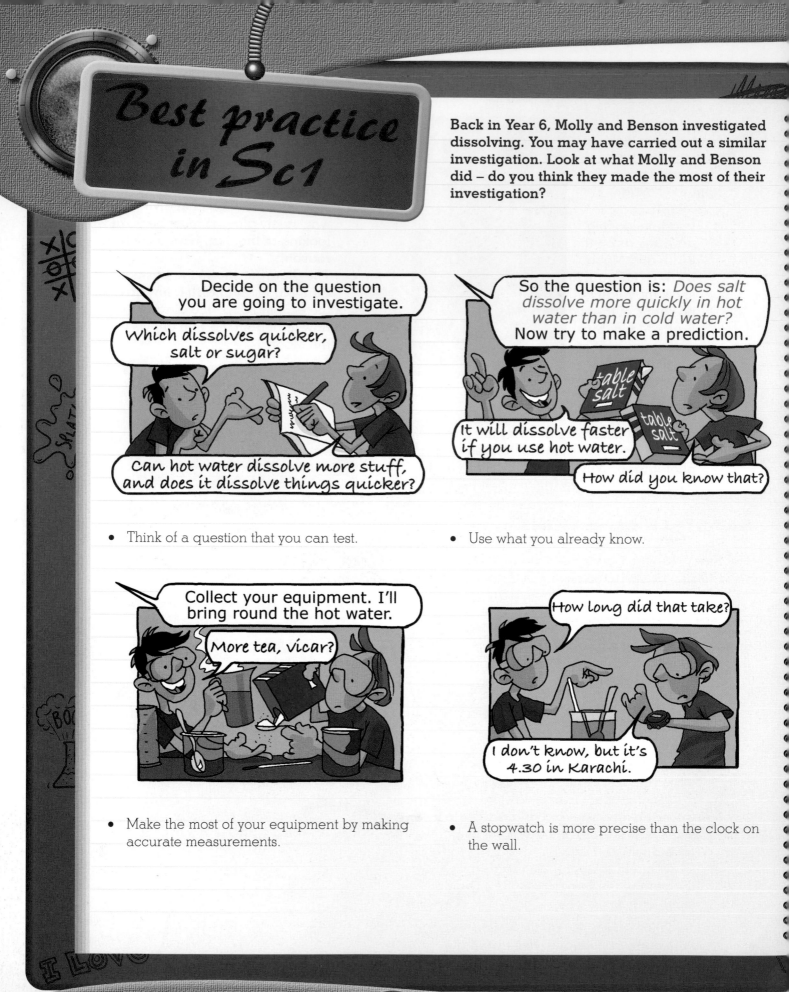

Decide on the question you are going to investigate.

Which dissolves quicker, salt or sugar?

Can hot water dissolve more stuff, and does it dissolve things quicker?

- Think of a question that you can test.

So the question is: *Does salt dissolve more quickly in hot water than in cold water?* Now try to make a prediction.

table salt

table salt

It will dissolve faster if you use hot water.

How did you know that?

- Use what you already know.

Collect your equipment. I'll bring round the hot water.
More tea, vicar?

- Make the most of your equipment by making accurate measurements.

How long did that take?
I don't know, but it's 4.30 in Karachi.

- A stopwatch is more precise than the clock on the wall.

Share your results with groups who used different temperatures.

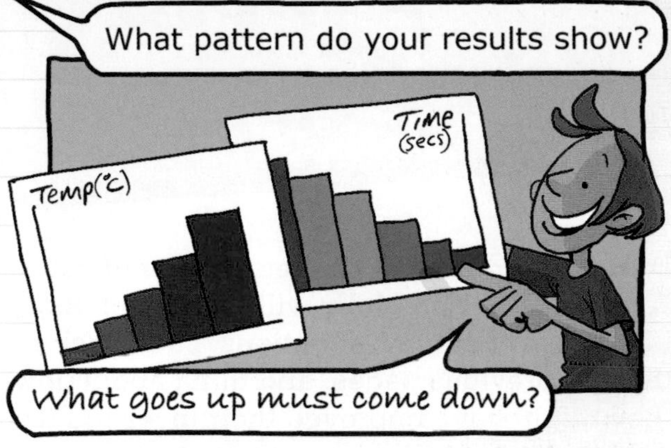

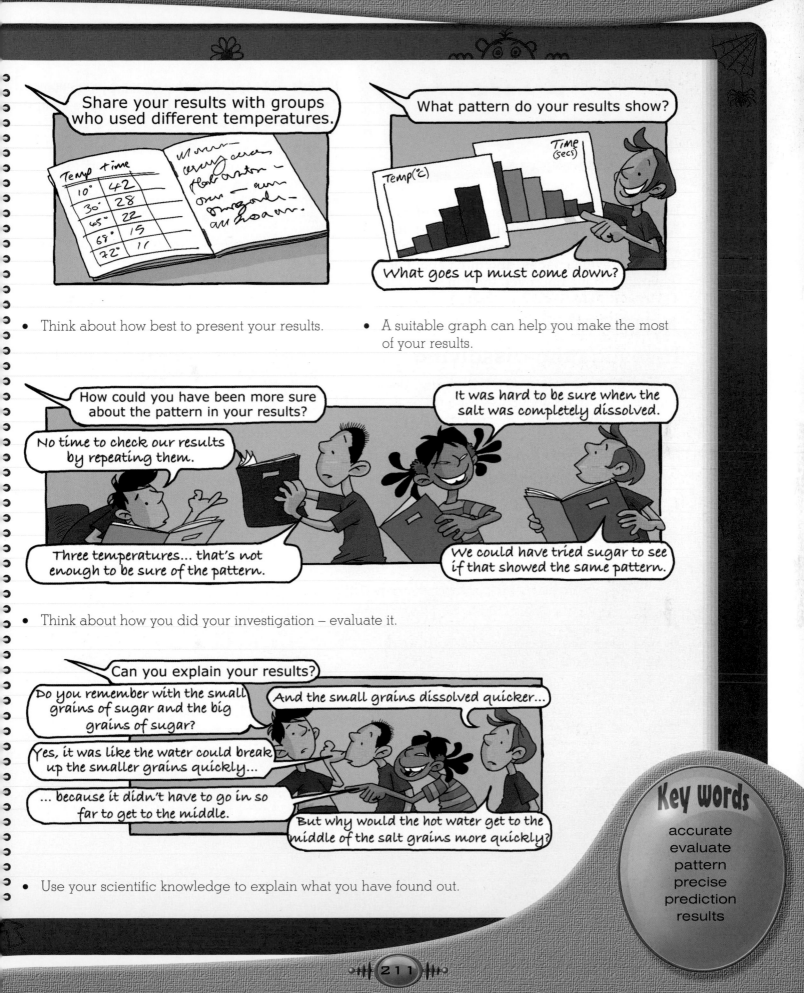

- Think about how best to present your results.
- A suitable graph can help you make the most of your results.

How could you have been more sure about the pattern in your results?

No time to check our results by repeating them.

It was hard to be sure when the salt was completely dissolved.

Three temperatures... that's not enough to be sure of the pattern.

We could have tried sugar to see if that showed the same pattern.

- Think about how you did your investigation – evaluate it.

Can you explain your results?

Do you remember with the small grains of sugar and the big grains of sugar?

And the small grains dissolved quicker...

Yes, it was like the water could break up the smaller grains quickly...

... because it didn't have to go in so far to get to the middle.

But why would the hot water get to the middle of the salt grains more quickly?

- Use your scientific knowledge to explain what you have found out.

Key words

accurate
evaluate
pattern
precise
prediction
results

During their science studies at Scientifica High, Benson and Molly will learn a lot about how to carry out investigations. Look back at the two previous pages, and think about how they might have improved their investigation.

ACTIVITY
Investigating dissolving

Molly and Benson investigated dissolving. There are lots of questions about dissolving which they could have investigated. Their question was:

Does salt dissolve more quickly in hot water than in cold water?

- Suggest another question about dissolving which Benson and Molly might have investigated.

Scientists try to think ahead. They make a **prediction**, saying how they think their investigation may turn out.

- What prediction did Benson and Molly make?
- What **evidence** can you provide to support their prediction?

(Remember, evidence can come from anywhere – from your scientific knowledge and from everyday life.)

Benson and Molly weren't very happy with their equipment. They thought it might not give them very **accurate** measurements.

- Look at the equipment they used. How could it have been improved, to give them more accurate measurements?
- What should they have done to make sure their investigation was a fair test?

Scientists try to use the best equipment, but they also try to use it as carefully as possible, to ensure that their results are as accurate as possible.

- How could Benson and Molly have made their results more reliable?
- Benson and Molly had cold water from one tap, and hot water from a jug. They mixed them to make warm water. How could they have improved their investigation by including higher and lower temperatures?

Benson and Molly made a mess of presenting their results.

- Show how they could have written down their results, so that the **pattern** was easier to see.
- Other groups in the class investigated the same question. Benson and Molly combined their results with the results from the other groups. Why was this a good idea? Why might it lead to problems?
- What type of graph would have been a good way to show their results? Draw the graph.
- Write a sentence to describe the pattern in the results.
- Can you use ideas about particles to explain the pattern?

Pete and Reese are investigating burning. Look at how they carried out their investigation – are they better at investigating than when they were in Year 6?

On page 215, Pip and Mike are investigating how the temperature changes during the day. They are using electronic equipment to collect data, but they still have to think just as hard about what their results mean.

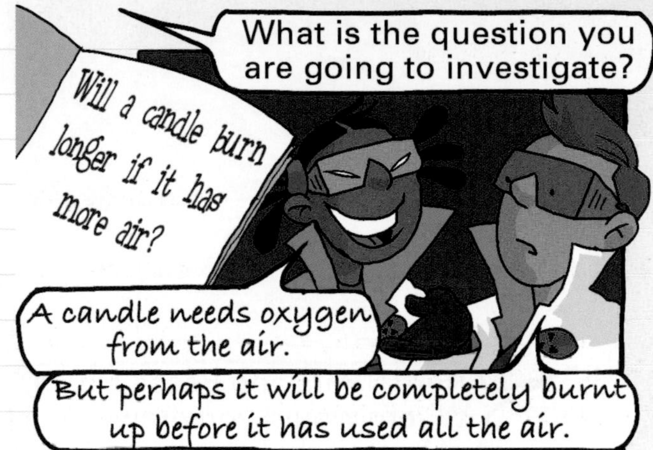

What is the question you are going to investigate?
Will a candle burn longer if it has more air?
A candle needs oxygen from the air.
But perhaps it will be completely burnt up before it has used all the air.

- Think ahead – can you imagine the pattern of your results? Use your scientific knowledge.

When should I start the clock?
00.00
As soon as the beaker touches the sand.

- It can help to have a trial run.

It's tricky to judge just when the flame goes out.

Better just write 28 seconds, then.

- Repeat readings can help you to judge how reliable your measurements are.

How good is your evidence?
We've only got values for two sizes of beaker.
size
time
We needed some more beakers to be sure of the pattern... and we needed more time!

- Think about the strength of the evidence you have collected.

Key words

accurate
evidence
pattern
prediction
reliable

- A graph will help you test your prediction.

Here's Pete and Reese's data. Where would you draw a line of best fit through the points?
Time
We had just two points on our graph.
A perfect straight line!

- A line of best fit has the points scattered on either side of it.

ACTIVITY
Better, stronger evidence

In a scientific investigation, you have to make the most of what you've got – equipment, materials and ideas. Pete and Reese did their best, but they needed more time.

They had to measure the time for which the candle burned.

- Why was it a good idea to have a trial run?
- Why was it a good idea to make **repeat readings**? How did this help them to decide whether their results were reliable?

The teacher showed the graph of Pete and Reese's results. A graph can also help you to decide whether your results are **reliable**.

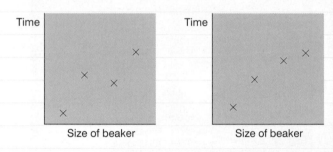

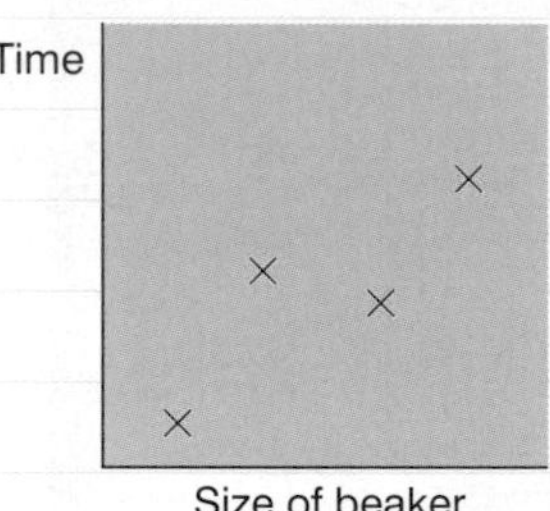

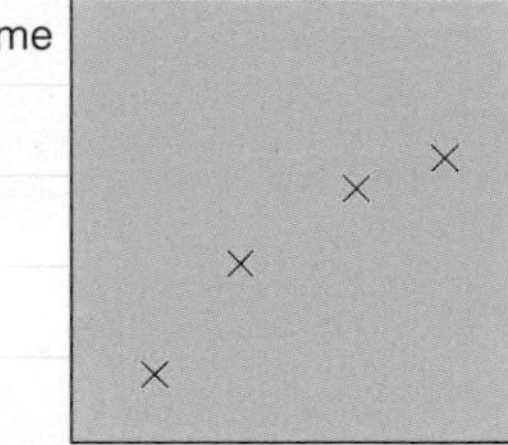

- Look at the two graphs shown here. Do they both show the same pattern? How does a graph help you to decide whether you results are reliable?
- How does a **line of best fit** help to show the pattern in some results? How could it help you to make predictions?

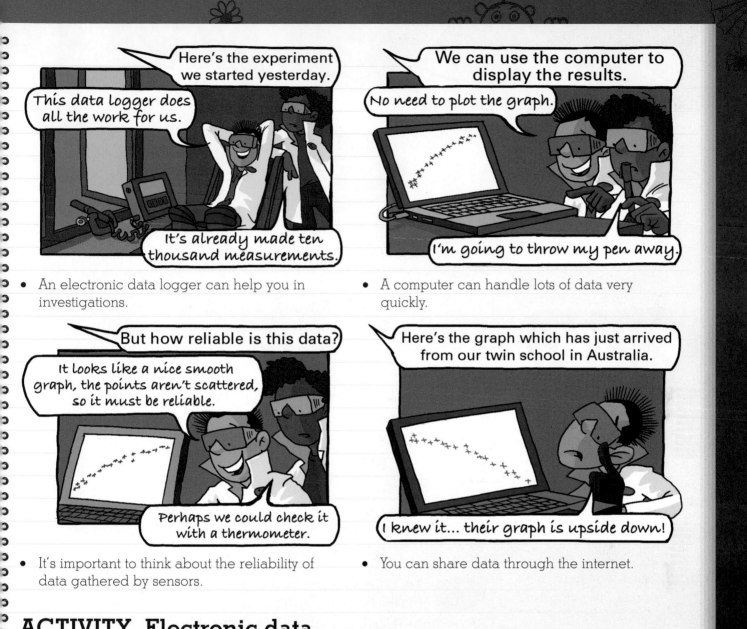

- An electronic data logger can help you in investigations.
- A computer can handle lots of data very quickly.

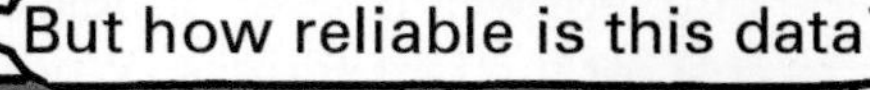

- It's important to think about the reliability of data gathered by sensors.
- You can share data through the internet.

ACTIVITY Electronic data

An electronic data logger, equipped with sensors, can help in an investigation.

- Explain why a data logger was useful in this experiment.

Data loggers collect data automatically. They can do it over a long period of time. They can also collect data very quickly.

- Suggest an experiment where a data logger would be useful to collect data quickly.

If you use sensors and a data logger, you need to check their reliability.

- How could Pip and Mike have used a thermometer to assess the reliability of the data from the data logger?

The class had some secondary data, from Australia.

- How could this help the class to understand the pattern in their own data?

Key words

data logger
line of best fit
reliability
repeat readings
sensors

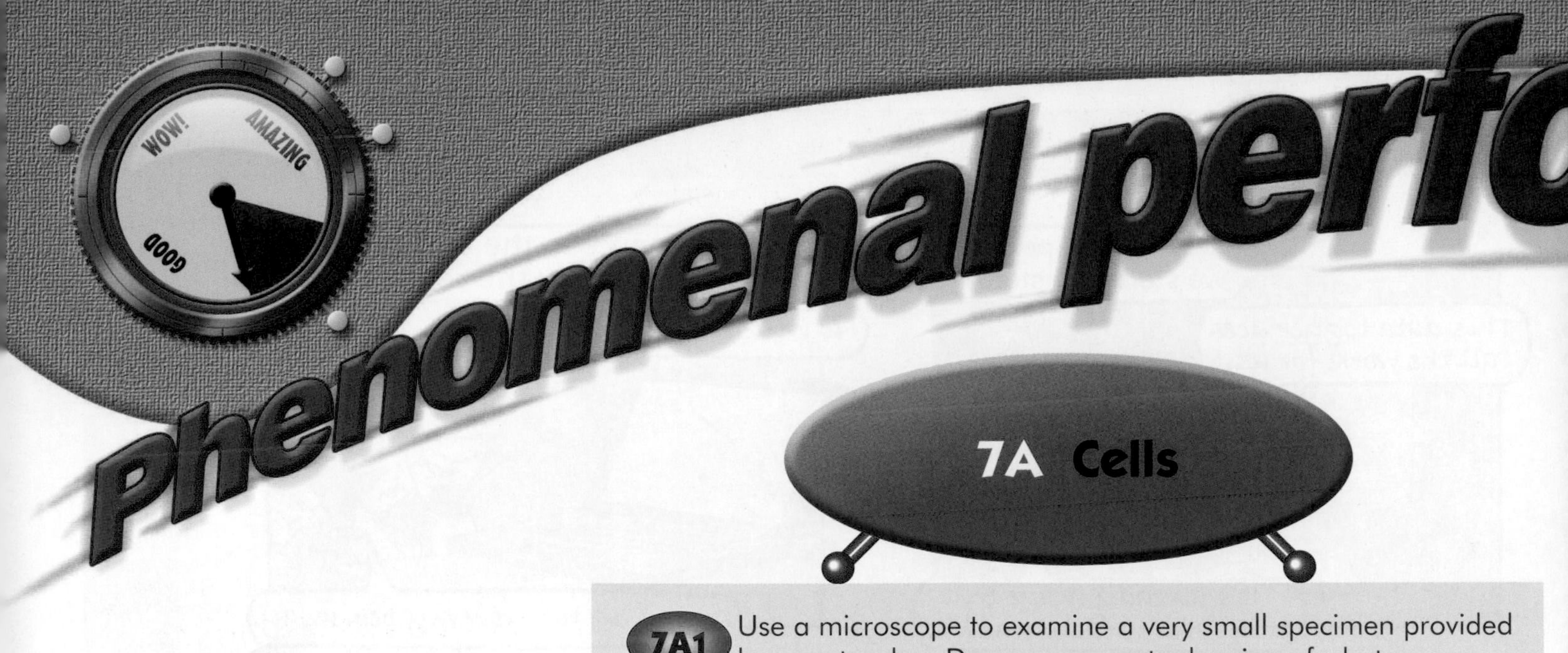

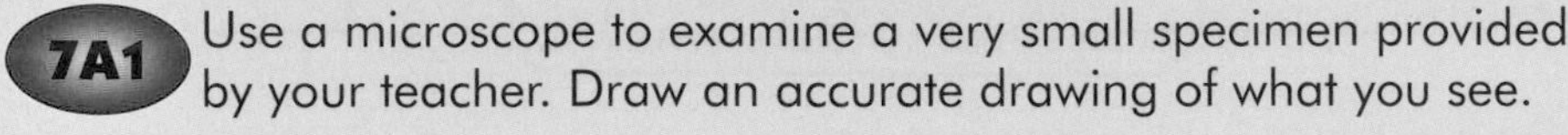

7A Cells

7A1 Use a microscope to examine a very small specimen provided by your teacher. Draw an accurate drawing of what you see.

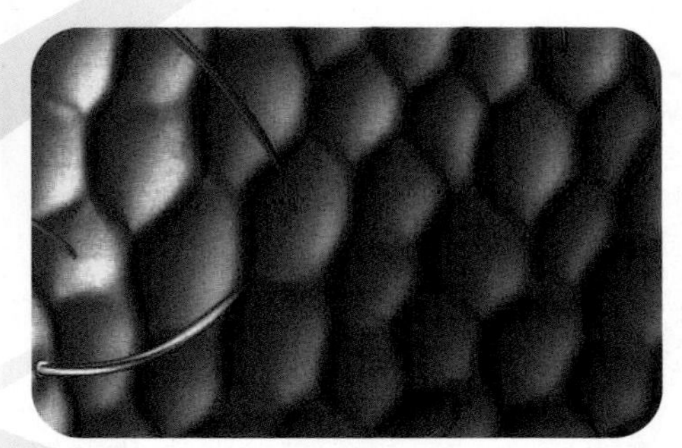

7A2 Paint the underside of a leaf with a layer of pale pink nail varnish to make a 'cast' of the leaf surface. When it has dried, peel it off carefully and use your microscope to look at your 'cast' of the leaf surface.

a) What shape are the cells making up the surface?

b) Can you see hairs on the leaf? You should be able to see holes, called **stomata** that allow air into a leaf.

7A3 Make a hay infusion from some grass or hay and a small amount of water from a pond, if possible. Use a binocular microscope to investigate the microscopic pond life that develops.

7A4 One of your most important organs is your liver. Sometimes it is called the 'body's chemical factory'. Find out what your liver does.

7A5 It is less than 100 years ago since we really began to understand what cells are and how we make more. Find out about the important discoveries made by the following people:

a) Theodor Schwann (1810–1882), a German zoologist,

b) Oscar Hertwig (1849–1922),

c) Rudolf Virchow (1821–1902).

7A6 Use a microscope to examine the pollen basket on a honeybee's leg:

a) What does it use the pollen basket for?

b) Why does a honeybee collect pollen?

7B Reproduction

7B1 Compose an 'Agony Aunt' page for a magazine aimed at teenagers. Write some letters about the problems of going through puberty and adolescence. Write short, but sensible, replies to the letters.

7B2 Your chromosomes determine whether you are a boy or a girl. Find out how your chromosomes decide your sex.

7B3 Women have begun their periods earlier and earlier. At the time of World War I, girls had their first period when they were 16 or 17; by the 1970s girls were starting their periods at age 13. By 2000, Miss Average had her first period when she was 12. What factors have led to earlier puberty?

7B4 Pregnant women have regular check-ups during their pregnancy. Find out what other checks are done during pregnancy in antenatal care.

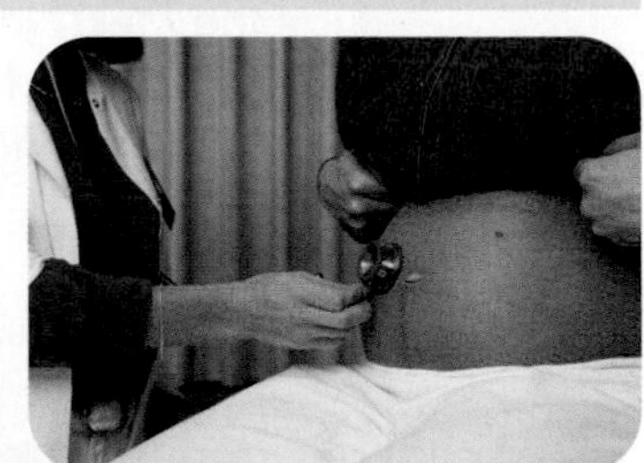

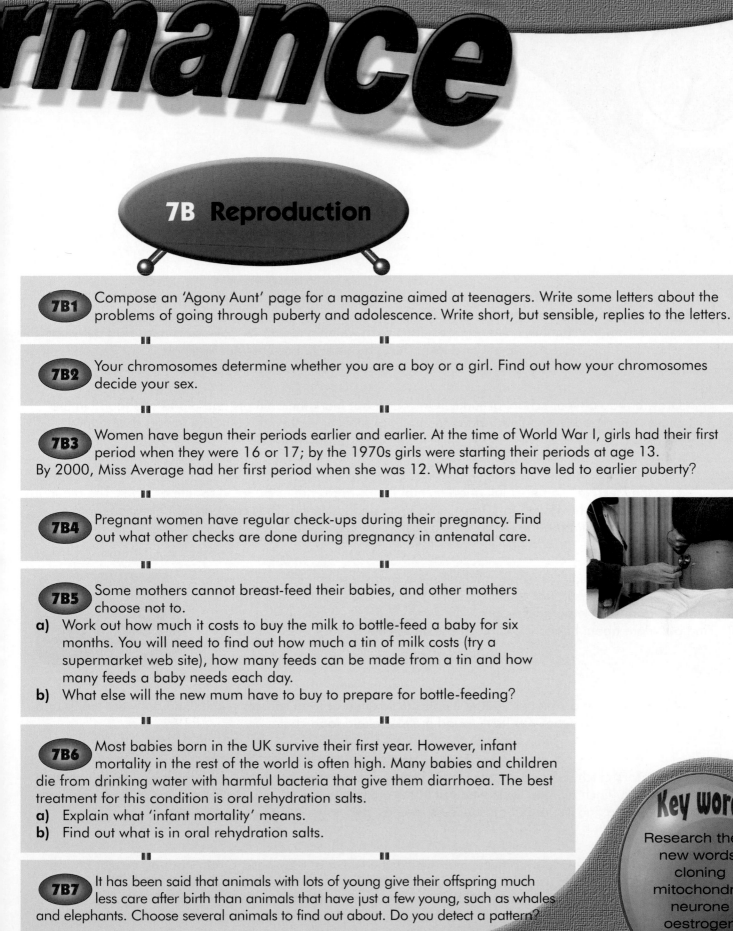

7B5 Some mothers cannot breast-feed their babies, and other mothers choose not to.

a) Work out how much it costs to buy the milk to bottle-feed a baby for six months. You will need to find out how much a tin of milk costs (try a supermarket web site), how many feeds can be made from a tin and how many feeds a baby needs each day.

b) What else will the new mum have to buy to prepare for bottle-feeding?

7B6 Most babies born in the UK survive their first year. However, infant mortality in the rest of the world is often high. Many babies and children die from drinking water with harmful bacteria that give them diarrhoea. The best treatment for this condition is oral rehydration salts.

a) Explain what 'infant mortality' means.

b) Find out what is in oral rehydration salts.

7B7 It has been said that animals with lots of young give their offspring much less care after birth than animals that have just a few young, such as whales and elephants. Choose several animals to find out about. Do you detect a pattern?

Key words

Research these new words:
cloning
mitochondria
neurone
oestrogen
protozoa

7C Environment and feeding relationships

7C1 Cars and lorries, factories and power stations all burn fossil fuels such as oil, gas and diesel for power. When these fuels are burnt, traces of other substances in the fuel make acid gases that enter the atmosphere from the chimneys. These gases dissolve in water in the air to make acid rain. Find out what happens when acid rain falls on a forest or a lake. Make a poster to present your findings.

7C2 Draw a map of your school grounds. On your map, mark the animals and plants you found in the places the class investigated. Add a comment or label to explain the physical factors that helped them to live there.

7C3 Play the 'Yes/No' game. Think of an animal that is nocturnal or adapted for life at night. The others in your group can ask up to 10 questions to try and identify it. They can only ask questions with a 'Yes' or 'No' answer. What are the most useful questions to ask?

7C4 Brine shrimps, sold as 'sea monkeys' in the shops, are small crustaceans that live in salty lakes in hot countries. Brine shrimps are adapted to a habitat that changes from salty water to drought.

a) Find out more about how brine shrimps are adapted.

7C5 What is the world's biggest eater? It eats the smallest of food sources – krill. Find out what krill is and what eats it. Use what you have found out to make a food chain.

7C6 **Predators** catch, kill and eat their prey. However, **parasites** need their prey to stay alive and provide them with lunch all their lives. Find out about a parasite and how its body and way of life is adapted for its diet. You could find out about mosquitoes, leeches, bed bugs, head lice or cat fleas.

7C7 Are there any new developments near where you live, e.g. a by-pass, a new housing estate, an old industrial site being used for a shopping centre, etc.?, for example, the development likely to affect local food webs and the environment?, will there be any good outcomes for local wildlife? Briefly describe the effects you expect to see.

7D Variation and classification

7D1 During the last 300 million years many more species have become extinct than are alive today. We know about these through fossilised traces. Find out about how fossils are made and what sorts of things can become fossilised.

7D3 Animals move about from place to place but plants do not. However plants do move. The daisy's flowers open in the morning and close at night. The sensitive mimosa's leaves droop instantly when they are touched. Find out what these plant movements are called and describe some more examples of plant movement.

7D4 Many of our features are inherited. Do a survey in the class of the distribution of inherited features, such as a small gap between the two front teeth and free or fixed ear lobes. If you have fixed ear lobes, your ear lobe goes smoothly into the jaw and you cannot fasten clip-on earrings to them very well. Free ear lobes have a small or large rounded flap at the bottom.

7D5 The colour of a cat's coat is inherited as genes. The gene for ginger colour is more rare than the gene for black. Ginger colour is carried on a particular chromosome called the X chromosome. Boys, and boy cats, have only one X chromosome, whereas girls, and girl cats have two. If a boy kitten inherits ginger on his X chromosome, he will be a ginger tom. If a girl kitten inherits ginger on one of her X chromosomes she will probably inherit black on the other, and be a tortoiseshell colour. She would need to inherit two ginger genes to be a proper ginger colour. Survey your class and find out if there are more ginger toms than female cats, as would be expected.

7D6 As long as 7000 years ago, farmers in Central America were improving crops of corn by planting hybrid corn seeds that had improved features. Many modern varieties of plants are described as **hybrid**, but pedigree dogs are **pure bred**.
Find out what these two terms mean.

Key words

Research these new words:
decomposer
deforestation
mutation
mutualism
ruminant

Phenomenal perfo

7E Acids and alkalis

7E1 **a)** Carry out some research to find out how substances are classified by their E numbers.

b) Write a few sentences about each category, giving examples and explaining why we add them to food.

7E2 Magnesium powder is very reactive. In a fire it burns vigorously. If water gets on it, the metal will give off flammable hydrogen gas. Design a hazard warning sign for a road tanker carrying a cargo of magnesium powder.

7E4 Some people say that bee stings are acidic, so you can ease the pain by treating the sting with a weak alkali, such as bicarbonate of soda. However, others say that this is 'an old wives' tale'. Do some research to find out whose view you support.

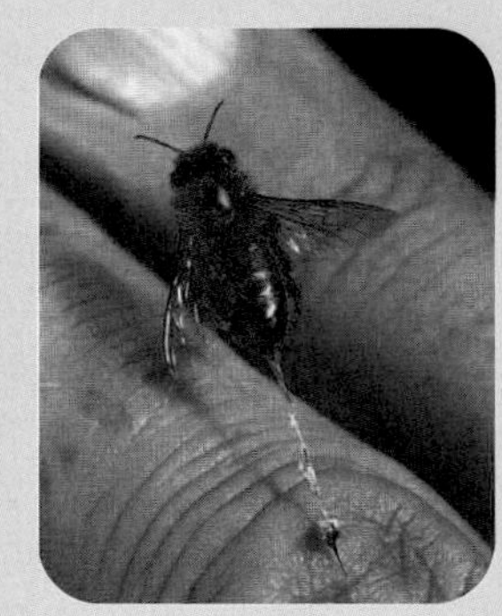

7E5 In the experiment on p.88, you looked at the change in pH as dilute sodium hydroxide was added to dilute hydrochloric acid.

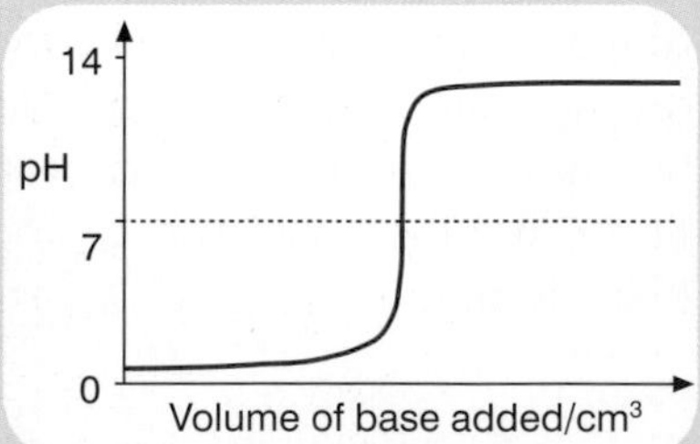

a) Predict the shape of the graph you would get if you added the acid to the alkali in the beaker instead.

b) What do you think the graph would look like if you used the same acid and alkali, but solutions that were 10 times more dilute?

c) How would you use these graphs to see exactly how much acid and alkali are needed to neutralise each other?

7F Simple chemical reactions

7F1 Carry out some research into the rockets we see in firework displays. Try to find out how all those beautiful colours are made, how it takes off, and how firework makers can make different patterns when the rocket explodes in the air.

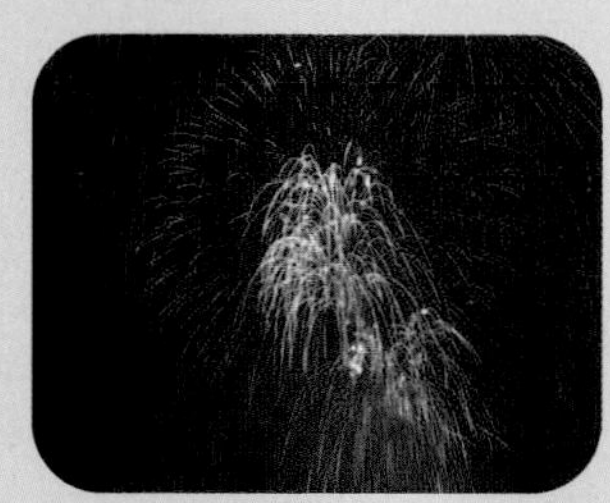

7F2 When 4 g of magnesium ribbon reacts completely with dilute hydrochloric acid, we get 4000 cm^3 of hydrogen gas produced at room temperature and pressure.
If you want to make just 200 cm^3 of hydrogen, how much magnesium would you use?

7F3 You know that the test for carbon dioxide is to see if it turns limewater milky.

a) Why does the limewater go cloudy?
b) Find out what limewater is and how it reacts with carbon dioxide gas.

7F4 On p.102, you learned about the fire triangle. Use your knowledge to decide on the best way to extinguish the following types of fire, and explain your reasoning:

a) an oil-rig fire **b)** an aeroplane fire **c)** a forest fire
d) an electrical fire **e)** a chip-pan fire

In this demonstration of nineteenth century fire extinguishers, pressurised carbon dioxide was used to force water onto flames

7F5 **a)** Predict which of these three candles will go out first.
b) Justify your choice and try out the experiment if you have time.

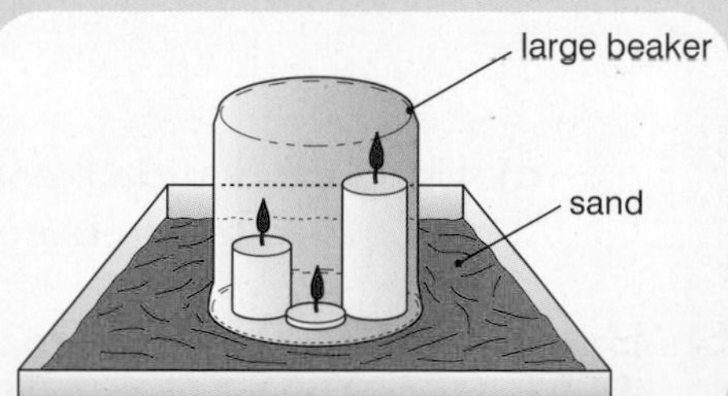

Key words

Research these new words:
ammonia
buffer solution
hazcards
oxidation

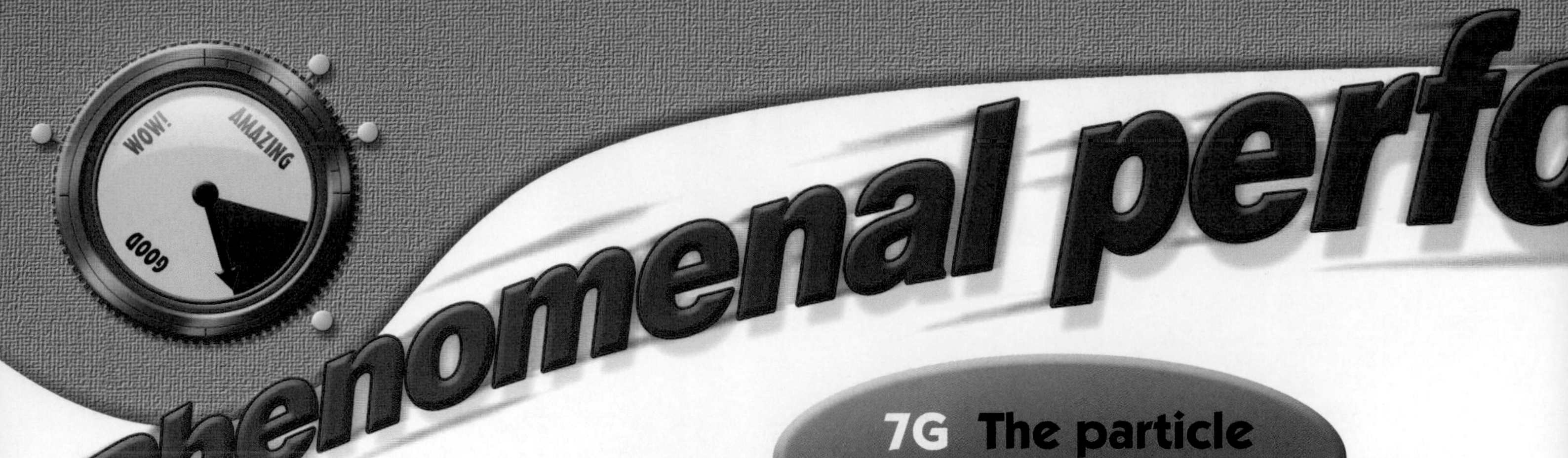

7G The particle model

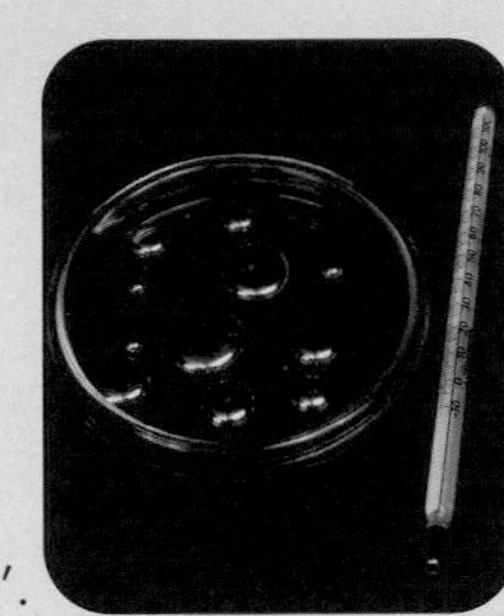

7G1 Liquids expand when you heat them up. That explains why we have liquid thermometers. Two common liquid thermometers contain mercury and alcohol.

a) Give an advantage and a disadvantage of each of these thermometers.

b) Do some research to find out about mercury and write a brief article for a magazine entitled 'Mercury – the weird metal'.

7G2 There are three states of matter – solid, liquid and gas. Imagine that all matter were made up of a fundamental substance called 'gloop'.
Invent a model that will explain the differences between solids, liquids and gases using the theory of 'gloop'.

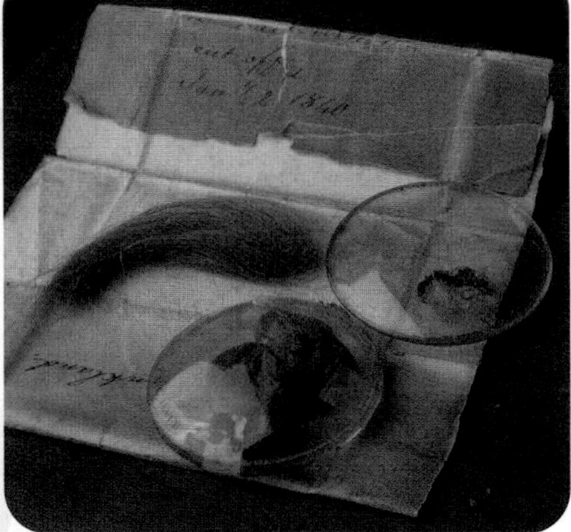

John Dalton's eyes (on the watch glass) and a lock of his hair. His eyes were taken out on his death as he requested. He wanted a doctor to check out a theory he had about his colour blindness – unfortunately his theory proved incorrect.

7G3 **a)** Write an account of the life of John Dalton. Make sure that you include the way he worked as a scientist.

b) Do you think scientists working today use the methods favoured by John Dalton? How do you think they might differ?

John Dalton (1766–1844)

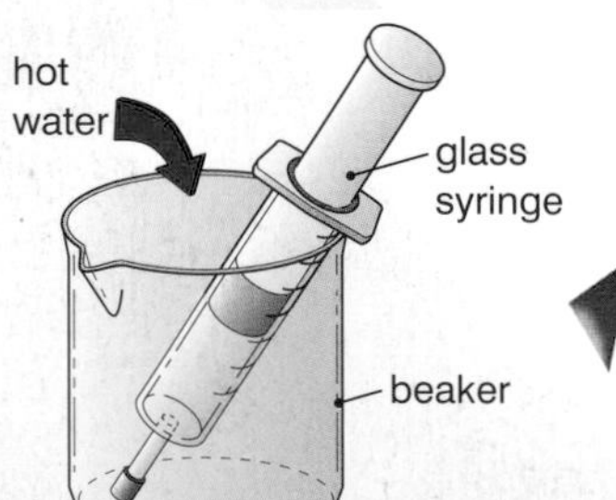

7G4 **a)** Using the particle theory, explain what you think will happen to the pressure as you heat a fixed volume of a gas.

b) Explain what would happen to the sealed glass syringe opposite, if you pour hot water from a kettle into the beaker.

7H Solutions

7H1 Find out how the rock salt under Cheshire was originally formed. What does this tell us about the change in climate in Britain since the formation of rock salt?

7H2 In the experiment on p.129 you listed all the factors that affect how quickly copper sulphate dissolves. You explained the effect of the factor you chose to investigate.
Now use the particle theory to explain the effect of each of the other factors.

7H4 Chromatography can be used to identify unknown substances using tables of R_f values. You can work out the R_f value as shown opposite:

a) What is the R_f value of substance B?
b) Draw a chromatogram that shows a substance with an R_f value of 0.8.
c) Why do tables of R_f values quote a particular temperature and state which solvent was used?

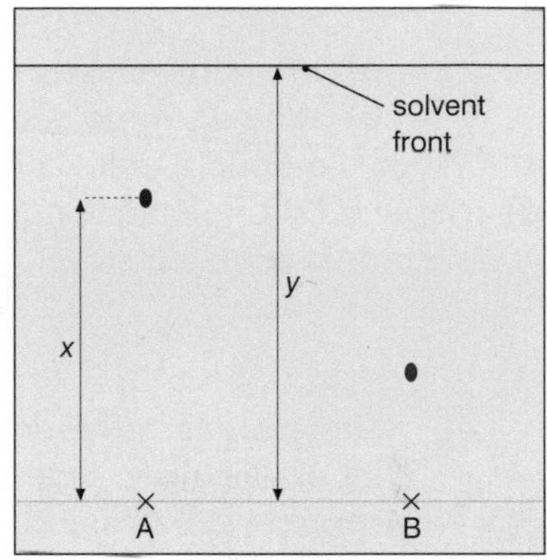

$$R_f \text{ value} = \frac{\text{distance spot moves}}{\text{distance to solvent front}} = \frac{x}{y} = 0.7$$

7H5 Look at the solubility curves opposite:

a) Which is the most soluble substance at:
i) 10 °C, ii) 40 °C?
b) At what temperature is the solubility of sodium chloride the same as that of potassium nitrate?
c) Which substance has its solubility affected the most by changes in temperature?
d) Describe what happens to the solubility of potassium sulphate as the temperature is changed.
e) 50 g of copper sulphate were dissolved in 100 g of water at 90 °C. The solution was then allowed to cool.
i) At which temperature would crystals first appear?
ii) What do we call the solution at this temperature?
f) How much potassium sulphate will dissolve in 20 g of water at 70 °C?

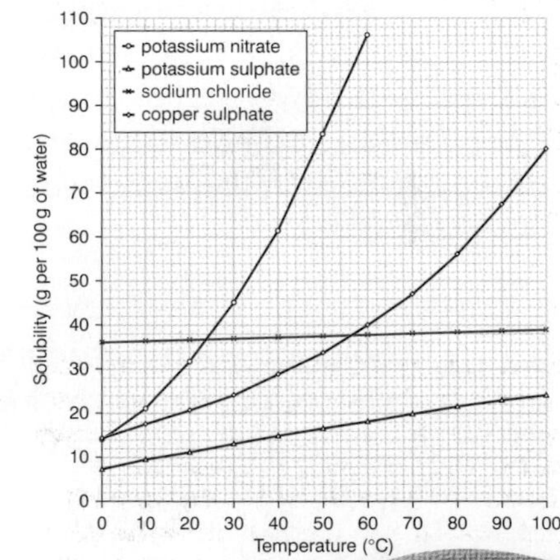

Key words

Research these new words:
benzene
crystal gardens
fractional distillation
plasma

71 Energy

711 **a)** Why do we use petrol or diesel in cars, rather than coal?
b) Why do some people heat their houses with gas, but others use wood?
c) What is a good fuel for a barbecue?
d) Make a list of all the things you would take into account when choosing a fuel for a particular purpose, such as a camping stove.

712 There are large reserves of coal underground, but eventually they will run out. In China and India, a lot of electricity is generated from coal, and demand is rising.
a) Why should we be careful about how we use coal?
b) Discuss whether or not we can ask people in other countries to use less coal.

713 Geothermal energy is energy from hot rocks underground. In some places, the rocks are hot enough to boil water; the steam produced is used in a power station to generate electricity.
Imagine that you had to go prospecting for new sources of geothermal energy. Where in the world would you look?

714 Solar power is becoming cheaper, and it is used more and more. Explain why solar cells are a good way of providing electricity for:
a) a communal television set in an Indian village,
b) a refrigerator in a clinic in the African bush,
c) a roadside telephone in the Australian outback.

Pasta as energy food

715 Different people need different amounts of energy from their food.
a) Suggest a person who doesn't need much energy; suggest someone else who needs very large amounts of energy from their food.
b) Your daily intake of energy varies throughout your lifetime. Sketch a graph to show how you imagine your energy needs change through your lifetime.

7J Electrical circuits

7J1
a) A car has many parts that work with electricity. List as many as you can.
b) The electrical parts work from the battery. A wire comes from one terminal of the battery, and divides up to go to the different places where it is needed. The electricity comes back to the battery through the metal body of the car, instead of using more wires. Why is this a good idea?

7J2 Electrons are the tiny particles that move through a metal when an electric current flows. Scientists have learned to control how electrons move, and that's how we have 'electronics'. Think of some of the things that have electronics in them. How has the science and technology of electronics helped to change our lives?

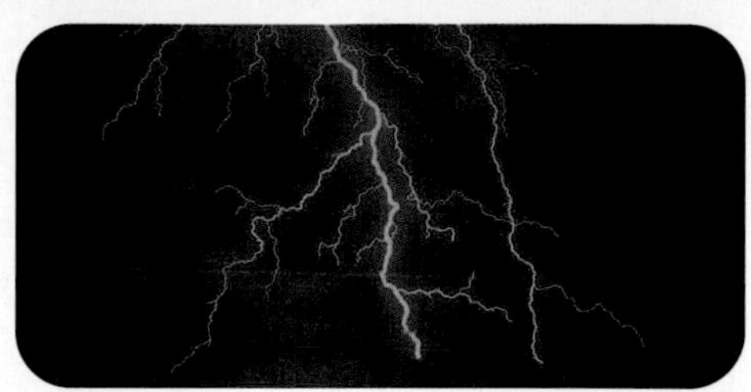

7J3 A car battery gives 12 V. It is made of several 2 V cells. Draw a circuit symbol to represent this.
a) Find some battery-operated devices, such as a mobile phone, laptop computer, calculator, watch, camera. What voltage do they require? (You may have to look in the instruction book.)
b) Do they have a single cell or a battery of several cells?

7J4 Some batteries are rechargeable. When they run down, you can recharge them with electricity from the mains. The chemical reaction that made electric current flow from the battery is reversed. Here are some places where rechargeable batteries are used: invalid cars, mobile phones, milk floats, laptop computers. People don't use rechargeable batteries as much as they might. They prefer to use ordinary batteries and throw them away when they are flat. Why do you think this is?

7J6 Electricity is dangerous, especially at high voltages. Perhaps you have seen hazard-warning signs at electricity sub-stations, or on the pylons that carry high-voltage power lines. Think about where you have seen parts of the electricity supply system in your neighbourhood.
a) Where are there warning signs?
b) How is the public kept safe from danger?

Key words

Research these new words:
energy footprint
fuel cell
photovoltaic
semiconductor
thermistor

7K Forces and their effects

7K1 Two magnets attract or repel each other. The forces they exert on each other depend on how far apart they are.

a) Think about this, and sketch a graph to show how you think the force one magnet exerts on another depends on how far apart they are.

b) Design an experiment to find out about the force.

7K2 Robert Hooke devised a way of keeping secret his law of springs. Here is his law, in modern English: 'The greater the force stretching a spring, the greater the extension of the spring.'
Devise your own way of coding this law to keep it secret.

7K3 If you go to the Moon, your mass stays the same but your weight is a lot less. People think that, one day, there will be holiday trips to the Moon. The photo shows an idea for a Moon hotel. Design a brochure to encourage people to come and stay in the hotel. Describe the facilities, and any activities for visitors.

7K4 **a)** If you dive into a swimming pool, you will float back to the surface. What does this tell you about your density?

b) If you float vertically at the deep end, you will find that the water level is just below your nose. That's handy – you'll be able to breathe. Some people stick out of the water more than others. Why do you think this is?

7K5 Think of a sport, for example, ice-skating, roller-blading, cycling. Make a list of aspects of the sport where a lot of friction is necessary, and another list of aspects where friction can be a nuisance.

7L The solar system – and beyond

7L1 A sundial is a kind of clock that makes use of light from the Sun. The part of the sundial that sticks up is called the 'gnomon'. How does the shadow of the gnomon move during the day? How does the length of the shadow change?

7L2 There are craters all over the surface of the Moon. They were formed at different times in the life of the Moon.

a) How are these craters formed?
b) Sometimes we can tell that one crater was formed more recently than another. Make a sketch of two overlapping craters, and explain how you can tell which one formed more recently.
c) Why isn't the Earth covered in craters like the Moon?

7L3 You have learned the scientific explanation of why we have seasons; but, in the past, people had different explanations.

a) Try to forget what you have learned, and think up as many alternative explanations as you can for the seasons. Why is it hotter at some times of the year than others?
b) Then think of evidence for and against your explanations.

7L4 The ancient Greeks realised that they could learn something about the Earth from their observations of eclipses of the Moon. They saw that the shadow of the Earth had a curved edge, and deduced that the Earth must be spherical. However, other shapes could also cast a curved shadow. Suggest some. In fact, the Earth's shadow on the Moon is *always* curved. What does this suggest?

7L5 Imagine that you were about to set off to explore the solar system, but you had forgotten to buy a map. Explain why a printed map would be of little use to you. Why would a computerised map be better?

Key words

Research these new words:
annular eclipse
neutron star
planetesimal
space telescope
tribology

GLOSSARY

acid a substance that forms a solution with a pH of less than 7. **p.80**

adapted having specialisations to be able to do a particular activity, or to cope in particular conditions. **pp.8, 42**

air resistance similar to drag; the force of friction when an object moves through air. **p.185**

alkali a substance that forms a solution with a pH greater than 7. **p.84**

ammeter an instrument for measuring electric current. **p.160**

amniotic fluid the fluid that supports and cushions a growing foetus in the uterus. **p.28**

asteroid a rock in orbit around the Sun. **p.202**

atmosphere the layer of gas surrounding any planet. **p.202**

axis the imaginary line through the middle of the Earth, about which it turns. **p.198**

balanced forces two or more forces whose effects cancel out. **p.182**

battery two or more cells connected together. **p.162**

biomass living material that can be burned to release energy. **p.146**

calcium carbonate the main substance in limestone, chalk and marble. Pure calcium carbonate is a white solid that fizzes in dilute acid releasing carbon dioxide gas. **p.101**

carbon a chemical element that exists as diamond and graphite, as well as in charcoal and soot. **p.104**

carbon dioxide a gas that makes up about 0.04% of the air. It is produced as a product when we burn fossil fuels. **p.100**

cell the small structures that living material is made of. **p.6**

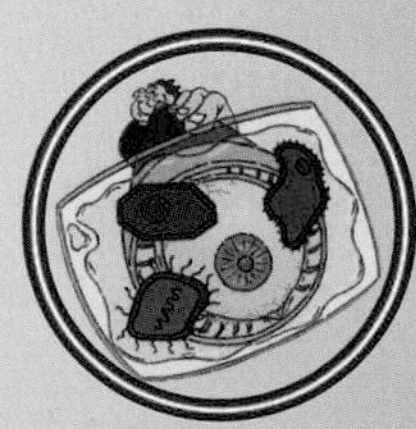

cell a single component that provides a voltage in an electric circuit. **p.158**

cell division the process a cell undergoes when it divides to make two new cells. **p.12**

cell membrane the outer surface layer of a cell that controls the entry and exit of materials from cells. **p.6**

cell wall a tough outer layer surrounding plant cells that gives them strength and shape. **p.7**

characteristic a distinctive feature that is found on members of a species. **p.62**

chloroplast structures within plant cells that make food by photosynthesis. **p.7**

chromatogram the paper that shows the separated substances after the solvent has run up it during chromatography. **p.132**

chromatography the process whereby small amounts of dissolved substances are separated by running a solvent along a material such as absorbent paper. **p.132**

chromosome a structure found in the nucleus of cells that carries genes. **pp.12, 70**

classification arranging organisms in groups with similar features. **p.63**

circuit diagram a way of showing how the components of a circuit are connected together. **p.158**

clone a group of identical cells. **p.13**

comet a lump of ice and dust in orbit around the Sun. **p.203**

competition this takes place when two animals or plants both need the same resource. Each finds it harder to get what they need. **p.54**

conserving energy resources making careful use of energy resources, so that they don't get used up too quickly. **p.149**

consumer an animal that gains its energy by eating other animals or plants. **p.50**

corrosive describes substances that attack and destroy living tissues, including eyes and skin. **p.82**

cytoplasm the material making up most of a cell's contents. **p.6**

density calculated using density = mass/volume. **p.183**

diffusion the automatic mixing and movement of one substance through another, without the need to stir up the substances. **p.118**

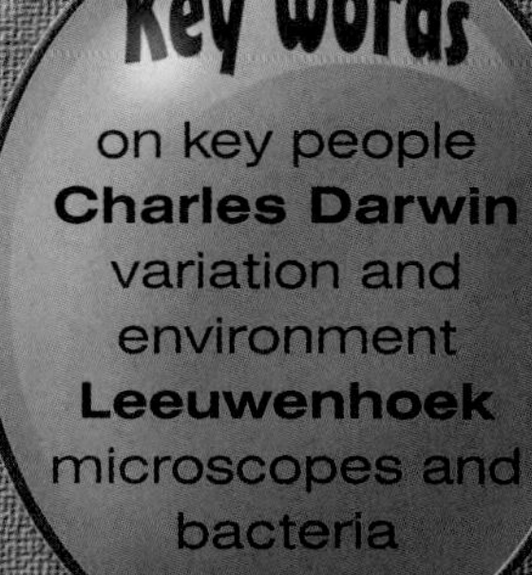

distillation	the process of separating a pure liquid from a mixture by boiling the mixture containing the liquid, then condensing the gas and collecting the pure liquid. **p.130**
dormant	plants survive the winter by becoming dormant. They are alive but do not grow until spring. **p.49**
drag	the force of friction when an object moves through a liquid or a gas. **p.185**
eclipse	when the Sun is hidden because it passes behind the Moon, or when the Moon passes into the Earth's shadow. **pp.200–1**
electric circuit	a complete path around which electric current can flow. **p.158**
energy resources	anything from which we can get energy. **p.146.**
energy	the ability to make things happen. For example, burning fuels release, allowing us to do things. **p.142**
equation	a way of describing a chemical reaction that shows what we start with and what we finish with after the reaction. **p.103**
evidence	data (measurements and observations) collected by scientists that supports or challenges a theory/prediction/conclusion. **p.114**
external fertilisation	sperm fertilise eggs outside the body. **p.35**
fertilisation	occurs when the nucleus of a male sex cell joins with the nucleus of a female sex cell to make a cell that can grow into an embryo. **p.15**
fertilisation	occurs when a sperm nucleus passes into the egg carrying its genes. **p.25**
field of view	the area that you can see when looking down a microscope. **p.5**
filtration	separating insoluble solid from a mixture of the solid and a liquid by passing it through filter paper. **p.127**
foetus	a baby developing in the uterus. It is not called a baby until it has been successfully delivered. **p.28**
food web	a set of linked food webs that show the feeding relationships between animals and plants in a habitat. **p.50**

force a push or pull which acts on one object, caused by another. **p.174**

forcemeter a device for measuring forces. **p.176**

fossil fuel a fuel formed from materials that were once alive. **p.144**

friction a force which opposes movement. **p.184**

fuel a material burned to release energy. **p.142**

fuse a component that melts ('blows') when the current flowing through it is too great. **p.168**

gas pressure the force per unit area exerted as gas particles collide with the walls of their container or other objects. **p.119**

gravity the pulling effect of any object that has mass. **p.178**

habitat the place where an animal or plant lives and reproduces. **p.44**

harmful describes substances that cause some damage to the body if swallowed, breathed in or absorbed through the skin. **p.82**

hazardous potentially dangerous substances. **p.82**

hibernation spending adverse winter conditions in a secure, sheltered place. Body activity is slowed to the bare minimum. **p.48**

hormones chemicals made by glands that pass round the body in blood and affect the activity of many body structures. **p.23**

humidity the amount of moisture in the air. **p.45**

hydrochloric acid a common acid found in school laboratories. **p.84**

hydrogen a gas that is the lightest of all the chemical elements. A lighted splint burns with a squeaky pop when applied to the mouth of a test tube of the gas. **p.99**

in parallel components connected side-by-side are in parallel. **p.166**

in series components connected end-to-end are in series. **p.166**

indicator a substance that changes colour depending on the pH of the solution it is in. **p.84**

insoluble does not dissolve in a particular solvent. **p.126**

Key words
on key people
Democritus
particles
Robert Brown
particle motion
Antoine Lavoisier
burning

insulation material that prevents you from accidentally touching electricity, because it doesn't conduct. **p.159**

invertebrates eight very different groups of animals, none possess a backbone. **p.64**

joule (J) the scientific unit of energy. **p.150**

kilogram (kg) the scientific unit of mass. **p.180**

limewater turns milky/cloudy when carbon dioxide is bubbled through it. **p.100**

luminous describes an object that is a source of its own light. **p.194**

magnesium a grey metal (silver beneath its outer coating) that burns in air with a bright, white light. **p.103**

magnification a measure of the number of times an image is enlarged by the use of lenses. It is calculated by multiplying the magnifying power of the eyepiece lens by the magnifying power of the objective lens. **p.4**

mass how much matter an object is made of. **p.180**

methane the main constituent of natural gas. It contains the elements carbon and hydrogen. **p.104**

migration animals moving to more favourable areas when conditions become severe. **p.48**

model a 'picture' constructed by scientists to help explain the way the things work. **p.114**

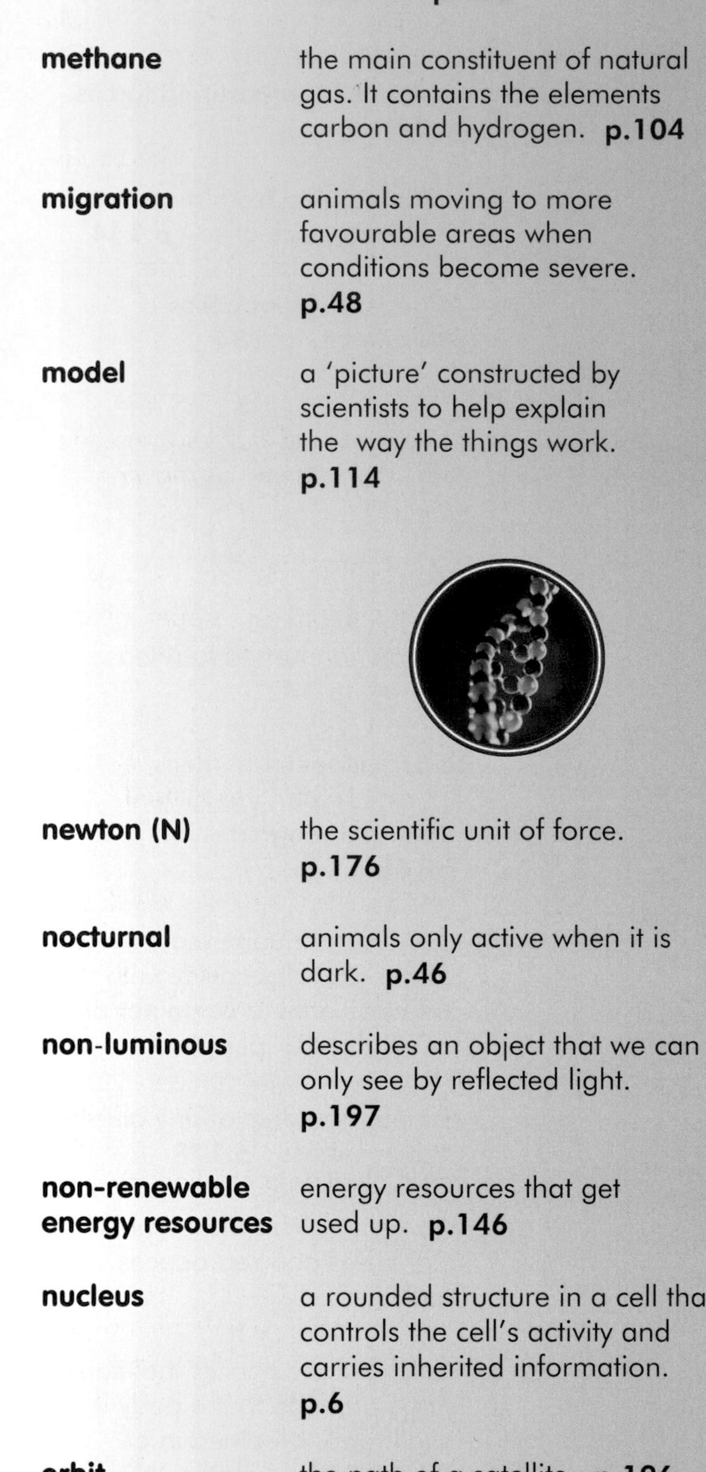

newton (N) the scientific unit of force. **p.176**

nocturnal animals only active when it is dark. **p.46**

non-luminous describes an object that we can only see by reflected light. **p.197**

non-renewable energy resources energy resources that get used up. **p.146**

nucleus a rounded structure in a cell that controls the cell's activity and carries inherited information. **p.6**

orbit the path of a satellite. **p.196**

orbit the track followed by one object as it travels round another object. **p.203**

organs structures that carry out a specific job that is necessary for life, such as obtaining oxygen from the air. They have components that do different parts of the job. **p.10**

ovulation the process of the release of the egg from the ovary. **p.26**

ovule found in flowers. It forms a seed after it has been fertilised by pollen. **pp.14–15**

oxygen the gas that is essential for breathing and burning, making up 21% of the air. A glowing splint re-lights in the gas. **pp.102–3**

palisade cell a cell found in the upper layers of a leaf, specialised for photosynthesis. **p.8**

particle a tiny, individual piece of a substance that is too small to be seen. **p.115**

pH value a number on the pH scale that indicates how acidic or alkaline a solution is; a pH value of 7 is neutral. Values below 7 are acidic (the lower the number the more acidic a solution is), whereas pH values above 7 are alkaline (the higher the value the more alkaline a solution is). **p.85**

pollen found in flowers. It carries a nucleus to the female part of a flower for fertilising ovules. **p.14**

producer plants are producers because they use light energy to make foods. **p.50**

product a substance that is formed in a chemical reaction. **p.97**

puberty the time during which we complete the development of our reproductive organs and sexual features. **p.22**

react when substances undergo a chemical change and form new substances. **p.96**

reactant a substance that we start with before a chemical reaction takes place. **p.97**

renewable energy resources energy resources that will never run out. **p.146**

resistance how much a component opposes the flow of electric current. **p.161**

rubella a virus that harms foetuses. **p.32**

satellite a smaller object travelling around a larger object. **p.196**

saturated solution a solution in which no more solute will dissolve at that particular temperature. **p.134**

on key people
Robert Hooke
springs and clocks
Isaac Newton
Laws of Motion

section a thin slice of material cut to examine under a microscope – or similar. **p.5**

selective breeding each generation of animals or plants with the best combination of features for local conditions are kept to be the parents of the next generation (gradually the desirable features are spread through the population). **p.72**

sodium hydroxide the most common alkali found in school laboratories. **p.84**

soluble describes a substance that dissolves in a particular solvent. **p.126**

solute a substance that dissolves in a particular solvent. **p.126**

solution the mixture formed when a substance dissolves in a liquid. **p.126**

solvent a liquid that dissolves a substance. **p.126**

speed how quickly something is moving, often measured in metres per second (m/s). **p.186**

stain a chemical that is taken up by cells in a section and makes parts of the cell show up more clearly. **p.5**

theory a set of ideas that we use to explain things. Theories can change in the light of new evidence. **p.114**

tissue a group of specialised cells that carry out a particular job. **p.10**

upthrust the upward force of an object in a liquid such as water, or in a gas. **p.182**

vacuole a fluid-filled structure found in plant cells. **p.7**

vertebrates five groups of animals with a bone or cartilage backbone that protects the main part of the nervous system, a head, and a tail. This group includes humans. **p.64**

vibration movement back and forth. **p.117**

voltage a measure of how much a cell or battery pushes current. **p.163**

weight the force of the Earth's gravity on an object. **p.180**

word equation a way to describe a chemical reaction, showing reactants and products written out in words. reactants $\rightarrow$ products. **p.103**